Treatment and Prevention of Alcohol Problems

A Resource Manual

Treatment and Prevention of Alcohol Problems
A Resource Manual

Edited by

W. Miles Cox

Psychology Service and Alcohol Research Laboratory
Richard L. Roudebush Veterans Administration Medical Center
and Department of Psychiatry
Indiana University School of Medicine
Indianapolis, Indiana

1987

ACADEMIC PRESS, INC.
Harcourt Brace Jovanovich, Publishers
Orlando   San Diego   New York   Austin
Boston   London   Sydney   Tokyo   Toronto

ACADEMIC PRESS, INC.
Orlando, Florida 32887

United Kingdom Edition published by
ACADEMIC PRESS INC. (LONDON) LTD.
24–28 Oval Road, London NW1 7DX

Library of Congress Cataloging in Publication Data

Treatment and prevention of alcohol problems.

(Personality, psychopathology, and psychotherapy)
Includes index.
1. Alcoholism—Treatment. 2. Alcoholism—Prevention.
3. Psychotherapy. I. Cox, W. Miles. II. Series.
[DNLM: 1. Alcoholism—prevention & control. 2. Alcoholism
—therapy. WM 274 T7836]
RC565.T73 1987 616.86'106 86-10758
ISBN 0—12—194470—0 (alk. paper)

PRINTED IN THE UNITED STATES OF AMERICA

86 87 88 89   9 8 7 6 5 4 3 2 1

For my colleagues who work to treat and prevent alcohol problems.

Contents

**1   An Overview of Treatment and Prevention of
      Alcohol Problems**

W. Miles Cox

I   Initiating Treatment

2   Beginning Treatment for Alcohol Problems

Michael R. Liepman and Ted D. Nirenberg

**3   The Assessment of Multiple Conditions in Persons
      with Alcohol Problems**

Kenneth Wanberg and John L. Horn

4 Medical Aspects of Alcoholism

David H. Knott, James D. Beard, and Robert D. Fink

II Specific Treatment Techniques

5 Behavioral Treatment of Alcohol Problems: A Review and a Comparison of Behavioral and Nonbehavioral Studies

Diane M. Riley, Linda C. Sobell, Gloria I. Leo, Mark B. Sobell, and Felix Klajner

6 Building Self-Confidence, Self-Efficacy, and Self-Control

Susan G. Curry and G. Alan Marlatt

III Associated Problems and Special Populations

11   Alcohol, Gender, and Sexual Problems: An Interface

Edith S. Lisansky Gomberg

12   Culture-Specific Treatment Modalities: Assessing Client-to-Treatment Fit in Indian Alcoholism Programs

Joan Weibel-Orlando

IV   Early Intervention and Prevention

13   Theory and Methods for Secondary Prevention of Alcohol Problems: A Cognitively Based Approach

Martha Sanchez-Craig, D. Adrian Wilkinson,
and Keith Walker

14 Prevention of Alcohol Problems

Peter E. Nathan and Raymond S. Niaura

Preface

With the enormous strides that have recently been made in our knowledge and attitudes about alcohol problems, it is time now to pause. We need to determine how the new information gained through clinical experience and research can best be utilized for the treatment and prevention of these problems. The present volume attempts to accomplish this purpose. As its title indicates, the book is intended to be a resource manual for the treatment and prevention of alcohol problems. The book is a *manual* in the sense that it provides information and instruction, giving details about specific procedures to follow. It is a *resource* manual in the sense that it is not intended to be a "one-shot" lesson on how to treat and prevent alcohol problems. The book may well serve as the basis for implementing a treatment program, but it is also intended to be a guide to which the clinical worker may refer as new problems and questions arise with individual clients.

The contributors to the book represent the major innovators of treatment and prevention programs for alcohol problems. Their chapters are organized into four major parts. Part I deals with *initiating treatment*. Under this rubric, Michael Liepman and Ted Nirenberg give guidelines to beginning treatment of persons with alcohol problems, focusing on inpatient programs that involve patients' families. Kenneth Wanberg and John Horn present guidelines for assessing whether or not a person has an alcohol problem that needs treating and the various factors that comprise the problem if one exists. David Knott, James Beard, and Robert Fink discuss the medical aspects of alcohol problems, describing the medical symptoms that characterize the various stages of an alcohol problem and how these symptoms should be attended to.

Part II proceeds with *specific treatment techniques*. Diane Riley, Linda Sobell, Gloria Leo, Mark Sobell, and Felix Klajner discuss various behavioral treatments for alcohol problems and compare the relative efficacy of behavioral and nonbehavioral approaches. Susan Curry and Alan Marlatt present their program for preventing relapses following treatment, a program which aims to build clients' self-confidence, self-efficacy, and self-control during its three respective phases. Next, Eric Klinger discusses mental imagery and logotherapeutic techniques that have been used enthusiastically by a substantial number of clinicians as a supplement to other procedures for helping persons to overcome their alcohol problems. Richard Thoreson and Frank Budd discuss group therapeutic procedures for persons with alcohol problems, giving special attention to the self-help groups administered by Alcoholics Anonymous (AA) and suggesting ways in which professionals and AA can work better together. The concept of craving for alcohol is central to AA's disease model of alcoholism, but in the final chapter of Part II, Laurence Baker, Ned Cooney, and Ovide Pomerleau discuss craving from an empirical rather than a disease perspective, describing the physiological indices of craving and therapeutic procedure to deal with it.

Part III deals with *associated problems and special populations*. Here, Timothy O'Farrell discusses his techniques for resolving marital and family problems associated with alcohol problems, including procedures to motivate clients to change, to bring about changes, and to maintain changes that have been effected. Next, Edith Gomberg considers the sexual and gender problems that are frequently interrelated with alcohol problems, providing recommendations for clinicians who work with persons with both alcohol and sexual/gender problems. Finally in Part III, Joan Weibel-Orlando describes culture-specific treatment modalities, highlighting her work with native Americans and suggesting ways to match particular clients with the most appropriate treatment modality.

The focus of Part IV is on *early intervention and prevention*. Martha Sanchez-Craig, Adrian Wilkinson, and Keith Walker describe their secondary prevention program, which identifies and treats drinking problems before they become severe and offers clients alternatives to the traditional disease model of alcoholism which mandates total abstinence. Peter Nathan and Raymond Niaura review a variety of prevention efforts that have been undertaken in the United States (ranging from programs for persons at risk to those for persons with well-developed alcohol problems), with special attention given to the employee assistance programs with which Nathan has worked.

These chapters are not intended to be mere reviews of the relevant literature. The procedures described are based on solid theoretical and empirical foundations, and the book attempts to uphold the highest scholastic standards. Nevertheless, a primary intent of the book is to instruct clinical workers in what techniques are available to them and how these techniques can be put to practical use. Accordingly, much of the writing is based on the authors' own clinical experiences.

It is expected that the book will be useful to a variety of professionals: psychologists, psychiatrists and other physicians, social workers, nurses, and counselors, as well as to paraprofessional alcoholism counselors. The book will also be appropriate as a text for courses dealing with alcohol problems. In addition, many others should find the book helpful, especially those who have had personal experience with alcohol problems and want to understand and better help persons with these problems.

Many persons helped to make this book possible. I thank the contributors for the time and effort that they put into writing their chapters. I am indebted to William Miller, Peter Nathan, and Sharon Wilsnack for their invaluable suggestions for the book when it was being planned. I am grateful to Joseph Blount, Colleen Donagher, and Eric Klinger for their encouragement and support during the preparation of the book. Finally, I acknowledge the expert secretarial assistance of Yvonne Storck and Charlotte Syverson.

1

An Overview of Treatment and Prevention of Alcohol Problems

W. MILES COX

Psychology Service and Alcohol Research Laboratory
Richard L. Roudebush Veterans Administration
*   Medical Center*
and
Department of Psychiatry
Indiana University School of Medicine
Indianapolis, Indiana 46202

I. INTRODUCTION

The treatment and prevention of alcohol problems do not enjoy a favorable history. Before the decade of the 1970s, persons with alcohol problems were given very little attention by professional therapists, physicians, or research scientists. Alcoholism had long been stigmatized as a problem associated mainly with the lower social classes (the stereotypical "skid-row bum"), moral weakness, and lack of willpower. Professionals, moreover, when they did work with alcoholics, did not have effective treatment techniques available to them; consequently, their endeavors were largely unsuccessful. In short, alcoholics were poorly understood, and they were not seen as rewarding persons with whom to work.

The 1970s saw a dramatic change in this sad state of affairs. There was a vast increase in governmental support of alcohol education, research, and treatment that began with the establishment of the National Institute on Alcohol Abuse and Alcoholism (NIAAA) in 1971. The consequences of the NIAAA for the treatment and prevention of alcohol problems have been far-reaching. Treatment facilities for alcohol problems have proliferated, basic and applied research has burgeoned (Cox & Thornton, 1986), and promising treatment techniques have been developed. Concurrent with the

1

progress in our knowledge about alcohol problems and how to deal with them, people's attitudes about these problems have changed. It has become increasingly recognized that persons from any socioeconomic status can develop problems with alcohol, that these problems are not an indication of moral weakness, and that there are effective treatments for them.

Our goal in this volume is to compile the latest techniques for treating and preventing alcohol problems that have been identified through the trailblazing work of the preceding years. The book is divided into four sections as follows:

II. INITIATING TREATMENT

In the first section, we deal with the initial phase of treatment. Here we discuss how to begin treatment for persons with alcohol problems, how to assess their problems, and how to deal with the medical complications related to them.

In Chapter 2, Michael Liepman and Ted Nirenberg present guidelines to begin treatment for persons with alcohol problems. They focus on inpatient treatments that emphasize involvement of the patient's family, but much of their advice is applicable to other forms of treatment as well.

Liepman and Nirenberg believe that two matters must be attended to when alcoholic patients enter a treatment program. First, therapists need to establish the affective tone of the therapeutic relationship that will prevail throughout subsequent treatment. The relationship should be based on warm, respectful, and empathic regard for the patient, but it should be one in which the therapist, not the patient, determines the direction that the treatment will take. Second, the therapist needs to assemble a "treatment team" to work to solve the patient's problems with alcohol. The team should comprise the various persons in the problem drinker's life who are concerned about his or her recovery but who may have unwittingly promoted the problem drinking in the past.

According to Liepman and Nirenberg, a treatment plan should be devised for the patient which should aim to make the positive aspects of sobriety outweigh those of drinking. Such a plan should not be confined to patients' drinking problems but should consider their medical, psychological, family, and social problems as well. The treatment should focus on small, readily achievable goals that lead to the achievement of larger goals. Finally, the goals of treatment should be clearly specified in a treatment contract that should be agreed upon by all persons involved in the treatment.

Before we can effectively treat a person's alcohol problems, we must first carefully assess the problems. Thus, in Chapter 3, Kenneth Wanberg and John Horn present guidelines for assessing whether or not a person has an alcohol problem that needs treating and the various factors that comprise the problem if one exists. Their multiple condition theory of alcoholism was developed from years of research with the Alcohol Use Inventory (AUI), a self-report instrument that yields scores on 18 primary scales, 6 second-order factors, and a general factor.

The AUI provides detailed information about five facets of a person's use of alcohol. (1) The various benefits that a person might derive from drinking, including positive reinforcement (e.g., enhancement of sociability, mental functioning, and positive emotions) and negative reinforcement (e.g., alleviation of stress, negative emotions, or somatic pain). (2) The person's manner and style of drinking (e.g., gregarious versus solo, sustained versus periodic, compulsive versus impulsive, and daily quantity). (3) Concepts indicating disruptive consequences of drinking (loss of control over behavior, social role maladaptation, physical and psychological withdrawal, disruptions in emotions and relationships). (4) Self-concerns about disruptive consequences (anxiety and stress related to drinking and prior efforts to change the pattern of drinking). (5) Acknowledgment of drinking problems (awareness of impaired control and readiness for treatment). Combinations of these five broad concepts define patterns of alcohol use that seem to point to various types of alcoholism, some examples of which are discussed by Wanberg and Horn.

Wanberg and Horn use these and various other measures to develop an assessment profile for each patient. The ultimate purpose of this profile is to match patients with available treatment modalities, such as those that are described in subsequent chapters in this volume.

Wanberg and Horn's AUI can be used to assess medical problems resulting from alcohol use — six primary medical factors have been identified. However, these conditions are better identified with medical tests and examinations than with questionnaires. Hence, Chapter 4 by David Knott, James Beard, and Robert Fink on the medical aspects of alcoholism tells us how physicians assess and attend to medical problems related to alcohol abuse.

In Knott, Beard, and Fink's view, alcoholism can be seen as occurring in three distinct phases: The *acute phase* includes intoxication, the withdrawal syndrome, and toxic psychoses associated with alcohol use. The *subacute phase* includes multiple medical and psychological problems associated with alcohol use that often disguise themselves as disorders other than alcoholism. The *chronic phase* includes various social, psychological, and vocational problems that may be either antecedents or consequences of alcoholism.

To assist readers with the medical management of persons with alcohol problems, Knott, Beard, and Fink carefully delineate the medical symptoms that characterize each of the three stages. They give details about the body systems that are affected by alcohol and provide guidelines for medical treatment during each phase. In their view, primary responsibility for treatment during the acute and subacute phases should be assumed by medical professionals, whereas responsibility for treatment during the chronic phase should be delegated to nonmedical professionals. Nevertheless, both medical and nonmedical professionals should actively participate in planning and implementing treatment during all three phases.

III. SPECIFIC TREATMENT TECHNIQUES

After discussing the preliminary aspects of treatment in Part I, we turn to specific treatment techniques in Part II. These techniques include behavioral treatments that are based on the principles of learning and conditioning, cognitive treatments that attempt to alter clients' thought processes, and treatments that utilize mental imagery, logotherapy, and group procedures.

In Chapter 5, Diane Riley, Linda Sobell, Gloria Leo, Mark Sobell, and Felix Klajner review the literature on behavioral treatments for alcohol problems over a 6-year period, including a discussion of the theoretical underpinnings or rationales of the various treatments. These treatments include aversive conditioning, relaxation training, skills training (drinking, interpersonal, vocational, and cognitive skills), marital and family behavioral therapy, contingency management, behavioral self-management, and multimodal behavioral approaches. Their review is not intended to be exhaustive for two reasons. First, this body of literature has been reviewed in several other publications. Second, Riley et al. chose to review studies that meet a basic set of criteria for scientific rigor, the most important of which is a minimum 6-month follow-up period.

The review suggests that behavioral techniques are differentially effective across subpopulations of alcohol abusers who differ in severity of alcohol dependence and socioeconomic factors. For example, behavioral self-control techniques seem to be more appropriate for not severely dependent alcohol abusers. Also, evidence from one study suggests that cognitive skills training may be too difficult for severely dependent alcohol abusers with neurological impairment.

A second aim of the chapter is to compare the methodology and relative efficacy of behavioral and nonbehavioral treatment studies published during this same 6-year period. Although the review shows that behavioral studies are methodologically more sophisticated then nonbehavioral studies, the foremost conclusion of the comparison is that "treatments for alcohol problems with demonstrated enduring effectiveness do not exist, regardless of treatment orientations or treatment goals" (p. 107). The review further concludes that relapse following treatment is a very real and frequent phenomenon for all treatments. In view of this fact, Riley et al. think that it would be productive for future treatments to focus on techniques to prevent relapse.

The prevention of relapse is the very topic of Chapter 6 by Susan G. Curry and Alan Marlatt. Their program is divided into three phases, during which clients are taught self-confidence, self-efficacy, and self-control, respectively, in order to prevent relapses from occurring.

It is primarily during the first phase of treatment that clients are helped to develop self-confidence. Various techniques are used to allow clients to explore their self-image as a drinker and what their self-image would be if they were to stop drinking. Clients are also helped to identify the immediate and long-term positive and negative consequences of their drinking, and thus to understand what benefits would accrue if they were to stop drinking. By imagining what they could achieve, clients begin to feel more self-confident and become motivated to change.

During the second phase of treatment, Curry and Marlatt help clients to achieve self-efficacy vis-à-vis their drinking. That is, clients develop a sense of being able to control their drinking in problematic situations. Clients are helped to recognize situations that pose a risk for drinking and to acquire skills for coping with these high-risk situations. Thus, during the second phase of treatment, actual changes in clients' pattern of drinking are initiated.

The focus of the third phase of treatment is on teaching clients self-control of their urges to drink. However, it is important for clients to recognize that although they might sometimes acquiesce to their urges, such lapses are not irreversible. By realizing that slips can be the occasion for growth, understanding, and learning, clients can prevent lapses from escalating into full-fledged relapses.

The techniques used by Curry and Marlatt to instill self-confidence, self-efficacy, and self-control are largely cognitive in nature; clients are taught to think differently about themselves and the situations that promote drinking. By contrast, Chapter 7 by Eric Klinger deals exclusively with mental imagery and logotherapeutic techniques for helping clients to gain control over their use of alcohol.

Klinger discusses three imagery techniques for dealing with alcohol problems. First, *covert sensitization* is a variation of aversive conditioning in which clients first imagine themselves involved in aversive scenes with alcohol and then imagine themselves making a response to escape from the aversive situation, thereby experiencing relief and presumably learning to avoid alcohol in the future. Second, *psychodrama* is a form of group therapy in which the members act out the roles that are psychologically important to them in their real lives. The interaction among characters allows them to clarify their feelings and identify previously unrealized possibilities for themselves in life. The third imagery technique is *guided affective imagery*.

During a therapy session in which this technique is used, clients are instructed to imagine a scene and allow their imagery to unfold from the scene. The method is psychodynamic and the mental imagery serves as the medium for emotional relearning, personal growth, growth in ego resources, and restructuring of interpersonal relationships. Guided affective imagery has become a major therapeutic movement in Europe and has been used there with alcoholic clients. Although it is clear that these three imagery techniques cannot be used alone to solve clients' complex problems with alcohol, they have been used enthusiastically by a substantial number of clinicians as an adjunct to treatment.

Logotherapy is a form of existential therapy that seems to be especially appropriate to use with persons with alcohol problems. In Klinger's view, dependence on alcohol is associated with a lack of meaning in one's life, and relinquishing that dependence requires commitment to satisfying alternative goals. Logotherapy has been used with alcoholic clients to help them achieve that very purpose: to find meaningful goals in their lives.

Many of the preceding techniques can be used in both individual and group therapy. In Chapter 8, Richard Thoreson and Frank Budd specifically discuss how group procedures are used to treat persons with alcohol problems. In their view, group therapy for persons with alcohol problems both helps to compensate for the paucity of trained professionals and makes unique contributions to alcoholics' recovery.

Various forms of groups are used to treat persons with alcohol problems and their families. These include (1) traditional therapy groups that attempt to resolve members' problems and concerns, (2) informational groups that instruct members about alcohol problems, (3) activity groups that engage members in recreation and other light-hearted activities, and (4) self-help groups.

The self-help groups administered by Alcoholics Anonymous (AA) are the most common type of group treatment for alcohol problems. According to Thoreson and Budd's description, AA groups are an important component in the long-term recovery of many alcoholics, providing them with a practical, daily behavioral program for maintaining sobriety. Nevertheless, professional and self-help endeavors sometimes appear to be opposed to each other, and Thoreson and Budd offer suggestions for a rapprochement between professionals and the AA community.

A central tenet of the disease concept of alcoholism that is promulgated by AA is that alcoholics' craving for alcohol causes them to lose control over alcohol. In Chapter 9, Laurence Baker, Ned Cooney, and Ovide Pomeleau discuss the concept of craving and describe empirical studies of the phenomenon and procedures to modify craving and prevent relapse.

These authors provide evidence that craving is a very real phenomenon. However, they account for craving in terms of classical conditioning and cognitive mediational processes, rather than seeing it as a symptom of alcoholics' disease. Baker, Cooney, and Pomeleau show that physiological indices of craving reliably distinguish alcoholics from nonalcoholics and predict alcoholics' drinking behavior and responses to treatment.

Baker et al. discuss two kinds of procedures that have been used to deal with craving: Procedures that decrease the likelihood of the onset of craving and those that decrease the intensity and duration of craving when it occurs. Both kinds of procedures have been found to be most successful when used in the context of an overall treatment program.

IV. DEALING WITH ASSOCIATED PROBLEMS AND SPECIAL POPULATIONS

In Part III, we consider some problems that are commonly interrelated with alcohol problems that need to be treated: marital, family, and sexual problems. In this section, we also consider the special needs of ethnic minority groups who develop problems with alcohol and how their needs can best be met.

Because alcohol problems frequently arise within the context of a marriage or family, it is often productive for marital or family therapy to be undertaken concurrently with treatment for alcohol problems. It has been shown, in fact, that treatment outcome for alcohol problems is positively related to marital and family adjustment.

In Chapter 10, Timothy O'Farrell discusses the techniques that he has developed for resolving marital and family problems. They include procedures for (1) motivating a commitment to change, (2) producing changes in drinking and marital/family relationships, and (3) maintaining the changes that have been accomplished. The interventions to improve the marital and family relationships include procedures to increase positive feelings, good will, and commitment to the relationship and procedures to resolve conflicts and negotiate desired changes. O'Farrell's experience with families and couples with alcohol problems indicates that serious marital and family problems sometimes first become apparent only after drinking has stopped, and if these problems are not resolved they may lead to further drinking or divorce.

Despite the value of the procedures that O'Farrell uses, he sees a need to develop additional marital and family interventions: those specifically for adolescents, females, homosexuals, families with more than one alcoholic, and persons whose drinking problem is less severe than that of diagnosed alcoholics. He also sees a need for marital/family preventive interventions, including education about responsible drinking practices and the fetal alcohol syndrome and work with high-risk groups prior to or early in marriage.

In Chapter 11, Edith Gomberg considers how alcohol problems are interrelated with sexual and gender problems. She first discusses the wide variations in human responses to alcohol and in human sexual responses, and then considers the effect that alcohol has on human sexual responses. She finds that the use of alcohol affects sexual activity, responsivity, and pleasure.

Gomberg describes the sexual and gender problems that are frequently found among persons with alcohol problems. Many of these problems have to do with problem drinkers' sexual functioning, sexual orientation, or their sex-role conflicts. In some cases, the sexual and gender problems appear to precede and contribute to the development of the alcohol problems. In other cases, sexual and gender problems appear to have been caused by alcohol problems. However, regardless of which problem occurred first, alcohol and sexual/gender problems seem to augment each other. Consequently, Gomberg provides recommendations for working clinically with persons with both alcohol and sexual/gender problems.

Members of ethnic minority groups who develop alcohol problems often need special consideration. In some cases, these persons' alcohol problems seem to result from the stress associated with membership in the minority group. In other cases, the alcohol problems may result from the unhealthy drinking practices of a particular minority group. Thus, the special difficulties of these groups that augment their problems with alcohol need to be dealt with and overcome.

To help accomplish this end, in Chapter 12 Joan Weibel-Orlando considers culture-specific treatment modalities, with special attention to her work with Native Americans. Based on their field work with various Native American groups, Weibel-Orlando and her colleagues have developed a continuum of treatment typologies that in varying degrees make use of indigenous healing practices (e.g., curing rituals and herbal medicines administered by indigenous healers). In addition, Weibel-Orlando presents a continuum of client types (that range from highly traditional to highly contemporary) and a method for matching clients with the most appropriate intervention. Finally, Weibel-Orlando advocates using her method of matching clients and treatments with ethnic groups besides Native Americans.

V. EARLY INTERVENTION AND PREVENTION

Where appropriate, the chapters in the first three sections of the book discuss the prevention of alcohol problems, but their emphasis is clearly on treating alcohol problems. By contrast, Part IV focuses on early intervention and prevention. The two chapters in this section highlight the arbitrary boundary between the treatment and prevention of alcohol problems.

In Chapter 13, Martha Sanchez-Craig, Adrian Wilkinson, and Keith Walker present conceptual models of alcohol abuse and relapse, upon which their treatment procedures are based. Their program is for secondary prevention in the sense that it is used to identify and treat drinking problems before they become more severe. These authors suggest that such programs should be implemented away from specialized alcoholism clinics. Early-stage problem drinkers have been reluctant to seek help at traditional treatment centers that subscribe to the disease concept of alcoholism and insist that abstinence is the only appropriate goal of treatment. In contrast to the traditional approach, Sanchez-Craig, Wilkinson, and Walker view problem drinking as a learned behavior that can be modified, and for which moderate drinking can be an appropriate and achieveable goal of treatment.

These authors have found that excessive drinking frequently represents either attempts to cope with events appraised as aversive, or an important source of recreation. Thus, Sanchez-Craig, Wilkinson, and Walker seek to modify drinkers' cognitions about alcohol and to teach them new ones that will help them change their behavior. Their techniques (similar to some of the cognitive and behavioral procedures discussed earlier in the book) have been quite successful at attracting early-stage problem drinkers into treatment, helping them to set appropriate drinking goals, and assisting them to develop coping responses in situations where they have been likely to drink excessively.

In Chapter 14, Peter Nathan and Raymond Niaura give an overview of prevention efforts in the United States, with special attention to the employee assistance programs with which the senior author has worked. In contrast to Sanchez-Craig, Wilkinson, and Walker, Nathan and Niaura believe that the customary distinction among primary, secondary, and tertiary prevention is not appropriate for alcohol problems, and they choose not to make such a distinction. They describe a variety of approaches aimed at groups ranging from those at risk to those with fully developed alcohol problems.

These authors discuss several categories of efforts to reduce the prevalence of alcohol problems: (1) efforts that focus of the individual, including women, youth, minorities, and the elderly; (2) efforts that focus on the host, including efforts to prevent drunk driving and the fetal alcohol syndrome; (3) efforts that focus on the agent, including efforts to control the consumption of alcohol by controlling pricing and the legal drinking age; (4) efforts that focus on the environment, including efforts to control drinking through education and the mass media; and (5) efforts in the workplace to prevent alcohol problems.

For all of the categories, Nathan and Niaura conclude that efforts to prevent alcohol problems have been largely unsuccessful. Whereas prevention programs typically increase levels of information about alcohol and its effects and sometimes change attitudes about excessive drinking, they rarely change actual patterns of consumption of alcohol. These authors believe that viable prevention programs have been hampered by a lack of financial support and debilitating political struggles.

VI. CONCLUSIONS

One theme resounds throughout this volume. In order to surmount problems with alcohol, there are two things that need to be accomplished. First, problem drinkers must give up their excessive drinking and must learn skills to prevent them from resuming excessive consumption of alcohol in the future. Second, problem drinkers need to find meaningful sources of enjoyment in their lives that will compete sufficiently with the satisfaction that they have derived from drinking alcohol. To a large extent, achievement of this goal requires that persons with alcohol problems correct the other problems in their lives that caused and were caused by their excessive drinking. A variety of procedures that can be used to help problem drinkers achieve these two goals are presented in this volume. A theoretical model that is based on the theme that emerges in the present volume is presented in greater detail elsewhere (Cox & Klinger, in press).

REFERENCES

Cox, W. M., & Klinger, E. (in press). Incentive motivation, affective change, and alcohol use: a model. In W. M. Cox (Ed.), *Why people drink: Parameters of alcohol as a reinforcer.* New York: Gardner Press.

Cox, W. M., & Thornton, A. (1986). Some recent trends in the quantity of alcohol and other drug publications. Manuscript in preparation.

I
Initiating Treatment

2

Beginning Treatment for Alcohol Problems

MICHAEL R. LIEPMAN AND TED D. NIRENBERG

Alcohol Dependence Treatment Program
Davis Park Veterans Administration Medical Center
and
Department of Psychiatry and Human Behavior
Center for Alcohol Studies
Brown University
Providence, Rhode Island 02908

I. INTRODUCTION

The beginning of treatment is likely to be a critical turning point for patients with alcohol problems and for their families. During initial contact, as the therapist is evaluating the patient and family, they are evaluating the therapist. Potential clients form first impressions about their compatibility with the therapist concerning styles, goals, values, and world views, and these initial impressions may affect subsequent therapeutic contacts. Because it is common for alcohol abusers to drop out of outpatient treatment before their fourth session (Nirenberg, Sobell, & Sobell, 1980), initial impressions may be very important to continuation of treatment.

This chapter has three purposes. First, it focuses on the elements of the beginning phase of treatment that are important in building a therapeutic alliance that is sufficiently strong to weather the stresses of recovery. Second, it identifies the factors that must be assessed early in treatment to establish the direction of change. Third, the chapter offers an approach for anticipating pitfalls that abort treatment.

13

TREATMENT AND PREVENTION
OF ALCOHOL PROBLEMS: A RESOURCE MANUAL

II. THERAPEUTIC RELATIONSHIP

Patients initially ask themselves such questions as "Will this therapist or program care about me, understand me, accept and respect me? Will my therapist be competent? Can I trust my therapist with my innermost secrets?" It is imperative that the therapist do everything possible to foster affirmative answers to these questions, especially if this patient has had prior unsuccessful treatment experiences.

A. Establishing Affective Tone

The affective tone of subsequent treatment is set by the initial contact. The therapist who approaches a patient and family in a sterile, impersonal manner rather than with a warm, respectful style may elicit a defensive response from them. Even the manner in which trivial matters such as insurance forms or program rules are discussed may set the tone of the working relationship. Initial discussion of such mundane topics as the weather or the slow elevators may help to communicate that the therapist is approachable and "down to earth."

The communication of empathy must be combined with a toughminded firmness that communicates that the therapist intends to challenge the patient and family to change. Constructive therapeutic intentions must be distinguished from a disrespectful approach to alcohol abusers and their families which is apparent among some health professionals (Liepman, Whitfield, & Landeen, 1981; Whitfield, 1980). Patients who have been treated indignantly by a prior clinician may be especially reluctant to trust a new therapist.

Comments by the therapist that counter social stigma usually associated with alcohol problems will enhance the therapeutic alliance. Often, alcoholics feel guilty about their behavior and have low self-esteem. Likewise, relatives may blame themselves for the drinking problems. Stigma and guilt may be reduced by reassuring them that they are merely a "family with a problem" for which no individual is solely responsible. Many families with depressed members have difficulty acknowledging their own assets (Beck, Rush, Shaw, & Emery, 1979). Instead of merely focusing on the negative consequences of alcohol problems, patients and their families should be encouraged to evaluate each others' negative and positive attributes in a balanced fashion. This approach may serve to reduce blaming, boost self-esteem, and enhance mood.

The family usually comes to therapy with some notion of what is wrong, but until they are able to trust the therapist, they will probably resist new ideas for dealing with their problems. To gain their trust, the therapist must diminish the perceived differences between the therapist and the family

(Minuchin, 1974). The therapist may then challenge the family's behavior with less concern that they will terminate treatment (Doherty & Baird, 1983). However, in individual therapy, changes made by the patient may meet with defensive resistance by other family members (Liepman, Nirenberg, & White, 1985; Liepman, Wolper, & Vazquez, 1982).

Therapist disclosure of similar background or experiences to that of the patient and family is one way to reduce the perceived distance. However, such self-disclosure must be undertaken cautiously and only when the therapist is comfortable discussing it.

Respect for the patient and family is communicated by the manner in which the therapist exercises control over the patient. For instance, when the therapist makes a decision that is unpopular with the patient or relatives, they should be offered an opportunity to express their objections. After hearing them, the therapist should consider the therapeutic implications of upholding or reversing the decision and explain the final decision in relation to treatment goals.

B. Assembling a Therapeutic Team

Most problem drinkers do not voluntarily seek help. Their excessive drinking may have hurt relatives, friends, co-workers, and neighbors, and it is often these persons who encourage the drinker to seek help. Yet these same persons may indirectly encourage or enable the problem drinking (Johnson, 1980; Koppel, Stimmler, & Perone, 1980). Through genuine concern for the alcohol abuser, they attempt to help him or her to escape from difficult situations caused by the drinking. Paradoxically, such support actually interferes with the drinker's own attempts to change.

Family involvement in recovery improves prognosis (Janzen, 1977; Kaufman, 1980; Levy, 1972; Stanton, 1979). Thus, early in treatment it is helpful to recruit the aid of persons who influence the alcoholic. Family involvement spreads the responsibility for change among more people and offers each of them the opportunity to influence the directions of change.

When family members are reluctant to participate in treatment, the therapist may be able to recruit them by offering a promising approach that they have never tried such as restricting their support of the alcoholic to actions that facilitate growth while discontinuing behavior that fosters the patient's drinking problem (Johnson, 1980; Koppel et al., 1980; Liepman, 1983, 1984a; Thomas & Santa, 1982). It is essential to engender optimism that treatment will be worthwhile and to enlist the family's assistance in planning and executing treatment. Family members must become aware of the importance of their contribution to the problems and the recovery if they are to be expected to support treatment. It is also helpful to arrange meetings with other families who have experienced similar problems (Kaufman & Kaufmann, 1977) and who thus are in a position to lend peer support. When patients block the therapist from communicating with the family or other enablers, it is important to confront the blocks as unhealthy (Van Deusen, Stanton, Scott, Todd, & Mowatt, 1982) because they prevent the enablers from being shown the destructive impact of their misdirected help. Insofar as practical, it is best to include in treatment all persons who have actively participated in the patient's addiction to alcohol (Liepman & Tauriainen, 1980). If these attempts fail, the alternative, less desirable approach is to counsel the alcoholic to avoid contact with his or her enablers.

Although the responsibility for recovery remains primarily with the patient, others must share the responsibility. Thus, the alcoholic must decide whether or not to drink, irrespective of provocation, but provocateurs must be held accountable for their actions. The therapist also must accept responsibility if he or she guides the patient or family into high-risk situations when they have not been adequately prepared for them.

C. Directing Family Treatment

The therapist has the difficult task of rapidly altering the behavior of a group of people who have consistently reinforced one another for maintaining the status quo. Whitaker (1982) contends: "the therapeutic team will be wise to regard the beginning of psychotherapy as a political process . . . [because the family's] unity is reinforced by excluding the rest of the world . . . therefore, it's necessary for the therapist to mobilize great power to bring about any change." The therapist, rather than the family, must determine the direction of treatment. The therapist must challenge current behavior and encourage experimentation with new behavior. Because the family's current desire for change may be transient, the therapist must work quickly and efficiently. If the family fails to follow the therapist's suggestions, they should be confronted about their motivation to change.

Nevertheless, the initiative for change must remain with the family (Whitaker, 1982). If some family members are ambivalent about treatment, the therapist may choose to work with those who are most committed. At the same time, the therapist must be wary of other family members who may encourage the patient to relapse or terminate treatment (Johnson, 1980; Liepman et al., 1982). If it is clear that no family member is committed to change, the therapist should consider individual therapy for the alcoholic, with a secondary goal of motivating the family into treatment. If the family interferes with individual therapy, it may be best to terminate treatment with the offer that the family may return when they are ready for change (Whitaker, 1982).

Many alcoholic families blame particular individuals for general family problems. Thus, if family therapy is undertaken, family members should be encouraged at the outset to suspend blaming and begin supporting constructive changes. Restating unilateral accusations interactively helps to achieve this goal. For example, "She's always nagging at me" could be restated as "We seem to upset each other repeatedly."

III. DEFINING RECOVERY

Alcohol dependence results from a variety of interacting factors, some of which the patient and family might be unable to control (e.g., genetic predisposition, ethnic background, or concurrent psychiatric or medical problems). Recovery entails gaining control over those factors that can be modified (e.g., marital and family conflicts, job, social skills, social support network).

A. Changing

People are unlikely to alter their behavior unless a crisis motivates them to do so (Smilkstein, 1980). In the case of alcoholics, the crisis must be painful enough to break through defensive denial. Once the patient is motivated to change, new patterns of behavior can be tried and refined until they become self-reinforcing. While suggesting new behaviors to replace old ones, the therapist should emphasize the benefits of change and the harm of stagnation because once complacency begins, therapy ends until the next crisis.

Long-term recovery must be distinguished from temporary reduction or cessation of drinking (Steinglass, 1981) or substitution of another drug for alcohol. Many alcoholics temporarily cease drinking several times before lasting recovery. These transient episodes of "improvement" without substantive behavior change might be a means of temporarily escaping external pressures to recover.

It is important for the patient and family to view recovery as made up of small, readily achievable segments. Impatient alcoholics and their families may express disappointment at their failure to achieve full recovery in a short time. To counteract the disappointment, they can be reminded that the addiction developed over many years and that recovery will be similarly gradual. It is helpful to set initial short-term goals and to suspend long-term goals until later. In some cases, the patient and family can be provided with a series of progressive steps, with projected dates of completion, that they will need to take to complete treatment. By reinforcing small changes in the right direction, the therapist can gradually change undesirable behavior. The therapist can also teach family members to shape one another's behavior (Thomas & Santa, 1982).

B. Relapse

Many alcoholics get caught in a vicious cycle of alternating episodes of problem drinking and abstinence. Unless a treatment plan can be established and implemented whereby the positive aspects of sobriety outweigh those of drinking, the patient will probably continue to relapse. Relapse in the recovering alcoholic may reflect either an inadequate treatment plan or poor compliance with it. Although relapses bring costly medical, psychological, and social consequences, when the relapsing patient continues to pursue treatment, the relapse can lead to constructive changes in the treatment plan or improved adherence to it.

It is helpful to teach the patient and family to recognize high-risk situations that lead to relapse and how to deal with them. For instance, if in the past family arguing often precipitated drinking, as soon as bickering begins the family should seek help. If being around alcohol triggers urges to drink, and staying away from alcohol is part of a patient's plan for recovery, then attending a wake where drinking occurs would be a high-risk situation needing special caution. Similarly, patients who discontinue taking disulfiram or attending AA meetings would be engaging in high-risk behaviors of which their families should be wary. In general, high-risk behaviors by any family member should be viewed as a danger signal for the entire family, and appropriate action should be taken to counteract them. If family members fail to do so, they must share some responsibility for a relapse that might ensue.

C. Setting Goals

The goals of recovery should be made explicit and should be agreed to by all members of the treatment team (Sobell, Sobell, & Nirenberg, 1982). For instance, if an alcoholic wants to return to nonproblem drinking, his wife wants him to stop beating her when he is intoxicated, and his therapist wants him to remain abstinent, these individuals will not be able to work effectively together as a team unless they compromise their goals.

The quality of recovery is not measured merely by the patient's drinking status. Unresolved problems in other areas of life (e.g., sexual dysfunction, erratic employment, depression, anxiety, family problems) must also be considered in goal setting. A patient may be unwilling or unable to modify his or her drinking if these other problems persist. Some of the problems may resolve spontaneously as problem drinking ceases; others may require intensive therapy to resolve; and still others may not be resolvable. The therapist should help the patient and family identify their problems, discover which can be resolved, and agree on how to address them.

IV. TREATMENT CONTRACTS

Treatment contracts are useful in assuring that patient and therapist understand each other. Contracts provide structure and direction for therapy. It is often important to complete a treatment contract early in treatment (even before a thorough assessment has been completed) because many patients and families drop out of treatment if they feel that they are getting little from it (Nirenberg, Sobell, & Sobell, 1980). An early contract may allay impatience and set the stage for early interventions while further assessment is done.

A. Monitoring Feelings and Behavior

A treatment contract may specify ways for the patient and family members to collect data, including those related to drinking behavior (Nirenberg, Sobell, & Ersner-Hershfield, 1983). Keeping track of feelings will be a new experience for some people who may need help even to name their feelings. Information gathering becomes a way to involve the patient and each family member actively in recovery and enhances communication. For instance, if an alcoholic wife is asked to tell her husband whenever she feels an urge to drink, he may learn to anticipate her urges, appreciate her commitment to abstinence despite her urges, and notice aspects of his own behavior that provoke her urges to drink.

B. Contingency Contracts

Contingency contracts are agreements between therapist, patient, and family that specify treatment goals and the consequences of meeting or failing to meet these goals (Anker & Crowley, 1982; Nirenberg, Ersner-Hershfield, Sobell, & Sobell, 1981). Contingency contracts may be used to extinguish unwanted behavior and/or increase the frequency of more healthy behavior.

Bigelow, Strickler, Liebson, and Griffiths (1976) examined the efficacy of contingency contracts with outpatient alcohol abusers. Patients posted monetary deposits that were refunded if they took disulfiram (Antabuse) daily. Patients reported longer periods of abstinence after this program was implemented than during the previous 3 years. Crowley (1984) reported similar improvements when drug-abusing physicians, nurses, and dentists instructed their therapist to mail to their licensing board a letter in which they admitted to drug abuse if they ever failed to pass a urine toxicology test.

Through contingency contracts, the patient and treatment team jointly determine treatment goals and ways to achieve them, specifying criteria for evaluating progress, procedures for monitoring it, and the consequences of breaking the contract. For example, contingency contracts can be used to improve family relations. By setting negative consequences for blaming and positive consequences for accepting responsibility, contracts can defuse family tension.

Because only a small proportion of patients are able to maintain abstinence or nonproblem drinking for extended periods (Polich, Armor, & Braiker, 1980), the consequences of relapse should be clearly specified through the contingency contract. A plan should be formulated to abort the relapse early before more severe damage is done. The cause of the relapse should be determined and the degree of therapeutic structure might be temporarily increased (e.g., through restriction of passes, disulfiram administration, increased frequency of counseling sessions). The contract should specify that the patient and family report any ingestion of alcohol, urges to drink, and conditions that may have increased the risk of relapse. This information will allow the treatment team to identify high-risk situations with which the patient and family will need to learn to cope. The contract should also specify a procedure for quickly stopping drinking once it has started.

Some patients are coerced into treatment by community agencies after the drinker violates a law or endangers others. Conflicts of interest can develop when an agency insists on obtaining information about a patient's progress in treatment. In such cases, a therapist must neither alienate the patient nor allow the patient and family to escape responsibility for their actions (Koppel, Stimmler, & Perone, 1980). If the patient or family perceives the therapist to be aligned with the authorities, they are likely to be less than totally honest in their interactions with the therapist. Hence, the conditions under which information about the patient will be divulged should be clearly specified in the contingency contract.

V. ASSESSMENT

A detailed assessment of the multidimensional problems of the alcohol abuser is critical for effective treatment (Nirenberg, 1983; Wanberg & Horn's chapter in this volume). The assessment should address problem analysis, treatment goal setting, and the patient's motivation for treatment.

A. Problem Analysis

Information about patterns of drinking and consequences of alcohol use can be gathered through a focused clinical interview, standardized drinking scales, self- and collateral reports, toxicology tests, and biochemical indicators of body damage (Liepman, 1984a, 1984b; Sobell et al., 1982). Ingestion patterns over time provide information about physical and psychological dependence and also reflect the patient's attempts to alleviate problem drinking. A functional analysis of alcohol problems should include evaluation of factors that sustain the drinking pattern or stimulate relapse. It is also important that the therapist be aware of the patient's ingestion of drugs in addition to alcohol.

In addition to alcohol problems per se, an assessment of the alcohol abuser must consider the patient's medical, psychiatric, family, and social problems. The patient might have problems that interfere with treatment, limiting the realistic options that a therapist may offer. A thorough assessment of patient handicaps and resources provides a basis for individualizing the treatment plan. Alcohol frequently interacts with a multiplicity of physical, psychological, and social factors to prevent permanent moderation or cessation of drinking without troublesome side effects. The extent of the patient's physical dependence will determine whether medical attention is necessary during detoxification to prevent the dangers of severe physiological withdrawal. Alcoholics who suffer from anxiety and phobic disorders while sober are particularly vulnerable to drinking for temporary symptomatic relief, although alcohol consumption probably impairs long-term recovery from these disorders (Cameron, Liepman, Curtis, & Thyer, in press; Mullaney & Trippett, 1979). Patients with personality disorders who react to alcohol by expressing pent-up emotions may learn that periodic drinking seems helpful, even though the unrestrained release of these feelings may cause social problems. Patients with bipolar affective disorders may lose control of their drinking during manic episodes, or drinking may precipitate a manic episode. Because alcoholism mimics certain psychiatric disorders, it is important to scrutinize the interaction between psychiatric symptoms and drinking to guard against misdiagnosis (Freed, 1975; Schuckit, 1973).

Barriers to treatment such as cognitive impairment, medical or psychiatric instability, legal problems, employment responsibilities, or inadequate social support must be overcome. For example, if a patient has Korsakoff's dementia, individual psychotherapy with an educational thrust would be inappropriate, but family education might be helpful. If a patient repeatedly drinks impulsively, disulfiram or inpatient/residential care may need to be considered as part of the initial treatment plan. Finally, a patient whose primary enabler is a homebound elderly mother should be encouraged to include the mother in family therapy sessions during home visits.

Resources valuable to recovery should be incorporated into the treatment plan. A primary resource is social support. Through structured interviews (Hartman & Laird, 1983), the therapist can identify the roles that various persons play in a patient's social support network (Johnson, 1980; Koppel et al., 1980). These roles should be taken into account during treatment planning. For example, the mother who rescues her son repeatedly from the consequences of his drinking will probably try to rescue him from the demands of treatment. Involvement in family therapy and attending Al-Anon may help her to curb her rescuing behavior and take control of her own life.

Alcoholic families may endure the painful consequences of alcoholism in order to maintain family stability (Billings, Kessler, Gomberg, & Weiner, 1979; Jacob, Dunn, & Leonard, 1983; Steinglass, Davis, & Berenson, 1977). The family's alternation between drinking and abstinence may be their way of coping with stress and achieving family flexibility (Davis, Berenson, Steinglass, & Davis, 1974; Jacob et al., 1983; Minuchin, 1974). Thus, unless the family is taught new coping skills, recovery may pose a serious threat to the family structure (Steinglass, 1980). By examining interpersonal deficits during abstinence that are remedied by drinking, the therapist may identify coping skills needed by the abstinent family members (Liepman, Nirenberg, & Broffman, 1985; McCrady, 1982). It may be helpful to observe the family both when the alcoholic is intoxicated and when sober. Such assessments have focused on communication patterns (Gorad, McCourt, & Cobb, 1971; Hersen, Miller, & Eisler, 1973; Jacob, Ritchey, Cvitkovic, & Blane, 1981), problem-solving techniques (Billings et al., 1979; Frankenstein, Hay, & Nathan, 1985), roles (Kogan & Jackson, 1963), and affective expression (Orford, Oppenheimer, Egert, Hensman, & Guthrie, 1976).

Consider the example of a male who is found to be shy and passive when sober but aggressive and violent when intoxicated. It is likely that he has difficulty expressing his angry feelings when sober, so he builds up resentments and vents them through violence when he is drunk. His wife may dominate him by instilling guilt when he is sober and provoke angry confrontations when he is drinking. This couple would benefit from assertiveness training so that their sober interactions would not lead to domination or resentment, and their interactions during drinking would not lead to aggression.

B. Treatment Goal Setting

After a patient's psychological, social, and biomedical problems have been identified, treatment should be planned to meet the patient's individual needs. For instance, a patient might need vocational retraining and placement to gain financial security and bolster self-esteem. Training to refuse drinks might be needed by a patient who must work or socialize with people in drinking settings. Sex therapy might be needed by a patient with sexual difficulties. The patient who suffers from chronic back pain might need instruction in pain-management techniques.

Planning a sequence of steps toward recovery helps the therapist to structure treatment, monitor progress, and identify resistance. To minimize discouragement, patients should focus on short-term, readily attainable goals. For instance, although marital harmony (a long-term goal) may take several months to achieve, reduction in blaming might be achieved in a matter of hours or days and might be regarded as a first short-term goal. Subsequent short-term goals might include becoming less defensive, increasing affective expression, and sharing resentments.

C. Motivation for Treatment

Many people enter treatment for alcohol problems while they are in crisis (Liepman, 1983, 1984a; Liepman, Wolper, & Vazquez, 1982; Smilkstein, 1980), and appear motivated to change. However, some people contemplate or experiment with change without making a firm commitment (Prochaska & DiClemente, 1982). Some alcoholics mislead others into believing that they are willing to change in order to avoid the unpleasant consequences of drinking. This reaction is typical among people who have been referred to treatment by the courts.

One schema for classifying patient's motivation for treatment has been devised by Prochaska and Di Clemente (1982) and includes five sequential stages of change: (1) contemplation of change, (2) decision to change, (3) change in behavior, (4) maintenance of new behavior, and (5) relapse to old behavior. Only patients who are in stages 1 or 2 are open to suggestions for change. A crisis may motivate transition from the maintenance to relapse stage, from the relapse to contemplation stage, or from the contemplation to decision stage (Smilkstein, 1980). Prochaska and Di Clemente's (1982) schema is discussed in greater detail in Curry and Marlatt's chapter in this volume.

A family's prior treatment record may predict their current motivation for treatment. It might be helpful to identify the variables that interfered with or facilitated prior treatment plans. Nevertheless, therapists must guard against prejudging families based on their prior performance in treatment.

Initial motivation for treatment may not be sustained. The therapist should remain alert to changes in motivation which may be reflected, for example, in changing rates at which short-term goals are achieved. While the patient or family may verbally endorse the long-term goal of recovery, they may not actually be willing to alter their behavior. When the therapist and family reach an impasse, it might be best to refer them to another therapist or to discontinue treatment altogether, with the option to resume treatment if they change their minds. The authors' experience shows that in the latter case, patients return to treatment with a new respect for the therapist.

VI. SUMMARY

The beginning of treatment is crucial in setting the tone for recovery. Establishing a strong, empathic, respectful, yet firm and objective alliance with the patient and family enhances the chances for successful treatment. Thorough medical, psychological, and social assessment of the patient and family provides the basis for a treatment plan and ensures that the needs of the entire family will be met. After the assessment, each family member is made aware of his or her contributions to the problems of the family so that each member can assume some responsibility for change. Treatment planning should seek to meet the needs of the patient and family in an incremental fashion, rewarding achievement of successive small short-term goals that comprise ultimate long-term recovery. Motivation for treatment should be assessed before and during treatment to ensure that the patient and family are cooperating with the treatment plan.

REFERENCES

Anker, A. L., & Crowley, T. J. (1982). Use of contingency contracts in specialty clinics for cocaine abuse. *National Institute on Drug Abuse Monograph Series, 41,* 452–459.

Beck, A. T., Rush, A. J., Shaw, B. F., & Emery, G. (1979). *Cognitive therapy of depression.* New York: Guilford.

Bigelow, G., Strickler, D., Liebson, I., & Griffiths, R. (1976). Maintaining disulfiram ingestion among outpatient alcoholics: A security-deposit contingency contracting procedure. *Behavior Research & Therapy, 14,* 378–381.

Billings, A. G., Kessler, M., Gomberg, C. A., & Weiner, S. (1979). Marital conflict resolution of alcoholic and nonalcoholic couples during drinking and nondrinking sessions. *Journal of Studies on Alcohol, 40,* 183–195.

Cameron, O. C., Liepman, M. R., Curtis, G. C. Jr. & Thyer, B. (in press). Ethanol retards desensitization of simple phobias in nonalcoholics. *British Journal of Psychiatry.*

Crowley, T. J. (1984). Contingency contracting treatment of drug-abusing physicians, nurses, and dentists. In J. Grabowski, M. L. Stitzer & J. E. Henningfield (Eds.), *Behavioral intervention techniques in drug abuse treatment* (National Institute on Drug Abuse Monograph Series, #46, DHHS Publication No. ADM 84-1282, pp. 68–83). Washington, DC: US Government Printing Office.

Davis, D. I., Berenson, D., Steinglass, P., & Davis, S. (1974). The adaptive consequences of drinking. *Psychiatry, 37,* 209–215.

Doherty, W. J., & Baird, M. A. (1983). *Family therapy and family medicine.* New York: Guilford.

Frankenstein, W., Hay, W. M., & Nathan, P. E. (1985). Effects of intoxication on alcoholics' marital communication and problem solving. *Journal of Studies on Alcohol, 46,* 1–6.

Freed, E. X. (1975). Alcoholism and schizophrenia: The search for perspectives. *Journal of Studies on Alcohol, 36,* 853–881.

Gorad, S. L., McCourt, W. F., & Cobb, J. C. (1971). A communications approach to alcoholism. *Quarterly Journal of Studies on Alcohol, 32,* 651–658.

Hartman, A., & Laird, J. (1983). *Family-centered social work practice.* New York: The Free Press.

Hersen, M., Miller, P. M., & Eisler, R. M. (1973). Interactions between alcoholics and their wives: A descriptive analysis of verbal and nonverbal behavior. *Journal of Studies on Alcohol, 34,* 516–520.

Jacob, T., Dunn, N. J., & Leonard, K. (1983). Patterns of alcohol use and family stability. *Alcoholism: Clinical and Experimental Research, 7,* 382–385.

Jacob, T., Ritchey, D., Cvitkovic, J. F., & Blane, H. T. (1981). Communication styles of alcoholic and nonalcoholic families when drinking and not drinking. *Journal of Studies on Alcohol, 42,* 466–482.

Janzen, C. (1977). Families in the treatment of alcoholism. *Journal of Studies on Alcohol, 38,* 114–130.

Johnson, V. (1980). *I'll quit tomorrow* (2nd ed.). New York: Harper & Row.

Kaufman, E. (1980). Myth and reality in the family patterns and treatment of substance abusers. *American Journal of Drug and Alcohol Abuse, 7,* 257–280.

Kaufman, E., & Kaufmann, P. (1977). Multiple family therapy: A new direction in the treatment of drug abusers. *American Journal of Drug and Alcohol Abuse, 4,* 467–478.

Kogan, K. L., & Jackson, J. K. (1963). Role perception in wives of alcoholics and nonalcoholics. *Quarterly Journal of Studies on Alcohol, 24,* 227–238.

Koppel, F., Stimmler, L., & Perone, F. (1980). The enabler: A motivational tool in treating the alcoholic. *Social Casework, 61,* 577–583.

Levy, B. (1972). Five years after: A follow-up of 50 narcotic addicts. *American Journal of Psychiatry, 7,* 102–106.

Liepman, M. R. (1983). Recognizing and managing the family at high risk for alcoholism. In J. W. Hess, M. R. Liepman, & T. J. Ruane (Eds.), *Family practice and preventive medicine: Health promotion in primary care* (pp. 210–237). New York: Human Sciences Press.

Liepman, M. R. (1984a). Chemical dependence in the family. In J. Christie-Seely (Ed.), *Working with the family in primary care: A systems approach to health and illness* (pp. 422–448). New York: Praeger.

Liepman, M. R. (1984b). Finding substance abusers. In M. R. Liepman, R. C. Anderson, & J. V. Fisher (Eds.), *Family medicine curriculum guide to substance abuse* (pp. 3.1–3.17). Kansas City, MO: Society for Teachers of Family Medicine.

Liepman, M. R., Nirenberg, T. D., & Broffman, T. E. (1985, October). *Drinking associated family behavior: Key to relapse and recovery.* Paper presented at the 43rd Annual and Second International Conference of the American Association for Marriage and Family Therapists, New York City.

Liepman, M. R., Nirenberg, T. D., & White, W. T. (1985). Family-oriented treatment of alcoholism, *Rhode Island Medical Journal, 68(3),* 123–126.

Liepman, M. R., & Tauriainen, M. (1980). Factors contributing to success and failure of family coercive interventions on alcoholics. *Alcoholism: Clinical and Experimental Research, 4,* 78.

Liepman, M. R., Whitfield, C. L., & Landeen, R. (1981, April). *Inadequate knowledge, skills, and attitudes about alcoholism in medical school faculty.* Paper presented at the 12th Annual Medical–Scientific Conference of the National Council on Alcoholism, New Orleans.

Liepman, M. R., Wolper, B., & Vazquez, J. (1982). An ecological approach for motivating women to accept treatment for drug dependency. In B. G. Reed, G. M. Beschner, & J. Mondonaro (Eds.), *Treatment services for drug dependent women* (Vol. 2) (National Institute on Drug Abuse Monograph Series, DHHS Publication No. ADM 82–1219, pp. 1–61). Washington, DC: U.S. Government Printing Office.

McCrady, B. S. (1982). Marital dysfunction: Alcohol and marriage. In E. M. Pattison & E. Kaufman (Eds.), *Encyclopedic handbook of alcoholism* (pp. 673–685). New York: Gardner Press.

Minuchin, S. (1974). *Families and family therapy.* Cambridge, MA: Harvard University Press.

Mullaney, J. A., & Trippett, C. J. (1979). Alcohol dependence and phobias: Clinical description and relevance. *British Journal of Psychiatry,* **135,** 565–573.

Nirenberg, T. D. (1983). Treatment of substance abuse. In C. E. Walker (Ed.), *The handbook of clinical psychology: Theory, research & practice* (Vol. 2) (pp. 633–665). Homewood, IL: Dorsey Press.

Nirenberg, T. D., Ersner-Hershfield, S., Sobell, L. C., & Sobell, M. B. (1981). Behavioral treatment of alcohol problems. In C. K. Prokop & L. A. Bradley (Eds.), *Medical psychology: Contributions to behavioral medicine* (pp. 267–290). New York: Academic Press.

Nirenberg, T. D., Sobell, L. & Ersner-Hershfield, S. (1983, November). *Self-monitoring of alcohol consumption: Reactivity and reliability.* Paper presented at the meeting of the World Congress on Behavior Therapy, Washington, DC.

Nirenberg, T. D., Sobell, L. C., & Sobell, M. B. (1980). Effective and inexpensive procedures for decreasing client attrition in an outpatient alcohol treatment program. *American Journal of Drug and Alcohol Abuse,* **7**(1), 73–82.

Orford, J., Oppenheimer, E., Egert, S., Hensman, C., & Guthrie, S. (1976). The cohesiveness of alcoholism-complicated marriages and its influence on treatment outcome. *British Journal of Psychiatry,* **128,** 318–339.

Polich, J. M., Armor, D. J., & Braiker, H. B. (1980). *The course of alcoholism: Four years after treatment.* Santa Monica, CA: Rand Corporation.

Prochaska, J. O., & DiClemente, C. C. (1982). Transtheoretical therapy: Toward a more integrative model of change. *Psychotherapy: Theory, Research and Practice,* **19,** 276–288.

Schuckit, M. A. (1973). Alcoholism and sociopathy: Diagnostic confusion. *Quarterly Journal of Studies on Alcohol,* **34,** 157–164.

Smilkstein, G. (1980). The cycle of family function: A conceptual model for family medicine, *Journal of Family Practice,* **11,** 223–232.

Sobell, L. C., Sobell, M. B., & Nirenberg, T. D. (1982). Differential treatment planning for alcohol abusers. In E. M. Pattison & E. Kaufman (Eds.), *Encyclopedic handbook of alcoholism.* New York: Gardner.

Stanton, M. D. (1979). Family treatment approaches to drug abuse problems. *Family Process,* **18,** 251–280.

Steinglass, P. (1980). A life history model of the alcoholic family. *Family Process,* **19,** 211–226.

Steinglass, P. (1981). The alcoholic family at home: Patterns of interaction in dry, wet, and transitional stages of alcoholism. *Archives of General Psychiatry,* **38:** 578–584.

Steinglass, P., Davis, D. I., & Berenson, D. (1977). Observations of conjointly hospitalized "alcoholic couples" during sobriety and intoxication: Implications for theory and therapy. *Family Process,* **16,** 1–16.

Thomas, E. J., & Santa, C. A. (1982). Unilateral family therapy for alcohol abuse; A working conception. *American Journal of Family Therapy,* **10,** 49–58.

Van Deusen, J. M., Stanton, M. D., Scott, S. M., Todd, T. C., & Mowatt, D. T. (1982). Getting the addict to agree to involve his family of origin: The initial contact. In M. D. Stanton, T. C. Todd & Associates (Eds.), *The family therapy of drug abuse and addiction* (pp. 39–59). New York: Guilford.

Whitaker, C. A. (1982). Power politics of family psychotherapy. In J. R. Neill & D. P. Kniskern (Eds.), *From psyche to system: The evolving therapy of Carl Whitaker* (pp. 272–277). New York: Guilford.

Whitfield, C. L. (1980). Medical education and alcoholism. *Maryland State Medical Journal,* **29**(10), 77–83.

3

The Assessment of Multiple Conditions in Persons with Alcohol Problems

KENNETH WANBERG

Private Practice
Denver, Colorado 80219
and
Division of Youth Services
State of Colorado
Denver, Colorado 80236
and
Horizon Hospital
Denver, Colorado 80218

JOHN L. HORN

Department of Psychology
University of Southern California
Los Angeles, California 90089-1061

I. OVERVIEW

Our aim in this chapter is to provide guidelines for assessing persons who are said to be alcoholic. These guidelines are developed at two levels. First, we discuss criteria for determining whether a person does or does not have alcohol problems that need treatment. Second, we describe a number of distinctly different factors that can be used in assessing persons with alcohol problems.

Today, 66% of the adult population in the United States uses alcohol (Ray, 1983). Yet, only a portion of this group develops problems with alcohol that

27

need treatment. Most diagnostic systems are designed only to make the distinction between alcohol use and misuse (i.e., "alcohol" and "not alcoholic"). Such diagnostic approaches regard alcoholism as a single condition or disease determined by a set of symptoms an individual does or does not have.

Deciding that a person is to be included in an alcohol-misuse (alcoholism) category does not mean that one has obtained a valid description of the different conditions that are associated with that misuse. To describe such conditions, we move to a second level of assessment—a level that goes beyond merely using inclusion criteria for treatment of a single condition. Guidelines at this level are based on our multiple-condition theory of alcoholism, which holds that there are many distinct factors that define different kinds of alcoholism. We describe these factors objectively and indicate how they can be used to understand a person with problems related to alcohol use.

Our multiple-condition theory is built on factors defined by several self-report instruments that were developed in empirical and analytical studies conducted over a period of 17 years. This research led to the development of the Alcohol Use Inventory (AUI) (Horn, Wanberg, & Foster, 1986a). This instrument contains 17 primary scales, each providing measures of a specific condition of alcohol use and misuse. Six second-order factors define broad yet independent dimensions of alcoholism, and a general factor provides a conglomerate measure of the use and misuse of alcohol. The scales of the AUI are presented in Table 1. An acronym (e.g., SUSTAIND for sustained drinking) is used to identify each scale (factor). The methods and procedures used to develop the AUI are found elsewhere (Horn, Wanberg, & Foster, 1986b; Wanberg, Horn, & Foster, 1977). The concepts derived from the AUI scales provide a structure for a varigated approach to the assessment of persons with problems associated with alcohol use.[1]

II. THE CASE FOR MULTIPLE-CONDITION THEORIES

There is widespread belief that alcoholism represents a single condition of fundamental and invariant symptoms. The influential work of Jellinek (1952) and Glatt (1976) presents this case. In most clinical settings, the objective is to diagnose a single condition of alcoholism and often to assume there is only one treatment for this condition. Much of the research on alcohol problems has sought merely to identify differences between alcoholics and nonalcoholics (e.g., Barnes, 1983; Knox, 1976). Textbooks of

[1]The computerized and paper-pencil versions of the Alcohol Use Inventory are distributed by National Computer Systems, Inc., P.O. Box 1416, Minneapolis, MN 55343.

abnormal psychology (e.g., Harmatz, 1978; Gallatin, 1982) discuss alcoholism as a single abnormality. In short, among clinicians, researchers, theorists, and laypersons it is widely believed that alcoholism is best characterized by a single condition.

Widespread belief, however, does not indicate strong scientific support. Our reading of the evidence leads us to conclude that single-condition theories are incorrect. Support for this conclusion was indicated in our early study of self-reported problems and behaviors associated with the use of alcohol (Horn & Wanberg, 1969). It was impossible to represent our data with a Spearman one-common factor model; more than one principal component was needed to account adequately for the interrelationships. A simple-structure model was found to be reasonably appropriate, and 13 factors were identified. Eight of these 13 factors were invariant (as discussed in Horn, McArdle, & Mason, 1983) across gender and ethnic groupings. Results from our subsequent studies repeatedly failed to conform to single-condition theories (Foster, Horn, & Wanberg, 1972; Horn & Wanberg, 1970, 1973; Horn, Wanberg, & Adams, 1982; Horn, Wanberg, & Appel, 1973; Wanberg & Horn, 1970, 1973, 1983; Wanberg, Horn, & Foster, 1977). The various forms of alcoholism identified by these studies have different construct validities (Wanberg & Horn, 1983).

Several other investigators have found support for a multiple-condition theory of alcoholism (Caddy, 1978; Hyman, 1976; Pattison, 1982; Pattison, Sobell, & Sobell, 1977). Pattison and Kaufman (1982a) concluded that the scientific evidence best supports a multivariate model of assessment. They note that single-condition theories or "binary diagnostic methods have utility for screening, triage referral, and limited epidemiologic research. However, multivariate diagnostic methods are required for treatment selection, evaluation, and research" (p. 22). It is practical and empirically sound, therefore, to base the assessment of persons with alcohol problems on the assumption that there are a number of distinctly different conditions associated with the misuse of alcohol.

III. INCLUSION CRITERIA

Regardless of whether one favors a single-condition or a multiple-condition concept of alcoholism, the first level of assessment involves the utilization of criteria in order to identify individuals who have problems in the use of alcohol. These inclusion criteria, specified mostly by single-condition theories, adumbrate conditions that call for treatment. We now examine the inclusion criteria of a few well-established theories.

TABLE 1

Alcohol Use Multiple-Condition Measurement Concepts: Scales of the Alcohol Use Inventory

Primary scales

Benefits of alcohol use:

1. SOCIALIM—Drink to improve sociability: drinking helps to socialize, make friends, feel less inferior, relax socially, overcome shyness, feel more important, get along with people, relate better to opposite sex, and better express ideas.
2. MENTALIM—Drink to improve mental functioning: drink to be mentally alert, think better, work better, reach higher goals.
3. MANGMOOD—Drink to manage and change moods: drink to let down, relieve tension, to forget, get over being depressed, change moods, because things pile up; swing from periods of happiness to periods of despair.
4. MARICOPE—Drinking follows marital problems: marital problems before drank, spouse unfaithful, spouse jealous, changes in spouse and marital problems have led to drinking.

Styles of alcohol use:

5. GREGARUS—Gregarious versus solo use: drink at bars, parties, with friends, not alone, not at home, with opposite sex; most friends drink; most drinking done with acquaintances; usually drink with same group; social life requires drinking.
6. COMPULSV—Obsessive–compulsive drinking: drink throughout day; always think about alcohol; drink same time daily; carry bottle; sneak drinks; bottle by bedside; fear won't have drink.
7. SUSTAIND—Sustained versus periodic use: drink daily; drink weekends and during week; no abstinent periods; intoxicated daily; drinking daily last 6 months or more; do not go on wagon after drunk; long drinking periods.

Disruptive consequences of alcohol use:

8. LCONTROL—Loss of control over behavior when drinking: blackouts, pass out, get mean and belligerent, stagger, and stumble, harm to others, suicide attempts, all when drinking; gulp drinks.
9. ROLEMALA—Social role maladaptation: loss of job, live alone, driving offenses, miss work, move a lot, detained by authorities, unemployed, not in a marriage situation, all as a result of drinking.
10. DELIRIUM—Psychoperceptual withdrawal: fuzzy thinking, see, hear, feel things, weird and frightening sensations, all when sobering up; have had delirium tremens.
11. HANGOVER—Psychophysical withdrawal: convulsions, shakes, hangovers, physically sick, hot and sweaty, rapid heartbeat, all when sobering up.
12. MARIPROB—Marital problems in consequence of drinking: spouse angry and irritated over drinking; belittle and argue with spouse when drinking; physically abusive when drinking; spouse nags when drinking; drinking a factor in marital problems.

Self-concerns about disruptive consequences:

13. QUANTITY—Quantity of daily use when drinking: much wine, beer, spirits a day when drinking.
14. GUILTWOR—Guilt and worry associated with drinking: worried drinking getting worse, occurring at unaccustomed times; drink causing noticeable fear, depression, anxiety; avoid talking about drinking; make excuses to cover up drinking; guilt after drunk; drinking causes hardships with family and friends.
15. HELPBEFR—Prior attempts to stop drinking: used Antabuse, have been detoxified, attended AA, sought religion to stop, have sought help many times, used tranquilizers to sober up.

TABLE 1 (*Continued*)

Acknowledgement of alcohol use problems:

16. RECEPTIV—treatment readiness: recent crisis led to help; need help now; give month's salary to stop drinking; will do what a counselor suggests; feel that will be able to stop drinking.

17. AWARENES—Awareness of problems: am sure have problems with drinking; unable to regulate time, amount drunk; realize drinking interferes with living responsibilities.

Second-order scales

A. ENHANCED—Drinking to enhance functioning: drink to have fun, to be mentally alert, to have better ideas, to meet people, for ideas to come more freely, to work better, to get along with people, to better express thoughts to opposite sex, to be happier; go to parties to drink; social life requires drinking; most friends drink; do most drinking at bars; most drinking done with friends and acquaintances; encourage others to drink with me; drink to work better;

B. OBSESSED—Obsessive-sustained drinking: do not drink, sober up and drink again; drinking daily last six months or more; don't go on the wagon; drink during week and on weekends; dwelling on alcohol constantly; keep alcohol close at hand; drink to go to sleep at night; sneak drinks; hide bottles; intoxicated daily; little or no time between drinking periods; carry a bottle; fear may not have drink when need it; long drinking periods; drinking during work day.

C. DISRUPT1—Uncontrolled, life-functioning disruption: drinking much spirits, wine or beer each day when drink; as a result of drinking; have had a convulsion, long blackouts, been physically sick, had delirium tremens, passed out, stumbled and staggered, saw and heard things not there, felt things not there, moved from place to place, lived alone, charged with drunken driving, missed work, lost a job, detained for public drunkenness, had medical help to sober up; gulp drinks; drank in morning to relieve hangovers.

E. ANXCONCN—Anxious concern about drinking: drink causes hardships on family, excessive worry, guilt, shame, depression, mood changes, vague fears and anxieties; show resentments when drinking; afraid drinking getting worse, is occurring at unaccustomed times; drink to get over depression, to relieve tension, to forget, to let down, because things pile up; make excuses to cover drinking; avoid talking about drinking; guilt and depression after bout; moods different when drinking than when not drinking; sad when drinking; drink to change moods.

F. RECPAWAR—Awareness of alcohol problem: unable to regulate and control time and amount of drinking; frequency and amount recently increased; drinking definitely a problem now; difficult living without alcohol; present drinking interferes with responsibilities; recent crisis increased awareness of need for help; sure have drinking problem; sought help on own; need assistance now; willing to stay in treatment several weeks; worth more than one month's salary to correct problem; will do anything to stop; will try whatever counselor suggests; am confident can stop drinking.

A Third-order Alcoholism Factor

G. ALCINVOL—Broad alcohol involvement: Drinking much distilled spirits; unable stop after one or two; shakes, fuzzy thinking, hangovers, physically sick, noticeable fears, blackouts, see things not there, hear things not there, feel things not there, hot and feverish, rapid heart beat, weird and frightening sensations, miss work, pass out, lose control over what do, all when drinking or sobering up; drink to relieve hangover; drink in order to feel important, overcome shyness, relieve tension, to forget, when things pile up, to get over depression, to sleep at night; drink throughout day, keep somewhat intoxicated daily; keep alcohol close at hand, constantly think about alcohol, gulp drinks; make excuses or lie to cover up drinking; show marked resentments when drinking; moved geographically to stop drinking; feel depressed after a bout; always have drinks at a bar or party.

31

A. Phase Progression Theories

Jellinek (1952) provides the best-known example of a phase progression theory. He identified four phases of alcoholism: pre-alcoholic, prodromal, crucial, and chronic. Glatt (1957) further developed this model and specified that the phases follow a quadratic curve of deterioration that leads to "bottom level," from which reversal of the curve through stages of recovery can occur. The defining features of the phases of this theory are indicated in the lower part of Table 2.

In Table 2, we also list several AUI factors (described in detail in Table 1) along with the numbers and letters corresponding to the symptoms and behaviors of the phases of the Jellinek–Glatt theory. The table illustrates how factors defining multiple conditions of alcohol use relate to the Jellinek–Glatt phases. Most factors comprise drinking symptoms and behaviors from each of the various phases of the Jellinek–Glatt theory. These factors are statistically and mathematically independent (though correlated). The factor-analytic results thus indicate that the phases of this single-condition model do not represent distinct symptom clusters.

In addition to statistical problems, some of the assumptions of phase theories do not seem logical. For example, blackouts (associated with the prodromal phase) occur with some people only when they have experienced other severe alcoholic symptoms after extended periods of drinking, but occur among other individuals who have drunk to excess on only one occasion. Despite the many problems of the phase theory (Pattison, 1982), the symptoms of the various phases indicate important problems of alcohol misuse which provide a useful framework for defining inclusion characteristics.

B. Definitional Diagnostic Systems

There have been three major attempts to define alcoholism in terms of sets of diagnostic criteria:

1. The World Health Organization (WHO) Definition

An objective of WHO (1952, 1964) has been to depict alcohol problems in a manner that permits comparison across different cultures, ethnic groups, and communities. The 1964 WHO report defined *dependency* as involving a compulsion to use alcohol to "experience its psychic effects," or to "avoid the discomfort of its absence."

A WHO Task Force (Edwards, Gross, Keller, & Moser, 1976) defined the Alcohol Dependence Syndrome (ADS), the essential feature of which is "impaired control" and includes increased tolerance to alcohol, repeated withdrawal symptoms, drinking to avoid withdrawal, compulsion to drink,

TABLE 2

Relationship between Psychometrically Independent Factors of the Alcohol Use Inventory (AUI) and Variables Defining the Single-Condition Phase Theories

| | COMPULSV | SUSTAIND | Variables of the phase theories that define AUI Scales | | | | |
			LCONTROL	ROLEMALA	DELIRIUM	HANGOVER	GUILTWOR
	Scale 6	Scale 7	Scale 8	Scale 9	Scale 10	Scale 11	Scale 14
	Obsessive–compulsive drinking	Sustained vs. periodic	Loss of behavior control	Social role breakdown	Psychological withdrawal symptoms	Physical withdrawal symptoms	Postdrinking fear, worry and guilt
	A,F,G	I	C,D			B	E,H
	11,14	7	1,3,4,8	2,12,13		15,16	5,6,9,10
	i,j,n	a,b	e,k	h,k,m	c,f	g,l	d

Phases of alcoholism

Pre-alcoholic and prodromal phases	Crucial phase	Chronic phase

A. Surreptitious drinking
B. Physically sick
C. Gulping drinks
D. Blackouts
E. Feelings of guilt
F. Drink at specific time
G. Preoccupation with drinking
H. Avoidance of reference to drinking
I. Avid drinking

1. Loss of control over drinking
2. Loss of jobs, work problems
3. Antisocial acting out
4. Resentments
5. Shame and remorse
6. Drinking hard on family and friends
7. Go on the wagon
8. Aggressive behavior
9. Depressed, self-pity, outside interests abandoned
10. Make excuses for drinking (rationalizations, alibis)
11. Alcohol hoarding
12. Abandoned by family
13. Geographic cure
14. Alcohol-centered life
15. Morning drinking
16. Tremors and shakes

a. Benders (prolonged)
b. Drink daily during day
c. Hallucinations (DTs)
d. Unreasonable fears (indefinable fears)
e. Belligerent anger
f. Fuzzy thinking (thinking impaired)
g. Convulsions
h. Living alone due to drinking
i. Panic when nothing to drink
j. Keep alcohol around all the time
k. Chronically unemployed
l. Rapid heartbeat on withdrawal
m. Ethical deterioration
n. Obsessive thinking about alcohol

reinstatement of symptomatic drinking after abstinence, and obsession with drinking-related activities. Many of the characteristics of ADS described by WHO are empirically represented among AUI first-order scales 6, 10, 11, and 13 in Table 1.

Recognizing that some persons develop problems from their use of alcohol but do not present the criteria that defines ADS, a WHO study (Edwards, Gross, Keller, Moser, & Room, 1977) recommended that two separate classifications be used: (1) ADS and (2) a condition labeled "alcohol-related disabilities" (ARD). Many of the characteristics of ARD are empirically represented by AUI scales 8, 9, 12, and 14 in Table 1.

Both ADS and ARD are represented in our second-order factor that we labeled alcoholic deterioration in a previous report (Wanberg, Horn, & Foster, 1977) and is the DISRUPT1 scale in Table 1. Skinner and Allen (1982) demonstrated that a one-factor solution accounted for most of the reliable variance of DISRUPT1. Considering these results and the international thrust of the WHO definitions, we (Horn, Skinner, Wanberg, & Foster, 1984) put forth a separate scale that provides a measure of the WHO ADS concept, discussed below.

The rationale of the WHO definition is that if enough of the symptoms in ADS are reported, a person can be said to be "alcoholic." It is important to note that while there is unifactor evidence for the ADS concept, it is only one of several second-order factors found among alcohol-use characteristics that indicate alcoholism as defined by various theories.

2. The National Council on Alcoholism (NCA) Definition

The NCA (1972) system is based on 86 dichotomous indicators, divided into two tracks: (1) physiological dependence/clinical and (2) behavioral/ psychological/attitudinal. The Track I physiological indicators include withdrawal symptoms (tremors, hallucinations, seizures, and delirium tremens), tolerance, and blackouts. *Tolerance* is defined as (1) a blood alcohol level (BAL) of 150 mg/% without gross evidence of intoxication and (2) the body-weight-adjusted equivalent of an 180-pound person consuming one-fifth of a gallon of distilled alcohol daily, or the equivalent in beer or wine. A *blackout* is defined as a drinking-related loss of awareness for extended periods of time. Most of the Track I physiological indicators are found in AUI Scales 6, 10, 11, and 13 of Table 1. The clinical indicators of Track I involve illnesses associated with alcohol use (e.g., alcoholic hepatitis, Wernicke-Korsakoff syndrome, alcoholic cardiomyopathy).

Track II is defined by problems in behavioral, psychological, and attitudinal functioning. An important feature of Track II is that the individual drinks despite strong medical contraindication or despite strong social contraindication (job loss, marriage disruption, arrest for driving while intoxicated). Many of the Track II indicators are found in AUI Scales 8, 9, 12, and

14 of Table 1. The symptoms of the NCA system are also classified as major and minor. To be diagnosed as alcoholic, one must display at least one major symptom and several minor symptoms.

There are problems with reliability and validity in the NCA system (Pattison & Kaufman, 1982a). For example, with respect to validity, Breitenbucher (1976) found that of 70 persons identified as alcoholic with criteria external to the NCA system, only 5 matched the NCA physical criteria. Ringer, Kufner, Antons, and Feuerlein (1977) found that only 38 of the 86 items of the NCA system discriminated between an alcoholic-identified group and a control group; there were many (47.5%) false positives in the control group. Although these and other problems exist in the NCA system, the NCA indicators do provide a basis for inclusion criteria.

3. The American Psychiatric Association (APA) Definition

The *Diagnositic and Statistical Manual of Mental Disorders* (DSM-III, APA, 1980) classifies a number of conditions under three broad categories that lead to two diagnoses: alcohol abuse and alcohol dependence (see Table 3). Alcohol dependence represents the traditional concept of alcoholism, while alcohol abuse refers to "probable alcoholism" (Robins, 1982).

As can be seen in Table 3, alcohol abuse encompasses Categories 1 and 2, the symptoms occurring for at least 1 month; alcohol dependence encompasses the conditions of either Category 1 or 2, in addition to the conditions of Category 3. Alcohol abuse is best represented by AUI Scales 6, 7, 8, 9, 12, and 13, and the tolerance and withdrawal criteria for alcohol dependence are best represented psychometrically by AUI Scales 10, 11, and 14 in Table 1.

There are problems with some of the DSM-III criteria used to define alcohol dependence and alcohol abuse. For example, it is difficult to reliably identify tolerance (Gitlow, 1982; Robins, 1982). Gitlow (1982) observed that while it is assumed that alcoholics drink more than social drinkers, this assumption is not well-supported by clinical experience. The total ethanol intake of some who are identified as alcoholic may be less than the intake of some social drinkers. People vary considerably in the absolute amount they drink and the amount they drink before showing overt signs of intoxication. As well, in terms of some measures (such as reaction time), the physiologically deteriorated alcoholic is likely to show decreased (not increased) tolerance. Although tolerance may be an important concept in defining certain alcohol use patterns, it may not be a reliable indicator for determining an alcohol dependence diagnosis.

The APA system does not provide clear concepts for defining the psychological and affective disruptions—e.g., guilt, remorse, fear, anxiety—that can occur as a result of alcohol misuse, disruptions that are represented by AUI Scale 14. The APA model does provide guidelines for inclusion criteria. Its main problem, however, is subjectivity—a topic discussed next.

TABLE 3

Summary of DSM-III Criteria with Alcohol Use Inventory Scales Representing These Criteria

	Category I	Category II	Category III
	Pattern of pathological alcohol use	Impairment in social/occupational functioning	Tolerance or withdrawal secondary to alcohol use
DSM-III criteria	1. Daily need for use 2. Unable to stop or cut down on use 3. Repeated efforts to stop or control use 4. Binges (two days or more) 5. Consumption of fifth of spirits or beer/wine equivalent 6. Blackouts 7. Drinking in spite of exacerbation of physical disorders 8. Drinking nonbeverage alcohol	1. Violence when drinking 2. Absence from work when drinking 3. Legal problems resulting from drinking 4. Loss of job due to drinking 5. Arguments or difficulties with family/friends when drinking	1. Tolerance: need for markedly increased amounts to achieve the desired effects or markedly diminished effect with regular use of same amounts or 2. Withdrawal including: tremor of hand, tongue, eyelid; one of following: nausea/vomiting, malaise/weakness, autonomic hyperactivity(e.g., sweats), orthostatic hypertension, or depression, anxiety.
AUI diagnosis	SUSTAIND COMPULSV QUANTITY	ROLEMALA LCONTROL MARIPROB	HANGOVER GUILTWOR QUANTITY

ALCOHOL ABUSE

ALCOHOL DEPENDENCE

C. Measures of Alcoholism

The WHO, NCA, and APA systems require that clinical observations be used to determine whether or not the inclusion conditions for a category have been satisfied. Subjectivity is intrinsic to such assessment. In clinical observation, different clinicians often do not agree about the presence or absence of a defining condition; the same clinician on different occasions can render different conclusions; critical items can be overlooked; the clinician may be biased and make a judgment on the basis of only a few items or symptoms.

One approach to dealing with the problem of subjectivity is to combine a variety of indicators that are as objectively determined as possible and to all of which the subject is required to respond. This approach permits the subjective and idiosyncratic features of the separate indicators to cancel out as the reliable and valid features of the indicators accumulate in the composite. This is the principle on which most psychological measurement is based (Horn, 1971).

Horn, Skinner, Wanberg, and Foster's (1984) Alcohol Dependence Scale measures the ADS features of the WHO definition, as well as many of the features of the NCA and DSM-III criteria. It incorporates several assessment procedures that tend to reduce subjectivity such as that of combining several indicators. Skinner and Allen (1982) found that almost one-third of the total variance produced by the items of AUI Scales 6, 8, 10, and 11 could be accounted for by the first principal component; 29 items of this scale provided a homogeneous measure of this component with an internal consistency reliability of .90. This indicates that by combining 29 items of information, the idiosyncratic variance associated with any single item is reduced. Because the Horn et al. (1984) scale reduces several subjective influences, it is referred to as the ADSO (O for objective).

While measures such as ADSO reduce or eliminate several subjective influences associated with ratings and clinical observations, they do not eliminate the subjectivity that is inherent in self-ratings. A person can be unaware of her/his own condition or can consciously falsify the true condition. Adding over items helps to reduce this form of subjectivity.

While the ADSO provides a good measure of the major component of the first-order factors, it is not a measure of the major component among all of the first-order factors of the AUI. There is evidence for at least four second-order dimensions, each of which involves some of the alcoholism indicators specified in the phase progression, WHO, NCA, and APA systems. A third-order factor can be identified among the second-order dimensions of the AUI. This broad alcohol involvement dimension (ALCINVOL in Table 1) has about 50% of its items in common with DISRUPT1 and therefore,

ADSO. The variance of ALCINVOL, then, is larger than the variance of ADSO and taps influences that are not obvious indicators of alcoholism. These influences help to cancel out some of the subjective features of the ADSO.

For example, a person may be less defensive about subscribing to the alcohol use behaviors of ALCINVOL that are not as face-valid with respect to alcoholism, yet which contribute to a general alcohol involvement measure. Evidence for the value of ALCINVOL is accumulating but is now incomplete. Its internal consistency reliability ranges from .93 to .95.

There are problems in using measures of alcoholism in specifying criteria that will enable treatment staffs to sensibly, objectively, reliably, and validly determine who does or does not need treatment. The main problem is the question of what indicators, and how many, are counted in measures such as those suggested by WHO, NCA, and APA definitions, or in the more objective measures of ADSO or ALCINVOL.

Data presented in Figure 1 illustrate an inclusion guideline, and some problems with using the symptom-counting method for specifying the inclusion condition. All samples of Figure 1 would be regarded (by some) as representing persons with alcohol problems. Samples A, B, and C are groups of patients voluntarily hospitalized because of diagnosed alcoholism: Sample A from the state hospital serving metropolitan Denver; Sample B from a private hospital in Denver; and Sample C from the Denver Veterans Administration Medical Center. Sample D is from an alcohol-education program designed for court-referred individuals convicted of an alcohol-related driving offense.

The distributions of Samples A, B, and C are similar to each other but are notably different from Sample D. In samples A, B, and C, about 90% of the subjects score above a raw score of 15 on ALCINVOL; in Sample D, only 20% score this high. If it were assumed that a large percentage of Sample D (say, 80%) should not be classified as alcoholic, then a cut-score of 15 could be accepted as a reasonable point at which to draw the line between alcoholics and nonalcoholics. This divider would classify about 10% of the people in samples A, B, and C as not alcoholic.

The obvious problem comes with assuming that sample D contains fewer persons with alcohol problems than the other groups. It may be that many of the court-referred people have alcohol problems, but are unwilling (or unable) to acknowledge them. Thus, a raw score lower than 15 could be accepted as the point of dividing alcoholics from nonalcoholics. If the items of ADSO had been scored rather than the items of ALCINVOL, then fewer items would be counted, but a higher proportion of the items would be considered as face-valid for alcoholism.

The fundamental problem of symptom-counting diagnosis is thus indi-

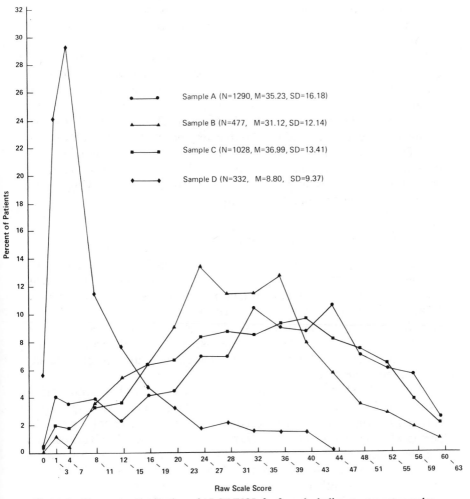

Figure 1. Frequency distribution of ALCINVOL for four alcoholism treatment samples.

cated: which symptoms, and how many, should be counted? A cut score based on broad measures such as ADSO or ALCINVOL can provide the clinician with guidelines, but this information alone does not provide a sufficient basis for generally applicable, inclusion criteria.

D. The Impaired-Control Negative Consequences Cycle

Alcohol use is governed by the same laws that govern other behavior: it is purposeful. People use alcohol either (1) to bring about positive consequences or (2) to turn off or attenuate feelings and thoughts associated with negative life consequences. These uses encompass the benefits of drinking outlined in Table 1.

For some people, at some point in their drinking careers, negative consequences result from alcohol use (e.g., loss of job, physical problems, as represented in Scales 8 through 14 of Table 1 and indicated in the preceding outlined diagnostic systems). *Impaired control* over alcohol use is indicated when such notable negative consequences occur. The *impaired control cycle* begins when alcohol is used to solve the very problems that result from its use. If we define problem drinking on the basis of the occurrence of negative consequences, then all persons in Sample D of Figure 1 would be considered as meeting our inclusion criteria (e.g., an alcohol-related driving offense would be considered a negative consequence of drinking).

E. Self-Selection and the Relationship Identifier

Even though an individual can be classified as having problems with alcohol, it does not follow necessarily that the individual will enter treatment. Two additional factors are usually involved. First, the individual must be aware that there are problems related to alcohol use and then acknowledge the need for treatment. The basis of this self-selection process is found in Scales 16 and 17 of the AUI. Such self-selection is enhanced when the individual experiences some emotional concern about the disruptive quality of drinking (Scale 14).

Second, self-selection is often precipitated by a relationship identifier (RI) (Wackwitz, Diesenhaus, & Foster, 1977). A RI is a person who forges a link between life-role disruptions and conditions of using alcohol. Often, the person who makes this connection is not the alcohol user. The RI concludes that the undesirable behaviors of the drinker are a direct consequence of the drinker's use of alcohol (although the major determinants of the life-role disruptions may be other than alcohol use). Thus, there is a pattern of alcohol use (e.g., compulsion to drink), and disruptions in role functions; an RI links these together. The drinker accepts the RI's analysis and enters treatment. Until the link between drinking and role disruption is established, the drinker is not likely to enter alcoholism treatment no matter how many other indicators of alcoholism may be present.

F. Determining Entry into Treatment

No one set of criteria uniquely defines the improper use of alcohol. There are several different alcoholisms. We have seen that the phase progression, single-condition theories do not provide an adequate basis for inclusion criteria. We are led to consider, therefore, some form of multiple-condition basis for inclusion in treatment. The following three sets of criteria can help to provide an improved basis for treatment selection:

1. Self-selection: The alcohol user must admit to having problems associated with the use of alcohol, and that these problems require treatment.

2. A relationship identifier: A person, or several people, forges the link between life-role disruptions and the use of alcohol and suggests that this condition is treatable.

3. Impaired control: This involves two essential features: (a) direct negative consequences resulting from alcohol use, evidenced by information gathered from the user and from others using an interview in accordance with a diagnostic system and objective measures (e.g., ADSO or ALCINVOL); (b) evidence of a negative-consequence cycle indicating that deterioration of life functions follows from use of alcohol and results in further use of alcohol.

IV. MULTIPLE-CONDITION CONCEPTS AND MEASURES

The second level of assessment involves the identification and description of specific conditions associated with alcohol misuse. We define several multiple-condition concepts and measures that can be used at this level in assessing persons with alcohol problems. The main focus here is on four domains of information: alcohol use, background, current life-adjustment, and personality.

A. Alcohol Use

A number of concepts help us to understand why and how alcohol is used, the results of its use, and the degree to which a person is concerned and willing to do something about unfavorable consequences of its use. The scales of the AUI provide the empirical basis for assessing these concepts. Five sets of measures provide a basis for organizing our thinking: benefits from use, styles of use, negative consequences of use, concerns about use, and acknowledgment that use is causing problems. Figure 2 provides a system for describing the five concepts and their specific expressions. As each concept is discussed, the reader is referred to the AUI measurement definition (using the scale acronym) in Table 1 that represents the concept.

1. Benefits from Alcohol Use

The benefits of alcohol use refer to producing positive effects and alleviating negative conditions. One area of positive benefit is that of using alcohol to *improve sociability*—to help one better relate to others, to improve the ability to express feelings and thoughts, and to deal with feelings of inferiority

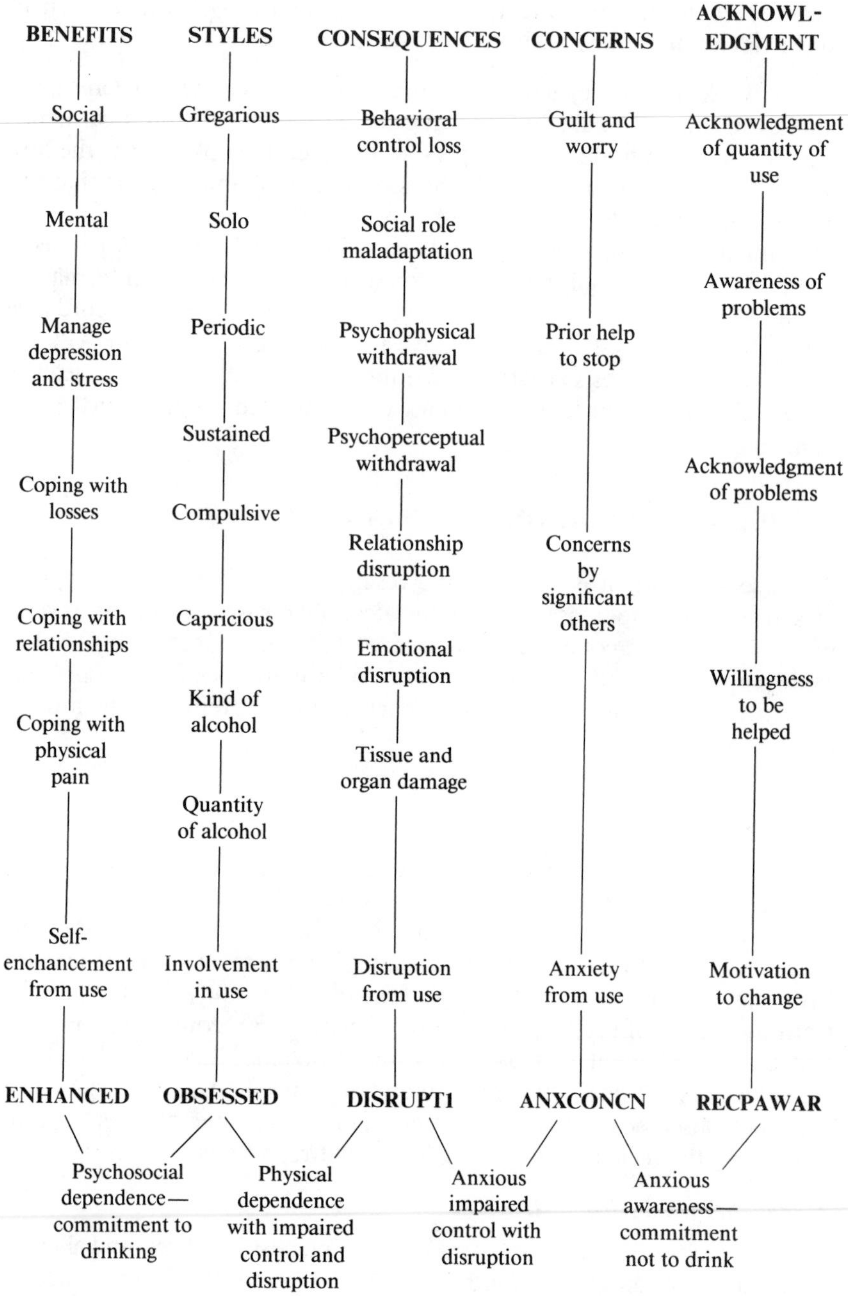

Figure 2. Conceptual framework for describing alcohol use multiple conditions.

(SOCIALIM in Table 1). Drinking is also used *to improve mental functioning* (MENTALIM). Although alcohol is a central nervous system depressant, people often believe that they think better, are more mentally alert, can reach higher goals, and can work better while drinking. People also *drink to feel good emotionally*—to achieve a high, to feel euphoric, and to experience a "warm glow." This benefit is measured by both the SOCIALIM and MENTALMP scales.

Several scales help the clinician to identify the use of alcohol to alleviate negative life conditions. People report that drinking helps to cope with, or escape from, internal stress and the discomfort of life problems and disruptions. They *drink to manage negative* moods, tension, or depression. This use is measured by the MANGMOOD scale. Others report using alcohol to help *cope with stressful relationships* and problems associated with marital stress (MARICOPE).

Alcohol is often used to deal with *somatic pain*. It is commonly reported by patients that they drink to alleviate headaches, back pain, muscle tension, and arthritis. However, this benefit is not directly assessed in the current version of the AUI.

The negative conditions that drinking alleviates prior to problematic drinking can also be a consequence of alcholism. For example, the use of alcohol to cope with marital stress (MARICOPE) correlates positively (about .30) with marital stress resulting from drinking (MARIPROB). The use of alcohol to cope with negative moods (MANGMOOD) correlates .60 with negative moods and stress caused by drinking (GUILTWOR). Thus, the benefits and consequences of alcohol use are more closely related in the intrapersonal than the interpersonal domain of functioning.

A broad second-order dimension among the benefits scales is measured by the ENHANCED factor of the AUI (Table 1). This measure indicates the degree to which the person is committed to drinking and hence psychologically dependent on alcohol. It is separate and independent from other dimensions of alcoholism, particularly those dimensions that point to the control alcohol can have in a person's life. Thus, it may warrant attention during treatment.

2. Styles of Use

The styles of use refer to the manner in which alcohol is used. The dimensions that describe use styles are illustrated in Figure 2 and described in Table 1.

The first of these dimensions distinguishes between *gregarious and solo drinking*. It is common to find people who consistently follow only one of these two patterns throughout their drinking career; they are either gregarious or solo drinkers. Others begin their drinking in a gregarious manner and then change to a solo, isolative pattern in later years; or the gregarious, convivial drinker may shift to a solo pattern during times of stress. A continuum from gregarious to solo drinking is measured by the GREGARUS scale (Table 1).

The second style of use distinguishes sustained from periodic alcohol drinking and is measured by SUSTAIND (Table 1). Several distinct patterns can be identified by using the periodic and sustained concepts. One is the sustained daily user who each day maintains a consistent level of alcohol intake in order to prevent withdrawal symptoms. The daily amount might cause intoxication in the average person, but the drinker does not appear intoxicated because of having developed behavioral or pharmacological tolerance. Although a high score on SUSTAIND points to maintenance drinking style, other concepts combine to define this pattern — a high score on compulsive drinking (COMPULSV) and at least a moderate score on daily quantity (QUANTITY). There is also a sustained, but not necessarily daily, user, represented by moderate to high scores on SUSTAIND. A score in the middle to lower range of SUSTAIND indicates sporadic use of alcohol with clear-cut, alcohol-free periods. The drinking can be daily binges that continue for several weeks. Even when binges are short — 1 to 2 days — the pattern can be seriously disruptive.

A third style of use is an obsessive — compulsive pattern: preoccupation with alcohol, planning daily activities around drinking, drinking at the same time each day, keeping alcohol close at hand, and drinking during the work day. This concept is measured by COMPULSV (Table 1). A low score on this scale represents a capricious user who drinks on impulse, under the press of a particular mood, or under particular circumstances. This pattern, too, can have serious consequences. For example, such a drinker may impulsively get very drunk resulting in unpredictable negative consequences (e.g., arrests for drunken driving, fighting, arguing with spouse).

Daily quantity can also be viewed as a style of use. The amount of daily use when drinking, as measured by QUANTITY scale in Table 1, provides important qualifiers for understanding other conditions of use. If QUANTITY is high and there is evidence of sustained use (a high score on SUSTAIND), then there is indication of a dependence (addictive) pattern that is likely to be seriously disruptive of role functions and physical health. On the other hand, if QUANTITY is low and SUSTAIND is high, there may be dependence on alcohol, which may not present serious problems of adjustment or adaptation. Low SUSTAIND, indicating a periodic pattern, coupled with high daily intake points to disruptive binge drinking. A moderate to low amount of daily use, coupled with evidence of withdrawal symptoms (HANGOVER and DELIRIUM in Table 1), indicates a person who may be experiencing decreased tolerance to alcohol, suggesting again an alcohol-dependence pattern.

OBSESSED is a broad second-order dimension that accounts for a large proportion of variance among the scales measuring styles of use. This scale represents a separate and unique expression of alcoholism, and although correlated with the other second-order scales, its statistical independence warrants special attention during treatment.

3. Concepts Indicating Disruptive Consequences of Drinking

Six disruptive conditions have been reliably defined in our studies (Figure 2). *Loss of control over behavior* when drinking (LCONTROL) is one of the most important of these. A high score on this scale indicates blackouts, loss of psychomotor coordination, passing out, belligerence, and inflicting physical harm on self or others, all when drinking. Obviously, the pattern indicates a dangerous and potentially lethal condition.

Another disruptive consequence occurs when, as a result of drinking, there is notable loss of ability to meet the required role expectations of work, social living, family life, legal behavior, and residential stability. This *social role maladaptation* (ROLEMALA) is sometimes referred to as a Skid Row syndrome, but the condition can occur in persons from all walks of life.

Two disruptive conditions involve impaired psychological and physical functioning occurring where there is suspension of use of alcohol following a period of excessive and continuous use. The *psychological withdrawal* condition involves mental confusion, hallucinations (auditory, visual, or tactile), unusual sensations, and frightening dreams. This pattern is measured by DELIRIUM, representing the psychological symptoms associated with delirium tremens (DTs).

The physical withdrawal condition, HANGOVER, involves "morning after" complaints and, in more severe forms, disruption in central and autonomic nervous system functioning. Indicants of this withdrawal pattern are psychomotor tremors, tachycardia, diaphoresis, pyrexia, vomiting, and epileptic seizures. DELIRIUM and HANGOVER have enough independence (statistical and mensurational) to be treated as separate conditions even though they are correlated .62 (have 36% of their variance in common). Clinical observation supports this finding. Patients in detoxification often are observed to have the physical symptoms of DTs without the psychological symptoms.

As a consequence of alcohol use, individuals can experience fear, depression, and anxiety. Such emotional disruptions are measured by GUILT-WOR. Postdrinking depression and guilt can be very debilitating, yet they can become an impetus for treatment.

The use of alcohol often causes *disruptions in relationships.* For example, one of the most common reasons for entering treatment for alcoholism is to accommodate to a spouse's complaints. MARIPROB measures marital problems resulting from drinking, but the disruption is also found in other relationships.

The second-order dimension among the disruptive consequence factors is

DISRUPT1.[2] As discussed in a previous section, DISRUPT1 provides the clinician with an idea of the breadth of uncontrolled disruption associated with alcohol use. It is a composite of the separate conditions of behavioral loss of control, social role maladaptation, relationship disruptions while drinking, and the psychological and physical disruptions that occur when drinking is discontinued. Although this concept is commonly construed as the essence of alcoholism and often becomes the only focus in treatment, it is only one of several independent dimensions of alcohol misuse.

The impact of drinking on hepatic, muscular, gastrointestinal, cardiovascular, respiratory, body defense, and neurological functions is well documented (see Pattison & Kaufman, 1982b; Knott, Beard, & Fink's chapter in this volume). Although these conditions are best identified with medical tests and examinations, they can also be assessed with questionnaires. Using a 67-item medical status questionnaire completed by a physician on 1891 patients, we identified six primary medical factors: liver pathology, cardiovascular problems, peripheral neuropathy, respiratory problems, malnourishment, and gastrointestinal difficulties. A liver pathology factor clearly emerged among 12 blood chemistry tests taken from this sample. It was defined primarily by elevations of three liver enzymes: alkaline phosphatase; serum glutamic oxaloacetic transaminase; and lactic dehydrogenase.

These results indicate that there are several distinct physical conditions associated with alcohol misuse. Excessive use of alcohol may result in liver pathology for one patient, neurological impairment for another patient, malnutrition for another patient, and no medical problems for still another patient. Such findings call for a multiple-condition approach to assessing the patient's medical condition.

4. Self-Concerns about Disruptive Consequences

The recognition that drinking is occurring at unaccustomed times, is getting worse, and/or is causing hardships on family and friends can cause anxious concern for the individual. Such anxiety may result in the individual's wanting to avoid talking about drinking or even making excuses to cover up drinking. This anxious concern and defensiveness is measured by GUILTWOR. As noted, this factor also represents a negative consequence of drinking. A high score on GUILTWOR indicates high internal stress about alcohol use. The extent to which the person *perceives others as being concerned* about his or her drinking is also an expression of self-concern. Are significant others in the patient's life perceived by the patient as wanting to be involved in treatment, being concerned about the patient's drinking, and supportive of treatment? Although these concerns are measured in part by

---

[2]There are two second-order disruptive consequence dimensions in the AUI—DISRUPT1 and DISRUPT2. The items in DISRUPT2 are not included in any of the AUI primary scales. It is correlated .84 with DISRUPT1. It is not included in discussion in this chapter.

GUILTWOR, more detailed assessment can be made through interviews with significant others.

Another expression of concern is the extent to which previous efforts have been made to change the pattern of drinking. These efforts of *prior help to stop* include detoxification treatment, use of Antabuse, use of drugs to manage hangovers, attending Alcoholics Anoymous, or seeking psychological treatment to deal with the drinking problem. HELPBEFR represents this concept.

A general measure of concern about drinking is provided by the second-order scale, ANXCONCN. The items on this scale indicate the overall degree of anxiety and stress that is related to the use of alcohol. ANXCONCN is an independent dimension of alcoholism that warrants separate treatment consideration.

5. Acknowledgment of Drinking Problem

In a society that rewards drinking but punishes drunkenness, it is difficult for people to acknowledge that they have lost control over the use of alcohol. Such acknowledgment, however, is an important first step toward changing the problem behavior.

Two concepts can be used to assess this acknowledgment. One is *readiness for treatment:* the recognition that help is needed, that recent crises or changes have led to this awareness, that one is willing to participate in treatment, and that significant sacrifices will be made in order to be involved in treatment. This readiness concept is measured by the RECEPTIV scale of the AUI.

Acknowledgment also involves *awareness of* the idea that one has *impaired control* over drinking and that drinking is interfering with living responsibilities. AWARENES measures this concept. Although AWARENES and RECEPTIV correlate .52, the variance in common in low enough to indicate that the two factors represent independent concepts.

An overall acknowledgment of an alcohol problem and an openness to treatment is measured with the combination of RECEPTIV and AWARENES. This broad concept is labeled RECPAWAR. Its correlations with other second-order scales are low enough to indicate that it also represents an independent dimension of alcoholism. An individual may score high on this scale and score low on any or all of the disruption scales. Acknowledgment that something is wrong with respect to alcohol use can represent a condition that needs attention during treatment. Specific disruptive conditions are indicated by elevated scores on other scales.

We have found that high scores on SUSTAIND tend to predict a return to a more continuous drinking pattern after treatment, even though it is positively correlated with RECPAWAR. Similarly, patients who were most likely to become involved in symptomatic drinking after treatment have scored high on QUANTITY, LCONTROL, HANGOVER, and ROLE-MALA, and each of these factors correlates positively with RECPAWAR.

There is, however, a significant correlation of about .20 between treatment receptiveness and posttreatment abstinence, suggesting that abstinence is somewhat predicted by motivation. However, many factors other than treatment receptiveness contribute to treatment outcome.

B. Some Derived Alcohol Use Concepts

Combinations of the five preceding broad concepts define patterns that may point to various types of alcoholism. These combinations are outlined at the bottom of Figure 2. One derived concept describes a person who is psychologically dependent on alcohol and who is committed to its use. Such a person would have moderate to high scores on ENHANCED and OBSESSED and low scores on the other second-order scales. Such a drinker is likely to be court-ordered into treatment because of alcohol-related driving offenses and is unlikely to be diagnosed as alcoholic.

A combination of OBSESSED and DISRUPT1 describes a person who is physically dependent on alcohol and who is experiencing significant impaired control over, and disruptive consequences from, alcohol use. Such a person may not be motivated for treatment if his or her use of alcohol does not cause anxiety. However, high scores on ANXCONCN, RECEPTIV and AWARENES portend well for readiness to enter and participate in treatment.

High scores on DISRUPT1 and ANXCONCN indicate a person who is experiencing significant disruption from alcohol use and is feeling a high degree of stress and anxiety. If this anxious patient is well motivated to change, a commitment not to drink often can result.

A combination of obsessive-sustained drinking, uncontrolled disruption, and anxious concern can point to an anxious, deteriorated individual who has been involved in maintenance drinking. However, a low score on the obsessive-sustained (OBSESSED) factor would indicate that the anxious, deteriorated pattern occurs within the context of periodic or binge drinking.

The reader is encouraged to use the concepts of Table 1 and the schemata of Figure 2 to describe particular drinkers with whom she/he is familiar.

C. Non-Alcohol-Use Conditions

The factors of the alcohol-use domain are not highly correlated with factors that are conceptually outside this domain (Horn, Wanberg, & Adams, 1982; Wanberg & Horn, 1983). Assessment of "outside" conditions can help to provide a comprehensive view of the patient. Three broad domains of such conditions have been identified: (1) background and life history, (2) the current life situation, and (3) personality and psychological status. A system for these conditions is presented in Figure 3.

1. Background Conditions

Several concepts related to background can be useful in specifying a basis for assessing current treatment needs. These conditions have been presented in detail in other papers (Horn, Wanberg, & Adams, 1982; Wanberg & Horn, 1986). The relevancy of background conditions to current treatment efforts will depend on whether or not the individual has unresolved issues from his or her past. The younger the person is, the greater impact these background conditions seem to have on adult life functioning. Significant disruption in the background factors in Figure 3 may need to be addressed in treatment.

A general childhood disruption measure, developed from the primary factors in Figure 3, correlates .24 with DISRUPT1 and .27 with ALCIN-VOL. The correlations indicate that childhood disruption is associated with (and possibly leads to) impaired control of the use of alcohol.

2. Current Life-Situation

The factors that provide the basis for assessing current life-situation are summarized in Figure 3. They are discussed in detail in other papers (Horn, Wanberg, & Adams, 1982; Wanberg & Horn, 1986), but some of their alcohol use covariates are reviewed here.

Younger patients express more alcoholic disruption than do older patients, but older patients report more depression, guilt, and loneliness. Women report less social role maladaptation, but more anxiety and depression (see Gomberg's chapter in this volume). Hispanics and Native Americans show greater acting out and social role dysfunction than do blacks or whites (Wanberg, Lewis, & Foster, 1978).

An unstable life situation is significantly correlated with DISRUPT1 (.46) and ALCINVOL (.38), indicating that alcohol disruption is related to problems in establishing a stable living pattern. The social instability factor is also positively correlated with ANXCONCN, DISRUPT1, and ALCINVOL, indicating that people with alcohol disruption also show interpersonal and social problems.

The job and economic adjustment factors are positively correlated with ANXCONCN, DISRUPT1, and ALCINVOL, indicating that as alcoholic disruption increases, so do problems with job productivity. Self-reported health problems correlate significantly with alcohol use, indicating that persons who report high disruption from alcohol use also report medical problems.

The use of drugs other than alcohol (prescription and illicit drugs) is an important consideration when assessing current status. The use of these drugs to manage the negative consequences of alcohol use should be distin-

50

Background Development

Current Life-Situation

Personality Structure

FAMILY CONDITION

Economic problems

Conflict with, rejection by parents

Family alcoholism

Family mental illness

EMOTIONAL–INTRAPERSONAL

Anxiety–neurotic disturbances

SOCIAL STRUCTURE

Age–gender–ethnic group
Income–education–marital status–religion

SOCIAL–INTERPERSONAL

Social withdrawal
Interpersonal conflict
Restricted interests
Residential instability

PRODUCTIVITY ADJUSTMENT

Poor job adjustment
Unemployed status
Occupationally unhappy
Low income

MEDICAL–HEALTH PROBLEMS

Patient's self-reported medical problems
Physician-diagnosed medical problems
Prescription drug abuse

MANNER OF RELATING

Aloof vs. sociable
Shy vs. bold
Self-debasing vs. confident
Restricted interests vs. broad interests

VIEW OF SELF

Tense vs. composed
Depressed vs. happy
Somatic complaint vs. perceived good health
Hesitant vs. decisive
Phobic vs. fearless
Strange thinking vs. conventional thought

VIEW OF SOCIETY

Tough vs. sensitive
Experimenting moral vs. traditional moral

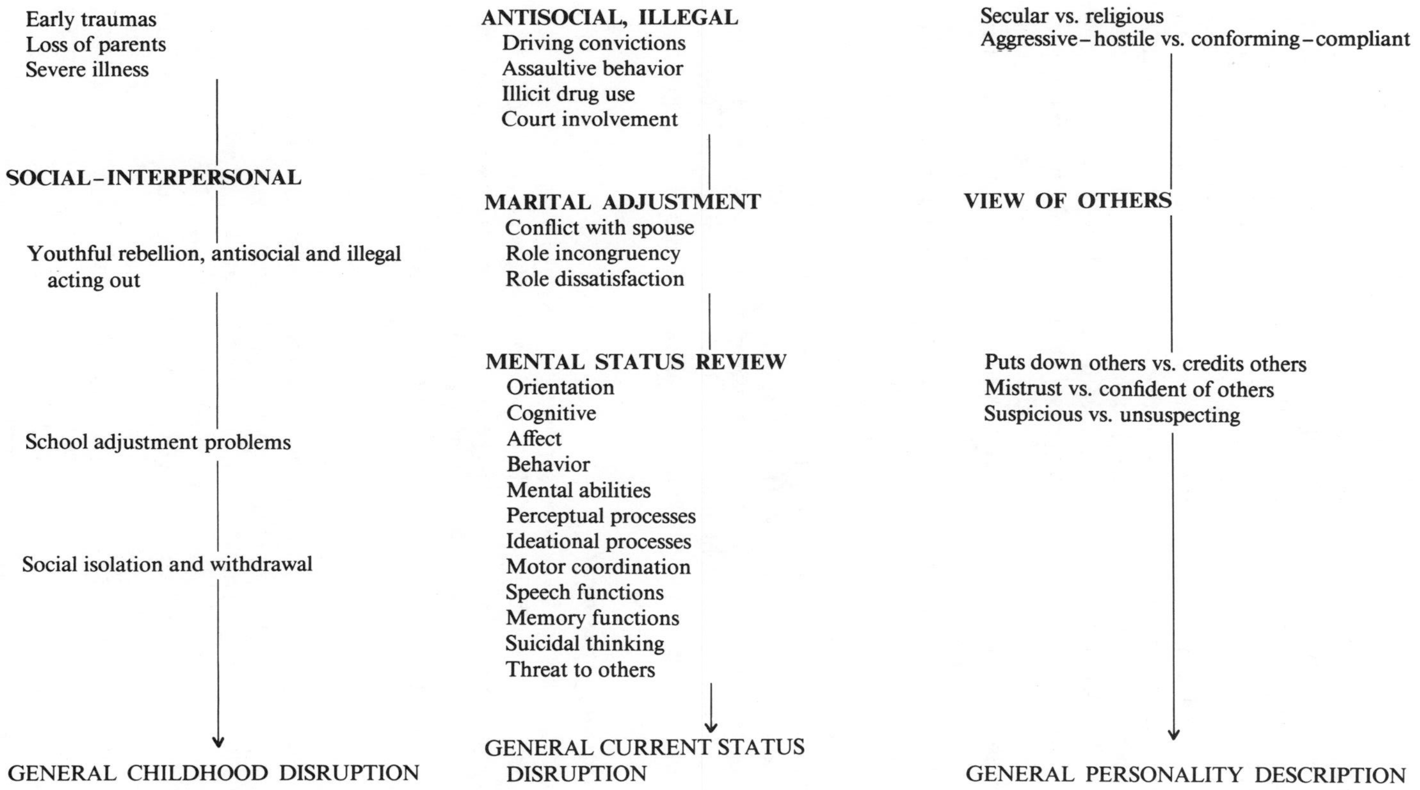

Figure 3. Conceptual framework for non-alcohol-use conditions.

Early traumas
Loss of parents
Severe illness

SOCIAL–INTERPERSONAL

Youthful rebellion, antisocial and illegal acting out

School adjustment problems

Social isolation and withdrawal

GENERAL CHILDHOOD DISRUPTION

ANTISOCIAL, ILLEGAL
Driving convictions
Assaultive behavior
Illicit drug use
Court involvement

MARITAL ADJUSTMENT
Conflict with spouse
Role incongruency
Role dissatisfaction

MENTAL STATUS REVIEW
Orientation
Cognitive
Affect
Behavior
Mental abilities
Perceptual processes
Ideational processes
Motor coordination
Speech functions
Memory functions
Suicidal thinking
Threat to others

GENERAL CURRENT STATUS DISRUPTION

Secular vs. religious
Aggressive–hostile vs. conforming–compliant

VIEW OF OTHERS

Puts down others vs. credits others
Mistrust vs. confident of others
Suspicious vs. unsuspecting

GENERAL PERSONALITY DESCRIPTION

guished from a pattern of multiple substance use (MSA). The MSA pattern represents the use of several drugs for their independent effects rather than using one drug to relieve the negative effects of another drug.

Antisocial and legal problems are positively correlated with the use of illicit drugs, with GREGARUS, and with LCONTROL, but negatively correlated with age. These correlations point to a broad alcohol-related personality disorder found mainly among younger, often court-referred patients.

A current-status factor measuring problems in marital adjustment is correlated .44 with MARICOPE and .32 with MARIPROB of the AUI. The magnitude of these correlations suggests that marital problems among persons with alcohol problems do not result simply from the use of alcohol. These problems can be dealt with by using the techniques discussed in O'Farrell's chapter in this volume.

In our studies, several interviewing psychiatrists completed a 45-item mental status inventory on 1500 alcoholic patients. From these results, we have identified the 12 independent mental status factors that are listed in Figure 3. These dimensions can be assessed by a person trained to do mental status evaluations. In evaluating the mental status of alcoholic patients, special attention should be given to depression and physical threat to self or others. It is important to differentiate between three potential kinds of depression found among alcohol patients: alcohol-determined, endogenous, and exogenous. Each patient should be carefully assessed for suicidal and homicidal ideations.

3. Personality Assessment

Prior attempts to develop personality dimensions among alcoholic patients have used personality tests developed on samples of nonalcoholics (see Cox, 1983, 1985). In our work, however, we have developed a set of personality items for specific use with alcoholic patients (Horn, Wanberg, & Appel, 1973; Wanberg & Horn, 1983). The factors developed from these items are shown in Figure 3. These factors are used to assess how the patient relates to the world, describes himself or herself, conceptualizes society, and views others.

Alcohol patients vary considerably with respect to how they *relate to the world.* Some are aloof, shy, restricted and self-deprecatory, whereas others are sociable, bold, self-confident, and interested in intellectual and aesthetic aspects of the world. Several independent factors describe how alcohol patients *view themselves.* These include seeing oneself as tense, anxious, depressed, in poor health, indecisive and hesitant, fearful and phobic, and having unusual and bizzare thoughts. Alcohol patients also vary as to how they *view society and the world.* Some see society as a place for experimentation, where one achieves goals through expedient means with little respect for the welfare of others. Others regard the world in a secular, nonspiritual manner. Still others see the world as a place where one must be tough and insensitive, and where one gets what one wants, even if it involves aggressive, acting out behavior. Some alcohol patients *view others* as distrustful, suspicious, and discrediting — attitudes that hinder the development of a positive therapeutic relationship.

V. SUMMARY — THE RAISON D'ÊTRE OF ASSESSMENT

The concepts outlined in this chapter provide a conceptual – empirical framework for identifying and describing persons with alcohol problems. The reliable and valid measures within this framework represent conditions associated with alcohol use and misuse, background and development, current status, and personality structure. These measures can be used to build a profile of the multiple conditions of the person who might have problems associated with alcohol use. In building a profile, a clinician will usually want to begin with an analysis of a person's use of alcohol and then describe the person's current life condition and personality. Both linear and nonlinear combinations of factors can be used to indicate complex patterns of involvement with alcohol.

The raison d'etre of the assessment profile is to guide treatment. The clinician must use logic and common sense in determining which treatment is best for any condition defined by the assessment profile. There is little empirical basis to guide decisions in this area. Instead, the clinician must depend on practical judgment and good reasoning to systematically match particular patients with the available treatment approaches. In this chapter, we have described some concepts and methods used to assess persons with problems associated with alcohol use, and in subsequent chapters in this volume, a variety of treatment approaches that can be used with such persons are discussed. Our goal now is to obtain a scientific coalescence of the concepts of assessment and the methods of treatment.

REFERENCES

American Psychiatric Association. (1980). *Diagnostic and statistical manual of mental disorders* (3rd ed.) Washington, DC: Author.
Barnes, G. E. (1983). Clinical and prealcoholic personality characteristics. In B. Kissin & H. Begleiter (Eds.), *The biology of alcoholism. Vol. 6. The pathogenesis of alcoholism: Psychosocial factors* (pp. 113–196), New York: Plenum.
Breitenbucher, R. B. (1976). The routine administration of the Michigan Alcoholic Screening Test to ambulatory patients. *Minnesota Medicine, 59,* 425–429.
Caddy, G. R. (1978). Toward a multivariate analysis of alcohol abuse. In P. E. Nathan, G. A. Marlatt, & T. Løberg (Eds.), *Alcoholism: New directions in behavioral research and treatment.* New York: Plenum.

54
Kenneth Wanberg and John L. Horn

Cox, W. M. (Ed.). (1983). *Identifying and measuring alcoholic personality characteristics.* San Francisco: Jossey-Bass.

Cox, W. M. (1985). Personality correlates of substance abuse. In M. Galizio & S. A. Maisto (Eds.), *Determinants of substance abuse: Biological psychological, and environmental factors* (pp. 209–246). New York: Plenum.

Edwards, G., Gross, M. M. Keller, M., & Moser, J. (1976). Alcohol-related problems in disability perspective: A summary of the consensus of the WHO group of investigators on criteria for identifying and classifying disabilities related to alcohol consumption. *Journal of Studies on Alcohol, 37,* 1360–1382.

Edwards, G., Gross, M. M., Keller, M., Moser, J., & Room, R. (1977). *Alcohol-Related Disabilities* (offset publication N. 32). Geneva: World Health Organization.

Foster, F. M., Horn, J. L., & Wanberg, K. W. (1972). Dimensions of treatment outcome. *Quarterly Journal of Studies on Alcohol, 32,* 1079–1098.

Gallatin, J. (1982). *Abnormal psychology: Concepts, issues, trends.* New York: Macmillan Publisher Co., Inc.

Gitlow, S. E. (1982). The clinical pharmacology and drug interactions of ethanol. In E. M. Pattison & E. Kaufman (Eds.), *Encyclopedic handbook of alcoholism.* (pp. 354–364), New York: Gardner Press.

Glatt, M. M. (1957). Group therapy in alcoholism. *British Journal of Addiction, 54,* 120–128.

Glatt, M. M. (1976). Alcoholism disease concept and loss of control revisited. *British Journal of the Addictions, 71,* 135–144.

Harmatz, M. (1978). *Abnormal psychology.* Englewood Cliffs, NJ: Prentice-Hall.

Horn, J. L. (1971). Discussion of models in personality theory. *Proceedings: XIX International Congress in Psychology.* London: British Psychological Society, 191–192.

Horn, J. L., McArdle, J. J., & Mason, R. C. (1983). When is invariance not invariant: A practical scientist's look at the ethereal concept of factor invariance. *The Southern Psychologist, 1,* 179–188.

Horn, J. L., Skinner, H. A., Wanberg, K. W., & Foster, F. M. (1984). *Alcohol Use Questionnaire (ADS).* Toronto, Canada: Addiction Research Foundation.

Horn, J. L., & Wanberg, K. W. (1969). Symptom patterns related to excessive use of alcohol. *Quarterly Journal of Studies on Alcohol, 30,* 35–58.

Horn, J. L., & Wanberg, K. W. (1970). Dimensions of perception of background and current situation of alcoholic patients. *Quarterly Journal of Studies on Alcohol, 31,* 633–658.

Horn, J. L. & Wanberg, K. W. (1973). Females are different: On the diagnosis of alcoholism in women. In M. E. Chafetz (Ed.), *Proceedings of the First Annual Alcoholism Conference of the National Institute on Alcohol Abuse and Alcoholism,* Rockville, MD: U.S. Department of Health, Education and Welfare.

Horn, J. L., Wanberg, K. W., & Adams, G. (1982). Diagnosis of alcoholism. In E. M. Pattison (Ed.), *Selection of treatment for alcoholics.* New Brunswick, NJ: Rutgers Center of Alcohol Studies.

Horn, J. L., Wanberg, K. W., & Appel, M. (1973). On the internal structure of the MMPI. *Multivariate Behavioral Research, 8,* 131–171.

Horn, J. L., Wanberg, K. W., & Foster, F. M. (1986a). *The Alcohol Use Inventory (AUI):* Minneapolis, MN: National Computer Systems, Inc.

Horn, J. L., Wanberg, K. W., & Foster, F. M. (1986b). *Guidelines for understanding alcohol use and abuse: The Alcohol Use Inventory (AUI).* Minneapolis, MN: National Computer Systems, Inc.

Hyman, M. M. (1976). Alcoholics 15 years later. *Annals of the New York Academy of Sciences, 273,* 613–623.

Jellinek, E. M. (1952). Phases of alcohol addiction. *Quarterly Journal of Studies on Alcohol, 13,* 673–684.

Knox, W. J. (1976). Objective psychological measurement and alcoholism: Review of literature, 1971–1972. *Psychological Reports*, **38**, 1023–1050.

National Council on Alcoholism, Criteria Committee, (1972). Criteria for the diagnosis of alcoholism. *American Journal of Psychiatry*, **129**, 127–135.

Pattison, E. M. (1982). The concept of alcoholism as a syndrome. In E. M. Pattison (Ed.), *Selection of treatment for alcoholics.* New Brunswick, NJ: Rutgers Center of Alcohol Studies.

Pattison, E. M., & Kaufman, E. (1982a). The alcoholism syndrome: Definitions and models. In E. M. Pattison & E. Kaufman (Eds.), *Encyclopedic handbook of alcoholism.* (pp. 3–30), New York: Gardner Press.

Pattison, E. M., & Kaufman, E. (Eds.) (1982b). *Encyclopedic handbook of alcoholism.* New York: Gardner Press.

Pattison, E. M., Sobell, M. B., & Sobell, L.C. (1977). *Emerging concepts of alcohol dependence.* New York: Springer.

Ray, O. S. (1983). *Drugs, society, and human behavior.* Saint Louis: C. V. Mosby Company.

Ringer, C., Kufner, H., Antons, K., & Feuerlein, W. (1977). The NCA criteria for the diagnosis of alcoholism: An empirical evaluation study. *Journal of Studies on Alcohol*, **38**, 1259–1273.

Robins, L.N. (1982). The diagnosis of alcoholism after DSM-III. In E. M. Pattison & E. Kaufman (Eds.) *Encyclopedic handbook of alcoholism* (pp. 40–54), New York: Gardner Press.

Skinner, H. A., & Allen, B. A. (1982). Alcohol dependence syndrome: Measurement and validation. *Journal of Abnormal Psychology*, **91**, 199–209.

Wackwitz, J. H., Diesenhaus, H. & Foster, F. M. (1977). *A model for defining substance "abuse".* Paper presented at the National Drug Abuse Conference, San Francisco, CA.

Wanberg, K. W., & Horn, J. L. (1970). Alcoholism symptom patterns of men and women. *Quarterly Journal of Studies on Alcohol*, **31**, 40–61.

Wanberg, K. W. & Horn, J. L. (1973). Alcoholism syndromes related to sociological classifications. *International Journal of the Addictions*, **33**, 1076–1098.

Wanberg, K. W. & Horn, J. L. (1983). Assessment of alcohol use with multidimensional concepts and measures. *American Psychologist*, **38**, 1055–1069.

Wanberg, K. W., & Horn, J. L. (1986). *The scales of the Life-Situation Questionnaire—LSQ.* Denver, CO: Center for Alcohol-Abuse Research and Evaluation.

Wanberg, K. W., Horn, J. L., & Foster, F. M. (1977). A differential assessment model for alcoholism: The scales of the alcohol use Inventory. *Journal of Studies on Alcohol*, **38**, 512–543.

Wanberg, K. W., Lewis, R, & Foster, F. M. (1978). Alcoholism and ethnicity: A comparative study of alcohol use patterns across ethnic groups. *International Journal of the Addictions*, **13**, 1245–1262.

World Health Organization. (1952). *Expert Committee Report* 48. Author: Geneva.

World Health Organization. (1964). *Expert Committee Report on Mental Health.* (Technical Report Series, N. 273). Author: Geneva.

4

Medical Aspects of Alcoholism

DAVID H. KNOTT,[*,‡,§] JAMES D. BEARD,[†,‡,§]
AND ROBERT D. FINK [‡,§]

*Clinical Services
†Alcohol Research Center
‡Memphis Mental Health Institute
§Department of Psychiatry
University of Tennessee
Center for the Health Sciences
Memphis, Tennessee 38174-0966

I. INTRODUCTION

Seldom in the history of medicine has a disease concept attracted the diverse energy and attention of the nonhealth segment of our society as has alcoholism. The disease concept was originally promulgated in 1788 by a physician, Benjamin Rush. However, since that time, a variety of opinions about the nature of alcoholism have been generated which still prevail today among both professionals and the general public. Some of these opinions are as follows: (1) alcoholic drinking is nothing more than heavy social drinking, (2) alcoholic drinking is a self-inflicted disorder caused by a lack of will-power, (3) alcoholic drinking is a social problem, not a medical–psychiatric one, (4) alcoholic drinking is a symptom of an underlying psychiatric disorder, (5) alcoholic drinking is symptomatic of the disease alcoholism, which ranks with heart disease and cancer as the major threats to the public health.

Nevertheless, the disease concept of alcoholism has gained substantial popularity and credibility during the past 25 years. Unfortunately, the disease concept implies an understanding of the etiology, clinical manifestations, and appropriate treatment of alcoholism, that we do not have even though some advances have been made.

57

TREATMENT AND PREVENTION
OF ALCOHOL PROBLEMS: A RESOURCE MANUAL

II. THE DISEASE TRAJECTORY OF ALCOHOLISM

In order to delineate which aspects of treating the alcoholic that medical and other professionals should assume responsibility for, it is helpful to divide the disease trajectory into three distinct categories, or phases. Such phases represent the major components of the disease trajectory of alcoholism. The acute phase includes alcohol intoxication, the alcohol abstinence (withdrawal) syndrome, and the toxic psychoses associated with alcohol use. This phase involves the acute effects of alcohol and alcohol withdrawal, and treatment of this phase is termed detoxification. The subacute phase includes the multiple medical and psychological problems associated with alcohol use, which frequently masquerade in a more subtle (subacute) manner as disorders other than alcoholism. The chronic phase includes such problems as social, family, and vocational ones which may have existed a priori but which are usually consequential to the alcoholisms.

Treatment during the acute and subacute phases frequently requires that physicians assume primary responsibility, with secondary responsibility assumed by nonmedical care providers. On the other hand, the chronic phase demands the attention of both health professionals (psychologists, social workers, counselors) and lay persons.

III. ACUTE PHASE (Knott, Fink, & Morgan, 1978)

The acute phase of the alcohol dependence syndrome (tolerance and physical dependence) includes episodes of intoxication and withdrawal which, in many instances, can be adequately managed in a nonmedical setting with physician consultation. However, during the acute phase, patients have a high degree of morbidity and mortality, and medical services are often essential. In these cases, skillful management of the patient during detoxification will diminish the morbidity and may expedite the formulation of a long-term care plan and encourage the patient to become involved in such a plan.

Recognizing some of the epidemiological aspects of the acute phase is helpful in understanding the natural history of this phase (Denhartog, 1982).

1. The severity of the alcohol withdrawal syndrome — particularly alcohol withdrawal delirium — is correlated with the amount of alcohol (particularly distilled spirits) consumed prior to withdrawal.

2. Unemployment, low income, low educational achievement, multiple alcohol-related arrests, and receiving welfare payments all increase the likelihood of an individual's being admitted to a medical facility for detoxification.

3. The older the individual (above age 40), the more severe the alcohol abstinence syndrome is likely to be.

4. Persons who are under 40 with a history of heavy drinking of less than 10 years are less likely to suffer alcohol withdrawal delirium than those with a greater than 10-year history of heavy drinking or among those over 40 (at which age the 10-year history is less important).

5. If a patient relapses to alcohol dependence, the recurrence rate of alcohol withdrawal delirium is approximately 43%. This appears to be a predictor in determining the level of intervention necessary for optimal patient care.

6. Any concomitant serious medical disorder, whether or not it is alcohol-induced, is associated with an increase in the frequency and severity of alcohol withdrawal.

7. A history of a seizure disorder from whatever cause is associated with an increase in frequency and severity of alcohol withdrawal.

A. Alcohol Intoxication

The depressant effects of alcohol on the central nervous system result in a variety of signs and symptoms ranging from mild (i.e., impaired judgment, emotional lability, eye problems that range from nystagmus to moderately dilated pupils which are slowly reactive to light, slurred speech, and muscular problems ranging from ataxia and other motor incoordination) to severe (i.e., convulsions, coma, and death). The degree of impairment depends on the duration, actual value, and rate of rise of the blood alcohol concentration.

Coma associated with alcohol intoxication alone occurs more frequently in children, adolescents, and the elderly than among the adult population aged 18–60. Coma associated with alcohol intoxication in other adults is usually accompanied and exacerbated by other complications such as head and spinal cord injuries, hypoglycemia, diabetic coma, cardiac arrhythmias, seizure activity, and concomitant use of other drugs, particularly sedatives.

Treatment considerations for alcohol intoxication should be guided by the recognition that humans have been getting drunk and sobering up for thousands of years without the assistance of physicians, nurses, detox centers, or drugs. Guidelines for the treatment of mild to moderate intoxication include good nutrition, vitamin therapy (especially thiamine B-1 and pyridoxine B-6), and close observation for the possible occurrence of withdrawal symptoms. Treatment of severe intoxication associated with coma includes mechanical support of ventilation, diagnosis and treatment of other complicating factors, gastric lavage and administration of activiated charcoal if this can be performed within 2 hours of the consumption of large amounts of alcohol, seizure precautions, and observation for the occurrence of withdrawal symptoms.

B. Alcohol Abstinence Syndrome (Alcohol Withdrawal and Alcohol Withdrawal Delirium)

The alcohol abstinence syndrome is responsible for most of the serious morbidity and mortality associated with the acute phase. Traditional diagnostic labels such as "DTs," "impending DTs," "incipient DTs," and "mild DTs" have little therapeutic or prognostic usefulness because such terms have been poorly defined. Instead, a more diagnostically descriptive approach to the alcohol abstinence syndrome encourages a more objective and less histrionic assessment and thus a more predictably effective treatment intervention. This can be accomplished by recognizing the three stages of the alcohol abstinence syndrome.

Stage I of the alcohol abstinence syndrome includes these symptoms: psychomotor agitation, autonomic hyperactivity – hypertension, tachycardia, diaphoresis, anorexia, insomnia, illusions.

The onset of Stage I can occur at any time from the point the blood alcohol concentration begins to decline up until 72 – 96 hours after the last drink. However, most frequently Stage I reaches peak severity 12 – 36 hours after the last drink. Stage I is usually self-limiting, lasting from a few hours to 1 to 2 days, depending on the intensity and duration of exposure to alcohol.

If the alcohol abstinence syndrome progresses, Stage II begins and is accompanied by the symptoms of Stage I in addition to hallucinations — visual, auditory, tactile, and/or olfactory. The hallucinations are usually mixed, transient, threatening, and followed by a partial or total amnesia of the psychotic event(s).

Stage III, accompanied by signs and symptoms of Stage I and Stage II, is characterized in addition by disorientation, delirium, and delusions, which are transient and usually followed by total or partial amnesia. Progression to Stage III is associated with a rapid escalation in morbidity and mortality. It is exceedingly rare that a patient suffering Stage III is experiencing only alcohol withdrawal. Instead, Stage III is usually caused by alcohol withdrawal plus other alcohol-related complications, which commonly include but are not necessarily limited to seizure activity, infection, trauma, hypoglycemia, pancreatitis, and multiple drug dependencies.

C. Alcohol-Related Seizures

Seizures (usually generalized motor — grand mal) are withdrawal complications which can occur during the acute phase and which may or may not be associated with the signs of alcohol withdrawal or alcohol withdrawal delirium (Stages I – II – III). It is estimated that seizures represent 2.5% of all alcohol-related illnesses requiring treatment. The incidence of various alcohol-related seizures appears to be (1) seizure during intoxication — 2%, (2) seizures during withdrawal — 23%, (3) "alcoholic" seizures (rum fits) —

45%—seizures which occur without significant, concomitant withdrawal phenomena, and (4) seizures associated with CNS pathology—that is, prior head trauma—30%

Factors which contribute to alcohol-related seizures include an altered transcellular membrane potential secondary to alcohol-induced intracellular accumulation of sodium in the central nervous system, acid–base changes secondary to respiratory alkalosis, and functional and relative hypoglycemia. Seizures during intoxication, seizures during withdrawal, and alcoholic seizures generally occur within the first 72–96 hours of the acute phase. If necessary, the seizure activity can be adequately controlled with intravenous diazepam. Patients with these types of seizures do not require long-term anticonvulsant therapy. However, seizures associated with CNS pathology can occur within or beyond 72–96 hours and may require long-term anticonvulsant therapy.

D. Treatment Considerations of the Alcohol Abstinence Syndrome

1. Rational Psychopharmacotherapy

The physician needs to determine whether or not a psychoactive agent is required because many patients in Stage I respond merely to vitamins and emotional support. However, if the morbidity of Stage I persists or increases, the short-term use of benzodiazepines or hydroxyzine is useful. Generally, the duration of medication does not have to extend beyond 72–96 hours. Patients suffering hallucinations (Stage II), disorientation, delusions, or delirium (Stage III) should receive a neuroleptic, the most effective one of which appears to be haloperidol. The patient in Stage III (alcohol withdrawal delirium) should have a complete diagnostic evaluation for associated and complicating medical disorders, and if these disorders are present, treatment should be instituted.

2. General Medical Management

a. Fluid and Electrolyte Metabolism (Beard & Knott, 1968)

The chronic, heavy use of alcohol produces an increase in total body water. Dehydration occurs only if there is serious malnutrition, or protracted vomiting and/or diarrhea. The overzealous use of intravenous fluids should be avoided, and, indeed, in certain cases of overhydration, short-term diuretic therapy is useful. In addition to fluid retention, alcohol causes a retention of sodium (Na^+) and an accumulation of Na^+ intracellularly in the CNS, cardiac muscle, skeletal muscles, and smooth muscles. The short-term oral administration of diphenylhydantoin for 3 to 4 days tends to correct this abnormality and improves the patient's overall level of functioning. Although there is a retention of Na $^+$, chronic alcohol use can lead to a renal loss of magnesium (Mg^{2+}); such loss contributes to the overall hyperexcitability of the central nervous system during withdrawal. Replacement of Mg^{2+} using intramuscular magnesium sulfate has proven beneficial.

b. Acid-Base Metabolism (Sargent, Beard, & Knott, 1979)

During periods of alcohol ingestion (acute and chronic), the drinker tends to develop both respiratory and metabolic acidosis. During alcohol withdrawal, respiratory alkalosis can occur. Acid–base disturbances thus result in a rather unpredictable manner. Diagnosis and treatment of these disturbances reduces the morbidity of the acute phase of alcohol dependence.

c. Nutrition

In general, the use of alcohol in amounts capable of producing intoxication and resulting in the abstinence syndrome is accompanied by an inadequate intake of balanced nutrients, including vitamins. Depleted glycogen stores can lead to hypoglycemia, and concomitant liver disease impairs protein metabolism. A high-carbohydrate and high-protein diet should be instituted in patients without alcoholic hepatitis or cirrhosis.

Excessive alcohol use decreases gastrointestinal absorption of vitamins, hepatic storage of vitamins, and conversion of vitamin precursors to active forms. Higher than normal doses of thiamine and pyridoxine (B-6) should be administered along with multivitamin replacement therapy. Megavitamin therapy has no demonstrable efficacy.

d. Infection

The patient suffering the alcohol abstinence syndrome is susceptible to many infections, the more common ones being respiratory tract infections, urinary tract infections, meningitis, tuberculosis, peritonitis, septicemia, and septic arthritis. Alcohol impairs the body's ability to combat infections effectively; when clinically indicated, the use of antibiotics should be instituted early.

e. Trauma

Complications can result indirectly from the fact that alcohol impairs motor control. These include acute and chronic head trauma, fractures (particularly rib fractures), and external blood loss. These complications, which occur frequently, need to be diagnosed and treated.

f. Other Conditions

These include esophagitis, gastritis, pancreatitis, and malabsorption syndrome. Additional problems commonly occur during the alcohol abstinence syndrome and should be treated.

E. Toxic Psychoses Associated with the Acute Phase of Alcohol Dependence

While the most frequent form of the alcohol abstinence syndrome is alcohol withdrawal and alcohol withdrawal delirium (Stages I, II, and III), other variants known as toxic psychoses can occur. Differential diagnosis is critical because the psychiatric and psychopharmacological treatments required for toxic psychoses may be different from these relating to alcohol withdrawal and alcohol withdrawal delirium.

1. Idiosyncratic Intoxication

Idiosyncratic intoxication is a psychosis associated with alcohol intoxication rather than with the abstinence syndrome. It is characterized by the sudden onset of disorientation and confusion associated with the consumption of small quantities of alcohol insufficient to produce obvious intoxication in another person. This disorder is also characterized by visual hallucinations and aggressive, hostile, destructive behaviors, and paranoid delusions. The psychotic episode can last from 2 to 24 hours, but usually terminates with somnolence and is followed by total amnesia. In some cases, the cause appears to be a temporal lobe dysrhythmia precipitated by alcohol, with EEG patterns similar to those observed with psychomotor seizures. Intravenous diazepam or phenobarbital have been helpful in controlling the agitated phase. Persons with seizure disorders and/or acute and chronic organic brain syndromes appear to be at higher risk for developing idiosyncratic intoxication. Also, if one suffers idiosyncratic intoxication, repeated episodes can be expected.

2. Alcoholic Hallucinosis

Alcoholic hallucinosis can occur as early as 72 to 96 hours after blood alcohol levels begin to decline. However, it may occur as late as 4 to 7 days after the last drink. It is characterized by auditory hallucinations (but rarely visual hallucinations), delusions, and paranoid ideations. The sensorium can be clear (the patient is oriented in all spheres), and autonomic hyperactivity and psychomotor agitation are frequently absent. There is little or no amnesia of the psychotic period, a point that should be considered when taking a history of previous episodes. A concomitant systemic infection is frequently present. Adequate treatment consists of the use of a neuroleptic in conjunction with diagnosis and treatment of any associated medical disorders.

3. Alcoholic Paranoid State

The alcoholic paranoid state is sometimes confused with paranoid schizophrenia. It can occur days after the last drink and can last from days to weeks. It may be insidious in onset and is related to both the amount of alcohol consumed and the duration of drinking. Frequently, it is characterized by suspicion, distrust, jealousy, paranoid delusions (especially of marital infidelity), and amnesia for the psychotic episode. While this condition responds well to neuroleptic medication, recurrence is unpredictably associated with resumption of alcohol ingestion.

These toxic psychoses must be differentiated from the alcohol abstinence syndrome because they demand aggressive administration of neuroleptics rather than sedatives. A disturbed premorbid personality and functional psychiatric disorders frequently are involved, thus necessitating more careful attention to psychiatric referral and follow-up.

The acute phase of alcohol dependence, although frequently existing in mild forms, is nevertheless a group of potentially serious disorders with a significant degree of morbidity and mortality. The physician and other health professionals should be aware of differential diagnostic approaches and skilled in treating the more serious aspects of the acute phase.

IV. SUBACUTE PHASE OF ALCOHOL DEPENDENCE

There are a number of medical problems which can persist after the acute phase and, more importantly, occur commonly in alcohol-dependent persons who never exhibit clinically significant withdrawal reactions. The chronic, heavy use of alcohol either causes, complicates, or exacerbates a number of common medical disorders. Unfortunately, all too often the medical complications are treated, but the underlying alcohol dependence is either overlooked or ignored. This alcohol-induced impairment of multiple physiological systems contributes in a major way to the morbidity associated with alcohol dependence.

A. Central Nervous System (Dreyfus, 1974)

The chronic effect of prolonged alcohol dependence on the CNS has been fairly extensively studied with resulting accurate descriptions of disorders which include Wernicke–Korsakoff psychosis, focal and generalized cerebellar degeneration, cerebral atrophy disparate for the patient's age, and the sequelae of head trauma associated with alcohol dependence. Direct neurotoxicity of alcohol, associated malnutrition, generalized metabolic abnormalities, and trauma have all been implicated as etiologic factors.

Recent studies, however, have revealed a more subtle, covert form of organicity which could best be termed *subclinical brain damage*. While intellectual functioning does not appear to be grossly impaired, there are demonstrable defects in sensory–motor performance, perceptual capacities, conceptual shifting, visual–spatial abstracting, and memory. These deficits can impair the overall adaptive abilities of alcohol-dependent persons. Assessment of these deficits is critical in formulating an initially realistic treatment approach. Vitamin therapy, adequate nutrition, and abstinence from alcohol are the cornerstones of medical therapy. Sedative medications are contraindicated.

B. Peripheral Nervous System

The direct neurotoxic effects of alcohol complicated by nutritional deficiencies cause axonal degeneration in both the sensory and the motor portions of the peripheral nervous system. Signs and symptoms include pain; a tingling, pins-and-needles sensation; and diminished vibratory sense. Initially, the distal portion of the lower extremities are affected, but in the latter stages, the upper extremities may be involved. The neuropathic changes are usually accompanied by muscular weakness. It is estimated that 10% of hospitalized, alcohol-dependent patients exhibit clear signs of peripheral neuropathy; however, recent evidence suggests that 70–75% of alcohol-dependent patients may suffer from subclinical forms of peripheral nerve damage. Abstinence from alcohol and nutritional and vitamin therapy frequently result in a course of improvement which often requires 6–12 months or even longer.

C. Respiratory System (Lyon & Saltzman, 1974)

The incidence of pulmonary pathology is increased in alcohol-dependent persons because of alcohol-induced impairment of the protective aspects of respiratory function. Specifically, alcohol depresses the cough reflex, causes dehydration of the mucous lining of the bronchial tree, and impairs phagocytosis by alveolar macrophages. As a result, bacterial and viral pneumonias, aspiration pneumonia, pulmonary abscess, tuberculosis, emphysema, fibrosis, and bronchiectasis occur more frequently among alcohol-dependent persons than persons from the general population. While heavy smoking is a contributing factor, alcohol itself plays a major role in the pathogenesis of pulmonary disease.

D. Cardiovascular System (Knott & Beard, 1982)

Among the millions of persons who have been diagnosed as having essential hypertension in the United States, there is a significant number whose hypertension is secondary to heavy drinking. The chronic, heavy use of alcohol affects blood pressure in two ways. First, it can cause an alcohol-induced hypertension which is reversible with abstinence, and, second, it can be a risk factor for the development of essential hypertension. The association between alcohol use and elevated blood pressure appears to be independent of age, sex, race, cigarette smoking, coffee use, past heavy drinking, adiposity, educational attainment, or regular salt use.

Alcoholic cardiomyopathy is a form of heart disease caused by alcohol. Biochemically, it is caused by an alcohol-induced deposition of lipid (primarily triglyceride) in the heart muscle that leads to a fatty heart. The hemodynamic consequences of alcohol cardiomyopathy include decreased contractility of the heart, decreased coronary blood flow, and decreased oxygen extraction. In many instances, the cardiomyopathy is subclinical and asymptomatic until there is a superimposed stress such as exercise or surgery. Clinical problems result because the response of the heart to this stress is impaired. Frequently, cardiomyopathy is completely reversible with abstinence from alcohol. In its most severe form, alcoholic cardiomyopathy is manifest as biventricular heart failure, which can be refractory to treatment and lead to death.

In contrast to the preceding conditions, there may be a negative association between alcohol use and atherosclerosis of the coronary arteries. This has led some to speculate that because alcohol increases high density lipoprotein cholesterol (HDL), a protective effect is afforded by alcohol use. There is evidence, however, that there may be extensive intramyocardial, small-vessel pathology associated with heavy drinking even in the absence of large-vessel pathology. Thus, on the whole, there is insufficient evidence to propose that alcohol use is protective and thus beneficial to cardiac functioning.

E. Liver (Korsten & Lieber, 1982)

Second to the CNS, the liver is the organ most sensitive to the effects of alcohol. The liver metabolizes 90–95% of ingested alcohol, and this process produces a system overload, resulting in marked alteration in normal metabolism, primarily of lipids—but secondarily of protein and carbohydrates.

The most common and frequently asymptomatic form of liver disease caused by alcohol is a fatty liver. Alcohol causes an increased production in and decreased release of lipids from the liver, thus leaving the hepatocyte swollen with fat. This condition can often be diagnosed on the basis of elevated liver function tests and on the basis of an enlarged liver. This condition is readily reversible with abstinence from alcohol.

A much more serious condition is alcoholic hepatitis, which can be either acute or chronic, and is characterized by destruction of liver cells. Alcoholic hepatitis frequently causes cirrhosis—more often in women than in men. The mortality rate over a 3-year period is 10 times greater in patients with alcoholic hepatitis than in non-alcohol-dependent persons of comparable age. Nutritional therapy and abstinence from alcohol are essential. Recent evidence suggests that the use of anabolic steroids decreases both morbidity and mortality associated with alcoholic hepatitis.

Cirrhosis, one of the leading causes of death in the United States, has always been closely associated with alcohol dependence. This relationship appears to be as follows: 90% of all persons who die from cirrhosis are alcohol-dependent, and 10% of all alcohol-dependent persons develop cirrhosis.

There are essentially four ways by which alcohol use and dependence can lead to cirrhosis: (1) cirrhosis associated with malnutrition plus chronic, heavy drinking; (2) postnecrotic cirrhosis resulting from alcohol plus another hepatotoxin such as a virus. In these cases, large amounts of alcohol do not necessarily have to be consumed. (3) cirrhosis caused directly by alcohol if 50% or greater of one's daily calories is derived from ethyl alcohol over a prolonged period of time; (4) cirrhosis which develops as a malignant progression of alcoholic hepatitis.

Abstinence from alcohol is absolutely essential as part of the medical management of the patient with cirrhosis.

F. Pancreas (Korsten & Lieber, 1982)

Excessive alcohol consumption, usually in combination with high-fat and high-protein diets found in 50% of the cases of acute pancreatitis. In addition to the acute forms of this disorder, many alcohol-dependent persons suffer subclinical pancreatic damage, which can result in various malabsorption syndromes and malnutrition. Nutritional therapy and abstinence from alcohol are generally effective in managing these patients.

G. Gastrointestinal Tract (Lorber, Dinoso, & Chey, 1974)

Excessive alcohol use impairs peristalsis in the distal two-thirds of the esophagus and also impairs the peristaltic response to swallowing. This leads to reflux esophagitis (return of stomach contents to the esophagus) and the common complaint of heartburn and indigestion. As much as 25–40% of alcohol can be absorbed directly through the stomach. Thus, alcohol interferes with gastric motility and emptying and increases gastric secretions that are high in acid. This results in hyperemia, hemorrhage, erosion, and ulceration of the gastric mucosa, causing the clinical signs and symptoms of acute and chronic gastritis.

Alcohol also affects motility patterns of the small intestine, resulting in diarrhea. Perhaps more importantly, chronic, excessive alcohol use produces structural damage in the small intestinal mucosa, which leads to malabsorption of vitamins and other essential nutrients.

H. Skeletal Muscle (Ferguson & Knochel, 1982)

Both directly and indirectly, excessive alcohol use can cause destruction of skeletal muscle tissue. This destruction can be manifest in the acute, subclinical, and chronic forms.

Acute alcoholic myopathy follows an alcoholic debauch frequently when the individual has also engaged in strenuous exercise. Signs and symptoms include pain and weakness in the proximal limb musculature with or without paralysis. This is a serious disorder and can lead to renal failure and death.

Subclinical alcoholic myopathy is more common and is frequently manifest as a generalized muscle weakness and diminished exercise tolerance. Chronic alcoholic myopathy is insidious in onset and development and involves symmetrical weakness with or without atrophy of the proximal musculature of the lower extremities.

Adequate nutrition and abstinence from alcohol provide symptom relief; frequently, the myopathic process is completely reversible.

I. Hematopoietic System (Chanarin, 1982)

The direct and indirect toxicity of alcohol on the hematopoietic system results in a number of clinical disorders—chiefly anemia, bleeding tendencies, and increased susceptibility to infection.

The anemias result from one factor or from a combination of factors, including liver disease, direct suppression of red-cell production, real and functional folate deficiencies, blood loss, and hypersplenism.

Alcohol-induced blood loss is usually occult and insidious and generally results from a decreased platelet production and aggregation, bleeding from esophagitis and gastritis and from liver disease, which interferes with factors essential for coagulation.

An increased susceptibility to infection has already been noted as a common medical complication in alcohol-dependent patients. Chronic, excessive alcohol use causes a decreased production and impaired chemotaxis of white blood cells and also a decreased plasma bactericidal activity. Infections should be regarded as a potential medical emergency in alcohol-dependent patients.

V. CONCLUSIONS

As research continues to define the toxicity of ethyl alcohol, medical problems associated with the use of and dependence on this drug will also be more clearly delineated. While treatment of the medical – psychiatric problems associated with the acute and subacute phases is certainly *not* synonymous with the treatment of alcohol dependence (alcoholism) per se, skillful and well-informed medical management is certainly an essential effort in the overall long-term rehabilitation and habilitation of the alcohol-dependent person.

While there is usually a degree of physiological stability achieved during the chronic phase, physicians and other health professionals should nevertheless actively participate in long-term treatment planning and implementation designed to deal with the multitude of psychosocial problems which need to be addressed.

REFERENCES

Beard, J. D., & Knott, D. H. (1968). Fluid and electrolyte balance during acute withdrawal in chronic alcoholic patients. *Journal of the American Medical Association, 204,* 135–139.
Chanarin, J. (1982). Effects of alcohol on the hematopoietic system. In E. M. Pattison & E. Kaufman (Eds.), *Encyclopedic handbook of alcoholism* (pp. 281–292). New York: Gardner Press.
Denhartog, G. L. (1982). *A decade of detox: Development of nonhospital approaches to alcohol detoxification—a review of the literature.* Substance Abuse Monograph Series, No. 2-82,1067, Division of Alcohol and Drug Abuse, State of Missouri.
Dreyfus, P. M. (1974). Diseases of the nervous system in chronic alcoholics. In B. Kissin and H. Begleiter (Eds.), *The biology of alcoholism* (Vol. 3) (pp. 265–286). New York: Plenum.
Ferguson, E. R. & Knochel, J. P., 1982. Myopathy in the chronic alcoholic. In E. M. Pattison and E. Kaufman (Eds.), *Encyclopedic handbook of alcoholism* (pp. 204–214), New York: Gardner Press.
Knott, D. H., Fink, R. D., & Morgan, J. C. (1978). Intoxication and the alcohol abstinence syndrome. In G. R. Schwartz, P. Sofar, & J. H. Stone (Eds.), *Principles and practice of emergency medicine.* Philadelphia: W. B. Saunders Co.
Knott, D. H., & Beard, J. D. (1982). Effects of alcohol ingestion on the cardiovascular system. In E. M. Pattison & E. Kaufman (Eds.), *Encyclopedic handbook of alcoholism* (pp. 332–342). New York: Gardner Press.
Korsten, M. A., & Lieber, C. S. (1982). Liver and pancreas. In E. M. Pattison & E. Kaufman (Eds.), *Encyclopedic handbook of alcoholism* (pp. 225–244). New York: Gardner Press.
Lorber, S. H., Dinoso, V. P., & Chey, W. Y. (1974). Diseases of the gastrointestinal tract. In B. Kissin & H. Begleiter (Eds.), *The biology of alcoholism* (Vol. 3) (pp. 339–356). New York: Plenum.

Lyon, H. A., & Saltzman, A. (1974). Diseases of the respiratory tract in alcoholics. In B. Kissin & H. Begleiter (Eds.), *The biology of alcoholism* (Vol. 3) (pp. 403–431). New York: Plenum.

Rush, B. (1788). An oration on the effects of spirituous liquors upon the human body. *American Museum, 4*, 325–327.

Sargent, W. Q., Beard, J. D., & Knott, D. H. (1979). Acid base balance following ethanol intake and during acute withdrawal from ethanol. In E. Majchrowicz & E. Noble (Eds.), *Biochemistry and pharmacology of ethanol.* New York: Plenum.

II

Specific Treatment Techniques

5

Behavioral Treatment of Alcohol Problems: A Review and a Comparison of Behavioral and Nonbehavioral Studies[1]

DIANE M. RILEY,*,† LINDA C. SOBELL,*,†
GLORIA I. LEO,* MARK B. SOBELL,*,†
AND FELIX KLAJNER*,†

*Behavioural Treatment Research
Clinical Institute
Addiction Research Foundation
Toronto, Ontario, Canada M5S 2S1
and
†Department of Psychology
University of Toronto
Toronto, Ontario, Canada M5S 2S1

I. INTRODUCTION

This chapter has multiple aims. First, the literature on behavioral treatment of alcohol problems from 1978–1983 is reviewed, including a discussion of the theoretical underpinnings or rationales of the various treatments. Second, based on studies published from 1978 through 1983, the methodology and (to the extent possible) relative efficacy of behavioral and nonbehavioral treatments are compared. Third, the state of the art is evaluated, and speculation is offered regarding the potential efficacy and cost-effectiveness of future treatment approaches.

[1]The views expressed in this chapter are those of the authors and do not necessarily reflect the views or opinions of the Addiction Research Foundation.

73

The present review of behavioral and nonbehavioral alcohol treatment research studies is based on peer-reviewed studies published in English from 1978 through 1983. This interval was chosen because earlier reviews of this literature covered time periods up to or shortly before 1978 (Costello, Biever, & Baillargeon, 1977; Emrick, 1979). Besides appearing in a peer-reviewed, English language publication, all studies had to meet the following criteria: (1) Subjects had to have a primary diagnosis of alcohol abuse; studies that reported data for both alcohol and other drug abusers were included only if data for the alcohol abusers were separately presented. (2) The report could not be merely a case study or series of case studies. (3) The study had to report a minimum of 6 months of treatment outcome data for all subjects from the time of discharge from an inpatient – residential program or from the time of admission to an outpatient program. This criterion eliminated numerous studies; a 6-month follow-up interval was regarded as the minimum for which results could be considered predictive of longer-term functioning (see Emrick, 1979; Marlatt, 1983; Miller, 1983). (4) The study must have assessed and reported specific drinking-behavior outcomes; for example, one excluded study (Zivich, 1981) merely reported that a statistically significant decrease in subjects' average daily alcohol consumption occurred, but no specific consumption data were given; another excluded study (Costello, 1980) evaluated drinking outcome in terms of a path analysis but presented no specific outcome data. (5) The treatment intervention had to be psychological rather than physiological in nature (i.e., no detoxification- or pharmacological-treatment-only studies). (6) The treatment had to be of a formal nature (i.e., no drinking driver, Alcoholics Anonymous, or alcohol education studies). (7) The study could not selectively exclude certain types of outcome data (e.g., Cernovsky, 1983, excluded heavy drinking outcomes). (8) Studies that failed to report codable outcome data for *all* four of Costello's (1975a,b) outcome categories (i.e., dead, lost, successes, failures) were excluded (e.g., Watson, Herder, & Passini, 1978). (9) Studies for which details pertaining to behavioral and nonbehavioral treatments could not be determined (e.g., Paredes, Gregory, Rundell, & Williams, 1979) or separated (e.g., Cronkite & Moos, 1978) were excluded.

An extensive search (e.g., computerized literature searches, *Current Contents*) of the published literature was conducted. Once a study was identified as eligible for inclusion, it was then evaluated by at least two of the present authors for the purpose of determining data from the study which could be included in the review. In cases where it was difficult to determine certain details or methodological aspects of a study, evaluators had to agree about whether the report included sufficient information to allow a judgment regarding what procedures or data had been reported. When details of a study were not clearly determinable, they were coded as such.

Although two previous reviews (Costello et al., 1977; Emrick, 1979) of the alcohol treatment outcome literature have cataloged studies according to different therapeutic orientations, neither of these reviews specified what was meant by "behavioral approaches" (Emrick, 1979, p. 73) or "behavior modification programs" (Costello et al., 1977, p. 315). However, based on the studies included in those two reviews, it was apparent that in order to qualify for inclusion as a behavioral treatment approach, a study had to have a predominant behavioral therapeutic orientation or focus. Therefore, similar criteria were used for the present review. In most cases, descriptions of behavioral treatment approaches were quite adequate to make such a determination. As was the case in the reviews by Costello et al. (1977) and Emrick (1979), several behavioral treatment studies involved behavioral treatments superimposed on nonbehavioral inpatient treatments (e.g., Chaney, O'Leary, & Marlatt, 1978; Elkins, 1980). In a few cases, judgments had to be made regarding whether the predominant focus was behavioral (e.g., Steinglass, 1979, used role playing and couples therapy and was classified as a behavioral study). In other cases, investigators included one behavioral technique in what otherwise would be considered milieu or eclectic therapy (e.g., relaxation training: Welte, Hynes, Sokolow, & Lyons, 1981).

Applying the preceding requirements, 68 studies (19 behavioral, 38 nonbehavioral, and 11 reporting outcome results separately for both behavioral and nonbehavioral treatments) published from 1978 through 1983 met our criteria for inclusion, and these are noted in the Reference section of this chapter with an asterisk. When a study was described in more than one publication (e.g., 1-year follow-up in one article and 2-year follow-up in another article), the article (primary reference) reporting data over the longest follow-up interval was referenced. If two articles reported data over similar follow-up intervals, the more comprehensive article was referenced. Studies that were reports of subsamples (e.g., Smart, 1978a) of a larger study (e.g., Smart, 1978b) were not considered primary references. Descriptive and other data (e.g., demographic, alcohol-use history), however, were obtained, when necessary, from other articles describing the same subject population and treatment program. Such secondary references do not necessarily appear in the Reference section, and when they do appear, they are not identified with an asterisk.

This chapter is not intended to be an exhaustive, cumulative review of the behavioral alcohol treatment literature for two reasons. First, that literature has been reviewed in several recent chapters (Caddy, 1982; Nirenberg, Ersner-Hershfield, Sobell, & Sobell, 1981; Pomerleau, 1982; Sobell, Sobell, Ersner-Hershfield, & Nirenberg, 1982). Second, one aim of this chapter was to compare the relative efficacy and methodology of behavioral versus nonbehavioral treatments of alcohol problems. Thus, with regard to behavioral studies, we chose to emphasize those that met a basic set of criteria for scientific rigor, and to discuss issues which in our view are important for the field. We begin by reviewing in some detail major behavioral treatment approaches and relevant studies published from 1978 through 1983.

II. BEHAVIORAL TREATMENT APPROACHES: RATIONALE AND FINDINGS[2]

A. Aversive Conditioning

1. Rationale

Aversive conditioning therapy is nominally based on the Pavlovian conditioning model and involves the pairing of a noxious stimulus (the aversive unconditioned stimulus such as shock, nausea-inducing chemicals, aversive imagery) with appetitive alcohol cues (the conditioned stimuli such as the smell, taste of alcohol), in order to condition an aversive reaction to the alcohol cues. This reaction is then presumed to lead the individual to avoid those cues in the future. Research on taste-aversion learning, similar to the preceding paradigm, indicates that for mammalian species including humans, taste and smell cues are very readily associated with nausea, and more so than with other noxious stimuli (e.g., shock; Garcia & Koelling, 1966). It has been suggested (e.g., Cannon, Baker, & Wehl, 1981) that these findings explain the apparent superiority of emetic (nausea-inducing) over electrical aversive conditioning. However, as discussed subsequently, this superiority may be more apparent than real.

Covert sensitization is a form of aversive conditioning where images of highly aversive events are paired with images of drinking (cf. the chapter by Klinger in this volume). A conceptual advantage of this technique is that it can be self-administered by the patient.

2. Data on Aversive Conditioning Techniques

During the period covered by this review, no studies were reported involving treatments that solely involved electrical aversive conditioning. Jackson and Smith (1978) compared chemical ($n = 287$) and electrical ($n = 57$)

---

[2] The outcome figures for the behavioral studies reported in Sections II are those presented by the authors of those studies. The figures reported in the text do not always sum to 100% because percentages of lost and/or deceased subjects were not usually included. Generally, such figures, were presented only if they were exceptionally high (i.e., of methodological concern). However, if the success and failure figures reported in the text do sum to 100%, this does not necessarily imply that there were no lost and/or deceased subjects in that study. Some authors included lost and/or deceased subjects in one of the other two outcome categories or excluded them from their analyses altogether.

methods (5 sessions each) in conjunction with hospital milieu treatment. A follow-up questionnaire was mailed to all subjects 2 years after treatment asking them if they were presently drinking alcohol. No significant differences were found between the two groups; overall, 21% reported they were not presently drinking alcohol. Although the authors asserted that their results favored the electrical aversion procedure because it was less expensive and less physically stressful, the results were confounded by nonrandom assignment of subjects to groups. Also, the poorly worded follow-up questionnaire and a high follow-up attrition rate (41%) cloud the interpretation of the results.

Cannon et al. (1981) randomly assigned male alcoholics to (1) a multifaceted inpatient alcohol treatment (MIAT: control group, $n = 6$), (2) the MIAT plus five emetic aversion therapy sessions ($n = 6$), and (3) the MIAT plus 10 shock-aversion sessions ($n = 7$). Although emetic subjects had more abstinent days than the shock and control group subjects at a 6-month follow-up, there was no difference between the control and the emetic groups at 12 months, and both of these groups had more abstinent days than the shock group. However, Cannon et al. (1981) advised caution in interpreting these results because of the small number of subjects.

In a study by Boland, Mellor, and Revusky (1978), 50 male alcoholics were given chemical aversion conditioning (lithium carbonate was paired with various alcohol cues) along with the standard hospital treatment. Subjects were sequentially rather than randomly assigned to experimental and control groups (i.e., admitted at different times). At a 6-month follow-up, 36% of the experimental subjects were abstinent, compared with 12% of the control group.

Both the Cannon et al. (1981) and the Boland et al. (1978) studies involved patients at public hospitals. A series of studies conducted at both private and public hospitals allows for comparison of patients with different sociodemographic characteristics. Neubuerger, Matarazzo, Schmitz, and Pratt (1980) compared clients treated at a private hospital ($N = 261$) with subjects treated at two public hospitals ($N = 275$ and $N = 290$, respectively). The treatment included detoxification, inpatient therapy, five chemical aversion sessions, and six posttreatment aversion booster sessions. The 12-month essential abstinence rates (no more than two drinks during the year) were 63% for the private sample (Wiens, Montague, Manaugh, & English, 1976) and 39% and 50%, for the two public hospitals (Neubuerger et al., 1980). Neubuerger et al. (1980) suggested that the differences were due to demographic differences between the two populations (e.g., Medicare, marital, and employment status).

Neubuerger and his associates further examined patient characteristics in two studies involving patients from various socioeconomic groups (Neubuerger, Hasha, Matarazzo, Schmitz, & Pratt, 1981; Neubuerger, Miller, Schmitz, Matarazzo, Pratt, & Hasha, 1982). In each study, the treatment was the same as that reported by Wiens et al. (1976). In the first (Neubuerger et al., 1981), data from 908 subjects treated over a 3-year period indicated that subjects with a Medicare disability status and various physical and psychiatric disorders had a relatively poor prognosis (i.e., a 33% abstinence rate during the 3 years compared to 53% for the total sample). Being married or employed at admission increased the likelihood of abstinence relative to the entire sample (62% and 65%, respectively), with the best outcome associated with being both married and employed (73%).

The second study (Neubuerger et al., 1982) examined four patient populations ($N = 1245$) and found similar results (overall abstinence rate of 54%) to those of Neubuerger et al. (1981). As before, subjects who were both married and employed had the best outcome (73% overall abstinence rate). Medicare patients on disability payments had a less favorable abstinence rate (36%), but older Medicare patients receiving retirement benefits had an abstinence rate (52%) similar to that of the total population. Older patients (> 49 years) had an abstinence rate of 57% compared with 41% for younger patients (< 30 years), suggesting that older patients are better candidates for private hospital treatment.

In another study of the same private hospital treatment, Wiens and Menustik (1983) investigated the effect of five chemical aversion sessions and boosters with 685 subjects. At a 1-year follow-up, 63% of the subjects were abstinent, with the figure dropping to 33% at 3 years. Although no differential treatment effect was found for patients with different educational levels, married males had more successful outcomes than unmarried males, replicating the findings of Neubuerger et al. (1981, 1982). As reflected in the studies just discussed, differences in abstinence rates between studies can largely be explained by examining differences in patient characteristics.

Mellor and White (1978) used motion (six sessions of passive, off-vertical rotation sitting in a chair blind-folded) as an alternative unconditioned stimulus producing sickness with 10 subjects. Although 20% of the subjects were totally abstinent at a 6-month follow-up, the small sample size, short follow-up interval, and no control group makes it impossible to draw conclusions from this study.

Imaginal aversive stimuli, both electrical and chemical, have been used to circumvent potential ethical problems arising from the use of actual aversive stimuli. Elkins (1980) used imaginal verbal stimuli in a covert sensitization treatment and attempted to maximize conditioning by combining Cautela's (1966) and Anant's (1967) procedures. The aversion therapy was given to 57 patients on an inpatient basis over a period of 1 to 1½ months. Although the amount of treatment needed to induce a conditioned aversive response varied among individuals, most received five or more sessions. At a 12-month follow-up, 40% of the subjects were reported as abstinent or engaging in nonproblem drinking (nonproblem drinking, it should be noted, seems inconsistent with the theoretical rationale for aversion treatment). The lack of a control group again renders the conclusions equivocal.

In a comparison of the long-term effects of covert sensitization and relaxation training with an insight-oriented therapy (transactional analysis, TA), Olson, Ganley, Devine, and Dorsey (1981) randomly assigned 148 hospitalized alcoholics to either a milieu treatment control group, or to one of three experimental groups each of which included milieu therapy: (1) a behavioral group, involving covert sensitization and relaxation training, (2) a TA group, and (3) a combined TA and behavioral group. Four-year follow-up interviews (n = 113) indicated no significant differences in abstinence rates among the groups at any point in the follow-up. In the first 6 months of follow-up, the overall abstinence rate was 73.5%, decreasing to 36.3% at a 4-year follow-up. The confounding between treatment type and length in this study (i.e., milieu therapy—6 days per week; behavioral and TA treatment—3 hours per week) could possibly account for the lack of significant effects.

3. Summary

In general, aversive conditioning procedures appear to be effective largely with those individuals who have a relatively good prognosis at the outset. However, because of the relatively poor long-term effectiveness of aversion techniques, it is difficult to justify their use, especially in light of their highly aversive and invasive nature. Although it has been suggested that the effectiveness of chemical aversion therapy might be improved by a pretreatment abstinence period (Elkins & Hobbs, 1979), this remains to be empirically validated. Also, while covert sensitization techniques may pose fewer ethical problems, the efficacy of these procedures has not been established. To date, such imaginal techniques appear to be only slightly more effective than no treatment, but even this conclusion is tentative given the lack of studies using no-treatment control groups.

The contribution of aversion techniques to the effectiveness of multimodal programs (reviewed later in this section) appears to be rather small, and Miller and Hester (1980) have suggested that in the case of shock aversion, the contribution may, in fact, be negative. The fact that aversion techniques, especially chemical aversion, produce substantially superior outcomes with older subjects who are of higher socioeconomic status suggests that the principal benefits of these techniques may relate to factors other than classical aversive conditioning (e.g., motivation, social stability, support systems).

B. Relaxation Training

1. Rationale

The theoretical rationale underlying applications of relaxation training techniques usually involves two assumptions: (1) the problem is caused or exacerbated by tension or anxiety, and (2) relaxation training can effectively deal with the problem either by reducing anxiety or by increasing the individual's sense of perceived control in stressful situations (reviewed in Klajner, Hartman, & Sobell, 1984). At the present time, the most popular relaxation training techniques are progressive muscle relaxation (Jacobson, 1938; Wolpe, 1958) and meditation (Benson, 1975; Marlatt & Marques, 1977); others include autogenic training, biofeedback, and hypnotically-induced relaxation (Benson, 1975; Taylor, 1978).

Although stress or anxiety may affect alcohol consumption, it does not necessarily follow that alcohol is consumed for its relaxation effects (Cappell & Greeley, in press). Marlatt (1976) has suggested that alcohol may be reinforcing under stressful conditions because it increases the individual's perceived sense of control over the stressor in the absence of other coping alternatives (e.g., Marlatt, Kosturn, & Lang, 1975). Thus, relaxation training techniques could be an effective treatment to the extent that they produce a sense of coping or increased perception of personal control rather than relaxation. Accordingly, it has been reported that drinking increases in situations involving social or interpersonal stress (Higgins & Marlatt, 1975; Miller, Hersen, Eisler, & Hilsman, 1974), and especially in those situations where coping responses other than drinking are not readily available (Marlatt et al., 1975). Such situations may be viewed as involving a relative lack of perceived control (Averill, 1973), and alcohol may then function to increase perceived control rather than to reduce anxiety per se (Marlatt & Marques, 1977; McGuire, Stein, & Mendelson, 1966).

Hull (1981) has proposed that alcohol serves to decrease an individual's level of self-awareness, and that stress reduction results from this effect. According to this view, alcohol reduces the individual's sensitivity to information regarding the self, including information about possible sources of tension. However, the explanatory power and validity of this theory has recently been challenged (Frankenstein & Wilson, 1984; Wilson, 1983).

Another departure from the traditional tension-reduction hypothesis was proposed by Jones and Berglas (1978) in their attribution theory of how ethanol consumption leads to an increase in perceived control. They suggested that drinking might be one of several self-handicapping behaviors used by individuals to avoid being viewed by others as lacking competence, and that intoxication provides a convenient justification for failure. If situations involving interpersonal stress and reduced perceived control actually increase alcohol consumption, then providing the individual with alternative coping responses for such situations should be effective in treating alcohol abuse. Relaxation training may provide coping responses that also increase the person's sense of control over the situation (Klajner et al., 1984).

Still another possibility is that drinking may be a means for promoting positive affect rather than reducing anxiety or increasing perceived control. There is evidence that this euphoria-incentive effect is greatest in individuals who have less initial anxiety and are heavy drinkers (Pihl & Yankofsky, 1979; Senter, Heintzelman, Dormeuller, & Hinkle, 1979). Relaxation training may not be an effective treatment for those individuals who putatively drink to obtain positive (euphoria) rather than negative (anxiety reduction) reinforcement.

2. Data on Relaxation Training Techniques

Using operant conditioning techniques, Watson et al. (1978) compared inpatient alcoholics given 10 days of 1-hour alpha biofeedback training sessions with those who received no such training. At an 18-month follow-up, the two groups differed on only 1 of 13 drinking outcome measures. However, the results of this study are weakened by several methodological problems.

In a study discussed earlier, Olson et al. (1981) failed to show any long-term significant differences on drinking measures between groups when comparing a behavioral package of covert sensitization and progressive relaxation with transactional analysis and milieu therapy.

3. Summary

Despite the popularity of relaxation training with alcohol abusers, very little unimodal research on relaxation techniques was reported in the period covered by this review. Relaxation techniques, however, are frequently included in multimodal studies. Evidence regarding the efficacy of relaxation as a treatment of alcohol abuse is equivocal, and numerous methodological problems preclude definitive conclusions. To meaningfully evaluate the efficacy of relaxation training, the degree to which clients actually practice the relaxation skills must be more closely assessed, and adequate control conditions must be used.

C. Skills Training

Although most behavioral techniques involve the acquisition of skills, some focus on teaching adaptive behaviors that are presumed to be deficient prior to the individual's problem drinking. Other skills-training approaches are directed at modifying the drinking behavior only, focusing on different parts of the behavioral chain eventuating in alcohol consumption.

The main assumption underlying skills-training techniques is that alcohol abusers have deficiencies in such skills. At present, however, there is a general lack of evidence to support this assumption. Although one study found that severely dependent alcohol abusers were relatively deficient in drink-refusal skills (Twentyman, Greenwald, Greenwald, Kloss, Kovaleski, & Zibung-Hoffman, 1982), they were comparable to a control group (firemen) in other skills. There is no evidence that less severely dependent alcohol abusers have skills deficits.

1. Drinking Skills

a. Rationale. Training in drinking skills is based on the view that excessive drinking is a learned response that has short-term effectiveness for the drinker in specific situations, particularly when the individual lacks effective nondrinking responses. Drinking skills training is used to teach alcohol abusers to drink in a nonabusive manner as an alternative to abstinence, and usually forms part of a more broad-based treatment program. Training in drinking skills has been accompanied by fairly extensive research on the drinking behavior of alcohol abusers and on the situational antecedents of drinking.

Blood alcohol level (BAL) discrimination training is another method used to teach appropriate drinking behavior. With this technique, subjects are given an alcoholic beverage to drink and then are asked to estimate their BAL. They receive feedback regarding their accuracy, and are often given general rules for computing their BAL based on the amount of alcohol consumed and the duration of consumption.

b. Data on Training in Drinking Skills. In the period under review, there were no unimodal studies of training in drinking skills, although such training has frequently been included in multimodal programs.

2. Interpersonal Skills

a. Rationale. The evidence on deficits in interpersonal skills among alcohol abusers is equivocal (e.g., P. Miller & Eisler, 1977; Monti, Corriveau, & Zwick, 1981; O'Leary, O'Leary, & Donovan, 1976). Some studies do suggest, however, that alcohol abusers may drink as a coping response to stressful interpersonal situations (e.g., Higgins & Marlatt, 1975; P. Miller et al., 1974). Also, alcohol abusers often retrospectively report that their relapses were initiated by stressful situations (Cummings, Gordon, & Marlatt, 1980). Therefore, it is possible that interpersonal skills training may increase the individual's real control over the stressor by compensating for skills deficiencies, or increase the individual's perception of control over the stressor, in either case leading to control over the consequent drinking.

b. Data on Interpersonal Skills Training. Chaney et al. (1978) evaluated social skills training treatment by randomly assigning alcoholics to three groups: a skills-training group ($n = 15$), a discussion group ($n = 13$), or a no-treatment control group ($n = 12$). All subjects also participated in an inpatient alcohol treatment program and had an abstinence goal. The skills-training condition (eight sessions) focused on assertiveness with behavioral rehearsal, modeling, and problem solving, while the discussion group discussed these topics without any specific training or rehearsal. At a 1-year follow-up, the skills-training subjects were superior to the discussion and control group subjects in terms of fewer drinking days, less total alcohol consumption, and shorter average length of drinking episodes. Because this difference had not been found at the 3-month follow-up, learning may have occurred during the following 9 months (Marlatt, 1983).

Jones, Kanfer, and Lanyon (1982) extended Chaney et al.'s (1978) behavioral skills training package to middle-class alcoholics. Subjects were randomly assigned to a skills-training group ($n = 24$), a discussion group that focused on emotions ($n = 23$), or a no-treatment control group ($n = 21$). Unlike Chaney et al. (1978), Jones et al. (1982) found that the skills-training and discussion groups did not differ and both were superior to the control group at a 1-year follow-up in terms of amount of alcohol consumed and number of days intoxicated. Although Jones et al.'s results suggested that different treatment components may be critical for different groups (e.g., higher-functioning alcoholics may require less concrete training), their results are weakened by a very high follow-up attrition rate (54%) and by less skills training than the Chaney et al. (1978) study (six vs. eight sessions).

In another investigation of interpersonal skills training, Cohen, Appelt, Olbrich, and Watzl (1979) studied 60 female alcoholics. In addition to the 3-month hospital treatment program, subjects participated in a multimodal behavioral treatment program, and aftercare was provided for 1 year following treatment. Follow-up conducted between 13 and 29 months posttreatment indicated that 52% of the subjects were abstinent or had significantly decreased their drinking. Unfortunately, the absence of a control group obviates clear conclusions. In a later study, Rist and Watzl (1983) investigated the manner in which female subjects' evaluations of their personal efficacy in problem situations were related to their drinking outcomes, but again no control conditions were used. At an 18-month follow-up, 50% of the subjects were either drinking in a controlled manner or were abstinent, although their self-efficacy ratings were not related to their drinking outcomes. Presently, little else is known about interpersonal skills deficits among female alcoholics.

Ferrell and Galassi (1981) conducted a controlled trial comparing assertion training and human relations training with 22 chronic hospitalized alcoholics who also received milieu therapy. Although both groups had comparable total abstinence rates at a 6-week follow-up (73%), only 2 subjects (from the assertion group) were totally abstinent for 2 years.

3. Vocational Skills

a. **Rationale.** Training in vocational skills is based on findings that many problem drinkers have a poor employment history and that employment status is a good predictor of treatment outcome. Such training usually involves assertiveness training and training in other skills for dealing with interactions with co-workers and employers.

b. **Data on Vocational Skills Training.** Generally, training in vocational skills has been used as one component in multimodal treatment programs. No unimodal studies meeting the present selection criteria were reported in the period covered by this review.

4. Cognitive Skills

a. **Rationale.** Cognitive-behavioral therapy has become a popular technique for dealing with a wide range of problems (e.g., drinking, depression, anxiety; see Beck, 1976; Mahoney, 1974; Sanchez-Craig, Wilkinson, & Walker in this volume). Cognitive-skills training for alcohol abusers is based on several assumptions: that drinking problems are often the result of maladaptive cognitions, that alcohol misuse is an attempt to solve such problems, and that training aimed at developing alternative, adaptive cognitions will decrease alcohol use. Unfortunately, cognitive skills are extremely hard to measure, and adequate assessment instruments are currently lacking.

b. **Data on Cognitive Skills Training.** Cognitive therapy, which was part of a multimodal behavioral treatment package, was tested with four male problem drinkers by McCourt and Glantz (1980). At a 12-month follow-up, all subjects were improved (abstinent or moderate drinking). According to the authors, however, this same type of treatment was, inexplicably, not successful when used as part of an inpatient program.

Oei and Jackson (1982), using a matching procedure, assigned 32 hospitalized subjects with mild to severe assertion deficits to four treatments: (1) social skills training (SST), (2) cognitive restructuring (CR), (3) CR followed by SST, and (4) a control group provided with traditional supportive therapy. Booster sessions were given at 3, 6, and 12 months posttreatment. At a 6- and 12-month follow-up, the CR, SST, and the CR–SST groups were superior to the control group on all measures, including drinking. The CR and CR–SST groups also reported significantly less alcohol consumption than the SST group at the two follow-ups. Although the results support the use of cognitive-skills training with this population, the major problem with this study is that the results for each follow-up interval are concerned with the immediately preceding 7 days (p. 533), an interval hardly representative of the entire follow-up period.

In two different studies, Sanchez-Craig and her colleagues (Sanchez-Craig & Walker, 1982; Walker, Sanchez-Craig, & Bornet, 1982; Sanchez-Craig et al. in this volume) trained halfway-house residents in the use of cognitive coping skills. In one study, 90 subjects were randomly assigned to three treatments (15 sessions each): (1) coping skills training, (2) covert sensitization, or (3) a discussion control group. No differences were found among the treatments on any outcome variables at 6, 12, and 18 months. The authors suggested that the failure to obtain differences may relate to memory deficits observed among 30% to 60% of the sample—most subjects could recite problem-solving strategies during the program, but were unable to recall the strategies at the follow-up interviews. These results, together with those of Jones et al. (1982), suggest that cognitive techniques may not be appropriate for cognitively impaired populations.

Longabaugh, McCrady, Fink, Stout, McAuley, Doyle, and McNeill (1983) assessed the cost-effectiveness of a day-treatment ($n = 114$) versus an inpatient treatment ($n = 60$) program. Although the day-treatment subjects went home at night and on weekends, the treatment content (primarily cognitive and social skills training) and goal (abstinence) were the same for both programs. At a 6-month follow-up, 40% of all subjects described their drinking as nil to moderate, but 32% of the subjects were lost to follow-up. Although both groups had comparable outcomes with respect to drinking and social and vocational functioning, it is possible that neither treatment would be more effective than either a less costly outpatient treatment or no treatment.

5. *Marital – Family Training*

a. **Rationale.** Because alcohol problems can result from or cause marital problems (Towle, 1974), there is often a need to recognize and address problems involving interactions with the spouse and other family members.

b. **Data on Marital – Family Training.** McCrady, Paolino, Longabough, and Rossi (1979) randomly assigned 33 couples to three inpatient treatments: group treatment for alcoholic husbands, group treatment for couples with an alcoholic husband but where only the husband was hospitalized, and group treatment for such couples with joint admission of both spouses. At a 6-month follow-up, the alcoholics involved in the couples groups had decreased their alcohol consumption, but there were no differences between these groups on other measures (e.g., marital problems, depression). At a

4-year follow-up (McCrady, Moreau, Paolino, & Longabaugh, 1982), no significant differences in drinking for the joint or individual therapy subjects were noted, with an overall success rate of only 24% (abstinent or controlled drinking).

Katz, Morgan, and Sherlock (1981) evaluated a family–marital treatment program carried out in an outpatient medical setting with 36 subjects. At a 6-month follow-up, 69% of the subjects were abstinent or controlled drinkers. The authors speculated that the high success rate was related to the individualized nature of the treatment. The intensive follow-up (once a week) may also have had a positive effect. However, because no comparison group was used, the relative efficacy of this treatment is unknown.

Steinglass (1979) evaluated inpatient and outpatient multiple couples group therapy for alcoholics. Part of the inpatient program involved an experimental investigation of how drinking affected the couples' interactions. Although only one subject (9%) remained abstinent during the entire 6-month follow-up, five of the nine alcoholics located "were drinking less at the 6-month follow-up than they were prior to treatment (reductions ranged from a modest 20% to total abstinence)" (Steinglass, 1979, p. 166). As with any pilot study ($N = 11$), a definitive evaluation of this experimental program will require a controlled trial and a longer follow-up.

6. Summary

While training in interpersonal skills appears to be a promising area for future research, few studies to date have been methodologically adequate. Furthermore, there is a lack of evidence that alcohol abusers are, in fact, deficient in interpersonal skills. Better documentation of the need for social skills training is necessary because such training is labor-intensive. It is possible that skills-training approaches may have benefits beyond skills acquisition (e.g., increasing patients' perceived self-efficacy), but it would still remain to be established that such skills training is the most efficient way to achieve these benefits.

The efficacy of training in cognitive skills for alcohol problems is also uncertain. Although cognitive-skills training may result in behavioral changes among clients with no cognitive deficits, such changes are much less likely for cognitively impaired clients (Wilkinson & Sanchez-Craig, 1981). Perhaps less cognitively demanding techniques will prove more suitable for the latter population.

D. Contingency Management

1. Rationale

In general, contingency management involves arranging the individual's environment so that positive consequences follow desired behaviors, and either negative or neutral consequences follow undesired behaviors. A substantial body of research supports the use of these techniques for individuals with alcohol problems. These techniques require other persons (e.g., spouses, employers) to enforce the contingencies and are often used as part of a multimodal treatment program.

2. Data on Contingency Management Techniques

Ahles, Schlundt, Prue, and Rychtarik (1983) used behavioral contracting in an attempt to increase participation in aftercare following treatment. Fifty patients were randomly assigned to either standard clinic aftercare or intensive aftercare. Both conditions had the same aftercare schedule, but intensive aftercare patients signed a behavioral contract for aftercare attendance and were given a calendar indicating their appointments for the next 6 months. Patients received reinforcers for complying with the contract. At a 12-month follow-up, 56% of the intensive aftercare group and 28% of the control group were either abstinent or nonproblem drinkers. Regardless of group assignment, those who attended aftercare had significantly decreased alcohol intake.

Pomerleau, Pertschuk, Adkins, and Brady (1978) also used behavioral contracting in an attempt to increase aftercare attendance, as well as participation in treatment and nondrinking activities. Subjects in multimodal behavior therapy paid a deposit of up to $300, which they could regain by complying with treatment requirements and forfeit if they left treatment prematurely. Although fewer subjects dropped out of the behavioral program (2 of 18) than the traditional treatment program not employing behavioral contracting (6 of 14), this finding may be due to several other differences between the groups (e.g., different treatment goals).

Contingency management has also been used to increase the use of disulfiram, a drug which produces an unpleasant aversive reaction if present in the body when alcohol is consumed. Azrin, Sisson, Meyers, and Godley (1982) randomly assigned 43 subjects to three groups: (1) traditional disulfiram treatment; (2) a socially motivated "disulfiram assurance program" —relatives supervised the taking of disulfiram and patients took the drug at each counseling session; subjects also identified and were given behavioral training to deal with situations that could lead to failure to take disulfiram; and (3) behavior therapy and disulfiram assurance—the same treatment as the disulfiram assurance group as well as other procedures (e.g., training in job finding skills, brief relaxation training). At a 6-month follow-up, the behavior therapy group had used disulfiram on significantly more days and was abstinent more days per month than the other two groups.

3. Summary

Contingency management involving deposit contracting or other forms of tangible reinforcement may be effective for increasing participation in treatment and aftercare sessions and may, therefore, serve as an important adjunct to treatment when feasible. Further research is needed to systematically examine the effects of various forms of contingency management, while controlling for factors such as treatment goal and therapeutic orientation.

E. Self-Management Procedures

1. Rationale

Self-management procedures require clients to implement their own treatment. The primary potential advantage of these procedures is that they can maximize the generalization of treatment effects during treatment and following the termination of treatment. The main problem with such techniques, however, is that they are likely to be feasible with only highly motivated individuals. Self-management programs generally have three main components: (1) self-monitoring, (2) functional analysis of drinking, and (3) manipulating the antecedents and consequences of drinking. Investigations of self-management procedures have generally examined self-control programs, self-administration of reinforcement and punishment, and the use of self-help manuals.

2. Data on Self-Management Procedures

Most of the research on self-management treatments has focused on middle class, self-referred problem drinkers who are not severely dependent on alcohol. In one such early study (W. Miller, 1978), 46 subjects were randomly assigned to three groups: (1) behavioral self-control training (BSCT), (2) BSCT plus BAL discrimination training, discriminated aversive counterconditioning, and self-monitoring (composite treatment); and (3) aversive counterconditioning only. The treatment goal was nonproblem drinking, and all subjects received 10 weekly treatment sessions. At a 12-month follow-up, all treatment groups showed a significant reduction in drinking, although the aversive counterconditioning group showed the least change. Unfortunately, these findings are difficult to interpret because a self-help manual (including discussion of self-control information and strategies) was given to a random sample of the subjects at the end of treatment and to all of the remaining subjects at the 3-month follow-up interview. Furthermore, it was not possible to determine the efficacy of the methods relative to no treatment because no control group was used. Although the efficacy of the treatments did not differ, W. Miller (1978) noted that the composite treatment was the most costly, involving four times more therapist contact, and offering no additional benefits to justify the additional cost.

Miller and Taylor (1980) examined various forms of self-management training by assigning 41 problem drinkers to four treatments: (1) bibliotherapy, involving the use of a self-help manual but no therapy sessions, (2) individual BSCT involving 10 individual sessions in addition to the self-help manual, (3) individual BSCT plus relaxation training, and (4) 10 sessions of group BSCT plus relaxation training. At a 12-month follow-up, there were no significant differences among the four groups, with an overall success rate of 39% (abstinent or controlled drinking). It can be tentatively concluded that, for middle class, self-referred problem drinkers, BSCT administered by a therapist offers no advantage over its self-help counterpart. Again, the lack of a no-treatment control or a comparison treatment precludes further conclusions.

In another study, Miller, Taylor, and West (1980) examined the relative effectiveness of focused versus broad-spectrum behavioral self-control approaches to controlled drinking by randomly assigning 41 problem drinkers to four groups: (1) bibliotherapy—subjects were given self-help materials but no other treatment, (2) individual BSCT over six weekly sessions, (3) individual BSCT plus 12 sessions of relaxation, communication, and assertion training, and (4) individual BSCT plus 12 sessions of broad-spectrum behavioral treatment modules. At a 12-month follow-up, 41% of all subjects were reported as abstinent or engaging in controlled drinking. The four treatments yielded similar results, with the only significant difference being that the subjects assigned to bibliotherapy spent more hours per week intoxicated than subjects in the other groups. Overall, for this population the broad-spectrum approach failed to produce an outcome superior to focused treatment.

Miller and Baca (1983) conducted a 2-year follow-up of the subjects involved in the preceding two studies (Miller & Taylor, 1980; Miller et al., 1980) and found that significant improvements in drinking and other measures were maintained at 2 years. In the Miller and Taylor (1980) study, 59% of the subjects were abstinent or engaging in controlled drinking, while for the Miller et al. (1980) study, 44% of all subjects had such an outcome. In both studies, subjects who were reported as successful were abstinent or engaging in controlled drinking. However, at certain points in their articles, Miller and his colleagues referred to much higher "favorable outcomes rates" than those just noted. These higher rates resulted because the authors included in their favorable-outcome category subjects whose drinking behavior was reported as improved. Improved subjects were defined as those who failed to meet the criteria for controlled drinking but showed "at least a 30% noncontradicted reduction from baseline" (Miller et al., 1980, p. 597). Because no data were presented regarding each subject's baseline drinking level, a variety of possible interpretations of the meaning of improved drinking is possible. For example, a 30% reduction in drinking could coexist with highly problematic drinking. Thus, to evaluate these two studies in a manner similar to other studies in this review, we designated only the abstinent and controlled drinking outcomes as successful.

As with the other studies reviewed here, neither of the preceding two studies included a no-treatment control group, precluding clear conclusions about the effectiveness of bibliotherapy. However, it does appear that adding other procedures to bibliotherapy does not enhance outcome. Finally, it should be noted that the results do not reflect subjects' functioning over the entire follow-up interval, but rather for 3 months (Miller & Taylor, 1980) or 2 to 6 months (Miller et al., 1980) preceding the 24-month follow-up interview.

3. Summary

Behavioral self-control training appears to be a cost-effective method for treating persons who are not severely dependent on alcohol. However, none of the behavioral self-control studies has included a no-treatment control group, and it is possible that not even self-management training is required for individuals who are only moderately dependent on alcohol. It is also not known which particular components of behavioral self-control training are related to improvement.

F. Multimodal Approaches

1. Rationale

Multimodal approaches are based on the rationale that the individual has multiple problems that are best treated by combining several treatment modalities. These approaches have the advantage of being more comprehensive than unimodal approaches, with the attendant disadvantage that for most studies, the contributions of specific treatment procedures cannot be evaluated, and thus the treatment may be unnecessarily intensive and costly.

2. Data on Multimodal Approaches

Sobell and Sobell (1973a) used a multimodal approach—"individualized behavior therapy (IBT)"—with 70 hospitalized alcoholics. After being assigned to either a nonproblem (controlled) drinking goal ($n = 40$) or an abstinence ($n = 30$) goal by the research staff, subjects within each goal group were randomly assigned to either an IBT program in conjunction with the standard hospital treatment program or to the hospital treatment alone. It was found that within the 2 years following treatment, the experimental subjects treated with a controlled drinking goal functioned significantly better than their respective control subjects with respect to both drinking and other measures of functioning (Sobell & Sobell, 1973b, 1976). In a subsequent independent double-blind third-year follow-up of 53 of the 70 subjects, Caddy, Addington, and Perkins (1978) found that the two groups of experimental subjects generally functioned better than their respective controls. Comparison of the two controlled-drinking groups showed that the experimental subjects functioned significantly better than their respective controls with respect to a number of drinking (including number of days of controlled drinking) and life functioning measures, supporting the two-year results of Sobell and Sobell (1976).

Pomerleau et al. (1978; partially reviewed earlier in Section II.D.2) compared a 12-session multimodal group behavioral treatment program ($n = 18$) for outpatient, middle-income problem drinkers with a 12-week traditional, confrontation approach ($n = 14$). The behavioral approach emphasized controlled drinking (provided that there were no medical or other constraints), whereas the traditional therapy emphasized abstinence. At a 12-month follow-up, no significant difference emerged between the two groups with respect to drinking. However, major differences between the two groups (e.g., use of contracting, different goals) make comparisons difficult.

Blake and Pigott (1979) studied 131 subjects who participated in a 4-week residential multimodal behavioral program. Follow-up was conducted through 12 monthly outpatient appointments. At the end of follow-up, only 24% of the subjects were totally abstinent or drinking without problems. However, a very high follow-up attrition rate (70%) and no comparison condition preclude clear interpretation of these results.

Freedberg and Johnston (1980) reported the results of a 3-week inpatient "multimodal behaviorally oriented treatment program" (p. 84) for 428 employed problem drinkers. At 1 year after discharge, 32% of the subjects were abstinent. However, the failure to report attrition and failure rates, coupled with no control group, again precludes a clear interpretation of these findings.

3. Summary

Multimodal studies have consistently supported the use of behavioral techniques for the treatment of alcohol problems. However, there remains a definite need for component analysis. Given the ever-increasing cost of health care, the cost-effectiveness of certain multimodal interventions and their various components is likely to be much examined in the near future. Because it is becoming increasingly evident that "more" or "more expensive" treatment is not necessarily "better" treatment, research should focus on the controlled evaluation of which components contribute to successful outcomes for which subjects.

III. COMPARISON OF METHODOLOGY AND RELATIVE EFFICACY OF BEHAVIORAL AND NONBEHAVIORAL TREATMENTS

Any comparison of the effectiveness of behavioral and nonbehavioral treatments is extremely difficult because outcome criteria, treatment content, follow-up intervals, patient characteristics, and many other important factors vary considerably across studies. Consequently, the main emphasis of the present comparison is on methodology rather than efficacy. The criteria for selecting behavioral and nonbehavioral studies in this review were noted in the introduction to this chapter. For clarity, behavioral and nonbehavioral studies are compared in a tabular format. Only those studies ($N = 68$) meeting all of the criteria previously mentioned in the introduction are included in the tables. Data are reported separately for three types of studies: behavioral-only studies ($n = 19$); nonbehavioral-only studies ($n = 38$); and studies that compared behavioral and nonbehavioral treatments ($n = 11$). Behavioral-only studies and studies comparing behavioral and nonbehavioral treatments represent 44% (30 of 68) of all studies in the present review. This figure indicates that behavioral treatment evaluations are well represented in the recent literature on alcohol treatment.

A. Subject Characteristics, Drinking Problem History, and Treatment Characteristics

All studies were evaluated on several dimensions. Table 1 shows the percentage of behavioral-only, nonbehavioral-only and behavioral–nonbehavioral comparison studies that report: (1) subject characteristics, (2) subjects' pretreatment drinking problem history, and (3) treatment characteristics.

Eligible studies were evaluated with respect to whether they reported data for five subject characteristics (age, sex, employment status, education, and ethnicity). These data are shown in Table 1. When studies reported pretreatment global scores derived from several variables (e.g., psychosocial adjustment), relevant variables were included only if data for them were presented separately. With regard to basic subject characteristics, nonbehavioral-only studies presented less complete data (except for ethnicity) than the behavioral-only studies. Many studies of all types failed to report subject characteristics and other basic population parameters. This failure limits conclusions not only concerning the generalizability of findings but also concerning direct comparisons among studies.

As discussed later in this chapter, subject's history of drinking problems is an important factor in research on alcohol treatment because the effectiveness of some treatments depends on the initial severity of drinking problems. Thus, the studies in this review were evaluated with respect to whether they reported data for five variables related to subject's pretreatment drinking history (years of problem drinking; formal diagnosis, such as DSM-III, NCA, MAST, WHO; pretreatment drinking behavior; prior alcohol-related treatment and/or hospitalizations; and pretreatment alcohol-related arrests). If a study used a global index, the same criteria as described for subject characteristics were used to determine whether data on the history of drinking problems were considered to have been reported. Generally, the behavioral-

TABLE 1

Percentage of Three Types of Studies Reporting Data on Various Subject Characteristics, History of Drinking Problem Variables, Treatment Characteristics, and Sources of Outcome Data

	Study type		
Variable	Behavioral-only ($n = 19$)	Nonbehavioral-only ($n = 38$)	Behavioral–nonbehavioral comparisons ($n = 11$)
Subject characteristics (% of studies)			
Age	95	79	100
Sex	95	71	100
Employment	68	55	55
Education	74	61	55
Ethnicity	26	45	18
Drinking problem history (% of studies)			
Years of problem drinking	58	24	82
Formal diagnosis	32	21	9
Pretreatment (Pre Tx) drinking behavior	90	97	91
Alcohol-related (AR) prior treatment and/or hospitalizations	63	32	91
Pre Tx AR arrests	16	8	36
Treatment characteristics (% of studies)			
Controlled trial	37	16	91[a]
Treatment setting	100	97	100
Treatment length/amount	84	79	82

(continued)

TABLE 1 (*Continued*)

Variable	Study type		
	Behavioral-only ($n = 19$)	Nonbehavioral-only ($n = 38$)	Behavioral–nonbehavioral comparisons ($n = 11$)
Drinking treatment goal: abstinence (ABST) only	68	79	73
Nonproblem drinking (NPD) only	16	0	0
ABST and NPD[b]	0	5	18
Not determinable	16	16	9

[a]One of these 10 studies reported two separate studies, one of which was a controlled trial.
[b]In some instances different goals were used with different subjects in the same study, while in other studies subjects were randomly assigned to a goal.

only and behavioral – nonbehavioral comparison studies, compared with the nonbehavioral-only studies, more often reported data for these variables, but the overall extent of reporting was not impressive for any type of study. The only exception was that some pretreatment drinking behavior data were reported in 94% (64/68) of all studies reviewed. Overall, this deficiency in reporting data greatly restricts the utility of published studies for clarifying the relationship between pretreatment problem severity and subsequent treatment effectiveness.

For each of the three types of studies, we also evaluated whether the study constituted a controlled trial and whether information was reported about the type of treatment setting (e.g., inpatient, outpatient) and the length – amount of treatment. These data appear in Table 1. Controlled trials were clearly far more frequent among the behavioral – nonbehavioral comparison studies than either the behavioral-only or nonbehavioral-only studies. The fact that 10 of the 11 behavioral – nonbehavioral comparison studies were controlled trials (i.e., used random or matched assignment to groups) is not surprising, because such a design is necessary for making valid treatment comparisons. However, the fact that there were very few controlled trials among the remainder of the studies makes it very difficult to draw conclusions about the relative efficacy of the various treatments. The three types of studies, however, did not differ markedly with regard to reporting the two basic treatment parameters. Overall, about one-fifth (13/68) of the studies failed to report the length/amount of treatment.

Another treatment characteristic that was examined was the type of drinking treatment goal used in the studies. Table 1 shows the percentages of behavioral-only, nonbehavioral-only, and behavioral – nonbehavioral comparison studies that specifically reported using an abstinence goal, a nonproblem drinking goal, or both goals (e.g., a comparison of treatment goals; patients chose their own goal) and the percentage of studies in which a treatment goal was not readily determinable. In some instances, a determination of an abstinence goal was based on statements in the article reflecting an abstinence orientation (e.g., AA was part of the treatment; subjects took disulfiram; subjects were instructed to attend AA after treatment; total abstinence or sobriety rates were assessed posttreatment). For the seven studies that used a nonproblem drinking treatment goal (10.3% of studies in this review: behavioral-only, $n = 3$; nonbehavioral-only, $n = 2$; behavioral – nonbehavioral comparisons, $n = 2$), the use of such a goal was specifically stated in the articles.

B. Follow-up Parameters, Outcome Variables, and Data Sources

All studies were also evaluated along several follow-up and outcome dimensions. Table 2 shows (1) the percentage of studies that reported using

TABLE 2

Percentage of Three Types of Studies Reporting Various Sources of Outcome Data Used, the Longest Interval over Which Follow-up Data Were Reported, and Various Descriptive Statistics for Studies Reporting Data for Outcome Variables Other Than Drinking Behavior

	Study type		
Variable	Behavioral-only ($n = 19$)	Nonbehavioral-only ($n = 38$)	Behavioral–nonbehavioral comparisons ($n = 11$)
Sources of outcome data (% of studies)			
Self-reports[a]	100	100	100
Collateral reports	90	61	82
Biochemical tests	26	11	9
Official records	26	11	45
Staff reports	26	21	27
Used ≥ 2 data sources	90	66	91
The longest interval over which follow-up data were reported (% of studies)[b]			
Follow-up months:			
6	21	24	27
7–11	5	5	9
12	32	29	36
13–17	5	8	0
18	5	3	0
19–23	5	3	0
24	16	11	9
25+	11	18	18
Descriptive statistics for outcome variables other than drinking behavior			
Mean number of variables used	2.6	3.7	2.7
Median number of variables used	3	4	1
Range of variables used	0–7	0–8	0–6
Percentage of studies using ≥ 1 such variable	74	84	91

[a]Includes self-monitoring.
[b]Due to rounding, not all figures sum to 100.

various sources of outcome data, (2) the percentage of studies reporting the longest interval over which follow-up data were reported, and (3) various descriptive statistics for studies reporting data for outcome variables other than drinking behavior.

All studies in this review used self-reports as one source of outcome data. A slightly higher percentage of behavioral-only and behavioral–nonbehavioral comparison studies used collateral reports than nonbehavioral-only studies. Biochemical tests, official records, and staff reports were not widely used by any of the three types of studies. Slightly over three-quarters (52/68) of all studies in this review used two or more data sources to assess treatment efficacy. This figure is somewhat higher than that reported in an earlier review (Sobell & Sobell, 1982), where only 57% (21/37) of the studies reviewed (published from 1976 through the early part of 1980) reported using two or more information sources for outcome data. The present finding is encouraging because no single source of outcome data is error free, and multiple outcome sources allow for a convergent determination of efficacy (Sobell & Sobell, 1980).

All studies were evaluated with respect to whether they reported data for 10 categories of outcome variables other than drinking behavior (e.g., vocational functioning, physical health, alcohol-related arrests). Studies (e.g., Gordis & Sereny, 1980; Pettinati, Sugerman, DiDonato, & Maurer, 1982) that reported a single global index and failed to report data on the individual variables constituting the global index, were classified as having a single other variable. Also, studies which reported that outcome data were gathered for a large number of variables but which failed to present any data were classified as not having reported on the respective outcome variables. However, a study was considered as having reported on a variable if the values for the variable were reported, or if the variable was involved in a statistical analysis that was reported, even if descriptive statistics for the variable were not presented.

Table 2 shows the mean number, median number, the range of outcome variables other than drinking behavior reported by the three types of studies. The percentage of studies within each study type reporting data for at least one nondrinking outcome variable is also listed. A high proportion of all studies in this review (82%, 56/68) reported data for at least one outcome measure other than drinking behavior. Across all three study types, nonbehavioral-only studies reported data for the highest mean and median number of outcome variables other than drinking behavior. Across all studies, the mean number of such outcome variables for which data were reported was 3.2. This figure compares favorably with results from a recent review of 37 alcohol treatment outcome studies where a mean of 3.5 outcome measures per study (excluding drinking behavior) was reported (Sobell & Sobell, 1982).

Two aspects of follow-up methodology were examined across all studies. Table 2 presents the percentage of studies reporting the longest interval over which follow-up data were reported for all three types of studies. For those studies that reported a mean number of months of follow-up, that mean was used, and for studies that reported a range for the number of follow-up months (e.g., 30 to 60), the lower bound was used as a conservative index. For inpatient programs, follow-up began at the time the subject was discharged. However, for several outpatient programs, follow-up began when treatment began (e.g., Ahles et al., 1983; Bulmer, 1980). For some inpatient programs (e.g., Cannon et al., 1981; Neubuerger et al., 1980), booster sessions occurred during the follow-up period. As well, some programs had aftercare components, and in several instances, follow-up was conducted during the aftercare (e.g., Chaney et al., 1978; Walker, Donovan, Kivlahan, & O'Leary, 1983). As shown in Table 2, differences in the length of follow-up among the types of studies are negligible. Although 71% ($n = 48$) of all studies conducted follow-up for 1 year or more, this figure does not necessarily reflect common research practices, because many studies were excluded from this review because they failed to provide follow-up data for even a 6-month period. Although there is some indication that an 18-month follow-up interval is sufficient for group results to reach stability (reviewed in Sobell & Sobell, 1982), this conclusion is based on a small number of studies. In this regard, only 34% (23) of all studies in this review reported follow-up data for 18 months or longer and 28% (19) reported outcome data for 24 months or longer.

It should be noted that although two different studies might have reported contacting subjects at the same point in time after discharge, the outcome data from the two studies did not necessarily cover the same time interval. The following are examples of what might be termed *abbreviated* or *partial* follow-up evaluations: (1) Miller and Baca (1983) followed subjects for 24 months in two studies, but in one study (Miller & Taylor, 1980) they reported drinking outcome data for the 90 days prior to the 24-month follow-up contact, and for the second study (Miller et al., 1980), they reported drinking outcome data for only 2 to 6 months prior to the 24-month contact; (2) Wilson, White, and Lange (1978) followed subjects for 15 months, but reported abstinence data for only the 3 months prior to the 15-month interview; (3) Edwards, Duckitt, Oppenheimer, Sheehan, and Taylor (1983) reported a 10- to 12-year follow-up, but much of their data, including drinking behavior, represented the 1-year period prior to the follow-up interview; (4) Vaillant, Clark, Cyrus, Milofsky, Kopp, Wulsin, and Mogielnicki (1983) followed subjects for 8 years, but reported outcome data for only the last 3 years prior to the follow-up; (5) Polich, Armor, and Braiker (1980) followed subjects for 4 years, but in several instances reported drinking outcome data for only the 30 days prior to the subjects' last drink; and (6) Oei and Jackson (1982) presented a 1-year follow-up, but actually reported data for only the 7 days preceding the interview. To our knowledge, the use of abbreviated follow-up intervals has not been discussed at length in previous reviews and is therefore discussed here.

The most serious problem with not collecting outcome data over the entire follow-up interval is that individual samples of drinking behavior typically do not represent the entire interval. Rather, an individual's drinking tends to vary over time and includes periods of abstinence, nonproblem drinking, and problem drinking (for a discussion see Emrick, 1974, 1975; Pettinati et al., 1982; Polich et al., 1980). Reports of partial outcome data also do not allow the temporal stability of outcome measures to be assessed. Unfortunately, a review of alcohol treatment studies found that many investigators present only partial outcome data in long-term follow-up studies (Sobell & Sobell, 1984c).

The second aspect of follow-up methodology that was examined across all studies was the number of follow-up contacts each study reported. Table 3 presents the percentage of studies that reported the number of follow-up contacts as well as the mean, median, and range of follow-up contacts for behavioral-only, nonbehavioral-only, behavioral–nonbehavioral comparison studies, and all studies combined. For the few studies that reported a mean number of actual follow-up contacts per subject, that figure was used, and for studies that reported a range of follow-up contacts across subjects (e.g., 5–10), the lower figure was used. For many studies, the number of contacts reported appears to refer to scheduled contacts, and it is unclear whether all scheduled contacts were achieved. Again, the differences across study types were not marked. Although the mean number of contacts for behavioral–nonbehavioral comparison studies was slightly higher than for the other two types of studies, the median figure indicates that this difference resulted from a few studies inflating the mean. Although the mean number of contacts per follow-up interval across all studies was 2.3, 71% of these studies collected data for 12 or more months. Thus, data collected over extended periods of time are often based on only a few follow-up contacts.

TABLE 3

Percentage of Studies Reporting Various Numbers of Follow-Up Contacts with Subjects and the Mean, Median, and Range of Follow-Up Contacts per each Study Type

Study type	Follow-up contacts						
	1[a]	2–5[a]	6–10[a]	ND[a,b]	Mean[c]	Median[c]	Range[c]
Behavioral-only (n = 19)	21	53	5	21	2.3	2	1–6
Nonbehavioral-only (n = 38)[d]	42	42	3	13	2.1	2	1–6
Behavioral-nonbehavioral comparisons (n = 11)	36	36	18	9	3.2	2.5	1–8.2
All studies (N = 68)[d]	35	44	6	15	2.3	2	1–8.2

[a]Due to rounding not all figures sum to 100.
[b]ND = Not determinable.
[c]Studies where the number of contacts was not determinable are excluded; the number of studies included in these figures are: behavioral only (n = 15), nonbehavioral only (n = 33), behavioral and nonbehavioral comparisons (n = 11), all studies (N = 68).
[d]Although the Edwards et al. (1983) study had 13 follow-up contacts during the first follow-up year, and 1 contact in the second year, only one follow-up contact was made to collect the 10–12-year outcome data reported in this study. Thus, the number of follow-up contacts listed for this study was one.

100 Diane M. Riley et al.

C. Relative Efficacy: Nature of Outcomes Reported

As might be expected on the basis of the wide differences in subject populations, treatment duration and procedures, and outcome methods and measures, it is difficult to compare the efficacy of various alcohol treatment studies. However, in an earlier attempt to do so, Costello (1975a, b) used the following four outcome categories to compare studies: percentage of original treatment cohorts reported as (1) *deceased,* (2) *lost* to follow-up, (3) *successful* [defined as "moderating or terminating their drinking" (1975a, p. 253) or "sober or drinking with no associated problem" (1975b, p. 858)], and (4) *failures* (defined as "still drinking with an associated problem"; 1975a, b, pp. 253 and 859, respectively). Because Costello's method of categorization has been reported in the literature, it was decided to use the same outcome classification system in the present review.

Even within Costello's (1975a, b) scheme, definitions for the four outcome categories varied immensely across studies. For example, some studies considered only total abstinence (i.e., *no* drinking over the entire follow-up interval), while other studies used an essential abstinence criterion. Examples of essential abstinence include (1) Heather, Rollnick, and Winton (1983), who used a category of "*mostly abstinent* but with one or two 'slips'" (p. 14); (2) Parker, Winstead, Willi, and Fisher (1979), who reported that "a slightly lower percentage of patients remained totally abstinent with time, yet a larger percentage of patients was either abstinent or had drunk less than three times" (p. 1180); (3) McLachlan and Stein (1982), who while reporting totally abstinent outcomes for 33% of their population also reported that "25% had brief relapses from which they recovered (with no more than 14 drinking days during the year), making a total of 58% who had stopped drinking at follow-up" (p. 265); and (4) Vaillant et al. (1983), who in an 8 year follow-up report stated "Our operational definition of *abstinence* was less than one drink a month and not more than one episode of intoxication —and that of less than a week's duration—in the past 24 months" (p. 456). Thus, although a number of investigators are defining and reporting essential abstinence outcomes, their definitions vary widely. Moreover, many investigators operationally defined *abstinence* only in their method and/or results sections, and in their discussion section *abstinence* often was unqualified. The recent reporting of essential abstinence outcome categories might be seen as an improvement, because enduring problem-free outcomes are rare, and successful outcomes most often involve occasional relapses.

In a similar vein, a previous review of the literature (Pattison, Sobell, & Sobell, 1977) showed that nonproblem drinking outcome definitions and criteria varied across studies. Consequently, other than for very general levels of analysis such as reported here, the lack of a consensus on all outcome definitions greatly restricts the ability to make comparisons among specific studies.

Although Costello (1975a, b) did not indicate whether his lost category was limited to only lost subjects, the *Lost/Refused* category in the present review includes subjects who were lost, for whom there were insufficient data, and who refused follow-up interviews. Finally, and somewhat surprisingly, many investigators did not indicate whether they searched records to identify subjects who were deceased. If there was no mention of subjects being lost or deceased in a particular study, we assumed that there were no such subjects. Consequently, data in these two categories are likely to be underrepresented.

A brief review of Costello's findings will be helpful for interpreting the findings of the present review. Costello's outcome profiles for subjects in his 58 studies ($N = 11,022$) with a 1-year follow-up published between 1951 and 1973 (1975a), and his 23 studies ($N = 5,833$) with a 2-year follow-up published between 1952 and 1972 (1975b) were as follows: *One Year Follow-up:* 1% *deceased,* 21% *lost,* 25% *successes,* and 53% *failures; Two Year Follow-up:* 3% *deceased,* 19% *lost,* 35% *successes,* and 43% *failures.* Additional reviews or evaluation studies have found similar or lower percentages of successes. The 4-year Rand study (Polich et al., 1980) found that 28% of the treated sample were long-term abstainers (6 or more months), with the figure falling to 7% abstinent throughout the entire 4 years. Furthermore, 18% of the sample were found to be drinking without problems or symptoms of dependence at the 4-year follow-up, and 15% were reported as deceased.

Table 4 shows the percentage distributions of behavioral, nonbehavioral, and all studies combined with respect to the number of subjects classified as *deceased, lost, failures* or *successes* (data for subjects in the 11 behavioral–nonbehavioral comparison studies were separated according to behavioral or nonbehavioral treatment and so classified). The outcome data used to compute these figures were those reported for the most recent follow-up contact. The investigators' original reports of their outcome variables (i.e., success, failure, dead, lost) were used whenever possible. Following the same procedure employed by Costello et al. (1977), if a study used a "floating *n,*" then the outcome variables were recalculated. For example, if the investigators' success rates were calculated from an *N* smaller than the original (i.e., adjusting for subject attrition or "experimental mortality"), the adjusted *N* would result in an inflated success rate. Thus, for comparability across studies, the four outcome parameters were calculated from the original number of subjects who completed the treatment phase of this study. As noted in Table 4, a small percentage of studies did not provide data for some of the outcome categories. Thus, under each outcome variable the overall sample size on which the figures are based is listed as well as the number of studies that reported such outcomes. Also, for some behavioral studies (e.g., Azrin, et al., 1982; Chaney et al., 1978), success and failure rates defined by Costello's (1975a, b) criteria could not be determined because these studies

TABLE 4

Percentage and Number of Subjects in Behavioral, Nonbehavioral, and All Studies Combined That Were Reported as Dead, Lost, Successes, and Failures

Study type (No. of studies/ no. of subjects in the studies)	Variable							
	Deceased		Lost/refused		Successes		Failures	
	%	$(n/N)^a$	%	$(n/N)^a$	%	$(n/N)^a$	%	$(n/N)^a$
Behavioral[b,c] (30 studies/4,894 subjects[c])	0.7	(36/4,863) 29 studies	16.2	(587/3,628) 26 studies	40.7	(1,951/4,795) 26 studies	39.6	(1,406/3,553) 23 studies
Nonbehavioral[b,c] (49 studies/9,652 subjects)	3.0	(272/9,231) 47 studies	24.7	(2,255/9,138) 45 studies	30.9	(2,920/9,456) 44 studies	39.9	(3,715/9,302) 42 studies
All studies[b,c] (68 studies/14,546 subjects)	2.2	(308/14,094) 66 studies	22.3	(2,842/12,766) 62 studies	34.2	(4,871/14,251) 63 studies	39.8	(5,121/12,855) 59 studies

[a] Some studies did not provide data for the various outcome categories. Thus, the percentage of subjects in each of the four outcome categories is based on the number of subjects reported as deceased, lost/refused, successes or failures over the total number of subjects in the studies for which data were reported for each category (n/N). The number of studies which the N is based on is listed below the outcome figures. Because of varying Ns, the percentage figures do not sum to 100 in all cases.

[b] There are 68 total studies in this review: 19 behavioral studies, 38 nonbehavioral studies, and 11 comparison studies which provided data for both behavioral and nonbehavioral subjects. For the behavioral and nonbehavioral studies presented separately in this table, the subject data for the appropriate treatment types in the 11 comparison studies are included in each of their respective categories (behavioral and nonbehavioral).

[c] In one study (Olson et al., 1981), 37 subjects could not be included in either of these groups, as behavioral and nonbehavioral therapies were combined in one treatment group. In another study (Seelye, 1979), the number of subjects in both the failure and success columns was a conservative estimate due to the fact that the deceased subjects had been included in these categories — i.e., their functioning before they died was used as outcome data.

presented their outcome results using a daily drinking disposition measure, and the follow-up period was partitioned into categories (e.g., number of days abstinent; number of days jailed for alcohol-related reasons; number of days consuming less than three ounces of absolute ethanol). Although these outcome data are more precise than the "abstinent, improved, same, or worse" categories and allow for pre – posttreatment comparisons, they cannot be included in Costello's (1975a, b) success/failure categories. However, because an increasing number of studies have assessed outcome by partitioning the follow-up interval into categories (e.g., days in different operationally defined drinking categories; see Sobell & Sobell, 1984a), future evaluations of treatment efficacy should seek ways to include such studies in outcome categories.

Caution is advised in comparing success rates between the behavioral and the nonbehavioral studies because of the great variability in the ways investigators defined success and because of the variable length of follow-up across studies in this review (range: 6 – 144 months). Although the data suggest a slight advantage for behavioral studies, a valid comparison would necessitate taking into account methodological and population differences. Such an evaluation was not undertaken in the present review because very few studies could be meaningfully compared.

Based on the 68 studies in this review, a total of 14,546 subjects were reported to have completed treatment and were scheduled for follow-up. Of that total, 4,894 were classified as behavioral subjects and 9,652 were classified as nonbehavioral subjects. Of the total sample, 2% were reported as deceased, 22% were either lost to follow-up, refused follow-up, or had insufficient follow-up data, 34% had successfully moderated or terminated (abstinent) their drinking, and 40% were still drinking and had (an) associated problem(s). The rates for all four outcome categories in the present review are strikingly similar to those reported by Costello (1975b) for alcohol treatment studies with a 2-year follow-up (3% deceased, 19% lost, 35% successful, and 43% failures). Despite the varying follow-up intervals in the present review (6 – 144 months), perhaps all that can be concluded is that alcohol treatment outcome results have not changed appreciably during the period 1978 through 1983. In essence, the effectiveness of our treatments seems to be static and is still not particularly impressive.

In terms of the percentage of subjects classified as deceased or as failures, the behavioral and nonbehavioral studies are generally similar. However, a slightly higher percentage of the behavioral than nonbehavioral subjects is reported as successful. Also, the behavioral studies collectively located 84% of their subjects for follow-up, versus 75% for the nonbehavioral studies. With respect to the percentage of subjects for whom data were unavailable (lost/refused), it still remains the case (as noted a few years ago by Sobell &

Sobell, 1982) that investigators need to make a more concerted effort to locate as many subjects as possible to avoid biasing their outcome results. Similarly, because mortality findings seem to be quite common in both short-term (see Costello, 1975a, b) and long-term (see Sobell & Sobell, 1984b) outcome evaluations, investigators should report whether records were checked for evidence of deaths as well as the number of subjects deceased.

Because Costello's (1975a, b) success category includes both abstinent and nonproblem drinking outcomes, studies in this review were evaluated for whether they reported nonproblem drinking outcomes. Inclusion of a nonproblem drinking outcome depended on an explicit mention of such an outcome or a report of drinking behavior that could be thus classified. Although the behavioral-only studies had the highest percentage of studies reporting nonproblem drinking outcomes (57.9%, 11 of 19 studies), they did not differ greatly from either the nonbehavioral-only studies (47.4%, 18 of 38 studies) or the behavioral–nonbehavioral comparison studies (45.4%, 5 of 11 studies) in this regard. Because nonbehavioral studies usually have an abstinence orientation, it was surprising that nearly half of the nonbehavioral-only studies reported explicit nonproblem drinking outcomes. Overall, one-half of all studies (50%, 34 of 68 studies) in this review reported nonproblem drinking outcomes. This finding suggests that, at least as an outcome category, nonproblem drinking is being used quite widely by both behavioral and nonbehavioral researchers.

Although it was not evaluated in the present review, other recent reviews (Heather & Robertson, 1983; Miller & Hester, 1980) show, as noted several years ago (Sobell, 1978), that less severely dependent alcoholics tend to be more likely to engage successfully in nonproblem drinking than more seriously dependent alcoholics. However, because there have been a number of reports of controlled drinking among chronic alcoholics (e.g., Sobell & Sobell, 1973a, b, 1976, 1978; Vogler, Compton, & Weissbach, 1975; for a review see Heather & Robertson, 1983), this issue is not yet resolved. Furthermore, much of the evidence on controlled drinking outcomes, especially for chronic alcoholics, derives from studies of abstinence-oriented treatments. Also, relatively few studies have used an experimental design to compare controlled drinking and abstinence-oriented treatments.

IV. STATE OF THE ART AND PROSPECTS FOR THE FUTURE

Based on the outcome results of the 68 studies in the present review, it would appear that the effectiveness of alcohol treatment programs in general has not progressed beyond that reported in previous reviews. However, a variety of problems prevent drawing strong conclusions from the current studies. Some generalizations concerning relative efficacy can be drawn from studies using essentially similar methodologies to compare different treatments, but these studies are few in number.

The lack of comparability across behavioral and nonbehavioral treatments also precludes drawing unequivocal conclusions about the relative efficacy of these treatment orientations. Only a handful of studies has directly compared behavioral and nonbehavioral treatments, while the results of studies with a single-orientation usually are subject to a variety of competing explanations other than those related to the difference in treatment orientation. Replication across different settings and by different investigators is fundamental to the scientific method in terms of establishing the robustness and generalizability of findings, but it is a research strategy that has been largely neglected by treatment researchers in the alcohol field, regardless of orientation.

Given the preceding limitations, a number of important methodological problems must be addressed before meaningful conclusions concerning treatment efficacy can be reached. In addition to the need for controlled trials and replication studies, other areas that need improvement are

1. Use of operationally defined, quantifiable, reliable, and valid measures;
2. Greater standardization of outcome assessment procedures and measures;
3. Closer analysis of within-subject treatment gains;
4. Collection of more pretreatment data;
5. Detailed specification of the population of alcohol abusers under study;
6. Specification of treatment components and evaluation of their contributions to treatment outcome;
7. Continued evaluation of the influence of extratreatment factors on treatment outcomes.

An important recent development in the alcohol field has been a reconceptualization of the relapse process (Curry & Marlatt, in this volume). While the traditional model of alcoholism suggests that alcohol problems and recovery from these problems are all-or-none phenomena, the treatment-outcome literature strongly indicates that alcohol problems tend to be recurrent, even when individuals show great improvement over time. Marlatt (Marlatt & George, 1984) has suggested that recovery is best conceptualized as gradual rather than abrupt; his theoretical conceptualization has spurred much research on the determinants of relapse, methods to prevent relapse, and ways to minimize the adverse consequences of relapses that do occur.

It is our view that relapse prevention eventually will be seen as a very important concept in the alcohol field. We speculate that the major impact of the concept of relapse prevention will be that it will make it respectable for clinicians to discuss the possibility of relapse with their clients and to make plans for dealing with relapses. Relapse prevention bridges the gap between scientific knowledge (which shows that relapses are commonplace) and clinical practice (where good outcomes are too often viewed as problem-free) and is particularly timely, given reports showing that alcohol problems tend to be highly recurrent (e.g., Pettinati et al., 1982; Polich et al., 1980). To acknowledge that alcohol problems are frequently recurrent would bring beliefs about the nature of alcohol problems closer to what the empirical evidence demonstrates (Madden, 1984).

Treatment goals for alcohol problems is another area currently undergoing considerable change and one that has become fraught with controversy. Despite the prevalence of the traditional view that abstinence is the only acceptable goal for treating alcohol problems, research has clearly established that a unitary goal of abstinence is neither sufficient nor necessary (Heather & Robertson, 1983) and that nonproblem drinking outcomes do occur.

The effectiveness of nonproblem drinking approaches must be compared with that of other treatment approaches (see Sobell & Sobell, 1984b). In this regard, abstinence versus nonproblem drinking treatment outcomes must not be confused with abstinence versus nonproblem drinking treatment goals. Long-term abstinence or totally problem-free drinking are both rare, whereas substantial improvement is a quite common outcome. At present, there is no definitive evidence on the question of whether abstinence or nonproblem drinking approaches differ in their capacity to produce improved long-term outcomes, even with chronic alcoholics, although we recognize that there are obvious cases where the risk of any drinking contraindicates anything other than an abstinence approach. In summary, considerable research is needed to understand the effect of treatment goals on treatment outcomes, and continued research is needed on the pressing issue of which individuals are best suited for either a nonproblem drinking goal or an abstinence goal.

A third area very much in need of further investigation is the effect of treatment intensity on treatment outcome. Whereas work such as that by Orford and Edwards (1977) and Stinson, Smith, Amidjaya, and Kaplan (1979) has questioned the necessity of intensive treatment for many alcohol problems, other studies (e.g., Smart & Gray, 1978; Welte et al., 1981) suggest that certain individuals may benefit from longer and/or more intensive treatment. However, the characteristics of clients requiring more intensive treatment remain to be clearly specified, and as Emrick (1982) has noted, intensive treatment "can be accomplished much less expensively in non-hospital, residential settings" (p. 1157). Similarly, research is needed to determine which individuals might require specialized treatment (e.g., neuropsychologically impaired; Miller & Hester, 1980).

In a related regard, because a number of studies (see Miller & Hester, 1980) suggest that severity of alcohol dependence may differentiate between subgroups in terms of the nature and intensity of treatment required, it may be important to assess the severity of dependence when assigning clients to different intensities of treatment. The Alcohol Dependence Scale (ADS; Skinner & Horn, 1984), a self-administered 25-item questionnaire, is one of several assessment instruments that can be used for this purpose. Although it seems logical to assume that the efficacy of treatments may well be enhanced if individuals are better matched to treatment, guidelines for matching can be gained only through rigorous experimentation with adequate controls and adequate follow-up intervals.

Finally, it appears that changes in behavioral treatments for alcohol problems have paralleled those in behavior therapy in general. The original behavioral treatments used simple aversive conditioning techniques and were followed by treatments based on operant conditioning (e.g., skills training). Most recently, cognitive-behavioral procedures have been used. Behavior therapy is also undergoing a general broadening of perspective to encompass not only the development of treatments based on behavioral technology, but also a more comprehensive conceptualization of behavior problems which includes the full range of variables that can influence behavior (e.g., genetics, information-processing). In short, the field of behavior therapy is becoming more complex, with increasing attention devoted to theory as well as technology, and our understanding of alcohol problems is accordingly becoming more complex and complete.

V. CONCLUSIONS

The conclusions reached in the present review do not diverge greatly from those of previous reviews. Our foremost conclusion is that **treatments for alcohol problems with demonstrated enduring effectiveness do not exist, regardless of treatment orientations or treatment goals.** Unfortunately, continuing debate over treatment goals has somewhat obscured this sobering reality (see section by L. Sobell in Marlatt et al., 1985).

While the "controlled drinking controversy" has clearly foreshadowed other issues in the alcohol field, what the present and previous reviews (e.g., Costello et al., 1977; Emrick, 1974, 1975; Heather & Robertson, 1983; Miller & Hester, 1980) reveal is that relapse following treatment is a very real and a very frequent phenomenon for all treatments. On the strength of the empirical evidence, recovery from alcohol problems seems best conceptualized as a gradual improvement which realistically encompasses some slips. The most salient aspect of the empirical findings is that slips derive almost entirely from treatment programs that have embodied an abstinence goal.

If we are committed to the treatment of individuals who have alcohol problems, then we must recognize that most outcomes, even good outcomes, are frequently interrupted by relapses, and we must learn how to help our clients constructively deal with such events. The state of the art for the alcohol field is that no current treatment works very well, and our energies can best be spent on developing alternative treatments with demonstrated effectiveness.

ACKNOWLEDGMENT

Special thanks are extended to Louise Amantea for her patience in typing the manuscript.

REFERENCES[3]

*Abbott, M. W., & Gregson, R. A. M. (1981). Cognitive dysfunction in the prediction of relapse in alcoholics. *Journal of Studies on Alcohol, 42,* 230–243.
*Adams, K. M., Grant, I., & Reed, R. (1980). Neuropsychology in alcoholic men in their late thirties: One-year follow-up. *American Journal of Psychiatry, 137,* 928–931.
*Ahles, T. A., Schlundt, D. G., Prue, D. M., & Rychtarik, R. G. (1983). Impact of aftercare arrangements on the maintenance of treatment success in abusive drinkers. *Addictive Behaviors, 8,* 53–58.
*Alford, G. S. (1980). Alcoholics Anonymous: An empirical outcome study. *Addictive Behaviors, 5,* 359–370.
Anant, S. S. (1967). A note on the treatment of alcoholics by a verbal aversion technique. *Canadian Psychologist, 1,* 19–22.
Averill, J. R. (1973). Personal control over aversive stimuli and its relationship to stress. *Psychological Bulletin, 80,* 286–303.
*Azrin, N. H., Sisson, R. W., Meyers, R., & Godley, M. (1982). Alcoholism treatment by disulfiram and community reinforcement therapy. *Journal of Behavior Therapy and Experimental Psychiatry, 13,* 105–112.
Beck, A. T. (1976). *Cognitive therapy & the emotional disorders.* New York: International Universities Press.
Benson, H. (1975). *The relaxation response.* New York: Morrow.
*Blake, B. G., & Pigott, P. (1979). A follow-up of alcoholics treated by multimodal therapy. *American Journal of Drug and Alcohol Abuse, 6,* 477–486.
*Boland, F. J., Mellor, C. S., & Revusky, S. (1978). Chemical aversion treatment of alcoholism: Lithium as the aversive agent. *Behaviour Research and Therapy, 16,* 401–409.
*Brissett, D., Laundergan, J. C., Kammeier, M. L., & Biele, M. (1980). Drinkers and non-drinkers at three and a half years after treatment: Attitudes and growth. *Journal of Studies on Alcohol, 41,* 945–952.
*Bulmer, D. R. (1980). Disability insurance for alcoholics. *Journal of Studies on Alcohol, 41,* 352–357.
Caddy, G. R. (1982). Evaluation of behavioral methods in the study of alcoholism. In E. M. Pattison & E. Kaufman (Eds.), *Encyclopedic handbook of alcoholism.* New York: Gardner Press.

[3]Studies which met the criteria presented in Section I and which are included in the tabular presentation of results in Section III are identified with an asterisk.

*Caddy, G. R., Addington, H. J., Jr., & Perkins, D. (1978). Individualized behavior therapy for alcoholics: A third year independent double-blind follow-up. *Behaviour Research and Therapy,* **16,** 345–362.

*Cannon, D. S., Baker, T. B., & Wehl, C. K. (1981). Emetic and electric shock alcohol aversion therapy: Six- and twelve-month follow-up. *Journal of Consulting and Clinical Psychology,* **49,** 360–368.

Cappell, H., & Greeley, J. (in press). Alcohol and tension reduction: An update on research and theory. In H. T. Blane & K. E. Leonard (Eds.), *Psychological theories of drinking and alcoholism.* New York: Guilford Press.

Cautela, J. R. (1966). Treatment of compulsive behavior by covert sensitization. *Psychological Record,* **16,** 33–41.

Cernovsky, Z. (1983). Dimensions of self-actualization and posttreatment alcohol use in fully and in partly recovered alcoholics. *Journal of Clinical Psychology,* **39,** 628–632.

*Chaney, E. F., O'Leary, M. R., & Marlatt, G. A. (1978). Skill training with alcoholics. *Journal of Consulting and Clinical Psychology,* **46,** 1092–1104.

*Cohen, R., Appelt, H., Olbrich, R., & Watzl, H. (1979). Alcoholic women treated by behaviorally oriented therapy: An 18-month follow-up study. *Drug and Alcohol Dependence,* **4,** 489–498.

Costello, R. M. (1975a). Alcoholism treatment and evaluation: In search of methods. *International Journal of the Addictions,* **10,** 251–275.

Costello, R. M. (1975b). Alcoholism treatment and evaluation: In search of methods. II. Collation of two-year follow-up studies. *International Journal of the Addictions,* **10,** 857–867.

Costello, R. M. (1980). Alcoholism aftercare and outcome: Cross-lagged panel and path analysis. *British Journal of Addiction,* **75,** 49–53.

*Costello, R. M., Baillargeon, J. G., Biever, P., & Bennett, R. (1979). Second-year alcoholism treatment outcome evaluation with a focus on Mexican-American patients. *American Journal on Drug and Alcohol Abuse,* **6,** 97–108.

Costello, R. M., Biever, R., & Baillargeon, J. G. (1977). Alcoholism treatment programming: Historical trends and modern approaches. *Alcoholism: Clinical and Experimental Research,* **1,** 311–318.

*Crawford, R. J. M. (1982). The use of videotape in the erosion of denial in alcoholism: Pilot study. *New Zealand Medical Journal,* **95,** 82–84.

Cronkite, R. C., & Moos, R. H. (1978). Evaluating alcoholism treatment programs: An integrated approach. *Journal of Consulting and Clinical Psychology,* **46,** 1105–1119.

Cummings, C., Gordon, J. R., & Marlatt, G. A. (1980). Relapse: Prevention and prediction. In W. R. Miller (Ed.), *Addictive behaviors: Treatment of alcoholism, drug use, smoking, and obesity.* New York: Pergamon Press.

*Edwards, G., Duckitt, A., Oppenheimer, E., Sheehan, M., & Taylor, C. (1983). What happens to alcoholics? *Lancet,* **2,** 269–271.

*Elkins, R. L. (1980). Covert sensitization treatment of alcoholism: Contributions of successful conditioning to subsequent abstinence maintenance. *Addictive Behaviors,* **5,** 67–89.

Elkins, R. L., & Hobbs, S. H. (1979). Forgetting, preconditioning CS familiarization, and taste aversion learning: An animal experiment with implications for alcoholism treatment. *Behaviour Research and Therapy,* **17,** 567–573.

Emrick, C. D. (1974). A review of psychologically oriented treatment of alcoholism. I. The use and interrelationships of outcome criteria and drinking behavior following treatment. *Quarterly Journal of Studies on Alcohol,* **35,** 523–549.

Emrick, C. D. (1975). A review of psychologically oriented treatment of alcoholism. II. The relative effectiveness of different treatment approaches and the effectiveness of treatment versus no treatment. *Quarterly Journal of Studies on Alcohol,* **36,** 88–108.

Emrick, C. D. (1979). Perspectives in clinical research: Relative effectiveness of alcohol abuse treatment. *Family and Community Health,* **2,** 71–88.

Emrick, C. D. (1982). Evaluation of alcoholism psychotherapy methods. In E. M. Pattison & E. Kaufman (Eds.), *Encyclopedic handbook of alcoholism.* New York: Gardner Press.

*Ferrell, W. L., & Galassi, J. P. (1981). Assertion training and human relations training in the treatment of chronic alcoholics. *International Journal of the Addictions,* **16,** 959–968.

Frankenstein, W., & Wilson, G. T. (1984). Alcohol's effects on self-awareness. *Addictive Behaviors,* **9,** 323–328.

*Freedberg, E. J., & Johnston, W. E. (1980). Outcome with alcoholics seeking treatment voluntarily or after confrontation by their employer. *Journal of Occupational Medicine,* **22,** 83–86.

Garcia, J., & Koelling, R. A. (1966). The relation of cue to consequence in avoidance learning. *Psychonomic Science,* **4,** 123–124.

*Gordis, E., & Sereny, G. (1980). Effect of prior narcotic addiction on response to treatment of alcoholism. *Alcoholism: Clinical and Experimental Research,* **4,** 34–39.

Heather, N., & Robertson, I. (1983). *Controlled drinking* (2nd ed.). New York: Methuen.

*Heather, N., Rollnick, S., & Winton, M. (1982). Psychological change among inpatient alcoholics and its relationship to treatment outcome. *British Journal on Alcohol and Alcoholism,* **17,** 90–97.

*Heather, N., Rollnick, S., & Winton, M. (1983). A comparison of objective and subjective measures of alcohol dependence as predictors of relapse following treatment. *British Journal of Clinical Psychology,* **22,** 11–17.

*Hesselbrock, M., Babor, T. F., Hesselbrock, V., Meyer, R. E., & Workman, K. (1983). "Never believe an alcoholic"? On the validity of self-report measures of alcohol dependence and related constructs. *International Journal of the Addictions,* **18,** 593–609.

Higgins, R. L., & Marlatt, G. A. (1975). Fear of interpersonal evaluation as a determinant of alcohol consumption in male social drinkers. *Journal of Abnormal Psychology,* **84,** 644–651.

*Hoffman, N. G., Harrison, P. A., & Belille, C. A. (1983). Alcoholics Anonymous after treatment: Attendance and abstinence. *International Journal of the Addictions,* **18,** 311–318.

Hull, J. G. (1981). A self-awareness model of the causes and effects of alcohol consumption. *Journal of Abnormal Psychology,* **90,** 586–600.

*Jackson, T. R., & Smith, J. W. (1978). A comparison of two aversion treatment methods for alcoholism. *Journal of Studies on Alcohol,* **39,** 187–191.

Jacobson, E. (1938). *Progressive relaxation.* Chicago: University of Chicago Press.

Jones, E. E., & Berglas, S. (1978). Control of attributions about the self through self-handicapping strategies: The appeal of alcohol and the role of under-achievement. *Personality and Social Psychology Bulletin,* **4,** 200–206.

*Jones, S. L., Kanfer, R., & Lanyon, R. I. (1982). Skill training with alcoholics: A clinical extension. *Addictive Behaviors,* **7,** 285–290.

*Jones, S. L., & Lanyon, R. I. (1981). Relationship between adaptive skills and outcome of alcoholism treatment. *Journal of Studies on Alcohol,* **42,** 521–525.

*Katz, A., Morgan, M. Y., & Sherlock, S. (1981). Alcoholism treatment in a medical setting. *Journal of Studies on Alcohol,* **42,** 136–143.

*Kish, G. B., Ellsworth, R. B., & Woody, M. M. (1980). Effectiveness of an 84-day and a 60-day alcoholism treatment program. *Journal of Studies on Alcohol,* **41,** 81–85.

Klajner, F., Hartman, L. M., & Sobell, M. B. (1984). Treatment of substance abuse by relaxation training: A review of its rationale, efficacy and mechanism. *Addictive Behaviors,* **9,** 41–55.

*Kliner, D. J., Spicer, J., & Barnett, P. (1980). Treatment outcome of alcoholic physicians. *Journal of Studies on Alcohol,* **41,** 1217–1220.

*Longabaugh, R., McCrady, B., Fink, E., Stout, R., McAuley, T., Doyle, C., & McNeill, D. (1983). Cost effectiveness of alcoholism treatment in partial vs. inpatient settings: Six-month outcomes. *Journal of Studies on Alcohol,* **44,** 1049–1071.

Madden, J. S. (1984). Whither alcoholism? (Editorial). *Alcohol & Alcoholism,* **19**, 91–95.

Mahoney, M. J. (1974). *Cognitive and behavior modification.* Cambridge, MA: Ballinger.

Marlatt, G. A. (1976). Alcohol, stress, and cognitive control. In J. G. Sarasan & C. D. Spielberger (Eds.), *Stress and anxiety* (Vol. 3). Washington, DC: Hemisphere Publishing.

Marlatt, G. A. (1983). The controlled-drinking controversy: A commentary. *American Psychologist,* **38**, 1097–1110.

Marlatt, G. A., & George, W. H. (1984). Relapse prevention: Introduction and overview of the model. *British Journal of Addiction,* **79**, 261–275.

Marlatt, G. A., Kosturn, C. F., & Lang, A. R. (1975). Provocation to anger and opportunity for retaliation as determinants of alcohol consumption in social drinkers. *Journal of Abnormal Psychology,* **34**, 652–659.

Marlatt, G. A., & Marques, J. K. (1977). Meditation, self-control and alcohol use. In R. B. Stuart (Ed.), *Behavioral self-management: Strategies, techniques and outcome.* New York: Brunner/Mazel.

Marlatt, G. A., Miller, W. R., Duckert, F., Goetestam, G., Heather, N., Peele, S., Sanchez-Craig, M., Sobell, L. C., & Sobell, M. B. (1985). *Bulletin of the Society of Psychologists in Addictive Behaviors,* **4**, 123–150.

McCourt, W., & Glantz, M. (1980). Cognitive behavior therapy in groups for alcoholics: A preliminary report. *Journal of Studies on Alcohol,* **41**, 338–346.

*McCrady, B. S., Moreau, J., Paolino, T. J., Jr., & Longabaugh, R. (1982). Joint hospitalization and couples therapy for alcoholism: A four-year follow-up. *Journal of Studies on Alcohol,* **43**, 1244–1250.

McCrady, B. S., Paolino, T. J., Jr., Longabough, R., & Rossi, J. (1979). Effects of joint hospital admission and couples treatment for hospitalized alcoholics: A pilot study. *Addictive Behaviors,* **4**, 155–165.

McGuire, M. T., Stein, S., & Mendelson, J. H. (1966). Comparative psychosocial studies of alcoholic and nonalcoholic subjects undergoing experimental intoxication. *Psychosomatic Medicine,* **28**, 13–26.

*McLachlan, J. F. C., & Stein, R. L. (1982). Evaluation of a day clinic for alcoholics. *Journal of Studies on Alcohol,* **43**, 261–272.

*Mellor, C. S., & White, H. P. (1978). Taste aversions to alcoholic beverages conditioned by motion sickness. *American Journal of Psychiatry,* **135**, 125–127.

Miller, P. M., & Eisler, R. M. (1977). Assertive behavior of alcoholics: A descriptive analysis. *Behavior Therapy,* **8**, 146–149.

Miller, P. M., Hersen, M., Eisler, R. M., & Hilsman, G. (1974). Effects of social stress on operant drinking of alcoholics and social drinkers. *Behaviour Research and Therapy,* **12**, 67–72.

*Miller, W. R. (1978). Behavioral treatment of problem drinkers: A comparative outcome study of three controlled drinking therapies. *Journal of Consulting and Clinical Psychology,* **46**, 74–86.

Miller, W. R. (1983). Controlled drinking: A history and a critical review. *Journal of Studies on Alcohol,* **44**, 68–83.

Miller, W. R., & Baca, L. M. (1983). Two-year follow-up of bibliotherapy and therapist-directed controlled drinking training for problem drinkers. *Behavior Therapy,* **14**, 441–448. (Presented data for two studies: Miller & Taylor, 1980; Miller, Taylor, & West, 1980).

Miller, W. R. & Hester, R. K. (1980). Treating the problem drinker: Modern approaches. In W. R. Miller (Ed.), *Addictive Behaviors.* New York: Pergamon Press.

*Miller, W. R., & Taylor, C. A. (1980). Relative effectiveness of bibliotherapy, individual and group self-control training in the treatment of problem drinkers. *Addictive Behaviors,* **5**, 13–24.

*Miller, W. R., Taylor, C. A., & West, J. C. (1980). Focused versus broad-spectrum behavior therapy for problem drinkers. *Journal of Consulting and Clinical Psychology,* **48**, 590–601.

*Moberg, D. P., Krause, W. K., & Klein, P. E. (1982). Posttreatment drinking behavior among inpatients from an industrial alcoholism program. *International Journal of the Addictions*, 17, 549–567.

Monti, P. M., Corriveau, D. P., & Zwick, W. (1981). Assessment of social skills in alcoholics and other psychiatric patients. *Journal of Studies on Alcohol*, 42, 526–529.

*Mueller, S. R., Sutter, B. H., Prengaman, T. (1982). A short-term intensive treatment program for the alcoholic. *International Journal of the Addictions*, 17, 931–943.

Neubuerger, O. W., Hasha, N., Matarazzo, J. D., Schmitz, R. E., & Pratt, H. H. (1981). Behavioral–chemical treatment of alcoholism: An outcome replication. *Journal of Studies on Alcohol*, 42, 806–810.

*Neubuerger, O. W., Matarazzo, J. D., Schmitz, R. E., & Pratt, H. H. (1980). One year follow-up of total abstinence in chronic alcoholic patients following emetic countercontioning. *Alcoholism: Clinical and Experimental Research*, 4, 306–312.

*Neubuerger, O. W., Miller, S. I., Schmitz, R. E., Matarazzo, J. D., Pratt, H., & Hasha, N. (1982). Replicable abstinence rates in an alcoholism treatment program. *Journal of the American Medical Association*, 248, 960–963.

Nirenberg, T., Ersner-Hershfield, S., Sobell, M. B., & Sobell, L. C. (1981). Behavioral treatment of alcohol problems. In C. K. Prokop & L. A. Bradley (Eds.), *Medical psychology: Contributions to behavioral medicine*. New York: Academic Press.

*Oei, T. P. S., & Jackson, P. R. (1982). Social skills and cognitive behavioral approaches to the treatment of problem drinking. *Journal of Studies on Alcohol*, 43, 532–547.

*O'Leary, M. R., Donovan, D. M., Chaney, E. F., & O'Leary, D. E. (1980). Relationship of alcohol personality subtypes to treatment follow-up measures. *Journal of Nervous and Mental Disease*, 168, 475–480.

*O'Leary, M. R., Donovan, D. M., Chaney, E. F., & Walker, R. D. (1979). Cognitive impairment and treatment outcome with alcoholics: Preliminary findings. *Journal of Clinical Psychiatry*, 40, 397–398.

O'Leary, D. E., O'Leary, M. R., & Donovan, D. M. (1976). Social skill acquisition and psychosocial development of alcoholics: A review. *Addictive Behaviors*, 1, 111–120.

*Olson, R. P., Ganley, R., Devine, V. T., & Dorsey, G. C., Jr. (1981). Long-term effects of behavioral versus insight-oriented therapy with inpatient alcoholics. *Journal of Consulting and Clinical Psychology*, 49, 866–877.

Orford, J., & Edwards, G. (1977). Alcoholism: A comparison of treatment and advice, with a study of the influence of marriage. *Maudsley Monographs*, 26.

*Ornstein, P. (1981). Psychometric test changes following alcohol inpatient treatment and their relationships to posttreatment drinking behaviors. *International Journal of the Addictions*, 16, 263–271.

Paredes, A., Gregory, D., Rundell, O. H., & Williams, H. L. (1979). Drinking behavior, remission, and relapse: The Rand Report revisited. *Alcoholism: Clinical and Experimental Research*, 3, 3–10.

*Parker, M. W., Winstead, D. K., Willi, F. J. P., & Fisher, P. (1979). Patient autonomy in alcohol rehabilitation. II: Program evaluation. *International Journal of the Addictions*, 14, 1177–1184.

Pattison, E. M., Sobell, M. B., & Sobell, L. C. (Authors/Eds.). (1977). *Emerging concepts of alcohol dependence*. New York: Springer.

*Pettinati, H. M., Sugerman, A. A., DiDonato, N., & Maurer, H. S. (1982). The natural history of alcoholism over four years after treatment. *Journal of Studies on Alcohol*, 43, 201–215.

Pihl, R. O., & Yankofsky, L. (1979). Alcohol consumption in male social drinkers as a function of situationally induced depressive affect and anxiety. *Psychopharmacology*, 65, 251–257.

*Polich, J. M., Armor, D. J., & Braiker, H. B. (1980). Patterns of alcoholism over four years. *Journal of Studies on Alcohol*, 41, 397–416.

*Pollak, B. (1978). A two year study of alcoholics in general practice. *British Journal on Alcohol and Alcoholism,* **13,** 24–35.

Pomerleau, O. F. (1982). Current behavioral therapies in the treatment of alcoholism. In E. M. Pattison & E. Kaufman (Eds.), *Encyclopedic handbook of alcoholism.* New York: Gardner Press.

*Pomerleau, O., Pertschuk, M., Adkins, D., & Brady, J. P. (1978). A comparison of behavioral and traditional treatment for middle income problem drinkers. *Journal of Behavioral Medicine,* **1,** 187–200.

*Rist, F., & Watzl, H. (1983). Self assessment of relapse risk and assertiveness in relation to treatment outcome of female alcoholics. *Addictive Behaviors,* **8,** 121–127.

*Sanchez-Craig, M., & Walker, K. (1982). Teaching coping skills to chronic alcoholics in a coeducational halfway house: I. Assessment of programme effects. *British Journal of Addiction,* **77,** 35–50.

*Schau, E. J., O'Leary, M. R., & Chaney, E. F. (1980). Reversibility of cognitive deficit in alcoholics. *Journal of Studies on Alcohol,* **41,** 733–740.

*Seelye, E. E. (1979). Relationship of socioeconomic status, psychiatric diagnosis and sex to outcome of alcoholism treatment. *Journal of Studies on Alcohol,* **40,** 57–62.

Senter, R. J., Heintzelman, M., Dormeuller, M., & Hinkle, H. (1979). A comparative look at ratings of the subjective effects of beverage alcohol. *Psychological Record,* **29,** 49–56.

Skinner, H. A., & Horn, J. L. (1984). *Alcohol Dependence Scale (ADS) user's guide.* Toronto: Addiction Research Foundation.

Smart, R. G. (1978a). Characteristics of alcoholics who drink socially after treatment. *Alcoholism: Clinical and Experimental Research,* **2,** 49–52.

*Smart, R. G. (1978b). Do some alcoholics do better in some types of treatment than others? *Drug and Alcohol Dependence,* **3,** 65–75.

*Smart, R. G., & Gray, G. (1978). Minimal, moderate and long-term treatment for alcoholism. *British Journal of Addiction,* **73,** 35–38.

Sobell, L. C., & Sobell, M. B. (1980). Convergent validity: An approach to increasing confidence in treatment outcome conclusions with alcohol and drug abusers. In L. C. Sobell, M. B. Sobell, & E. Ward (Eds.), *Evaluating alcohol and drug abuse treatment effectiveness: Recent advances.* New York: Pergamon Press.

Sobell, L. C., & Sobell, M. B. (1982). Alcoholism treatment outcome evaluation methodology. In National Institute on Alcohol Abuse and Alcoholism, *Prevention, intervention and treatment: Concerns and models:* (Research Monograph No. 3). Washington, DC: National Institute on Alcohol Abuse and Alcoholism.

Sobell, M. B. (1978). Alternatives to abstinence. Evidence, issues and some proposals. In P. E. Nathan & G. A. Marlatt (Eds.), *Experimental and behavioral approaches to alcoholism.* New York: Plenum.

Sobell, M. B., & Sobell, L. C. (1973a). Individualized behavior therapy for alcoholics. *Behavior Therapy,* **4,** 49–72.

Sobell, M. B., & Sobell, L. C. (1973b). Alcoholics treated by individualized behavior therapy: One-year treatment outcome. *Behaviour Research and Therapy,* **11,** 599–618.

Sobell, M. B., & Sobell, L. C. (1976). Second year treatment outcome of alcoholics treated by individualized behavior therapy: Results. *Behaviour Research and Therapy,* **14,** 195–215.

Sobell, M. B., & Sobell, L. C. (1978). *Behavioral treatment of alcohol problems: Individualized therapy and controlled drinking.* New York: Plenum.

Sobell, M. B., & Sobell, L. C. (1984a). Under the microscope yet again: A commentary on Walker and Roch's critique of the Dickens Committee's Enquiry into our research. *British Journal of Addiction,* **79,** 157–168.

Sobell, M. B., & Sobell, L. C. (1984b). The aftermath of heresy: A response to Pendery *et al.*'s

114

(1982) critique of "Individualized Behavior Therapy for Alcoholics." *Behaviour Research and Therapy,* **22,** 413–440.

Sobell, M. B., & Sobell, L. C. (1984c). *Study on the treatment outcome research project — Critical review of the state of research.* (Research Contract No. 19SV.3204503). Ottawa, Ontario: Department of National Defence.

Sobell, M. B., Sobell, L. C., Ersner-Hershfield, S., & Nirenberg, T. (1982). Alcohol and drug problems. In A. S. Bellack, M. Hersen, & A. E. Kazdin (Eds.), *International handbook of behavior modification and therapy.* New York: Plenum.

*Steinglass, P. (1979). An experimental treatment program for alcoholic couples. *Journal of Studies on Alcohol,* **40,** 159–182.

*Stinson, D. J., Smith, W. G., Amidjaya, I., & Kaplan, J. M. (1979). Systems of care and treatment outcomes for alcoholic patients. *Archives of General Psychiatry,* **36,** 535–539.

Taylor, C. B. (1978). Relaxation training and related techniques. In W. S. Agras (Ed.), *Behavior modification: Principles and clinical applications* (2nd ed.). Boston: Little Brown.

Towle, L. H. (1974). Alcoholism treatment outcome in different populations. *Proceedings from the Fourth Annual Alcohol Conference of the National Institute on Alcohol Abuse and Alcoholism.*

Twentyman, C. T., Greenwald, D. P., Greenwald, M. A., Kloss, J. D., Kovaleski, M. E., & Zibung-Hoffman, P. (1982). An assessment of social skills deficits in alcoholics. *Behavioral Assessment,* **4,** 317–326.

*Vaillant, G. E., Clark, W., Cyrus, C., Milofsky, E. S., Kopp, J., Wulsin, V. W., & Mogielnicki, N. P. (1983). Prospective study of alcoholism treatment: Eight-year follow-up. *American Journal of Medicine,* **75,** 455–463.

*Valle, S. K. (1981). Interpersonal functioning of alcoholism counselors and treatment outcome. *Journal of Studies on Alcohol,* **42,** 783–790.

*Vannicelli, M. (1978). Impact of aftercare in the treatment of alcoholics: A cross-lagged panel analysis. *Journal of Studies on Alcohol,* **39,** 1875–1886.

Vogler, R. E., Compton, J. V., & Weissbach, T. A. (1975). Integrated behavior change technique for alcoholism. *Journal of Consulting and Clinical Psychology.* **43,** 233–243.

Walker, K., Sanchez-Craig, M., & Bornet, A. (1982). Teaching coping skills to chronic alcoholics in a coeducational halfway house: II. Assessment of outcome and identification of outcome predictors. *British Journal of Addiction,* **77,** 185–196.

*Walker, R. D., Donovan, D. M., Kivlahan, D. R., & O'Leary, M. R. (1983). Length of stay, neuropsychological performance, and aftercare: Influences on alcohol treatment outcome. *Journal of Consulting and Clinical Psychology.* **51,** 900–911.

Watson, C. G., Herder, J., & Passini, F. T. (1978). Alpha biofeedback therapy in alcoholics: An 18-month follow-up. *Journal of Clinical Psychology,* **34,** 765–769.

*Welte, J., Hynes, G., Sokolow, L., & Lyons, J. P. (1981). Effect of length of stay in inpatient alcoholism treatment on outcome. *Journal of Studies on Alcohol,* **42,** 483–491.

*Westermeyer, J., & Peake, E. (1983). A ten-year follow-up of alcoholic native Americans in Minnesota. *American Journal of Psychiatry,* **140,** 189–194.

*Weins, A. N., & Menustik, C. E. (1983). Treatment outcome and patient characteristics in an aversion therapy program for alcoholism. *American Psychologist,* **38,** 1089–1096.

Wiens, A. N., Montague, J. D., Manaugh, T. S., & English, C. J. (1976). Pharmacological aversive counterconditioning to alcohol in a private hospital. *Journal of Studies on Alcohol,* **37,** 1320–1324.

Wilkinson, D. A., & Sanchez-Craig, M. (1981). Relevance of brain dysfunction to treatment objectives: Should alcohol-related cognitive deficits influence the way we think about treatment? *Addictive Behaviors,* **6,** 253–260.

*Wilson, A., White, J., & Lange, D. E. (1978). Outcome evaluation of a hospital-based alcoholism treatment programme. *British Journal of Addiction,* **73,** 39–45.

Wilson, G. T. (1983). Self-awareness, self-regulation, and alcohol consumption: An analysis of J. Hull's model. *Journal of Abnormal Psychology, 92,* 505–513.

Wolpe, J. (1958). *Psychotherapy by reciprocal inhibition.* Stanford, CA: Stanford University Press.

*Yalom, I. D., Bloch, S., Bond, G., Zimmerman, E., & Qualls, B. (1978). Alcoholics in interactional group therapy: An outcome study. *Archives of General Psychiatry, 35,* 419–425.

Zivich, J. M. (1981). Alcoholic subtypes and treatment effectiveness. *Journal of Consulting and Clinical Psychology, 49,* 72–80.

6

Building Self-Confidence, Self-Efficacy and Self-Control

SUSAN G. CURRY

Cancer Control Research Unit
Fred Hutchinson Cancer Research Center
Seattle, Washington 98104
and
Department of Psychology
University of Washington
Seattle, Washington 98195

G. ALAN MARLATT

Addictive Behaviors Research Center
Department of Psychology
University of Washington
Seattle, Washington 98195

I. OVERVIEW

The cornerstone of problem drinking is the inability to maintain alcohol consumption at a level where the individual is not experiencing physical, legal, social, or psychological problems as a consequence of drinking. People entering treatment for alcohol problems have either told themselves or have been told by others that they are unable to control their drinking. By seeking treatment, many clients are making a statement to the effect that, "I don't have the confidence to do this myself, I want somebody to *do something to me* so that I can control my drinking." It is not surprising, therefore, that both low self-confidence and poor self-control characterize samples of alcoholics and other problem drinkers (e.g., Cox, 1985; Rohsenow, 1983).

Recently, the concept of self-efficacy has been utilized to understand the

117

TREATMENT AND PREVENTION
OF ALCOHOL PROBLEMS: A RESOURCE MANUAL

lack of self-confidence and self-control among problem drinkers and persons with other addictive behaviors (Annis, 1982a; Condiotte & Lichtenstein, 1981). This concept has been elaborated by Bandura (1977, 1981, 1982), who stated that, "Self-efficacy is concerned with judgments about how well one can organize and execute courses of action required to deal with prospective situations that contain many ambiguous, unpredictable, and often stressful elements" (Bandura, 1981, pp. 200–201). As a situationally specific concept, *self-efficacy* differs from more global judgments of self-confidence and from general outcome expectancies. With regard to drinking, *self-efficacy* refers to a problem drinker's degree of confidence in his or her ability to control his or her drinking in situations that are generally associated with problem drinking.

The goal of this chapter is to describe the components of our relapse-prevention program that enhance problem drinkers' self-confidence, self-efficacy, and self-control. We cover (1) theoretical background, including conceptual stages of behavior change, models of helping, and the general assumptions of the relapse-prevention model; (2) assessment techniques and intervention strategies organized around three phases of treatment (enhancing self-confidence, enhancing self-efficacy, and building self-control). Readers who wish a more detailed description of our treatment model are referred to Marlatt and Gordon, 1985.

II. THEORETICAL BACKGROUND

A. Stages of Change

The stage model of behavior change (Prochaska & DiClemente, 1983) is a very useful framework for understanding the therapeutic process. According to this model, behavior change proceeds through distinct and separable stages: contemplation, decision, active change, maintenance, and relapse or maintained change. Individuals in the contemplation stage are considering altering their behavior (e.g., "Do I want to stop drinking?"). The decision stage begins when individuals make a commitment to change (e.g., "I am going to begin treatment for my drinking problem"). Efforts directed at actually changing one's behavior occur during the active change stage (e.g., "I will monitor my drinking for 2 weeks to see where and when I most often drink"). The maintenance stage begins when the behavior change has actually been implemented (e.g., "I have not drunk any alcohol for 1 week"). The fifth stage is identified primarily by relapse; however, it also encompasses long-term maintenance.

Different therapeutic strategies may be appropriate during different stages. For example, verbal therapies targeted at consciousness-raising and education may be most helpful with clients who are merely contemplating making a change, whereas behavioral therapies targeted at stimulus control and coping skills training may be more helpful for clients who are in the active-change stage.

B. Models of Helping

An effective treatment paradigm should not only pay explicit attention to where clients are in the behavior-change process, but it should also be explicit about the underlying assumptions of the treatment approach. Brickman, Rabinowitz, Karuza, Coates, Cohn, and Kidder (1982) categorize treatment approaches into four models of helping and coping on the basis of assumptions about (1) the client's responsibility for his/her problem and (2) the client's responsibility for the solution to the problem. The four models that they have defined are (1) *moral model:* People are responsible for problems and solutions; (2) *compensatory model:* People are not responsible for problems, but are responsible for solutions; (3) *medical model:* People are not responsible for problems or solutions; and (4) *enlightenment model:* People are not responsible for solutions, but are responsible for problems.

Alcoholics Anonymous (AA) (which is discussed in the chapter by Thoreson and Budd in this volume) is perhaps the best known and most widely recommended self-help program for individuals who have problems with alcohol. Brickman et al. describe AA as, "one of the most successful examples of an enlightenment model organization, [which] explicitly requires new recruits both to take responsibility for their past history of drinking . . . and to admit that it is beyond their power to control their drinking — without the help of God and the community of ex-alcoholics in Alcoholics Anonymous" (p. 374). However, they also point out that the "deficiency of the enlightenment model lies in the fact that it can lead to a fanatical or obsessive concern with certain problems and a reconstruction of people's entire lives around the behaviors or the relationships designed to help them deal with these problems. . . . Alcoholics Anonymous reorganizes people's lives so that they stay away from their old drinking places and drinking partners, but they retain their concern for drinking as an issue in their lives" (p. 374).

Relapse prevention offers an alternative, compensatory treatment model. The underlying assumption of this model is that the individual is not held responsible for the development of his or her problem with alcohol, but he or she must take responsibility for solving the problem. The relapse-prevention model assumes that problem drinking is the product of various learning and cognitive processes: classical and operant conditioning, observational learning, and acquired expectations about drinking. The critical role of the therapist is to teach individuals "how to change maladaptive cognitive processes and environmental contingencies" (Brickman et al., 1982, p. 380).

Failure to make assumptions regarding the client's and therapist's respective roles explicit to incoming clients could be problematic in those instances where clients have had previous exposure to the AA model. Individuals who believe that the key to solving their problems with alcohol successfully is to surrender control to a higher power would undoubtedly be resistant to the efforts of a therapist working within a compensatory model, with its emphasis on learning to take greater personal control.

C. Relapse-Prevention Model

The *relapse-prevention model* is a cognitive-behavioral approach to the understanding and treatment of addictive behaviors, derived from contemporary social-learning theory and self-control theory. The treatment model encompasses Prochaska and DiClemente's (1983) five stages of behavior change, with particular emphasis placed on (1) enhancement of motivation and commitment; (2) implementation of change in drinking (e.g., abstinence); and (3) maintenance of new behavior.

At the start of treatment, we help clients increase their self-confidence and commitment by helping them identify their motivations to change, their ambivalence regarding change, and by sharing our assumptions about the treatment process. During the initiation-of-change stage, our emphasis shifts to enhancing self-efficacy by helping individuals learn how to cope when faced with situations in which problem drinking is likely to occur. Finally, our emphasis during the maintenance stage is on helping individuals learn strategies for controlling urges to drink and for preventing lapses from escalating into complete relapses.

The theoretical model of the relapse process initially developed by Marlatt and Gordon (1980) is diagrammed in Figure 1.

The figure traces two possible outcomes of a high-risk situation. First, coping in response to the situation enhances self-efficacy and, thus, decreases the probability of relapse. Conversely, failure to cope triggers a chain of responses which make relapse more likely. Several key assumptions of the relapse prevention model are illustrated in this figure. Briefly, these assumptions are (1) Relapse is situation specific. Our research on the precipitators of initial use of alcohol (as well as other substances such as tobacco and heroin) has shown that relapse usually occurs in one of three situations. These situations involve (a) intrapersonal negative emotional states such as frustration, anger, depression, and boredom, (b) interpersonal conflict, or (c) social pressure to drink. (2) The use of coping strategies in high-risk situations is a critical determinant of the situation's outcome (maintenance or lapse). (3) Self-efficacy is enhanced by using coping strategies in high-risk situations. (4) The individual's reaction to an initial lapse is an important

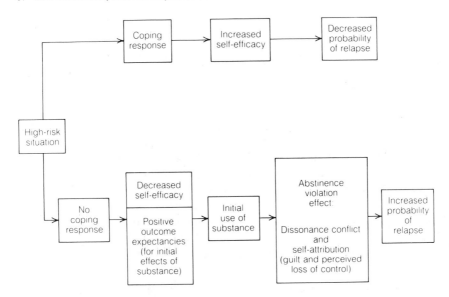

Figure 1. Cognitive-behavioral model of the relapse process.

factor in determining whether that lapse escalates into a full-blown relapse.

A common reaction to an initial lapse is called the abstinence violation effect (AVE). There are two components of the AVE: a cognitive attribution regarding the perceived cause of the lapse and an affective reaction to the attribution. The intensity of the AVE will increase to the extent that the individual attributes the cause of the initial lapse to internal, stable, and global factors that are perceived to be uncontrollable (e.g., lack of willpower and/or the emergence of the symptoms of an underlying addictive disease). The AVE decreases when the individual attributes the cause of the lapse to external, unstable (changeable), and specific factors that are perceived to be controllable (e.g., a transitory deficit in coping with a specific high-risk situation).

We turn now from the discussion of the basic concepts and definitions underlying our treatment approach to descriptions of assessment methods and intervention strategies used during the three treatment phases. Although we present assessment methods and intervention strategies by treatment phase, this organizational strategy does not reflect their interplay and balance during treatment. Self-confidence issues can and do arise throughout the change process, and skills taught during the initiation-of-change stage often need to be reviewed during maintenance.

III. INTERVENTION STRATEGIES

A. Phase I: Enhancing Self-Confidence

1. Decision Matrix

During the initial phase of treatment, we assess factors relevant to clients' motivation and commitment, including reasons why they wish to change their drinking behavior and the overall strength of their motivation to change. Motivation and commitment may or may not be highly correlated. For example, one may be motivated to stop drinking because of health reasons, but the motivation is not strong enough to spill over into an actual commitment to change one's drinking behavior.

Our goal during the initial phase of treatment is to help clients reach and exceed their *threshold of motivation* so that they can make a firm commitment to implement a plan for behavior change. There are many potential incentives or factors that can facilitate a threshold shift. They include increased risk or damage to one's physical or psychological well-being, feelings of guilt or dissatisfaction at being dependent on alcohol, social disapproval, and economic costs.

A *decision matrix* (Figure 2) is useful for helping clients to organize and prioritize their motivations for changing their drinking habits. With the therapist's assistance, clients can list the anticipated positive and negative consequences (both immediate and long-term) associated with the decision to change or maintain current drinking patterns. The decision matrix can help clients understand that they have been focusing exclusively on getting immediate gratification from drinking (e.g., reduced anxiety), while failing to take into account any long-range negative consequences (e.g., disrupted personal relationships). It should be noted that the decision matrix is similar in format to the "decisional balance sheet" developed by Janis and Mann (1977).

Once the decision matrix is completed, a copy should be given to the client as a reminder of his or her reasons for beginning treatment. The therapist should emphasize that reasons given prior to initiating a change in drinking will, in all likelihood, shift as treatment progresses. Certain negative consequences that apply *prior* to stopping drinking (e.g., shakiness, fatigue, gastrointestinal disorders) will lose their impact once the person has quit drinking. The former drinker mistakenly concludes that because these symptoms no longer occur, he or she may now resume drinking with impunity— forgetting that resumption of drinking will retrigger the problem. When motivational doubts occur during treatment, clients should be encouraged to consult and, if necessary, revise the original decision matrix as a reminder of all the relevant reasons why they changed their drinking patterns in the first place.

	IMMEDIATE CONSEQUENCES		DELAYED CONSEQUENCES	
	POSITIVE	NEGATIVE	POSITIVE	NEGATIVE
To moderate consumption or continue self-control	INCREASED SELF-EFFICACY AVOID ILLNESS FROM OVERDRINKING TENSION REDUCTION FINANCIAL GAIN SOCIAL APPROVAL FROM LIGHT & NONDRINKERS	WORK REQUIRED TO BREAK OLD HABITS SOCIAL PRESSURE FROM HEAVY DRINKERS INITIAL AWKWARDNESS WITH NEW HABITS	INCREASED SELF-CONTROL & SELF-CONFIDENCE IMPROVED HEALTH AVOID HANGOVERS WEIGHT LOSS CLOSER TIES WITH LIGHT & NONDRINKING FRIENDS DEVELOPMENT OF NEW HOBBIES & FRIENDS FINANCIAL GAIN	LOST FRIENDSHIPS WITH HEAVY DRINKERS DENIAL OF GRATIFICATION ASSOCIATED WITH BEING "BLASTED"
To continue or resume excessive drinking	IMMEDIATE GRATIFICATION CONSISTENT WITH PAST SELF-IMAGE APPROVAL FROM HEAVY DRINKERS EXCUSE FOR IRRESPONSIBILITY FASTER SLEEP ONSET PERCEPTIONS OF INCREASED PERSONAL POWER	ILLNESS FROM OVERDRINKING FINANCIAL LOSS SOCIAL EMBARRASSMENT SOCIAL DISAPPROVAL FROM LIGHT & NONDRINKERS IMPAIRED COORDINATION LESS ENJOYMENT OF DINING EXPERIENCES POSSIBILITY OF PERSONAL INJURY	CONSISTENT WITH OLD SELF-IMAGE FRIENDSHIPS WITH HEAVY DRINKERS MAINTAINED	DECREASED SELF-ESTEEM ADDED HEALTH PROBLEMS & RISKS FINANCIAL LOSS INTERPERSONAL CONFLICT OCCUPATIONAL DISRUPTION DEVELOPMENT OF PHYSICAL DEPENDENCY SOCIAL DISAPPROVAL HANGOVERS DWI ARRESTS

Figure 2. Decision matrix for moderating alcohol consumption.

2. Autobiography

In addition to articulating motivations for changing drinking habits, the client's *self-image* vis-à-vis drinking is an important topic to explore during the initial phase of treatment. Some clients have considerable difficulty imagining themselves as ex-drinkers.

The best way to explore the client's self-image is to ask him or her to compose an *autobiography* of his or her history as a drinker. In addition to providing an historical account of how they view themselves as a drinker, clients should be asked to describe how they see themselves as a nondrinker. The therapist should help those clients who have difficulty imagining future images of themselves, or who focus on aspects of deprivation or loss associated with not drinking. Using imagery and covert self-modeling techniques (such as those described in Klinger's chapter in this volume), the therapist and client may be able to construct a new self-image that focuses on the self as an active, coping, independent individual who has finally thrown away the crutch of dependency. Work on modifying the self-image should continue throughout the program until abstinence or new drinking patterns are well-established.

3. Past Experience

Clients with low self-confidence for changing their drinking behavior often base their estimates of failure on either their own track record of previous attempts to change and/or on descriptions of high relapse rates in alcohol treatment programs (i.e., they assume that unsuccessful prior attempts predict unsuccessful future attempts). To counter these expectations and increase general self-confidence, the therapist can point out that: (1) One predictor of eventual success may be the number of prior attempts to quit. From each attempt to quit a client probably acquires valuable information and experience that will assist him or her in future attempts. (2) Despite the probability of failure associated with any single treatment, recent evidence suggests that people are often successful in changing their own behavior over the long run. For example, Schachter (1982) reported that long-term smoking cessation and weight reduction are relatively common. Between 60 and 70% of the persons Schachter interviewed who had attempted to stop smoking or lose weight had succeeded and maintained their change. Relapse rates for alcohol treatments are similar to those for smoking cessation (Hunt, Barnett, & Branch, 1971). We might optimistically generalize from Schachter's findings that, over time, a high percentage of individuals could successfully discontinue their problem drinking.

4. Journey Metaphor

As we stated earlier, it is important for the therapist to explain clearly to the client the assumptions that underlie the treatment model being used. Providing an overall orientation to the treatment process can enhance motivation and commitment by encouraging the client to be an active participant. We use a *journey metaphor* to illustrate the major assumptions underlying relapse prevention.

With some imagination, therapists can create their own metaphors that include the following points: (1) By itself, the commitment to change cannot instantly transport clients to the journey's ultimate destination; clients must take the journey of change themselves; (2) The relapse prevention program is like a guide whom clients have hired to assist them on the journey by providing maps and navigational assistance, and by pointing out dangers and pitfalls along the route; (3) As with any journey into unknown territory, clients are bound to have some initial doubts (e.g., "Will I make it?" "What if I get lost or fail?"). These doubts are natural precursors of any important journey, and they can be reduced to the extent that clients are *prepared* in advance; (4) Advance preparation includes having the right tools (e.g., maps that show the location of various temptation situations, pitfalls, and danger-spots along the way that can throw a person off course), mastering the appropriate skills (e.g., knowing how to recognize early warning signals of possible relapse, methods of coping with stress such as relaxation or medita-tion, coping strategies or constructive ways of thinking and behaving to cope with urges and cravings for alcohol), and having the right attitude (i.e., knowing that it really is a journey with ups and downs and adventures along the way—and that it will take some time to reach one's destination); and (5) Not only is it important to have the necessary skills for coping with potential difficulties along the route; it is also important to be prepared for possible breakdowns (or relapses) along the route. Clients often embellish the journey metaphor with their own contributions, further personalizing the imagery.

B. Phase II: Enhancing Self-Efficacy

1. Identifying High-Risk Situations

During the second phase of treatment, clients actually undertake an active change in their drinking pattern. Assessment and intervention during this phase are targeted at helping clients (1) learn to recognize situations in which they will be at risk for problem drinking and (2) acquire skills for coping with those high-risk situations. Information on potential high-risk situations can come from several sources, including descriptions of previous relapse experi-ences and self-monitoring of drinking. If a client has past experience in trying to abstain from drinking, the therapist should ask him or her to describe, in as much detail as possible, the circumstances under which problem drinking first reoccurred. Relevant information includes thoughts and feelings asso-ciated with initial drinking; the setting, presence of others, and type of alcohol consumed; and whether or not a conscious decision was made to drink prior to the actual situation. Clients who are drinking at the start of therapy should be asked to monitor their drinking for at least 2 weeks, keeping track of the setting and amount consumed, their mood when drinking, and persons with whom they are drinking.

2. Assessing Self-Efficacy

In addition to assessing past experiences and current habits, assessment of self-efficacy can be used to provide the client with a list of potential "trouble spots." The assessment of self-efficacy is a relatively new endeavor, and the development of specific measurement procedures is ongoing. Readers who wish to review a variety of approaches to the general area of cognitive assessment can consult the volume by Merluzzi, Glass, and Genest (1981).

One self-efficacy scale for use with alcoholic clientele is The Situational Confidence Questionnaire (SCQ, Annis, 1982a). The SCQ consists of 100 items covering major areas of excessive drinking or relapse experienced by alcoholics. A pool of items was initially developed from a variety of sources, including existing questionnaires and discussions with other clinicians and former and current alcoholic clients.

Annis developed a parallel form of the questionnaire called the Inventory of Drinking Situations (IDS, Annis, 1982b). This inventory consists of the identical 100 items included in the SCQ, but clients are asked to indicate for each item whether they drank heavily in that situation during the past year, using a 4-point scale (never/rarely/frequently/almost always). The assumption is that situations associated with heavy drinking in the past will probably be high-risk situations for the future.

3. Assessing Coping Skills

The Situational Competency Test (SCT) was developed by Chaney, O'Leary, and Marlatt (1978) as a method of assessing coping ability in alcoholic clients entering treatment. The SCT requires a verbal response to a high-risk situation presented by a narrator on audiotape. Recorded oral responses were chosen in lieu of written responses for several reasons. Many clients are either unwilling or unable to provide a written description of what they would do when faced with a problematic situation because of deficits in motivation or writing skills. In addition, there is no easy way to monitor response latency or reaction time in a written format.

During the SCT, the client is presented with 16 different situations drawn from four major categories of high-risk situations: those involving frustration and anger, negative emotional states, and intrapersonal and interpersonal temptation. A sample situation is "You are eating at a good restaurant on a special occasion with some friends. The waitress comes over and asks, 'Drink before dinner?' Everyone orders one. All eyes seem to be on you." Each situation is followed with the request, "What would you do or say?" At the start of the test, the client is instructed to imagine that the situation was actually occurring and to say the words or describe the action that he or she would use in response to the situation.

Responses can be scored on the following measures: (1) *latency,* or elapsed time from the termination of the recorded situation to the beginning of the client's verbal response; (2) *response duration* as the frequency of words in the response; (3) *compliance,* or whether the client describes giving in to the situation without attempting to engage in an alternative coping response; and (4) *specification of new behavior,* or whether the description of the coping response was detailed enough so that someone else could use it as a guide.

The SCT can help the therapist identify both the types of situations in which the client is likely to have difficulty coping and specific areas to concentrate on in coping skills training. For example, a client may be able to generate a nondrinking response to each situation but take considerable time to do so. The longer it takes for a person to do something when in a high-risk situation, the greater the chances are that he or she will fall back on the easiest, most available behavior—drinking. In fact, Chaney, O'Leary, and Marlatt (1978) have found that duration of the delay period between being presented with a high-risk situation and being able to perform a coping response in a role-playing task was significantly related to measures of treatment outcome and relapse in male alcoholics. Thus, with clients demonstrating long latencies between presentation of the situation and generation of a coping response, the therapist can praise them for their ability to anticipate making nondrinking responses in the high-risk situations, and can encourage clients to respond more quickly.

An alternative assessment strategy is the use of *role-playing procedures.* With role playing, the client is asked to respond in a high-risk situation enacted with other clients and/or therapists. In order to gain access to the client's covert cognitions, the therapist can ask the client to verbalize, or think out loud, thoughts and reactions as they occur during the role play. The role plays can also be videotaped for later scoring and analysis.

An important advantage of role playing over the SCT is that it requires the performance of actual behaviors as opposed to the statement of intentions. Obviously, there is often a discrepancy between what people say they are going to do and what they actually do in a given situation. In some cases, individuals may be able to describe intended coping responses and yet when actually in a high-risk situation, their ability to cope without drinking is inhibited by anxiety. Such clients will show a marked discrepancy between their stated intentions to cope and their actual performance in a high-risk situation. Thus, to cope with the anxiety, the therapist can engage the client in an anxiety-reduction program such as systematic desensitization or other relaxation techniques (Goldfried & Davison, 1976).

4. Lifestyle Balance and Intervention

Behavior change in the area of lifestyle balance can be particularly important. We can think of *lifestyle balance* as a ratio between activities engaged in because one has to (shoulds) and activities engaged in because one wants to (wants). Problem drinkers may find that their daily lifestyle is characterized by a preponderance of shoulds, with drinking as their only counterbalancing want. Overreliance on drinking, both to alleviate stress and to increase pleasurable feelings, can result in low efficacy for coping without drinking.

A major goal of *lifestyle intervention* is to replace drinking with less harmful and more positive activities for alleviating stress and for balancing wants and shoulds. One such intervention is meditation (Marlatt & Marques, 1977), which is an easy activity to learn, and its continued practice has been related to an increased capacity to cope with a variety of stressful situations (Shapiro & Walsh, 1980). Another example is a regular program of exercise which can be a potent substitute for drinking as a self-indulgent time out or want.

Other lifestyle intervention procedures can be tailored to clients' individual needs and abilities. Self-efficacy can be enhanced by providing clients with feedback concerning their performance on any new task. For some clients, low self-efficacy engendered by their failure to cope with problem drinking has generalized to the extent that they feel incapable of dealing effectively with *any* problem area in their lives. In such cases, the therapist can involve the client in learning a new activity or task that enables the person to gain a new sense of mastery, thereby enhancing self-efficacy. Activities that involve acquiring new skills and that can be mastered with a high probability of success are recommended. They can range from everyday living tasks such as maintaining a balanced checkbook or completing a college course (Hay & Nathan, 1982) to developing a new hobby or artistic ability or volunteering at a social service agency. Clients should be encouraged to take on any new lifestyle activity slowly, one subtask at a time, under careful supervision and encouragement so as to minimize the chances of prematurely giving up or failing. Successful accomplishment, even of a relatively simple task, may greatly enhance the client's self-efficacy. Enhanced self-efficacy may then generalize to changing problem drinking as the client gains confidence in his or her capacity to master new skills.

As an example of how global lifestyle intervention can generalize to coping with problem drinking, consider the following article that appeared originally in the *Seattle Times* (February 23, 1982). Written by a staff reporter, Marjorie Jones, the headline for the article read "Alcoholics Go Over the Edge for New High":

> Scared and shaking, with hearts pounding and excitement pumping everyone into a natural high, the small group clustered at the top of the 100-foot, rocky precipice. The 13 would descend that cliff supported only by what appeared to be an inadequately thin rope

and a trust in their Maker and in those at the top, not necessarily in that order. None ever before had even contemplated belaying 100 feet down a jagged face of a cliff. The highest most ever had gotten before was on a bar stool. All but two of the 13 were alcoholics, residents of the Northwest Treatment Center. . . . They walked down the face of the cliffs backward, then walked down backward carrying each other in a rescue technique. This kind of activity is reserved normally for macho mountain climbers in top physical shape, not recovering alcoholics. It was all part of a new pilot program for alcoholics conducted here by the Northwest Outward Bound of Portland (Oregon). The idea is to give experiences that the alcoholics can work through and feel good about. They are placed in stressful, anxiety-filled situations. When they succeed, as in belaying down a cliff, the experience reinforces the idea that they don't have to turn to alcohol every time they face stress. They get an immediate payoff. Richard Ernst, Outward Bound projects director, said the three-day course was modeled after St. Luke's Hospital Alcoholism Outward Bound program in Denver. (p. B1).

Not everyone, of course, would be willing or able to participate in an Outward Bound program as a means of building confidence, although the preceding account clearly indicates that some individuals may greatly benefit from this approach.

5. Skill Training

In addition to general techniques for enhancing self-efficacy just described, skill training specifically to cope with high-risk situations is another crucial component of our treatment model. Our research (e.g., Cummings, Gordon, & Marlatt, 1980; Curry & Marlatt, 1985; Marlatt & Gordon, 1980) and that of other investigators in the area of addictive behaviors (e.g., Litman, 1974; Shiffman, 1982) indicates that training in coping skills is a vital component of treatment.

Once a client's high-risk situations have been identified (e.g., through self-monitoring, debriefing of past relapse experiences, self-efficacy assessment), the client can be taught to use coping strategies in response to cues that either anticipate or co-exist with a high-risk situation. The earlier in the chain of events leading up to a high-risk situation that one begins to use coping strategies, the easier it will be to prevent relapse. In many cases, it is possible to anticipate a high-risk situation far in advance of its actual occurrence. Examples include such events as an upcoming party, vacation period, or stressful work period. Clients should be trained to anticipate impending high-risk situations and to take preventive action at the earliest possible point. Once trained, clients are better equipped to make a relatively simple decision either to avoid a particular situation or to make advance plans about how they will deal with it when it occurs.

A coping strategy that many clients find helpful is once a week to go over the events that are likely to occur during the coming week. What situations are likely to prove difficult in terms of potential for relapse? What plans can be made in advance to deal effectively with each high-risk situation? What decisions can be made now to avoid particularly dangerous situations? Advance planning increases the client's sense of personal responsibility and self-efficacy by underscoring the advantage of early decision making in the process of relapse prevention.

Skill training is especially crucial inasmuch as not all high-risk situations can be identified in advance. Examples include unplanned access to alcohol, criticism from a friend or employer, a traffic accident, or the death of a loved one. Simply instructing a client which coping response to use in the preceding situations may not be adequate in helping him or her to avoid a relapse. In unexpected situations, the individual must rely on previously learned coping responses. Thus, skill training involves the actual acquisition of new behavior through overt practice and rehearsal. The individual must learn no longer to rely on the old coping habit but instead to learn a new and different method of dealing with the situation.

The approach we favor in skill training is to combine practice in general problem-solving skills with teaching specific coping responses. Clients are first trained to divide problem solving into several stages: (1) orientation to the problem situation; (2) definition of the problem itself; (3) generation of alternative solutions to the problem; and (4) verification of the effectiveness of a chosen alternative (cf. D'Zurilla & Goldfried, 1971; Goldfried & Davison, 1976). Following this, specific coping responses are taught utilizing a combination of behavioral training methods including direct verbal instruction, modeling of appropriate skills, and behavioral rehearsal and practice, combined with coaching and feedback provided by the therapist (cf. Curran & Monti, 1982; Eisler & Frederiksen, 1980; Goldstein, 1973; McFall, 1976).

The combination of general problem solving and teaching specific coping responses is well-illustrated by the skill-training procedures used by Chaney and his colleagues (1978) with chronic alcoholic patients in an inpatient setting. Their training consisted of eight, 90-minute, semiweekly sessions. Each group of three to five patients met with two therapists, a male and female. The sequence of group activities was (1) A therapist read a description of a problem situation. (2) Participants discussed how they viewed the situation and suggested ways of responding to it. (3) The probable consequences of different responses were discussed and, if necessary, the therapists proposed alternatives. (4) One therapist chose a response and modeled it for the group. For interpersonal situations, the cotherapist role-played the other person in the situation. For intrapersonal situations, the therapist outlined the steps he or she would take to implement the coping response. (5) After modeling by the therapist, each group member chose a particular response to rehearse. The therapist and other group members gave feedback and, if necessary, asked the participant to repeat his or her performance. (6) After each person had rehearsed, a group member summarized how to generate and evaluate an effective coping response for the target situation.

The preceding skill-training methods may be modified in several ways for use with a variety of client populations other than the one on which Chaney et al. developed their procedure. One useful modification is to take the client or a group of clients to an actual high-risk situation for a *dry-run* practice session. This can be done after clients have learned essential coping skills in the treatment setting. Clients are then taken to a real-life setting where they practice their new skills as a kind of graduation exercise.

An alternate to a dry-run practice session that may be useful with many clients is *covert modeling* (Kazdin, 1976, 1979; Klinger's chapter in this volume). This procedure is recommended when it is not practical or possible to practice new coping skills in a group session or in actual real-life settings. In the covert-modeling procedure, the client is asked to imagine him/herself encountering a high-risk situation and engaging in a successful coping response. The client is encouraged to visualize the scene as vividly as possible and to experience those thoughts and feelings that would occur if he or she were actually in the situation. The client should be instructed to imagine both the coping responses and the positive consequences of successful coping (e.g., increased self-esteem, social approval, absence of negative health consequences). The emphasis on positive consequences provides a positive self-image that contrasts sharply with the sense of loss or deprivation that might preoccupy the client who has recently given up drinking. Here, the focus is on the self-image of a person who has *gained something beneficial* by changing his or her drinking behavior, rather than of someone who has given up or lost something.

Clients learn and practice a range of coping strategies during the skill-training phase of treatment. Often the skills involve learning how to deal directly and constructively with problems in living such as conflict with family members, co-workers, or learning new ways of relaxing and socializing in settings other than bars. To the extent that individuals drink to avoid other problems, skill training can include training in social skills, assertiveness, relaxation, job-search skills, and so on.

C. Phase III: Building Self-Control

1. Control of Urges

The relapse-prevention program also includes training in general techniques for *control of urges*. These techniques enhance self-control by enabling clients to cope specifically with the craving experience that accompanies high-risk situations (see the chapter by Baker et al. in this volume). Once clients are able to control the craving, they can then use other coping strategies to control the situation. Strategies for controlling urges are particularly important during the maintenance stage because clients will often experience long stretches without any serious high-risk situations only to find themselves taken off-guard by an unexpected craving.

The first step in training urge-control is to correct common misbeliefs about urges and cravings. Misbeliefs include (1) All urges and cravings are due to physical withdrawal symptoms. (2) The occurrence of an urge indicates that treatment has failed or the effects of treatment have worn off. (3) Urges and cravings continue to increase in intensity and pressure until they are relieved by drinking. To counter these and other such beliefs, clients should be given an alternative explanation of the role of urges in the recovery process. The experience of urges following cessation of drinking is a normal reaction, and not a signal of treatment failure or an indication of imminent relapse. Cravings and urges are likely to recur whenever the individual is exposed to stimuli previously associated with drinking. These urges often are conditioned responses; if they are not reinforced by resumption of drinking, they will eventually become extinguished. In addition, urges can provide important feedback cues that something is wrong and needs attending to. Instead of attempting to block out these stress signals by an alcoholic haze, the client can use the urge as a cue for positive coping.

To counter the belief that an urge will increase in intensity unless it is indulged in, the therapist can describe the urge as a response that grows in intensity, finally peaks, and then subsides—as long as the individual does not respond by giving in. In this sense, the craving or urge response is metaphorically similar to an ocean wave. An imagery technique that we use to illustrate this analogy is *urge surfing.* The client is instructed to imagine that an urge is like a wave and that he or she is learning to be a surfer—to ride the wave with balance instead of being wiped out by its force. As with any new skill, urge surfing may take some time and practice before the client learns to keep his or her balance.

A related imagery technique is the *Samurai* image. With this technique, the client is instructed to visualize the urge as an externalized "enemy" or threat to his or her life. As soon as the Samurai warrior (the client) recognizes the presence of the urge, it is disposed of immediately with an active response (e.g., "beheaded with the sword of awareness"). The client as Samurai is warned that urges may assume a variety of "disguises" to avoid being detected. Although some urges may be easy to detect and deal with because they have tangible sources (e.g., an open bottle of liquor on a table), others may be more subtle and disguise themselves as an internal voice or prompt (e.g., having a thought such as "I could really use a drink at a time like this").

2. Coping with Slips and the AVE

We now turn to the problems that can arise if the client gives in to an urge and actually experiences a slip. The methods described in this section are used to prevent the lapse or initial setback from escalating into a total relapse. It is important for clients to realize that lapses are not irreversible, but that instead they can be the occasion for growth, understanding, and learning — a prolapse rather than a relapse.

To counter possible objections that preparing clients to anticipate and cope with potential slips is coddling and permissive, the following rationale is offered. Everyone who has been involved in the treatment of addictive behaviors is aware of the high relapse rates, often as high as 70 – 80% within the first 6 months following treatment (Hunt et al., 1971). It is therefore somewhat unrealistic and potentially self-defeating to assume that most clients will be totally successful in their attempts to maintain total abstinence. To the extent that a client adopts total abstinence as an absolute criterion for success, the first time a slip occurs he or she is likely to feel like a total failure, even though from a statistical standpoint the experience of an initial lapse is highly probable. If preparation for relapse is built into the treatment program, it may facilitate self-regulatory behavior that prevents a lapse from escalating into a relapse.

Despite the importance of the preceding argument, the therapist must at the same time warn clients about the possibility that they may be tempted to use preparatory information about slips as a rationalization to indulge. For example, a client may ask, "If it is possible to recover from a slip and it's not the end of the world if I have a lapse, then why shouldn't it be okay for me to go ahead and have a drink?" In response to such questions, we emphasize the necessity of assuming *personal responsibility* for the best use of the material. Being forewarned about the temptation to use the preparatory information as an excuse for relapse requires clients to assume personal responsibility for their behavior — they would be deceiving no one but themselves. In many ways, then, preparing clients for potential slips is parallel to conducting firedrills or other preparations for emergencies. We are teaching survival skills *in case* an emergency occurs; we are not giving permission to light fires.

Thus, whether or not an initial lapse escalates into a total relapse depends in part on the magnitude of the AVE or the individual's reaction to the slip. There are a variety of strategies to employ for coping with the AVE whenever a lapse occurs, and we summarize these strategies here in order of temporal priority, with the most important, immediate steps listed first. The same points can be summarized for clients in written form by the use of a "reminder card."

a. Stop, Look, and Listen. The first thing to do when a lapse occurs is to *stop* the ongoing flow of events and to *look and listen* to what is happening. Consult your *Reminder Card* for instructions.

b. Keep Calm. Your first reaction to the lapse may be one of feeling guilty and blaming yourself for what has happened. This is a normal reaction and is to be expected — it is part of the AVE. Give yourself enough time to allow the AVE reaction to arise and to pass away. Look upon the slip as a single, independent event, something that can be avoided in the future.

c. **Renew Your Commitment.** After a lapse, the most difficult problem to deal with is your motivation. You may feel like giving up, saying to yourself, "What's the use? I've blown it already." Again, this is a normal reaction (part of the AVE), and it can be remedied by the following steps. Think back over the reasons why you decided to change your drinking behavior in the first place. Look back at how far you have already come and reflect optimistically on your past successes in being able to change, instead of focusing pessimistically on your current setback.

d. **Review the Situation Leading up to the Lapse.** Look at the slip as a specific unique event. Ask yourself the following questions: What events led up to the slip? Were there any early warning signals that preceded the lapse? What was the nature of the high-risk situation that triggered the slip? Did you make any attempt to cope with the situation before the lapse occurred? Imagine the whole scene happening again, except that now, see yourself coping effectively. Beware of thoughts and feelings that suggest that the effects of the drink taken during the slip are going to overpower you and make it impossible for you to regain control. It is always easier to quit now, just after the slip, than to give in and postpone indefinitely your plans for recovery.

e. **Make an Immediate Plan for Recovery.** After a slip, it is important for you to renew your commitment and to take a plan of action immediately. Your options will depend on the situation, of course, but the following guidelines may assist you. First, get rid of all alcohol. Second, remove yourself from the high-risk situation if at all possible. If it is impossible to leave physically, leave psychologically — close your eyes and meditate for a few moments, or take a few deep breaths to clear your mind. Engage in robust physical exercise or other activity to drain off excessive energy and negative feelings. Do something good for yourself to help cancel the bad effects of the lapse. If you are overcome with guilt and self-blame, you might do something that will atone for your sin such as pay a fine or do a good deed for others. At the same time, avoid excessive self-punishment that might lead to thoughts that facilitate a relapse (e.g., "I'm no good, I deserve to die a hopeless drunk, so pass the bottle again").

f. **Ask for Help.** If you find that you need help, ask for it! For example, if you are with your friends, they might help by offering encouragement, providing alternative activities, or suggesting ways of coping. If you are alone, call your therapist (or a friend or relative) and seek out his or her assistance and support. Therapists may wish to set up a *relapse contract* with clients during treatment that would specify the steps to be taken in the event of a lapse. Some of the points that might be incorporated into a relapse contract are (1) costs or fines for drinking; (2) agreement to delay taking the first drink for a specified period (e.g., at least 20 minutes) after the initial temptation to give in; (3) agreement that the first lapse will involve a single "dose" of alcohol; (4) agreement to wait for a specified period (e.g., at least 1 hour) before continuing to drink. The client and therapist should each sign, date, and keep a copy of the contract. In addition, therapists should carefully prepare the clients for the expiration date of the contract, warning them of the possibility that they may experience temptations to relapse once the contract has expired.

IV. SUMMARY AND CONCLUSIONS

As any practitioner is aware, treatment for problems with alcohol is far from a unitary endeavor. Clients enter treatment with differing degrees of life disruption, physical addiction, prior treatment experience, motivation, and commitment to treatment. Additionally, clients progress through treatment at different rates and may find themselves stuck at any number of points along the way. Thus, attempts to apply a prepackaged, programmed treatment approach are unlikely to be successful. More likely, such attempts will be frustrating for both the therapist and client. Nevertheless, the components of the relapse-prevention treatment model that we have highlighted in this chapter for building self-confidence, self-efficacy, and self-control can be adapted for use with a wide variety of clients. We encourage therapists to individualize these components within their own treatment model for problem drinking.

REFERENCES

Annis, H. M. (1982a). *Situational confidence questionnaire.* Toronto: Addiction Research Foundation.
Annis, H. M. (1982b). *Inventory of drinking situations.* Toronto: Addiction Research Foundation.
Bandura, A. (1977). Self-efficacy: Toward a unifying theory of behavior change. *Psychological Review,* **84,** 191–215.
Bandura, A. (1981). Self-referent thought: A developmental analysis of self-efficacy. In J. H. Flavell & L. Ross (Eds.), *Social cognitive development: Frontiers and possible futures* (pp. 200–239). Cambridge: Cambridge University Press.
Bandura, A. (1982). Self-efficacy mechanism in human agency. *American Psychologist,* **37,** 122–147.

136

Brickman, P., Rabinowitz, V. C., Karuza, J., Coates, D., Cohn, E., & Kidder, L. (1982). Models of helping and coping. *American Psychologist,* **37,** 368–384.

Chaney, E. F., O'Leary, M. R., & Marlatt, G. A. (1978). Skill training with alcoholics. *Journal of Consulting and Clinical Psychology,* **46,**1092–1104.

Condiotte, M., & Lichtenstein, E. (1981). Self-efficacy and relapse in smoking cessation programs. *Journal of Consulting and Clinical Psychology,* **49 (5),** 648–658.

Cox, W. M. (1985). Personality correlates of substance abuse. In M. Galizio & S. A. Maisto (Eds.), *Determinants of substance abuse: Biological, psychological and environmental factors.* (pp. 209–246) New York: Plenum.

Cummings, C., Gordon, J. R., & Marlatt, G. A. (1980). Relapse: Strategies of prevention and prediction. In W. R. Miller (Ed.), *The addictive behaviors: Treatment of alcoholism, drug abuse, smoking and obesity.* (pp. 291–321). Oxford, United Kingdom: Pergamon Press.

Curran, J., & Monti, P. (Eds.). (1982). *Social skill training.* New York: Guilford Press.

Curry, S., & Marlatt, G. A. (1985). Unaided quitters' strategies for coping with temptations to smoke. In S. Shiffman & T. Wills (Eds.), *Coping behavior and substance abuse.* (pp. 243–265) New York: Academic Press.

D'Zurilla, T. J., & Goldfried, M. R. (1971). Problem solving and behavior modification. *Journal of Abnormal Psychology,* **78,** 107–126.

Eisler, R. M., & Frederiksen, L. W. (1980). *Perfecting social skills.* New York: Plenum.

Goldfried, M. R., & Davison, G. C. (1976). *Clinical behavior therapy.* New York: Holt, Rinehart & Winston.

Goldstein, A. P. (1973). *Structured learning theory.* New York: Academic Press.

Hay, W., & Nathan, P. (Eds.). (1982). *Clinical case studies in behavioral treatment of alcoholism.* New York: Plenum.

Hunt, W. A., Barnett, L. W., & Branch, L. G. (1971). Relapse rates in addiction programs. *Journal of Clinical Psychology,* **27,** 455–456.

Janis, I. L., & Mann, L. (1977). *Decision making.* New York: The Free Press.

Jones, Marjorie. (1982, February 23). Alcoholics go over the edge for new high. *Seattle Times,* p. B1.

Kazdin, A. E. (1976). Effects of covert modeling, multiple models, and model reinforcement on assertive behaviors. *Behavior Therapy,* **7,** 211–222.

Kazdin, A. E. (1979). Imagery elaboration and self-efficacy in the covert modeling of unassertive behavior. *Journal of Consulting and Clinical Psychology,* **47,** 725–733.

Litman, G. K. (1974). Stress, affect and craving in alcoholics. *Quarterly Journal of Studies on Alcohol,* **35 (1),** 121–146.

Marlatt, G. A., & Gordon, J. R. (1980). Determinants of relapse: Implications for the maintenance of behavior change. In P. O. Davidson & S. M. Davidson (Eds.), *Behavioral medicine: Changing health lifestyles* (pp. 410–452). New York: Brunner/Mazel.

Marlatt, G. A., & Gordon, J. R. (1985). *Relapse prevention: Maintenance strategies in the treatment of addictive behaviors.* New York: Guilford.

Marlatt, G. A., & Marques, J. K. (1977). Meditation, self-control and alcohol use. In R. B. Stuart (Ed.), *Behavioral self-management: Strategies, techniques and outcomes* (pp. 35–57). New York: Brunner/Mazel.

McFall, R. M. (1976). Behavioral training: A skill-acquisition approach to clinical problems. In J. T. Spence, R. C. Carson, & J. W. Thibaut (Eds.), *Behavioral approaches to therapy* (pp. 227–259). Morristown, NJ: General Learning Press.

Merluzzi, T. V., Glass, C. R., & Genest, M. (Eds.). (1981). *Cognitive assessment.* New York: Guilford.

Prochaska, J. O., & DiClemente, C. C. (1983). Stages and processes of self-change of smoking: Toward an integrative model of change. *Journal of Consulting and Clinical Psychology,* **51,** 390–395.

Rohsenow, D. J. (1983). Alcoholics' perceptions of control. In W. M. Cox (Ed.), *Identifying and measuring alcoholic personality characteristics* (pp. 37–51). San Francisco: Jossey-Bass.

Schachter, S. (1982). Recidivism and self-cure of smoking and obesity. *American Psychologist,* **37,** 436–444.

Shapiro, D., & Walsh, R. (Eds.). (1980). *The science of meditation: Theory, research and experience.* New York: Aldine.

Shiffman, S. (1982). Relapse following smoking cessation: A situational analysis. *Journal of Consulting and Clinical Psychology,* **50,** 71–86.

7

Imagery and Logotherapeutic Techniques in Psychotherapy: Clinical Experiences and Promise for Application to Alcohol Problems

ERIC KLINGER

Division of Social Sciences, Morris Campus
Department of Psychology, Minneapolis Campus
University of Minnesota
Morris, Minnesota 56267

I. INTRODUCTION

Virtually every new psychological treatment procedure that has impressed practitioners with its effectiveness is sooner or later applied to the treatment of alcohol problems. The same is true of the approaches described here. Neither the imagery group of techniques nor logotherapy was specifically designed to treat alcohol problems, but both have developed methods for use with alcoholic patients, and practitioners in both camps have proclaimed their approaches to offer the promise of effective treatment.

Of the two approaches, the imagery approach is really a highly diverse group of treatment procedures whose only common element is that they all require their clients explicitly to imagine something. What they are to imagine, in what relation to other procedures, and under what conditions vary widely. Some components of this group, such as sensitization therapy, have become rather well known and are included here for the sake of completeness. Guided imagery approaches, at least in the treatment of addictive

TREATMENT AND PREVENTION
OF ALCOHOL PROBLEMS: A RESOURCE MANUAL

disorders, are less well known in the United States and have been applied most widely in northern Europe.

Logotherapy, also of European origin, is a specific variant of existential psychotherapy and proceeds through a relatively unitary theoretical orientation and a small number of specific techniques. Its entry into the area of alcohol treatment is relatively recent.

II. IMAGERY METHODS AND TREATMENT FOR ALCOHOLISM

A. Theoretical Reasons for the Use of Imagery in Psychotherapy

Imagery may seem to be a weak reed on which to rest the burden of changing disordered behavior, especially behavior as notoriously hard to change as alcoholism. Psychology during the behaviorist era regarded imagery as at most an epiphenomenon — a subjective and imperfect reflection of the effective processes that govern behavior, one without causal effect and unworthy of scientific study. Furthermore, individuals vary widely in the subjective prominence of their imagery, with the result that some deny that they experience any imagery at all. What possible reason is there to believe that imagery provides a fruitful modality for psychological treatment?

To deal first with the second issue, it is true that individuals vary widely in the subjective prominence of their waking imagery, but this does not mean that they do not possess imaginal processes. First, virtually every intact individual experiences identifiably visual dreams during rapid-eye-movement (REM) sleep. Those dreams consist partially of imagery. Secondly, most individuals actively use mental imagery, even if they are unaware of doing so. Ask almost anyone to close his or her eyes and count the number of windows in his or her home, and the person will go through a procedure of imagining either walking around the outside of the house or through the various rooms, actively counting the windows. Such a counting procedure is possible only if the windows are represented in some kind of spatial — that is, visual — form. That is mental imagery. It is usually defined as sensory-like subjective experience in the absence of the stimuli that would normally arouse the corresponding sensations. In that sense, most people experience mental imagery.

The available information on the distribution of imagery in the population is a good deal more precise than that (e.g., Klinger, 1978–1979; Klinger & Cox, in press; Richardson, 1969; Singer & Antrobus, 1972), but it merely confirms the conclusion that mental imagery in general and the forms of it that most people call daydreaming are nearly universal human phenomena, at least within the populations studied to date.

The more challenging question regards the usefulness of employing imaginal techniques in psychological treatment. The answer is that mental imagery is a great deal more than incidental evidence of mental functioning. Rather, growing evidence indicates that the mechanisms that produce it overlap those used in everyday psychological functioning and that manipulating imagery can act on those mechanisms—on the individual's basic psychic apparatus—to produce psychological change. This evidence has been summarized elsewhere. Briefly, evidence summarized by Finke (1980) shows that a number of visual perceptual phenomena, such as the complex after-effect known as the McCullough Effect and the phenomena surrounding adaptation to distorting lenses, can be partially reproduced by having people imagine portions of the stimulus conditions instead of actually perceiving them. Other evidence (Klinger, 1981) indicates that the sequencing of imaginal content is determined by motivation and cues, as is much overt behavior, that images are conditionable, that images are accompanied by corresponding affect, and that images of one's own motor activity are accompanied by low-level activity of the muscles implicated in the imagined activity.

This evidence strongly suggests that mental imagery is part and parcel of the individual's larger psychological functioning because it shares at least some of the same mechanisms and, in the form of perceptual, motor, and affective activity, it generates some of the same correlates. Such a conclusion is strengthened by experimental demonstrations (reviewed briefly by Klinger, 1981) that mental practice of motor skills such as pursuit rotor tracking and athletic motions improves subsequent physical performance of those skills.

There is by now a sizable literature (reviewed by Singer, 1974; Singer & Pope, 1978) purporting to demonstrate the clinical utility of imagery techniques in psychotherapy. However, apart from the literature on desensitization methods, which is not reviewed here, there are relatively few well-controlled studies of therapeutic outcome and, indeed, few experimentally controlled studies of any kind. A small number, however, provide a basis for accepting imagery methods as powerful therapeutic tools in general psychotherapy. Thus, Kazdin (1979) has shown that assertiveness training is improved when clients are encouraged to elaborate their covert rehearsal of assertive behavior by their own spontaneous imagery. Lipsky, Kassinove, and Miller (1980) have shown that imaginal rehearsal improved the effectiveness of rational–emotive therapy. Wächter and Pudel (1980) demonstrated that guided affective imagery (a guided daydream method described in a later section) produced significant symptomatic and psychometric improvement in comparison with a waiting-list control group. Wilke (1980) found guided affective imagery to produce slightly better results than a standard psychoanalytically oriented psychotherapy (the significance of the difference remained untested) in the treatment of colitis patients. In a non-clinical context, Anderson (1983) showed that imagining oneself donating or not donating blood correspondingly changed subjects' actual intentions to donate or not to donate. The change in intentions persisted for at least 3 days following the imagery session.

B. The Range of Imagery Methods in Psychological Treatment

The use of mental imagery in treatment contexts has been as varied as the different approaches to treatment in general. Thus, Jung's active imagination (1964), which is one of the main precursors of modern imagery methods, consists in large part of completing in waking fantasy dreams experienced during sleep. Here, the emphasis is on permitting the client's imagery to unfold, often with dramatic and emotionally evocative changes. This process may take a considerable part of a therapeutic session. The second principal precursor, systematic desensitization (Wolpe, 1958), has clients focus on a series of narrowly specified images, each of which is to vary as little as possible, until the client feels comfortable with each image. The duration of each image may vary widely but may be quite brief.

These two precursors virtually define the extremes of application of imaginal methods, which vary according to whether clients are assigned a starting point for their imagery, whether the starting point is specified broadly or closely, whether the image is to remain constant or to change spontaneously, how long the imagery sequence is permitted to continue, to what extent the therapist contributes questions or suggestions regarding the imagery, whether the client reports the imagery continuously during its occurrence, the nature of the relaxation or hypnotic state induced prior to the imaging, and the extent to which the imaginal process is expected to produce psychological change by itself or to serve as a basis for discussion and articulated insights.

These dimensions of imagery methods vary to some extent independently of one another. Thus, in implosion therapy (Stampfl & Levis, 1967) the therapist specifies the target imagery closely and intervenes in its development, and the sequence may be fairly long. The experience is expected to generate desensitization of fear without the need for insight. In psychoimagination therapy (Shorr, 1983), the therapist specifies the outset of the imagery closely, allows it to change spontaneously, may intervene in its development, but keeps the average imagery period comparatively brief and uses the imagery as a basis for discussion and insight. Covert sensitization (Cautela & McCullough, 1978) specifies the imagery closely; it continues for relatively brief periods; and it is expected to generate aversion to undesirable activities without insight. Eidetic therapy (Ahsen, 1977) specifies the imagery closely, but chooses it on the basis of the client's individual experience, expects the client to focus heavily on particular scenes, often for protracted time periods, and makes little use of interpretation of the images but seeks to deepen the client's experience of them. Guided affective imagery (Leuner, 1978, 1980) broadly specifies a starting point for the imagery and allows the imagery to unfold spontaneously at length, but with frequent therapist intervention in the form of questions and occasional suggestions. Interpretation and insight are not considered essential to therapeutic effectiveness.

A further dimension of treatment, one that extends beyond covert imagery, is the extent to which the activity is purely mental. In contrast to the aforementioned methods, psychodrama (Moreno, 1972; Starr, 1977) involves groups of clients role-playing improvised scenarios. Role-playing has also been used in a wide variety of other contexts, including prominent use in assertiveness training. In conjunction with rational–emotive therapy it has been found comparable in effectiveness to covert imagery (Lipsky et al., 1980). Art therapy is used extensively as an adjunctive and primary therapy (Virshup & Virshup, 1981; Wadeson, 1980).

The imagery methods that appear to have been tried most systematically with alcoholic and other substance-abusing clients are covert sensitization, psychodrama, art therapy, and guided imagery. Except for art therapy, for whose effectiveness there does not seem to be any quantitative evidence, these are briefly described and the evidence for their effectiveness reviewed here next.

C. Covert Sensitization and Treatment for Alcoholism

Covert sensitization, originated by Cautela (1966), is an aversive conditioning method in which an unpleasant image (commonly of feeling nauseated and vomiting) closely follows an image of behavior the client wishes to give up. Clients are first introduced to the basic purposes and theory of the method. They then provide the details of their drinking behavior, which are incorporated into the imagery scenes that follow. In Wisocki's (1972, p. 106) words, "At every approach point (i.e., intending to drink, approaching the bar, touching the glass, etc.) the patient is told to imagine himself feeling sick and vomiting. After each presentation of a sensitizing scene, the therapist presents a 'relief' scene in which the patient imagines that alcohol is presented to him, but he refuses it and feels strong and virtuous." The aversion and relief scenes are alternated, with the patient closely following the therapist's previous description of the scene. The patient is also instructed to practice the scenes outside the clinical setting "whenever he is tempted to drink" (Wisocki, 1972, p. 106).

How well does this method work with alcoholics? In Wisocki's (1972) review, she concluded that "the covert sensitization procedure, as originally devised, has not yet been adequately examined in the treatment of alcoholic behavior" (p. 112). Despite repeated reports of therapeutic success in individual clinical instances, Wisocki was able to find only two controlled studies, one of which was seriously deficient in the duration of the treatment, the short follow-up period, and the imprecise application of the method. The other investigation (Ashem & Donner, 1968), which also used a sharply abbreviated course of treatment, found an abstinence rate of 40% 6 months after treatment (compared with 0% for the control group).

A literature search for the period subsequent to Wisocki's review turned up little additional work and none that would qualify as a competent test of Cautela's program. One experimentally controlled study (Newton, 1977) compared a group receiving a therapy regimen of four covert sensitization sessions with an untreated control group and found no treatment effect on alcohol consumption. Four sessions constitute a treatment duration drastically less than the regimen found clinically effective by Cautela. An investigation comparing several treatment methods administered to the same subjects found that eight covert sensitization sessions over 4 days produced little change in alcohol consumption during the following 4 days (Wilson & Tracy, 1976). Obviously, neither the treatment duration nor the criterion in this small-sample study represents adequate tests of the method. Furthermore, the mechanical, exclusive use of methods such as covert sensitization fall far short of dealing with the range of clinical issues presented by an alcoholic client.

From the literature turned up in this search, it is possible to conclude that (1) covert sensitization has been used in some alcoholic patients with successful treatment outcomes, (2) the treatment effect of a few sessions is modest to negligible, and (3) covert sensitization as a component of a clinically credible alcoholism treatment method of the kind originally proposed by Cautela has yet to be subjected to an adequate controlled test.

Covert sensitization has generally been conceptualized as a conditioning procedure. However, evidence suggests that, insofar as it is effective, it derives its effectiveness from some other principle. Thus, for instance, Ashem and Donner found no difference between a forward and a backward conditioning procedure for covert sensitization, and an analysis of the desensitization literature (Davison & Wilson, 1972) similarly argued against a conditioning interpretation.

D. Psychodrama

Psychodrama (Moreno, 1972; Starr, 1977) is a form of group therapy in which members role-play psychologically important scenes. For instance, the scene might depict the protagonist's interaction with a relative, spouse, or employer. The members of the group are on any one occasion divided into a director (therapist), a protagonist whose life is the focus of the scene, *auxil-*

iary egos (the other participants in the scene, who commonly play the protagonist's significant others), and the audience. All of the members, including the audience, interact to produce the therapeutic effect by helping the
protagonist and others to identify their feelings in the scene and to characterize the nature, limitations, and unrealized possibilities of the way the characters interact. The director assists the group in arriving at themes to explore
and works with the eventual protagonist to assure that the scene is likely to be
therapeutically productive but within limits the protagonist can withstand.
The auxiliary egos play their parts so as to meet the protagonist's specifica-
tions of those parts (the characteristics of his or her significant others) as
faithfully as possible. The audience responds by expressing its empathy and
its reactions honestly but supportively. The dramatization is followed by a
nonintellectualizing, open discussion of mutual reactions and insights.

Psychodrama has been applied to alcoholic populations with clinical results that have encouraged its practitioners. Thus, Blume (1974) characterized it as "a useful therapeutic adjunct in the rehabilitation of men and
women suffering from alcoholism" (p. 127). However, a literature search
turned up only one controlled evaluation of psychodrama with alcoholics.
Patients enrolled in a comprehensive treatment program at a U.S. Navy
Alcohol Rehabilitation Center received either psychodrama or small group
therapy as components of their treatment (Wood, Del Nuovo, Bucky,
Schein, & Michalik, 1979). The patients were assigned to psychodrama by
their group counselor rather than randomly, but the two groups were demo-
graphically similar. Treatment lasted typically 6 to 8 weeks. There was no
follow-up measure of alcohol consumption. The two groups did not differ
significantly on prognoses at discharge nor systematically on changes in
scores on the Minimult (short form of the Minnesota Multiphasic Personality Inventory), Comrey Personality Scales, or State–Trait Anxiety Inventory. Thus, psychodrama manifested neither advantages nor disadvantages
in comparison to a more conventional group therapy. However, because
there was no milieu or no-treatment control group, it is impossible to know
whether either treatment made a therapeutic contribution, and the selection
of outcome measures prevents drawing conclusions about effects on the
target behavior.

E. Guided Affective Imagery with Chemically Dependent
Patients

After Carl Jung's method of active imagination, the next major innovators
of guided imagery methods were the French engineer Desoille (1955), the
German psychiatrist Leuner (1955, 1978, 1980), and the American psychologist Shorr (1983). All of these proceed by suggesting to the client particular
starting points for an imagery sequence (a meadow, the entrance to a cave,

two animals walking down a road together, etc.) and let the client's imagery unfold from that point on, with the client describing the imagery to the therapist as it develops and the therapist intervening occasionally with questions, suggestions, and encouragment. In the methods of Desoille and Leuner, the imagery sequences are the centerpiece and typically take from 15 to 40 minutes to unfold. Shorr makes more ad hoc, fragmentary use of imagery in the context of a conversational therapy heavily influence by Sullivan.

Leuner's guided affective imagery (GAI) is the only one of the three for which a literature search found supportive quantitative evidence or a description of systematic applications to chemically dependent populations. The discussion that follows therefore focuses on GAI.

In northern and central Europe, GAI has taken on the status of a major therapeutic movement, complete with national organizations in West Germany, Austria, Switzerland, and Sweden, an international association, biennial training conferences and numerous other training seminars, a detailed training curriculum, a carefully controlled training evaluation and certification process for GAI therapists, training manuals (Leuner, 1981a, 1985), and a growing number of quantitative investigations.

GAI is rooted in classical psychoanalysis, and, although its methods depart widely from those of traditional psychoanalysis, its practitioners still overwhelmingly employ psychoanalytic concepts and language. It has nevertheless been influenced strongly by Jung and Rogers. GAI is actually divided into three variants or levels, called basic, intermediate, and upper or advanced. These are distinguished by the orientation and methods employed by the therapist and by the therapist's training level. Certification is separate for the three levels.

At the basic level, the therapist adopts a largely client-centered stance of facilitating the development of the client's imagery, protecting the client from undue amounts of anxiety, and avoiding confrontational tactics. Suggestions are limited to encouraging certain options in the imagery, such as following a stream to its source or mouth, or feeding and placating a threatening figure. The starting motifs for the imagery are limited to relatively ambiguous settings: a meadow, a brook, a mountain, a walk through an unspecified house, and watching the edge of a woods.

At the intermediate level, the therapist intervenes somewhat more directively, is prepared to help the client work through intense anxiety if necessary, may employ suggestions to confront threatening figures in the fantasy (for instance, by staring them down) or to instate guides (pacemakers), and chooses starting motifs more likely to address conflict themes directly: a lion, an ego-ideal figure, an interaction with a significant other, accepting a ride from a stranger, or scenes drawn from the client's dreams, waking life, body parts, et cetera. There is increased focus on the client–therapist relationship (the transference).

At the advanced level, which is open only to candidates with formal psychoanalytic training, GAI merges into conventional psychoanalysis, including heavy focus on transference, interpretation, possible suggestions to weaken threatening figures or to use magical fluids, and completely flexible use of starting motifs, including motifs such as cave entrances, swamp holes, volcanoes, and picture albums, all of which are intended to elicit repressed archaic material.

Each of these levels actually constitutes a separate, self-sufficient treatment program. Interpretation and intellectual insight are not regarded as necessary to therapeutic success. In each instance, imagery therapy sessions are opened with a brief conversation concerning reactions to the previous session and events since then. Following brief relaxation and one or more eyes-closed imagery periods of perhaps 15 to 40 minutes, the sessions are closed with brief conversations concerning reactions to the imagery just concluded, which also help to ease the client out of the altered state of consciousness normally induced by the imagery session. Clients are ordinarily asked to write down their recollections of their imagery and to paint or draw important scenes between sessions. These records are reviewed and discussed briefly during the opening conversation at the next session.

GAI sessions are normally scheduled once or twice a week. GAI treatment commonly takes from 15 to 120 imagery sessions, but it is increasingly recommended as an effective brief therapy — and even as a crisis therapy — requiring about 15 to 30 sessions.

Although GAI therapy has not been advertised as a method especially effective for alcoholism, it has been used extensively with alcoholic and other substance-abusing clients. Alcohol or other substance abuse occurs among neither the indications nor the counterindications for application of the method, although the latter include psychoses, organic disorders, deep depression, low intelligence, weak motivation for therapy, and, in general, certain kinds of compulsive neuroses, and cases with weak ego structures, including certain severe hysterical disorders.

Two outcome investigations using comparison groups and at least one other psychometric investigation have been reported for the use of GAI with general psychiatric and colitis samples (Kulessa & Jung, 1980; Wächter & Pudel, 1980; Wilke, 1980). The results support the efficacy of the method. No controlled outcome studies have been reported specifically for alcohol- or other substance-abusing samples. All that is available beyond case studies (Beck, 1968; Wächter & Leuner, 1978) is a sketchy description of group and individual GAI with substance-abusing adolescents at a child guidance clinic (Klessmann, 1983). Of a total 109 substance abusers (mostly polyabusers) known to the clinic, 35 entered individual GAI, and 35 entered group GAI. (Group GAI has evolved to a form in which up to about eight clients verbalize their imagery during each session interactively, thus generally forming a group fantasy.) Eleven of these GAI clients were needle users, and it is unclear how they fared, although it appears that four gave up "dropping out." About half of the remaining clients (predominantly marijuana and alcohol users) gave up their substance use; the other half were at the time of reporting occasional users. There was no comparison group and no indication concerning average duration of treatment or length of follow-up. Klessmann reports using client-selected music to help induce relaxation and imagery.

Leuner (1971; 1981b) has also developed a GAI-related psycholytic therapy using psilocybin and LSD to facilitate the imagery process. A literature review of pre-GAI psychedelic therapy with 1603 published cases with varying diagnoses found widely varying success rates (of "substantial" or "good" improvement) with different diagnoses, ranging from 70% for anxiety neuroses to 31% for alcoholic and other addictions (Mascher, 1967). In 82 cases treated by Leuner's group at the University of Göttingen Clinic (Mascher, 1966, reworked in Leuner, 1981b), a follow-up at 2 to 8 years after treatment obtained comparable results, ranging from success rates of about 80% for anxiety neuroses and phobias to only 25% (one case out of four) for alcoholics, and no success with two cases of infantile personalities.

Although these success rates for psycholytic therapy with alcoholics do not appear promising, controlled studies with alcoholics have also appeared (Kurland, Savage, Pahnke, Grof, & Olssen, 1971, described in Leuner, 1981b; Sarret, Cheek, & Osmond, 1966) and have reported positive results. However, the first of these studies compared two groups receiving two different levels of LSD, without a non-LSD group. The second relied on reports of male alcoholics' wives (an LSD versus a comparison treatment group, both small samples) and did not subject its results to significance tests. It is therefore hard to evaluate the positive results reported.

It should be noted that Leuner's (1981b) recommendations for psycholytic therapy are to use minimal (threshold) doses, with sessions embedded in a thoroughgoing verbal depth therapy. In this way, imaginal material can be optimally facilitated and subsequently worked through.

Alcoholism does not appear on the lists of indications for psycholytic therapy, but is also not regarded as an absolute contraindication, either. The low success rate from psycholytic therapy with alcoholics may be attributable to correlated features that do serve as contraindications (Leuner, 1981b), such as poor motivation for treatment, acting-out tendencies, psychopathy with little distress, personal self-neglect, a history of serious suicide attempts, and fragile defenses.

In summary, the evidence for the effectiveness of GAI with general clinical populations, combined with the uncontrolled results reported by Klessmann, suggests that GAI deserves to be investigated more systematically as a treatment for substance abuse, including alcoholism. However, the evidence now available permits no firm conclusions concerning extension of the method to alcoholics. Psycholytic therapy does not appear especially indicated for alcoholic and other substance abuse clients, although it may be effective with carefully selected cases.

III. LOGOTHERAPY AND TREATMENT FOR ALCOHOLISM

A. Theory and Methods of Logotherapy

Logotherapy is the Viennese psychiatrist Viktor Frankl's (1969) form of existential psychotherapy. In format—one-to-one conversation between client and therapist—it is a conventional talk therapy. Its orientation, however, departs sharply from the prevailing psychoanalytic, Rogerian, behavioristic, and cognitive alternatives.

The fundamental premise of logotherapy is that a human being's most fundamental need—one that transcends Freud's pleasure principle and Adler's will to power—is the need to experience one's life as meaningful, to believe that one's activities serve a sufficiently worthwhile purpose to be worth the effort and pain of daily existence. Frankl therefore posits a "will to meaning." The absence of a sense that one's life is meaningful constitutes an "existential vacuum" in which individuals cannot be happy or psychologically healthy. Frankl estimates that about 20% of the psychiatric patient population suffers from the "noögenic neuroses" (i.e., difficulties arising out of the lack of a sense of meaningfulness) that ensue.

In accordance with this central viewpoint, the task of logotherapy is to help clients find a sense of meaning. A sense of meaning is demonstrably associated with having committed oneself to striving for personally compelling goals, especially those including various aspects of personal relationships (Klinger, 1977). Thus, logotherapy may consist of helping clients to identify potential goals and to commit themselves to pursuing them.

Most people find their sense of meaning in their daily social relationships, vocations, education and self-development, and the like (Klinger, 1977; Lukas, 1972). If clients can be helped to establish satisfying personal relationships and vocational goals, they will have been helped.

Some of logotherapy's most striking successes, however, have been achieved with people such as the deeply bereaved and terminally ill who may, from their own and an outside observer's perspective, have little left to live for. Indeed, Frankl developed his therapy during 3 years as an inmate in Nazi concentration camps, where daily life was unimaginably wretched and the prospects for physical survival vanishingly small. Frankl concluded that more important than the physical availability of attractive incentives was the human's ability to choose what attitude to take toward one's own suffering. Thus, given the suffering, it can be reinterpreted as a test to be endured, as a humiliation to be surmounted through preserving one's own dignity, as an opportunity to demonstrate self-mastery to other sufferers and therefore to lend them strength, and so on. In each instance, the suffering is transformed from simply a meaningless burden that makes life miserable to an opportunity—even if a regrettable one—to achieve something personally worthwhile.

Logotherapy proceeds mostly through unstructured conversations that lead clients to discover new sources of meaning. No logotherapist can simply hand a client a meaningful goal. Beyond the preceding general orientation, however, supplemented by numerous case illustrations and clinical sophistication, Frankl's logotherapy has few concrete procedures to suggest to the beginning logotherapist. Two specific techniques, paradoxical intention and dereflection, seem at best only tangentially related to the central thrust of logotherapy. *Paradoxical intention,* which has received some quantitative empirical support (Ascher & Efran, 1978), is applied to very specific psychological symptoms and consists of the client exaggerating and thereby mocking any given target symptom. Thus, for instance, the heart phobic client plays out the fear or fantasy of a heart attack to the point of absurdity. *Dereflection* consists of leading a client who has already amply explored his or her symptoms and problems to focus away from them and onto personal strengths and possibilities instead.

B. Why Use Logotherapy for Alcohol Abuse?

Alcohol and other substance abuse syndromes are complex conditions that defy easy solutions. They are complex because the psychological and social factors that originally motivated the behavior are soon joined by social, motivational, and often physiological factors that stabilize and support the substance use (Klinger, 1977). First, the subjective effects of the substance give something that the user does not know how to get by other means, something that the user highly values—hope, relief from pain and depression, relaxation, oblivion, altered states of consciousness, orgasmic-like pleasure, and so on. Then, in the process of developing a pattern of use, including procuring the substance, sharing the experience, and paying for the substance, the user adopts a new set of substance-related goals that now constitute the user's main sources of meaning, and the user moves into a corresponding social network with its own norms and social pressures. When the substance is physically addictive, as in the case of alcohol, renouncing the substance means having to endure highly unpleasant and possibly dangerous withdrawal symptoms. Intoxicating substances also impair cognitive brain functions and therefore reduce the user's competence to make decisions. Furthermore, the user adopts and practices a set of self-attitudes and defenses that justify continued use and resist persuasion to stop.

Extricating the substance abuser from such a web of psychological forces is anything but easy. Despite the complexity, much of this web is motivational, which is to say that it relates to a sense of meaning and to choices of goals. Thus, students who use alcohol more heavily than others (Klinger, 1977) and people who patronize public amusement facilities (Lukas, 1972) report less meaningful lives than others. Anecdotally and statistically, many forms of substance abuse are inversely proportional to socioeconomic status, and therefore, presumably, to personal opportunity. Among U.S. military personnel in Viet Nam, alcohol and other drug use was strongly associated with symptoms of depression (Robins, 1974). When U.S. soldiers went to Viet Nam, narcotics use soared. Yet, after they returned, the prevalence of narcotics use returned to what it had been before (Robins, 1974). Presumably, when soldiers' personal opportunities were restored to them, they gave up the narcotic substitute. Compared with the power of other motivational factors, the fear of withdrawal symptoms plays a minor role in continued substance use.

To summarize, alcohol use is associated with a lack of meaning in one's life; substance use begins with the need to meet goals that were going unmet; and terminating substance abuse requires identifying and becoming committed to psychologically compelling alternative goals. Logotherapy, as a therapy concerned with meaning and goals, would thus appear to be a promising method for use with alcoholism.

C. Logotherapy and Alcoholism: Applications and Evidence

Consistent with this reasoning, logotherapy has been applied to relatively large numbers of alcoholic clients. One prominent logotherapist has even published a logotherapy self-help manual for problem drinkers (Crumbaugh, 1980). What is the scientific evidence for the effectiveness of logotherapy with alcoholics?

A literature search revealed only two quantitative studies. One of these (Estrada, 1981) obtained some posttreatment follow-up data on drinking and found no effects of logotherapy compared to a no-treatment group, but treatment was limited to a weekend retreat. The investigator did find that the treatment group increased their scores on awareness of purpose in life (Purpose in Life Test) and reported a greater increase in overall quality of life.

The other investigation (Crumbaugh, 1977) included substantial samples of actual logotherapy clients in a Veterans Administration Alcoholism Treatment Unit but reported no alcohol consumption outcome data. There are only three clues to the effectiveness of logotherapy in this report. First, 72% and 66% of the clients in two logotherapy samples were rated as having made a "good" (as contrasted with a "poor") recovery by the end of their therapy. Two nonlogotherapy samples were rated as having achieved a "good" level of adjustment in a 1-year follow-up in 51% and 54% of the cases. These percentages are lower than those of the logotherapy group, but the latter group consisted of selected cases and, in any event, the outcome measures used were different and applied at different time points for the two groups. A second clue for the effectiveness of logotherapy is that, between intake and exit, the logotherapy clients decreased their scores on the Seeking of Noetic Goals Test, which measures the extent to which subjects are searching for meaning. A decrease presumably means that the client has found some of the meaning he or she was seeking. In any event, the nonlogotherapy, general regimen clients increased their scores in the same time period. The difference between logotherapy and control subject changes was statistically significant. The third clue is that logotherapy clients whose recovery was rated poor ended therapy with lower purpose in life scores and higher seeking of noetic goals scores than those whose recovery was rated good. The result suggests concurrent validity for the two instruments and for the therapy outcome rating, but it says little about alcohol consumption after treatment.

In short, logotherapy is a theoretically highly attractive therapy for alcoholism because it is directed precisely at a motivational problem thought to lie at the root of alcoholism. However, there is little objective evidence available one way or the other concerning the effectiveness of logotherapy in changing the target behavior of alcoholic clients.

IV. SUMMARY AND CONCLUSIONS

This chapter reviewed the use of mental imagery methods and logotherapy in psychotherapy for alcohol problems. Most people experience mental imagery in some form. In fact, evidence suggests that mental imagery is part and parcel of the individual's larger psychological functioning. It shares some of the same mechanisms, generates some of the same correlates, and serves as a proxy for overt behavior, in that mental practice and other imaginal phenomena alter the individual's response repertoire on which the imagery is based.

A great variety of methods has evolved to harness mental imagery in the service of psychotherapy. A number of these have been shown to be effective in general clinical application. There is therefore good reason to hope that they can be adapted as components of alcohol treatment programs to improve the reliability, range, and effectiveness of treatment. However, controlled evidence of the effectiveness of existing imagery methods with alcohol problems is still very scarce, and the evidence that exists indicates at the very least that these methods do not promise a quick remedy for the complex, recalcitrant problems of alcoholism. Thus, although some behavior therapy uses of imagery have been supported in general clinical populations, the use of covert sensitization with alcoholics has yet to be adequately evaluated. It is possible to state only that its use has been associated with successful outcomes in individual cases and that the alcoholism treatment effect of sensitization therapy lasting only a few sessions is modest to negligible. Psychodrama has similarly convinced its practitioners of its usefulness with alcoholic clients, but the quantitative literature is insufficient to assess the value of the method. Guided affective imagery, whose effectiveness is supported by controlled outcome studies in general populations, has likewise not been evaluated by experimentally controlled studies with alcoholics and other substance abusers, although the method has been used apparently successfully with substantial numbers of adolescent polyabusers. Although its psycholytic variant, which uses hallucinogenic drugs to facilitate the imagery process, does not appear indicated for use with a substance abuse population, GAI as such merits further investigation in alcoholic populations.

Alcohol and other substance abuse disorders are associated with lack of a sense of meaning in life—i.e., with deficient engagement in satisfying goal pursuits. Logotherapy, a method concerned with meaning and goals, would on purely theoretical grounds therefore appear to be a method of choice with alcohol problems. Logotherapy has in fact been applied to large numbers of alcoholic clients with some claims of success. However, at this time there are no adequate data available with which to evaluate its effectiveness.

REFERENCES

Ahsen, A. (1977). Eidetics: An overview. *Journal of Mental Imagery,* **1,** 5–38.
Anderson, C. A. (1983). Imagination and expectation: The effect of imagining behavioral scripts on personal intentions. *Journal of Personality and Social Psychology,* **45,** 293–305.
Ascher, L. M., & Efran, J. S. (1978). Use of paradoxical intention in a behavioral program for sleep onset insomnia. *Journal of Consulting and Clinical Psychology,* **46,** 547–550.
Ashem, B., & Donner, L. (1968). Covert sensitization with alcoholics: A controlled replication. *Behavior Research and Therapy,* **6,** 7–12.
Beck, M. (1968). Rehabilitation eines chronischen Trinkers mit der Methode des Katathymen Bilderlebens [Rehabilitation of a chronic drinker with the Guided Affective Imagery method]. *Paxis der Psychotherapie,* **13,** 97–103.
Blume, S. B. (1974). Psychodrama and alcoholism. *Annals of the New York Academy of Sciences,* **233,** 123–127.
Cautela, J. R. (1966). Treatment of compulsive behavior by covert sensitization. *Psychological Record,* **16,** 33–41.
Cautela, J. R., & McCullough, L. (1978). In J. L. Singer & K. S. Pope (Eds.), *The power of human imagination: New methods in psychotherapy.* New York: Plenum.

Crumbaugh, J. C. (1977). The Seeking of Noetic Goals Test (SONG): A complementary scale to the Purpose in Life Test (PIL). *Journal of Clinical Psychology, 33,* 900–907.

Crumbaugh, J. C. (1980). *Logotherapy: New help for problem drinkers.* Chicago: Nelson Hall.

Davison, G. C., & Wilson, G. T. (1972). Critique of "Densitization: Social and cognitive factors underlying the effectiveness of Wolpe's procedure." *Psychological Bulletin, 78,* 28–31.

Desoille, R. (1955). *Introduction à une Psychothérapie rationelle* [Introduction to a rational psychotherapy]. Paris: L'Arche.

Estrada, S. C. (1981). The lifestyle recovery patterns of Mexican American male alcoholics. (Doctoral dissertation, United States International University, 1981). *Dissertation Abstracts International, 42,* 2052-B.

Finke, R. A. (1980). Levels of equivalence in imagery and perception. *Psychological Review, 87,* 113–132.

Frankl, V. E. (1969). *The will to meaning: Foundations and applications of logotherapy.* New York: World.

Jung, C. G. (1964). Die Beziehungen zwischen dem Ich und dem Unbewussten [The relationships between the ego and the unconscious]. In M. Niehus-Jung, L. Hurwitz-Eisner, & F. Riklin (Eds.), *Gesammelte Werke: Vol. 7. Zwei Schriften über analytische Psychologie.* Zürich: Rascher.

Kazdin, A. E. (1979). Imagery elaboration and self-efficacy in the covert modeling treatment of unassertive behavior. *Journal of Consulting and Clinical Psychology, 47,* 725–733.

Klessmann, E. (1983). Guided affective imagery in groups of young drug users. In H. Leuner, G. Horn, & E. Klessmann, *Guided affective imagery with children and adolescents.* New York: Plenum.

Klinger, E. (1977). *Meaning and void: Inner experience and the incentives in people's lives.* Minneapolis: University of Minnesota Press.

Klinger, E. (1978–1979). Dimensions of thought and imagery in normal waking states. *Journal of Altered States of Consciousness, 4,* 97–113.

Klinger, E. (1981). The central place of imagery in human functioning. In E. Klinger (Ed.), *Imagery: Vol. 2. Concepts, results, and applications.* New York: Plenum.

Klinger, E., & Cox, W. M. (in press). Dimensions of thought flow in everyday life. *Imagination, Cognition and Personality.*

Kulessa, C., & Jung, F. G. (1980). Effizienz einer 20-stündigen Kurztherapie mit dem Katathymen Bilderleben im testpsychologischen prae/post-Vergleich [Effectiveness of a 20-hour brief therapy with Guided Affective Imagery from the standpoint of a pre- versus posttherapy comparison of psychological test scores]. In H. Leuner (Ed.), *Katathymes Bilderleben: Ergebnisse in Theorie und Praxis* [Guided Affective Imagery: Results in theory and practice]. Bern: Huber.

Kurland, A. A., Savage, C., Pahnke, W., Grof, St., & Olssen, J. E. (1971). LSD in the treatment of alcoholics. *Pharmacopsychiatry, 4,* 83.

Leuner, H. (1955). Experimentelles Katathymes Bilderleben als ein klinisches Verfahren der Psychotherapie: Grundlegungen und Methoden [Experimental Guided Affective Imagery as a clinical procedure in psychotherapy: Foundations and methods]. *Zeitschrift für Psychotherapie und medizinische Psychologie, 5,* 185–203.

Leuner, H. (1971). Halluzinogene in der Psychotherapie [Hallucinogens in psychotherapy]. *Pharmakopsychiatrie, Neuro-Psychopharmakologie, 4,* 333–351.

Leuner, H. (1978). Basic principles and therapeutic efficacy of Guided Affective Imagery (GAI). In J. L. Singer & K. S. Pope (Eds.), *The power of human imagination: New methods in psychotherapy.* New York: Plenum.

Leuner, H. (Ed.) (1980). *Katathymes Bilderleben: Ergebnisse in Theorie und Praxis* [Guided affective imagery: Results in theory and practice]. Bern: Huber.

Leuner, H. (1981a). *Katathymes Bilderleben: Grundstufe* [Guided Affective Imagery: Basic level]. Stuttgart: Georg Thieme.

Leuner, H. (1981b). *Halluzinogene: Psychische Grenzzustände in* Forschung und Psychotherapie [Hallucinogens: Psychological borderline states in research and psychotherapy]. Bern: Huber.

Leuner, H. (1985). *Lehrbuch des Katathymen Bilderlebens* [Textbook of guided affective imagery]. Bern: Huber.

Lipsky, M. J., Kassinove, H., & Miller, N. J. (1980). Effects of rational–emotive therapy, rational role reversal, and rational–emotive imagery on the emotional adjustment of community mental health center patients. *Journal of Consulting and Clinical Psychology,* 48, 366–374.

Lukas, E. S. (1972). Zur Validierung der Logotherapie [Toward the validation of logotherapy]. In V. E. Frankl, *Der Wille zum Sinn: Ausgewählte Vorträge über Logotherapie* [The will to meaning: Selected lectures on logotherapy]. Bern: Huber.

Mascher, E. (1966). *Katamnestische Untersuchungen von Ergebnissen der psycholytischen Therapie* [Catemnestic investigation of outcomes of psycholytic therapy]. Unpublished M.D. Dissertation, University of Göttingen.

Mascher, E. (1967). Psycholytic therapy: Statistics and indications. In H. Brill, J. O. Cole, H. Hippius, & P. B. Bradley, *Neuro-psychopharmacology.* Amsterdam: Excerpta Medica Foundation.

Moreno, J. L. (1972). *Psychodrama* (Vol. 1) (4th ed.). Beacon, NY: Beacon House.

Newton, M. C. (1977). Early treatment of alcohol abuse through a brief program of covert sensitization and aversive olfactory conditioning. (Doctoral dissertation, University of Oregon, 1977). *Dissertation Abstracts International,* 38, 3288-A.

Richardson, A. (1969). *Mental imagery.* New York: Springer.

Robins, L. N. (1974). *The Viet Nam drug user returns.* Washington, DC: U.S. Government Printing Office.

Sarret, M., Cheek, F., Osmond, H. (1966). Reports of wives of alcoholics of effects of LSD-25 treatment of their husbands. *Archives of General Psychiatry,* 14, 171–178.

Shorr, J. (1983). *Psychotherapy through imagery* (2nd ed.). New York: Thieme-Stratton.

Singer, J. L. (1974). *Imagery and daydreaming methods in psychotherapy and behavior modification.* New York: Academic Press.

Singer, J. L., & Antrobus, J. S. (1972). Daydreaming, imaginal processes, and personality: A normative study. In P. W. Sheehan (Ed.), *The function and nature of imagery.* New York: Academic Press.

Singer, J. L., & Pope, K. S. (Eds.) (1978). *The power of human imagination: New methods in psychotherapy.* New York: Plenum.

Stampfl, T. G., & Levis, D. J. (1967). Essentials of implosion therapy: A learning-theory-based psychodynamic behavioral therapy. *Journal of Abnormal Psychology,* 72, 496–503.

Starr, A. (1977). *Psychodrama: Illustrated therapeutic techniques.* Chicago: Nelson Hall.

Virshup, E., & Virshup, B. (1981). An art therapy approach to the drug abuser, correlating behavioral, narcissistic, and laterality theory. In E. Klinger (Ed.), *Imagery: Vol. 2. Concepts, results, and applications.* New York: Plenum.

Wächter, H.-M., & Leuner, H. (1978). Kurztherapie eines Drogensüchtigen mit dem Katathymen Bilderleben [Brief therapy with a drug addict with Guided Affective Imagery]. In H. Leuner, G. Horn, & E. Klessmann, Katathymes Bilderleben mit Kindern und Jugendlichen [Guided affective imagery with children and adolescents]. Munich: Ernest Reinhardt.

Wächter, H.-M., & Pudel, V. (1980). Kurztherapie von 15 Sitzungen mit dem Katathymen Bilderleben [Brief therapy of 15 sessions with guided affective imagery]. In H. Leuner

156

(Ed.), *Katathymes Bilderleben: Ergebnisse in Theorie und Praxis* [Guided affective imagery: Results in theory and practice]. Bern: Huber.

Wadeson, H. (1980). *Art psychotherapy.* New York: Wiley.

Wilke, E. (1980). Das Katathyme Bilderleben bei der konservativen Behandlung der Colitis ulcerosa [Guided affective imagery in the conservative treatment of colitis ulcerosa]. In H. Leuner (Ed.), *Katathymes Bilderleben: Ergebnisse in Theorie und Praxis* [Guided affective imagery: Results in theory and practice]. Bern: Huber.

Wilson, G. T., & Tracy, D. A. (1976). An experimental analysis of aversive imagery versus electrical aversive conditioning in the treatment of chronic alcoholics. *Behavior Research and Therapy,* **14,** 41–51.

Wisocki, P. A. (1972). The empirical evidence of covert sensitization in the treatment of alcoholism: An evaluation. In R. D. Rubin, H. Fensterheim, J. D. Henderson, & L. P. Ullmann (Eds.), *Advances in behavior therapy.* New York: Academic Press.

Wolpe, J. (1958). *Psychotherapy by reciprocal inhibition.* Stanford: Stanford University Press.

Wood, D., Del Nuovo, A., Bucky, S. F., Schein, S., & Michalik, M. (1979). Psychodrama with an alcohol abuser population. *Group Psychotherapy, Psychodrama and Sociometry,* **32,** 75–88.

8

Self-Help Groups and Other Group Procedures for Treating Alcohol Problems

RICHARD W. THORESON AND FRANK C. BUDD

Department of Educational and Counseling Psychology
University of Missouri
Columbia, Missouri 65211

I. HISTORICAL DEVELOPMENT OF GROUP PROCEDURES

The use of group methods as a medium for personal and behavioral changes dates to the beginnings of recorded history. Religious healers used group forces to increase morale, inspire hope, and to counteract psychic and bodily ills. However, when the power to heal passed from the religious to the medical profession, the focus of treatment moved away from the group to the sanctity of the doctor–patient relationship (Lieberman, 1980).

The current proliferation of group methods owes its resurrection to several influential forces. The catalyst for the current use of group methods is usually attributed to Joseph Pratt, a Boston internist who organized classes for tubercular patients in 1907. Another influence was the use of group methods by an English psychoanalyst, Trigon L. Burrow. Burrow believed social forces played a role in the functioning of the individual and placed his patients into groups to analyze behavior disorders in relation to social forces. The term, *group analysis,* is attributed to Burrow's work. The first peak in the use of group methods occurred in the 1940s in response to the abundance of military personnel needing mental health services and the shortage of treatment personnel. The next and most recent peak occurred in the early 1970s with the encounter or self-enhancement movement. The uses and

157

TREATMENT AND PREVENTION
OF ALCOHOL PROBLEMS: A RESOURCE MANUAL

abuses of group methods during this period are described by Lieberman, Yalom, and Miles (1973).

At present, the use of group methods has reached such popularity that it now appears there is a group for any type of problem an individual may have (MacLennan, Beryce, & Levy, 1970). In general, however, a group can be broadly defined as a collection of individuals who meet at a predetermined place and time for a specified purpose. Groups may have designated leaders (therapists, facilitators, trainers) or be leaderless (such as the many self-help organizations, e.g., Alcoholics Anonymous, Narcotics Anonymous, Al-Anon, Over-Eaters Anonymous). They may focus on resolution of difficulties and personal change (usually referred to as therapy or counseling groups) or actualization of potential (variously termed T-groups, encounter groups, and growth groups). They may be short- or long-term, open (to new members) or closed (membership fixed at start), and they may focus on individual or interpersonal issues.

A. The Benefits of Group Methods for Alcohol Problems

At the present time, there is considerable enthusiasm for group methods for persons with alcohol problems (Albrecht, 1983; Flores, 1982; Ulrich, 1982). As Blume (1978) states, one of the most important reasons for the use of group methods concerns the dynamics of those it is used to help. Throughout the development of an alcohol problem, the individual becomes more and more alienated from others and from him/herself (Johnson, 1973). A sensitive and insightful description of the lonely and chaotic inner world of alcoholics is provided by Wallace (1977). The use of group methods provides a forum for the alcoholic to become resocialized and reintegrated into the world of other human beings. Through the use of interpersonal feedback and self-exploration, the group enables the person with alcohol problems to become aware of and appreciate his/her strengths. Focus is also placed on additional areas needed for growth. Hobbs (1951), speaking on group methods in general, states:

> It is one thing to be understood and accepted by a therapist, it is considerably a more potent experience to be understood and accepted by several people who are also honestly sharing their feelings in a joint search for a more satisfying way of life (p. 22).

The process by which one experiences acceptance and honest feedback is especially true for the interactional or "here-and-now" group method used by Yalom (1974, 1975; Brown & Yalom, 1977). In this type of group, the individual's fear of and repugnance for self-disclosure is wholly contradicted, and he/she learns the group therapeutic paradox that the more fears and inadequacies he/she shares with others, the more he/she is valued. In contrast, considerable force is generated in the group to confront the typical denial and rationalizing of members. While most alcoholic individuals can distort or dodge a single confrontation (as any family member can attest), the power and influence of the group as a whole often overcome any dishonesty or self-deception of the individual members.

Although clinical support abounds for the use of group methods, empirical support remains weak (Solomon, 1981). One point of controversy regards the efficacy of group methods with female alcoholics (Avery, 1976; Blume, 1978; Curlee, 1967; Lindbeck, 1975). Annis (1980), reviewing the outcome results of the various contradictory studies, states, "Group therapy characterized four of the five studies reporting better outcomes for females than males, and in one of these studies (Fox & Smith, 1959), group therapy was described as the backbone of the therapeutic program" (p. 131). She further concludes, "present evidence fails to provide any basis for concluding the inappropriateness of group techniques for the female alcoholic" (p. 131). While the inappropriateness of group methods for this subpopulation with alcohol problems can be ruled out, the overall appropriateness of group methods for the larger population needs further research support.

B. Types of Groups for Alcohol Problems

There are two primary considerations for the use of groups; one is the setting and the other is the process and goals. Groups for alcohol problems can be generally classified into self-help groups and therapy groups. Self-help groups such as AA typically meet in churches or schools, while therapy groups typically are held in formal settings, such as alcoholism treatment centers or alcoholism units in general hospitals. The primary self-help group for alcoholics, Alcoholics Anonymous, serves a primarily supportive function, focuses on alcohol use, and has as its goal a life without alcohol. In contrast, traditional therapy and counseling groups focus on the psychosocial processes underlying the maladaptive use of alcohol and have as their goal improvement in all areas of functioning. The remainder of the present section focuses on group methods in traditional treatment settings and their use with individuals whose health and happiness have become severely impaired by their alcohol problem, while the second section of this chapter discusses self-help group methods at length (using AA as a model).

1. Informational Groups

Informational groups are most often conducted during the initial phases of treatment. The use of this format allows the patients' and families' questions to be answered, allaying anxiety, and fostering realistic expectations and commitment to treatment. A variety of topics may be addressed (e.g., anger, assertiveness, family dynamics, the development of and recovery from alcohol problems). Because the typical alcoholic has spent most of his/her time while involved in the alcohol problem denying its existence, the opportunity provided by this group method serves to solidify commitment to treatment and to obtain much-needed cooperation and support from family members. Family members often need the information provided in this group method to counter the alcoholic's tendency to blame others and assuage their own guilt feelings and anxiety.

2. Activity Groups

Activity groups provide for a more light-hearted engagement of patients and their families. Various activities including dances, sporting events, picnics, and attendance at movies or shows are planned. Use of this group method also provides opportunities for patients and their families to practice planning enjoyable events together and, hopefully, fosters a positive attitude toward treatment. Individuals and their families faced with alcohol problems often lose their sense of joy in life and become depressed and/or apathetic. This group method offers everyone involved a chance to find enjoyment in daily living and for the family member in recovery to begin the process of finding enjoyable substitutes for alcohol.

3. Traditional Therapy Groups

Traditional therapy groups include patient groups, couples groups, spouses groups, family groups, and multiple family groups. The purpose of these various groups is to explore and resolve both individual and interpersonal difficulties or concerns. They usually adhere to the theoretical orientation of the group leader. Typical issues that may be addressed include resentments, how to increase intimacy, and traumas such as death, job loss, or divorce. These are life experiences that may have been covered up during an active alcohol problem. Whether or not abstinence is chosen during treatment, all these issues and many others must be successfully negotiated for full recovery from alcohol problems to occur. Traditional group therapy serves as an effective avenue for resolution of these issues.

4. Variations on a Theme

Two unique contributions to the group therapy literature are offered by Einstein and Jones (1965) and Sands and Hanson (1971). Einstein and Jones describe a heterogeneous group of drug-addicted and non-drug-addicted adolescents. Sands and Hanson used a variation of the couples group approach, pairing male alcoholics with women (other than their wives) who were married to alcoholics. Both approaches are viewed as successful ventures by their authors, who suggest further variations of the traditional therapy group.

The heterogeneous group method of Einstein and Jones (1965), when applied to alcohol problems, might successfully serve as a means to reintroduce the alcoholic to individuals with problems other than alcohol, while ideas, misperceptions, skills, and human foibles are shared among sometimes opposing groups of human beings. The alternate pairing group method of Sands and Hanson (1971), when applied to alcohol problems, offers individuals with alcohol problems a chance to deal with important emotional issues with a partner less directly emotionally involved and provides an opportunity to receive a second opinion on the experience of being involved with someone with an alcohol problem, and, one would hope, facilitating (under proper therapeutic supervision) greater understanding and acceptance for both partners.

C. Recurrent Issues in Group Psychotherapy for Alcohol Problems

1. Group Leader Issues

To implement effective group methods for individuals with alcohol problems, the group leader must overcome two obstacles: a lack of understanding of alcohol dependency and a lack of understanding for his or her own intellectual and emotional processes. A *lack of understanding of alcohol dependency* refers to the traditional search for the cause of alcohol dependency while deemphasizing the dependency itself. The private practitioner is especially vulnerable to this misperception (Glasscote, 1967) and may have pre-existing negative attitudes toward alcoholics or a sense of helplessness regarding their condition and may inappropriately prescribe antianxiety or antidepressant medication instead of referring them to more appropriate resources (Tamerin, Tolor, Holson, & Newmann, 1974). Overlooking the centrality of the alcohol problem and searching for intrapsychic causes is often doomed to failure (Pattison, 1979).

Potential group leaders frequently overcome a lack of self-understanding by becoming more keenly aware of both their impact on others and the impact of others on them. This awareness is emphasized by phenomenological psychotherapists (Jourard, 1964; Rogers, 1957; Truax & Carkhuff, 1967). Leaders must also consider the complexity of alcohol group member interactions as a result of concurrent needs, fantasies, and expectations (Stierlin, 1973). Yalom (1975) provides a cogent account of the dynamic interactions between the leader and the group members, and Flores (1982) specifically addresses group processes and alcohol problems. The importance of leader self-awareness is even more critical if he or she comes from or is currently involved in a family with alcohol problems. Black (1981) and Cermack and Brown (1982) comment on the tendency of children from alcoholic homes to assume certain rigid personality styles (roles) and to maintain these roles into adulthood. Friesen and Casella (1982) describe the "rescuing therapist," and Wegscheider (1981) describes the roles of various professional "enablers." Without leader self-awareness, both the *adult– child* group leader and the group members with alcohol problems will most likely become locked into a self-defeating yet comfortable group process in which the alcohol problem, feelings, growth, and change are all denied. Leaders of alcohol-problem groups need to take particular care of their most important therapeutic tool, themselves.

2. Group Member Issues

When conducting group therapy with individuals with alcohol problems, several recurring issues emerge. These can be generally termed: quasi-group cohesion, panic attacks, dual affiliation, subgrouping, and the intoxicated member.

Quasi-group cohesion (Sanguiliano, 1966) refers to the immediate identification and coming together of group members around the subject of their alcohol problems. An alcohol-free state is obviously an important goal of the group, yet a restricted focus by the group members on their commonality, if maintained past the first two sessions, represents an avoidance maneuver on both individual and group levels. Continued focus on member similarity denies the reality of individual differences and uniqueness.

Panic attacks are descriptive of the intense emotional turmoil that often follows the shift of focus away from alcohol use and "drunkalogs" into more sensitive psychosocial areas. If not prepared for in advance, members may revert to acting out behavior (missed sessions, alcohol use, suicide threats, psychosomatic reactions). For group members who seek abstinence, termination of alcohol use often results in feelings of emotional nakedness and vulnerability. These feelings provide an opportunity to desensitize the alcoholic's fear of intense emotions through the acceptance of the group.

Dual affiliation refers to group therapy members also being members of peer self-help groups (e.g., AA and/or Narcotics Anonymous). The effect of this dual membership often creates conflicting allegiances and can lead to "enemy camping," or the separation of the dual members against those only in the therapy group.

Subgrouping is often the result of escalating internal conflict stemming from dual affiliation, special cliques of certain members, or group members with alcohol problems excluding a group leader without these problems. The last phenomenon cannot go unchecked. To counteract it, we suggest that the group leader with no history of an alcohol problem should demonstrate increased sensitivity to the human bond of the group, to the ties of emotional pain, anguish, joy, and triumph that unite all human beings. The group leader who is unable to capitalize on these shared human features, through ignorance of alcohol problems or his/her own blocks to emotionality and growth, will likely remain excluded from the group.

The *intoxicated member* can be a special irritant to the group leader. If an intoxicated member is not challenged, the progress of the session and group as a whole may be stalemated. Vannicelli (1982) speaks of "drinking in the service of the group," describing how drinking can be a defensive function for both the individual and the group.

D. Strategies for Resolving Group Issues

The preceding group issues can often be resolved through confrontation and group structure created, for example, by specifying member goals and written agendas for each session. Effective confrontation: (1) necessitates the group leader's deep concern and willingness to become more deeply involved with the member(s) confronted and (2) involves an invitation to the member for self-examination (Egan, 1970). Two different approaches to the use of confrontation are provided by Bratter (1981) and Wallace (1978a). Bratter (1981) describes his confrontation group psychotherapy as "an educational-learning-based orientation" that "forces individuals to recognize the potentially annihilative aspects of their behavior." Bratter suggests that this style of confrontation can be applied almost immediately. In contrast, Wallace (1978a) describes working with the alcoholic's "preferred defense system" (PDS). Wallace sees the alcoholic PDS as "a collection of skills or abilities—tactics and strategies to be protected and capitalized upon." Wallace refrains from directly challenging the PDS until "two to five years of abstinence" have been obtained.

The group leader may work to prevent or eliminate unnecessary anxiety and confusion through careful pregroup orientation (Brown & Yalom, 1977), individual and group contracts regarding the ground rules and goals (Vannicelli, 1982), the use of written agendas for each session, videotape recordings and playback, written summaries of group sessions, and utilization of support systems (Brown & Yalom, 1977).

The most appropriate method for resolving the critical issues of group therapy for persons with alcohol problems thus seems to be to prevent them from occurring, through awareness of the special characteristics and behaviors in alcohol problem groups. Further details on how this may be achieved can be found in Wallace (1978b), Vannicelli (1982), Brown and Yalom (1977), Vogel (1957), and Mullan and Sanguiliano (1966).

II. SELF-HELP GROUPS

Since the mid-1970s, increased attention has been given to self-help groups as a means of effecting and maintaining behavioral change. Mutual-help groups cover a wide spectrum of problems and predicaments (e.g., Parents Without Partners, The Little People of America, Overeaters Anonymous, Gamblers Anonymous, and Alcoholics Anonymous [AA]). AA has been viewed in a variety of ways (e.g., an alternative form of caregiving, an intentional community support system, a social movement, an adjunct to therapy, a way of life, and a religious movement; see Gartner & Riessman, 1979; Killilea, 1976). In response to the devastating impact of alcoholism on family members, two additional self-help groups with programs based on the principles and steps of Alcoholics Anonymous have been developed—Al-Anon for families and close friends of alcoholics and Al-Ateen, the Al-Anon program for younger family members.[1]

In this section, we use AA as paradigmatic of mutual-help groups by looking at how AA works, with whom it works, and when it should be used. Specifically, we look at (1) the early history and development of AA; (2) the AA program, its meetings, steps, traditions, and literature; (3) the rationale, therapeutic dynamics, and factors in success of AA; and (4) components of effective liaison between AA and the professional treatment community.

A. A Brief History of AA

Alcoholics Anonymous, a movement characterized by Kurtz (1980, 1981) as having great, but infrequently noted intellectual significance, is undergirded by a fundamental axiom that alteration of major belief systems must precede behavior change (e.g., Vaillant, 1983). Thus, a radical life change is the underlying goal of the AA program, and spiritual revelation or spiritual awakening is an integral part of the process that leads to this radical change.

Alcoholics Anonymous started in 1934 when Bill W., its founder, was a patient in a hospital in New York City. His physician, William Silkworth, diagnosed Bill as a hopeless alcoholic. It was at this point that Bill W. reported a spiritual revelation or spiritual awakening: "All about me and through me there was a feeling of presence, and I thought to myself, 'so this is the God of the preachers.' A great peace stole over me and I thought, 'no matter how wrong things seem to be, they are still all right. Things are all right with God and his world'" (*Alcoholics Anonymous Comes of Age,* 1957/1983, p. 63). This "conversion experience" was to become a part of the basic formula of radical life change requisite to sobriety; Bill W. was to be recognized as its spiritual leader; alcoholism was to be viewed as a threefold disease of body, mind, and spirit; the achievement of sobriety was to be contingent upon maintaining a major change in belief system or personality.

Bill W.'s sudden change is not commonplace among AA members. Instead, the terms "spiritual experience" and "spiritual awakening" in the AA

[1]Al-Anon's *12 Steps and 12 Traditions* (1981) and other literature, pamphlets, books, booklets are available from Al-Anon Family Group Headquarters, Inc., 115 East 23rd Street, New York, New York 10010.

literature more accurately refer to personality change sufficient that recovery from alcoholism can occur. Changes typically involve a slowly developing transformation in outlook consisting of acquiring, through increased awareness, an appreciation of one's inner complexity or an "unsuspected inner resource" which members view as a power greater than themselves (*Alcoholics Anonymous,* 1939/1955/1984, pp. 569–570).

Thus, the concept of a spiritual awakening, frequently misunderstood by critics of AA as a religious concept, points to the recognition in the AA program that a radical change in outlook is a requisite for changing a deeply embedded involuntary habit. Although it clearly draws on religious principles, AA is not a religious program. It is a program directed toward attaining major changes in behavior and attitudes while maintaining a distinction between the spiritual elements of AA (emphasizing the inner nature of humans) and religious elements (referring to orthodox religious practice).

The AA program is described in *Alcoholics Anonymous Comes of Age* (1957/1983). The basic AA concepts are attributed to several specific influences from psychology, psychiatry, and religion. First, the program draws on William James' concepts of "surrender to a power greater than ourselves" and "deflation at depth" (James, 1978). Second, AA's principle architect, Bill W., was influenced by Carl Jung, the first of a number of twentieth-century humanistic psychologists to stress the deeper spiritual needs of men and women as pivotal to the process of developing into fully functioning persons. Jung concluded that in the case of alcoholics, the best means of attaining sobriety was through a spiritual experience *(AA comes of Age,* 1957/1983). This spiritual awakening or radical change in outlook was adopted as the goal of the AA program.

Third, the AA program was shaped by the movement of the Oxford Group, a religious revivalist organization. AA's basic doctrine is based on Oxford Group principles: (1) though we have behaved badly, (2) we can change; (3) confession is a prerequisite to change; (4) the person so changed will have direct access to God; (5) the age of miracles has returned; and (6) those who have changed must change others (*Alcoholics Anonymous Comes of Age,* 1957/1983). Although the Oxford Group principles are clearly religious in tone, their adaptation to Alcoholics Anonymous has clear implications for the medical treatment of alcoholism. In fact, Bill W. emphasized that alcoholism is a disease. Once the alcoholic admits to powerlessness over alcohol, he or she is responsible for following the program of AA in order to keep the disease in remission.

The Little Red Book (Hazelden Educational Services, 1957), a publication which serves to amplify the basic steps and traditions of AA, provides an excellent example of the total life change component as a requisite of sobriety and the paradox therein. "The AA program by which we effect our recovery is simple. Actually, it needs little interpretation. It will work if we live it" (p. 10). Although the basic steps and principles of AA are simple, "working" the AA program involves a radical change in lifestyle. The AA literature stresses that AA is designed for the uncontrolled drinker who sincerely desires to achieve sobriety and is "willing to go to any length" to get it. The latter point stresses the major commitment to change requisite to success in AA. In order to keep alcoholism in remission via the AA program, the alcoholic must show the capacity to maintain an open mind toward the key spiritual concept of AA—that is, that resources beyond those readily apparent or, in AA language, "a power greater than oneself" can lead to sobriety and a lifting of the compulsion to drink.

Contrary to the implications of its spiritual-religious language, the AA program is a direct, simple action program as indicated in the preamble to AA:

> The only requirement for membership is a desire to stop drinking. There are no dues or fees for AA membership; we are self-supporting through our own contributions. AA is not allied with any sect, denomination, politics, organization or institution; it does not wish to engage in any controversy; neither endorses nor opposes any causes. Our primary purpose is to stay sober and help other alcoholics to achieve sobriety. (*AA Grapevine,* 1984a, p. 1).

B. The AA Meeting: Accent on Action

The central focus of the AA program is its regular series of meetings of which there are two types. One type is the open meeting ("speakers' meetings") which is open to family, friends, and the alcoholics themselves. During these meetings, the recovered alcoholic describes how life was when he or she was drinking and compares it with how it is now that he or she is a sober AA member. The second type of meeting is the closed meeting, which is restricted to men and women who have a "desire to stop drinking."

Both the open and the closed meetings are usually limited to an hour. The time limit is important, as recovering alcoholics in AA often are restless, energetic people. Both types of meetings generally open with a reading of the AA preamble, sometimes followed by the reading of the Serenity Prayer (which is a short-hand version of the AA program): "God grant me the serenity to accept the things I cannot change, the courage to change the things I can, and the wisdom to know the difference" (Alcoholics Anonymous World Service, Inc., 1983, p. 18). The Serenity Prayer contains the essence of the AA program, including the key elements of courage, responsibility, acceptance, intelligent action, and humility.

These readings are sometimes followed by a reading of Chapter 5, "How It Works," from the book *Alcoholics Anonymous* (1939/1955/1984). The meetings often end with recitation of the Lord's Prayer while members join hands as a way to signify the mutuality of recovery—the giving, caring, and sharing of the strength of the group. However, each AA group is free to operate with considerable autonomy regarding the specifics of the meeting. This variability corresponds to the wide variation in sociodemographic characteristics (e.g., gender, age, vocation, ethnicity, and socioeconomic status) in AA membership, with powerlessness over alcohol as the common denominator.

The more frequent closed meeting provides the opportunity for alcoholics to share their experiences and, in this sharing of mutual vulnerabilities, to help each other learn to live comfortably without alcohol. In these meetings, one member volunteers to lead the meeting and discussion. Topics include practical ones such as how to deal with resentments, depression, anonymity, gratitude, holidays, old drinking companions, family relationships, dual addictions, responsibility, growth, and slips (relapses), and more abstract topics such as surrendering oneself to a higher power or the limits to personal power. In short, the meeting time is spent sharing experiences that help in living a new life free of alcohol.

C. The Behavioral Change Strategy

In a typical meeting, the volunteer leader might introduce the topic of "dealing with resentments" in this fashion: "I have been very resentful towards my husband/wife this past week. The Big Book (*Alcoholics Anonymous*, 1939/1955/1984) tells us that resentments are our number one offender. Resentment destroys more alcoholics than anything else. I have been burdened by resentments, and would like to know how others of you deal with this problem." Usually, each member is called on in turn, providing a nonthreatening but positive method for people to talk about their program of sobriety, to become known to other AA members, and to be active in the AA program. There are also "step meetings" in which each of the 12 AA steps (one per meeting) is read aloud and discussed (Alcoholics Anonymous World Services, Inc., 1953/1984).

D. The "Twelve Steps" of the AA Program and Their Therapeutic Analogues

The Twelve Steps of AA are the key to sobriety through AA. Chapter 5 of *Alcoholics Anonymous* (1939/1955/1984) describes the process of change: "Our story of what we were like, what happened to us, and finally, what we are like now." Chapter 5 goes on to underscore the vital importance of a strong commitment to the AA program and introduces the concept of the assumption of personal responsibility: "If you have decided you want what we have and are willing to go to any length to get it, then you are ready to take certain steps" (p. 58).

The twelve steps of the AA program, though couched in spiritual terms, can be seen to have direct therapeutic analogues. Step one is pivotal: "We admitted we were powerless over alcohol — that our lives had become unmanageable." It involves a vital paradox for recovery from alcoholism within the AA framework (i.e., "out of defeat comes victory, out of letting go comes control, out of powerlessness comes power"). Step one is analogous to the *problem identification stage* in psychotherapy.

Step two, "Came to believe that a power greater than ourselves could restore us to sanity," closely resembles William James' description of "healthy-mindedness": "It is summed up neatly in one sentence 'God is well and so are you — you must awaken to the knowledge of your real being.'" (James, 1978, p. 113). The therapeutic analogue is *admission of need for help*.

Step three, "made a decision to turn our will and our lives over to God as we understand Him," expresses a belief in the power of positive attitudes and in the efficacy of courage, hope, and trust accompanied by an awareness of the futility of doubt, fear, worry, and "all nervously precautionary states of mind" (James, 1978). The therapeutic analogue to step three is a *commitment to work with the therapist to solve the problem(s)*.

The first three steps are a basic recovery prescription. Their purpose is to help abate the alcoholic's self-centeredness. Again, James describes the necessity of "surrender," passivity, and giving up responsibility in order to experience success in experiencing the sense of "higher power" (1978, pp. 108–109).

Steps four through nine are the action steps. Step four, "made a searching and fearless moral inventory of ourselves," identifies the alcoholics' assets and liabilities and provides, in Thune's (1977) terms, "A model of 'what we were' in order to gain a model of 'what we can be in our new life.'" Admission of harmful traits leads paradoxically to their opposite. Step four's therapeutic analogue involves the *reformulation of the problem into root causes, assets, and liabilities*.

Step five, "admitted to God, to ourselves, and to another human being the exact nature of our wrongs," is the confession or "cleansing" step. It prepares the alcoholic to acquire the humility, honesty, and spiritual help necessary successfully to live the AA program. *Admitting to one's part in the problem and problem reformulation* with the therapist constitutes the therapeutic analogue for this step.

Steps six and seven are the AA steps that help define the alcoholic's readiness for radical change in attitude. Step six, "were entirely ready to have God remove all these defects of character," and step seven, "humbly asked Him to remove our shortcomings," stress the need for humility. This step again illustrates the AA paradox: through the recognition of limits to personal power and the acceptance of these limitations, one does not lose, but instead gains personal freedom and power through drawing on unsuspected inner resources. The therapeutic analogue is the *commitment to change and efforts to put this commitment into action.*

Step eight, "made a list of all persons we had harmed," and step nine, "made direct amends to such people wherever possible, except when to do so would injure them or others," are concerned with personal relationships. It is suggested that the alcoholic look backward to discover where he or she might have been at fault, to make a vigorous effort to repair the damage done, and after making appropriate amends with friends and family, to consider how, with the newfound knowledge of self, he or she can develop the best possible interpersonal relationships. *Taking responsibility for one's actions and feelings* constitutes the therapeutic analogue for these steps.

Step ten, "continued to take personal inventory and when we were wrong promptly admitted it," step eleven, "Sought through prayer and meditation to improve our conscious contact with God as we understood Him, praying only for knowledge of His will for us and the power to carry that out," and step twelve, "having had a spiritual awakening as the result of these steps, we tried to carry this message to alcoholics and to practice these principles in all our affairs," are referred to as the maintenance steps. The alcoholic "works" the first nine steps and prepares him or herself for the new life. Step ten is a daily extension and revision of step four where the alcoholic puts the AA program of living into daily practice.

Step ten underscores the importance of self-examination, responsibility, and the inner journey necessary to a program of growth and development. Although the fact of one's alcoholism is inescapable, once having accepted this as a condition, the alcoholic becomes responsible for rectifying wrongs done during the acute phase of his or her alcoholism and for maintaining sobriety. The therapeutic analog is the *task of incorporating therapeutic change into one's daily life.*

Step eleven stresses the importance of the inner journey from which unsuspected sources of wisdom and strength can be garnered. The therapeutic analog is the *use of daily meditation to help further integrate and facilitate those changes begun in therapy.*

Step twelve provides what is tantamount to an official sanction of the new lifestyle made possible through therapy. The therapeutic analog is the *recognition and acceptance of the changes brought about through therapy and the sharing of this new outlook with friends and family.*

E. The "Twelve Traditions"

The Twelve Traditions of AA are the rules that govern the organization. They spell out AA's position on such fundamental issues as anonymity, professional versus nonprofessional status, outside financing, promotion versus attraction of new members and membership requirements, opinions on outside issues, governing body, group welfare, and organizational principles. The history and development of the traditions are presented in three AA publications (*Alcoholics Anonymous Comes of Age: A Brief History of AA,* 1957/1983; *Twelve Steps and Twelve Traditions,* 1953/1984; and *Dr. Bob and the Good Oldtimers: A Biography with Recollections of Early AA in the Midwest,* 1984b). See Table 1 for a list of the Twelve Traditions.

F. The AA Sponsor

Fundamental to the AA program is the concept of the sponsor. New AA members are urged to seek as a sponsor one of the members who has had an extended period of contented sobriety. He or she is a confidant, an "older brother or sister," and lay therapist to one or more of his or her colleagues in AA. The sponsor–member relationship is a quasi-therapeutic one in which both the core facilitative conditions of trust, caring, respect, nurturance, and cognitive–behavioral strategies such as behavioral contracting (e.g., attend 30 meetings in the next 30 days) are present. Sponsorship epitomizes one of the key features of AA: In order to maintain contented sobriety, it is necessary for alcoholics to share their sobriety with others. This sharing of experi-

TABLE 1

The Twelve Traditions of AA

1. Our common welfare should come first: personal recovery depends upon AA unity;
2. For our group purpose, there is but on ultimate authority—a loving God as He may express Himself in our group conscience. Our leaders are but trusted servants; they do not govern;
3. The only requirement for AA membership is a desire to stop drinking;
4. Each group should be autonomous except in matters affecting other groups or AA as a whole;
5. Each group has but one primary purpose—to carry its message to the alcoholic who still suffers;
6. An AA group ought never endorse, finance, or lend the AA name to any related facility or outside enterprise, lest problems of money, property, and prestige divert us from our primary purpose;
7. Every AA group ought to be fully self-supporting, declining outside contributions;
8. Alcoholics Anonymous should remain forever nonprofessional, but our service centers may employ special workers;
9. AA, as such, ought never be organized; but we may create service boards or committees directly responsible to those they serve;
10. Alcoholics Anonymous has no opinion on outside issues; hence the AA name ought never be drawn into public controversy;
11. Our public relations policy is based on attraction rather than promotion; we need always maintain personal anonymity at the level of press, radio, and films;
12. Anonymity is the spiritual foundation of all our traditions, ever reminding us to place principles before personalities.

ence also serves to channel the restless energy of recovering alcoholics into action, giving them something constructive to do during the hours that they formerly spent drinking. Rules of sponsorship acknowledge the problems of mixing sexual/mentor relationships. In general, male–female sponsor– member pairings are discouraged.

G. AA Literature

The literature developed by AA is intended to be an integral part of the organization, to be used regularly at AA meetings and in daily living. The officially sanctioned, or conference-approved, literature of AA is limited. There are presently five books, two booklets, and approximately 40 pamphlets for sale and use by AA members and the general public. That the AA literature is limited actually is an advantage insofar as it provides the alcoholic with clear, direct exposure to the AA program of recovery without introducing the ambiguities and complexities of the disease as described in the vast array of publications available elsewhere. For example, Hazelden Press of Center City, Minnesota, publishes over 1000 books, pamphlets, and other educational materials all directly related to explicating the AA program of recovery (Hazelden Educational Materials Catalogue, 1984).[2]

The basic text for recovery, often referred to as the "Big Book" or "the Bible," is *Alcoholics Anonymous* (1939/1955/1984), which has religious overtones. Whitley (1977) perceives *Alcoholic Anonymous* as a "New Testament Gospel in 11 chapters" and in which Chapter 5, "How it Works," constitutes the pivotal New Testament chapter, one that helps AA members become initiated into the AA lifestyle. The "Big Book" also includes a section, "A Vision for You," which Whitley identifies as akin to the Book of Revelations. Whitley suggests that Part 2 of the "Big Book" (the stories) directly parallels the "Acts of Apostles," since the stories portray "the experiences of AA's early 'church fathers' in which battles of those, who against almost 'impossible odds,' won their way into the promised land of sobriety and the final victories of those whose cases seemed hopeless until the miracle happened" (p. 384). Although the tone of the "Big Book" is frankly religious, the program itself translates neatly into a practical recovery guide for alcoholics who wish to maintain sobriety.

Other literature commonly used in AA includes these "conference approved" books and booklets: *Alcoholics Anonymous* (1939/1955/1984), *Twelve Steps and Twelve Traditions* (1953/1984), *Alcoholics Anonymous Comes of Age* (1957/1983), *Dr. Bill and the Good Oldtimers* (1984b), *As Bill Sees It* (1967/1974), *Come to Believe* (1973/1980), *Living Sober* (1975). In addition, several texts published by Hazelden: *Stools and Bottles* (1955),

[2]Box 176, Pleasant Valley Road, Center City, MN 55012.

Twenty-Four Hours A Day (1975), and the *Little Red Book* (1957) are popular among AA members.[3] The AA approach, as exemplified in its literature, is both practical and behavioral. General behavioral strategies include making social approval contingent upon appropriate behavior leading to sobriety, rerouting social reinforcements via AA provision of personal friendships, and imitation or modeling through members serving as models of sobriety with whom the newcomer can identify (Burt, 1975).

H. Therapeutic Dynamics of AA

AA has been described by Oden (1972) as a "demythologized and secularized form of religious piety" specifically "tailored to the personality and the needs of recovered alcoholics." It contributes a particular kind of intensive small group experience, one that provides the alcoholic with mutual support through shared vulnerability.

AA is also a therapeutic community; there are norms for conduct, factors promoting cohesiveness, means for managing conflict, interpersonal learning, and competition (Gellman, 1964). It is, in the sociological sense, a special community with models, in the form of personal narratives, of "how it was," from which models for a new and joyful, spiritual life can be forged (Thune, 1977).

AA uses cognitive behavioral strategies such as self-monitoring of drinking, rerouting of social reinforcement, covert sensitization, restructuring irrational thoughts, modeling, and imitation (Burt, 1975). Vaillant (1983), pointing to the careful attention to the process of initiating the new learning paradigm for alcoholics, observes that "like the best behavior therapy, AA meetings not only go on daily, especially on weekends and holidays, but singlemindedly underscore the special ways that alcoholics delude themselves" (p. 301).

AA uses an existential, dialectic approach, which includes these components: taking personal responsibility, staying in the here and now ("one day at a time" — a 24-hour recovery program); observing polarities and paradoxes (e.g., in order to know true compassion, one needs to experience resentment and hatred); getting in touch with one's undesirable aspects (e.g., self-pity, grandiosity, fear, hate, greed, guilt) in order to truly know their opposites (e.g., acceptance, freedom from guilt and fear, honest thinking, and true happiness). The AA member who comes to understand these concepts acquires a sense of comfort and awe about the richness of life and the possibilities that it provides.

In summary, AA provides a complex, spiritual, behavioral–therapeutic

---

[3]A variety of pamphlets on AA recovery is available from AA World Services, Box 459, Grand Central Station, New York, New York 10163.

prescription for dealing with sobriety. As we noted, it uses religious principles although it is not religious in nature. It uses a special language, special literature, special doctrines and creeds, and special ceremonies that altogether constitute a special community or "cult."

I. Characteristics of AA Members

AA membership in the United States has been estimated at over 1,000,000 (Alcoholics Anonymous, 1976), with actual reported membership in the United States and Canada from registered groups at 476,000 (Alcoholics Anonymous, 1981). The latter report, from a 1980 membership survey, shows these demographic characteristics of AA members: 69% are males, 31% females (the percentage of women in AA has risen from 22% in 1968). The percentage sample in various age groups breaks down as: 30 or under— 15%; 31 to 50—51%; and over 50—32%. There has been a gradual increase in the number of young members in AA. Referral sources of members included other AA members—42%; self—27%, family—21%, counseling or treatment centers and physicians—9%. There has been a substantial increase in referrals from counseling and treatment centers from 19% in 1977 to 33% for those entering AA since 1977.

AA members are characterized, at point of entry into AA and as compared to their non-AA counterparts, as more likely to be unmarried, to be solitary drinkers, to be more verbal, less dysphoric, and more energetic (Alcoholics Anonymous, 1981). They also tend to have higher IQs and higher affiliation needs (Bailey & Leach, 1965; Gynther & Brilliant, 1967; Jackson, 1958; Jones, 1970; Leach & Norris, 1977; Robinson, 1979; Trice, 1959; Trice & Roman, 1972). Nevertheless, because of the likelihood of biased sampling, these generalizations should be accepted cautiously (Baekeland, Lundwell, & Kissin, 1975).

The aforementioned membership survey suggests that new members of AA are likely to be single, between the ages of 30 and 50, attend one or fewer meetings per week, are from the middle social class, and to have lost drinking friends, but to have supportive primary male or female relationships. Finally, new AA members are likely to be dependent, guilt-prone, orderly, and authoritarian and to use rationalization and reaction formation as defenses. However these characteristics do not apply to AA members with long-term sobriety in AA (DeSoto, 1983; Vaillant, 1983). Initial maladjustment followed by good long-term adjustment is consistent with the AA policy of urging new members to alter major character defects and replace them with the positive attributes that are made possible through working the AA program. A more detailed description of AA membership characteristics may be found in Bailey and Leach, 1965; and Robinson, 1979.

J. Factors in AA Success

Questions have been raised regarding the efficacy of AA with claims of its success challenged by Sobell and Sobell (1979) and Tournier (1979); and with AA vigorously defended by Madsen (1979), Rosenberg (1979), and Schulman (1979). Actually, AA members do not claim that AA is the best approach for getting sober; they often assert, in fact, that hospitals and clinics (many of which use the AA model) are more effective. Others, however, have concluded that AA is at least as effective as inpatient treatment (Bailey & Leach, 1965; Edwards, Hensman, Hawker, & Williamson, 1966). Still others have concluded that a combination of AA and formal treatment is most effective (C. Bill, 1965; Erickson, 1966). Vaillant (1983) observed that fundamental personality change occurs through AA attendance, but that it takes considerable time. Hoffman, Harrison, and Belille (1983) found that the alcoholic who attends AA is twice as likely to be abstinent as the alcoholic who does not attend.

DeSoto (1983) reported relatively severe maladjustment among new AA members with significantly decreasing patterns of maladjustment over time. In fact, at the 5-year mark, the adjustment of AA members was seen as remarkably healthy. It seems that AA is particularly attractive and useful for those alcoholics who have experienced significant life problems and at the point of entry into AA feel deep degradation and pain. Armor, Polich, and Stambul (1978), DeSoto (1983), Hoffman et al. (1983), and Vaillant (1983), all find that AA is an effective treatment for many alcoholics. Vaillant (1983) describes four requirements for changing deeply ingrained destructive drinking habits: (1) offer the alcoholic a nonchemical substitute dependency for alcohol, (2) remind him or her ritually that even one drink can lead to pain and relapse, (3) find a vehicle for the alcoholic to repair the social and physical damage that has been experienced, and (4) find a vehicle for restoring self-esteem. According to Vaillant, traditional psychotherapy usually provides only the first and third components, whereas AA provides all four.

AA is not appropriate for every alcoholic (e.g., those with severe psychiatric disorders, from low socioeconomic status, and early problem drinkers; Snyder, 1980; Tournier, 1979; Zinberg, 1977). However, AA support groups constitute an "important component of long-term recovery" for many alcoholics (Hoffman et al., 1983, p. 316). Kurtz (1981) maintains that Alcoholics Anonymous provides a means for the alcoholic to deal simply and successfully with the existential dilemma facing all of us: how to cope with the anguish that comes from knowing our finiteness and limitations. Kurtz argues that through involvement in the AA program, the alcoholic gains an understanding of the paradox that escapes most people—that is, that we delude ourselves into believing that we are near-gods seeking perfection, and in maintaining this delusion we are forever destined to frustration. The alcoholic who engages actively in the AA program comes to know this irrational part of the human experience and deals with it through the process of shared reflections of self found in other alcoholics. Thus, the alcoholic in good recovery in AA is thought to come to terms with a paradox of fundamental importance to contented sobriety: that one gains power precisely through accepting the limitations of personal power.

The acceptance of paradox is a key for contented sobriety in the AA model. The paradoxes of good and bad, ego and no ego, the notion that life defeats our efforts to contain it, and the Buddhist practice of gaining clear awareness of one's internal problems must be confronted. Alcoholics Anonymous teaches that the alcoholic should neither deny nor attempt to eliminate his or her dark or bad side, but rather to understand it, to savor it in order to enrich the good parts of the self. Anger and fear thus become acceptable rather than destructive. This comes as a great relief to the alcoholic who has been controlled and victimized by anger and fear. Kurtz believes that the intellectual significance of Alcoholics Anonymous found in this profound and rich philosophical heritage is often underrated or not seen at all by professional treaters. Yet it is precisely this philosophical heritage that makes AA attractive and palatable to many types of persons with a wide variety of alcohol problems (Kurtz, 1981; Thoreson, 1984).

K. Disease and Spiritual Elements of AA

Siegler and Osmond (1974) argue that the model of alcoholism used in AA, combining as it does both disease and spiritual elements, has a special utility for alcoholics. AA, in its focus on alcoholism as a disease of the spirit, deals directly with the basic dilemma presented to alcoholics—that is, that although not drinking is critical, it is not so much how one deals with problematic drinking as how one copes with sobriety that holds the key to remission.

AA suggests a solution to this dilemma in its insistence on a radical change in perspective toward the self and the world as a requisite to maintaining the disease in remission. In the AA formulation, the disease part of the model is outside the control of the alcoholic—an ego-alien force as it were. And the alcoholic is, through this formulation, both held accountable for keeping his or her disease in remission and spared from personal responsibility and guilt for acquiring the disease. For it is the severe guilt experienced by alcoholics which intensifies denial and increases their resistance to treatment. Alcoholics in AA, therefore, are encouraged to distinguish between their responsibility for sobriety and their responsibility for their alcoholism. This distinction stresses the fact that how the alcoholic got the disease is not important. What is important is that the alcoholic now practices a program that will keep his or her disease in remission. This approach serves to assuage the overriding guilt of alcoholics, to promote responsibility, and to help persuade them that the disease is bigger than they are, that they cannot with their own resources control it. The AA model, with both a spiritual and disease emphasis, focuses on the duties that the alcoholic has as a responsible patient. The alcoholic in recovery is also given a solution to the difficult decision regarding not drinking in a drinking society. He or she can now legitimately decide not to drink. In this sense, the AA concept of "hitting bottom" seems to refer to that moment when the alcoholic finds that it is no longer possible to be a participating member in a drinking society without pain exceeding pleasure.

L. AA and the Professional Community

AA and other self-help groups both help to compensate for the unavailability of professional services, and they contribute something that professional help cannot do. In the AA self-help program, the primary focus is on creating a new sober life rather than searching for the causes of alcoholism. This philosophy clearly separates AA from the professional domain where a search for causes is sine qua non of the scientific enterprise. In AA and other self-help groups, the emphasis is on sharing mutual vulnerabilities, which, according to Robinson (1979), involves two interrelated components: honestly reporting "how it was" during active drinking and seeking to put together a new life through radical life changes. Robinson notes further that AA is a fellowship of equals without any of the power and status differences that are evident in the professional–patient relationship. The process of simultaneously being helped and being a helper becomes an integral part of the recovering alcoholic's way of life.

One of the major strengths of AA as a mutual self-help modality is the way in which the sharing of mutual vulnerabilities increases the capacity of the alcoholic to listen, a capacity which has been greatly impaired during the period of active drinking. Listening is the key to the alcoholic's gaining contented sobriety. By listening to others, the alcoholic gains poignant glimpses of his or her own experiences.

Rapprochement between AA and the professional community is complicated by the unabashed religious tones in the basic text, *Alcoholics Anonymous.* This religious tone often makes it difficult for professionals to see the AA program as it mainly is — a practical, behavioral program for maintaining sobriety. It is important for professionals to understand that AA offers a daily behavioral prescription for the alcoholic to deal with his or her deeply embedded, largely involuntary alcohol habit. It is our thesis that a close liaison between professionals and AA members is possible and will lead to clearer awareness of the underlying behavioral emphases of Alcoholics Anonymous.

Thoreson (1978) described a small group method to assess attitudes toward AA and develop solutions for a better relationship between the AA community and the professional community. The group consisted of both professionals in alcoholism treatment and AA members. Members of the group listed positive and negative characteristics of AA and then provided these practical solutions for better rapprochement between professionals and AA members:

1. There needs to be better public relations in AA
2. AA needs to extend its public relations activity to the total alcoholic community, not merely to its own members
3. Professional counselors should go to open AA meetings, read AA literature, and in this way learn about AA
4. AA members can be helpful by being open about their recovery
5. There should be periodic "rap sessions" between the professionals and the AA members
6. The professional treatment staff should invite AA members to visit the alcoholic patient

Norris (1976) had made additional suggestions for coordinating professional treatment and posttreatment involvement in AA.

III. SUMMARY

Alcoholics Anonymous, with its fundamental emphasis on strength through shared vulnerability, freedom through acceptance of human limitations, and alcoholic equality in a group of equals who acknowledge their mutual vulnerability, represents a significant posthospital treatment and support system for many alcoholics. It contains the components necessary for changing the deeply ingrained destructive drinking habit. The insistence in the AA model that though alcoholics are not responsible for their disease, they are responsible for undertaking a program for recovery which will keep the disease in remission serves to allay guilt and promote responsibility for following a program of recovery.

REFERENCES

Al-Anon Family Group Headquarters, Inc. (1981) *Al-Anon's twelve steps and twelve traditions.*
Albrecht, J. (1983, Fall). Alcoholics in inpatient, short-term interactional group psychotherapy: An outcome study. *Group,* **7,** 50–54.
Alcoholics Anonymous World Services, Inc. (1939/1955/1984). *Alcoholics Anonymous* (3rd ed.). New York.
Alcoholics Anonymous World Services, Inc. (1953/1984). *Twelve steps and twelve traditions.* New York.

Alcoholics Anonymous World Services, Inc. (1957/1983). *Alcoholics Anonymous comes of age: A brief history of AA.* New York.

Alcoholics Anonymous World Services, Inc. (1967/1974). *As Bill sees it.* New York.

Alcoholics Anonymous World Services, Inc. (1973/1980). *Came to believe.* New York.

Alcoholics Anonymous World Services, Inc. (1975/1983). *Living sober.* New York.

Alcoholics Anonymous World Services, Inc. (1976). *Alcoholics Anonymous membership survey.* New York.

Alcoholics Anonymous World Services, Inc. (1981). *Alcoholics Anonymous membership survey.* New York.

Alcoholics Anonymous World Services, Inc. (1984a). *AA Grapevine, Inc.* New York, **41(6)**, 1.

Alcoholics Anonymous World Services, Inc. (1984b). *Dr. Bob and the good oldtimers: A biography with recollections of early AA in the Midwest.* New York.

Annis, H. (1980). Treatment of alcoholic women. In G. Edwards & M. Grant (Eds.), *Alcoholism treatment in transition.* Baltimore, MD: University Park Press.

Armor, D. J., Polich, J. M., & Stambul, H. B. (1978). *Alcoholism and treatment.* New York: John Wiley and Sons.

Avery, J. (1976). Special programs for women. In *Alcohol abuse among women: Special problems and unmet needs.* Washington, DC: Superintendent of Documents, U.S. Government Printing Office.

Baekeland, F., Lundwell, L., & Kissin, B. (1975). Evaluation and treatment methods in chronic alcoholism: A critical appraisal. In R. J. Gibbins, Y. Israel, H. Kolont, R. E. Popham, W. Schmidt, & R. G. Smart (Eds.), *Research advances in alcohol and drug problems* (Vol. 2) New York: John Wiley and Sons.

Bailey, M. B., & Leach, B. (1965). *Alcoholics Anonymous: Pathway to recovery: A study of 1058 members of the AA fellowship in New York City.* New York: National Council on Alcoholism.

Bill, C. (1965). The growth and effectiveness of Alcoholics Anonymous in a southwestern city, 1945–1962. *Quarterly Journal of Studies on Alcohol,* **26,** 179–184.

Black, C. (1981). *It will never happen to me.* Denver, CO: M.A.C.

Blume, S. (1978). Group psychotherapy in the treatment of alcoholism. In S. Zimberg, J. Wallace, & S. Blume (Eds.), *Practical approaches to alcoholism psychotherapy* (pp. 63–75). New York: Plenum.

Bratter, T. E. (1981). Some pre-treatment group psychotherapy considerations with alcoholic and drug-addicted individuals. *Psychotherapy: Theory, Research and Practice,* **18,** 108–151.

Brown, S., & Yalom, I. (1977). Interactional group therapy with alcoholics. *Journal of Studies on Alcohol,* **38,** 426–456.

Burt, D. (1975). A behaviorist looks at AA. *Additions,* **22,** 3, 56–69.

Cahn, S. (1970). *The treatment of alcoholics: An evaluative study.* New York: Oxford University Press.

Cermack, T., & Brown, S. (1982). Interactional group therapy with the adult children of alcoholics. *International Journal of Group Psychotherapy,* **32,** 375–389.

Curlee, J. (1967). Alcoholic women: Some considerations for further research. *Bulletin of the Menninger Clinic,* **31,** 154–163.

De Soto, C. B. (1983, August). Long-term changes in abstinent alcoholic professionals and nonprofessionals. Paper presented as part of a symposium on *Alcoholism: Issues in treatment and recovery of professionals,* the 91st annual meeting of the American Psychological Association. Anaheim, CA.

Edwards, G., Hensman, C., Hawker, A., & Williamson, V. (1966). Who goes to Alcoholics Anonymous? *Lancet,* **2,** 382–384.

Egan, G. (1970). *Encounter process for interpersonal growth.* Belmont, CA: Wadsworth.

Einstein, S., & Jones, F. (1965). Group therapy with adolescent addicts. In E. Haws (Ed.), *Drug addiction in youth* (pp. 132–147). New York: Pergamon Press.

Erickson, K. T. (1966). *Wayward puritans: A study in the sociology of deviance.* New York: John Wiley and Sons.

Flores, P. J. (1982, Spring). Modifications of Yalom's interactional group therapy model as a mode of treatment for alcoholism. *Group,* **6,** 3–16.

Fox, J., & Smith, M. A. (1959). Evaluation of a chemopsychotherapeutic program for the rehabilitation of alcoholics: Observations over a two year period. *Quarterly Journal of Studies on Alcohol,* **20,** 767–780.

Friesen, V., & Casella, N. (1982). The rescuing therapist: A duplication of the pathogenic family system. *The American Journal of Family Therapy,* **10,** 57–61.

Gellman, I. P. (1964). *The sober alcoholic: An organizational analysis of Alcoholics Anonymous.* New Haven, CT: College and University Press.

Gertner, A., & Riessman, F. (1979). *Self-help in the human services.* San Francisco: Jossey-Bass.

Glasscote, R.M. (1967). *The treatment of alcoholism: A study of programs and problems.* Washington, DC: Joint Information Service, American Psychiatric Association and National Association for Mental Health.

Gynther, M. D., & Brilliant, P. F. (1967). Marital status, readmission to hospital and interpersonal perceptions of alcoholics. *Quarterly Journal of Studies on Alcohol,* **28,** 52–58.

Hazelden Educational Services. (1955). *Stools and bottles.* Center City, MN.

Hazelden Educational Services. (1957). *The little red book.* Center City, MN.

Hazelden Educational Services. (1975). *Twenty-four hours a day.* Center City, MN.

Hazelden Educational Services. (1984). *Educational materials catalog.* Center City, MN.

Hill, M., & Blane, H. (1967). Evaluation of psychotherapy with alcoholics: A critical review. *Quarterly Journal of Studies on Alcohol,* **28,** 76–104.

Hobbs, N. (1951). Client-centered psychotherapy. In C. R. Rogers (Ed.), *Client-centered therapy.* Boston: Houghton Mifflin.

Hoffman, N. G., Harrison, P. A., & Belille, C. A. (1983). Alcoholics Anonymous after treatment: Attendance and abstinence. *International Journal of the Addictions,* **18(3),** 311–318.

Jackson, J. K. (1958). Type of drinking pattern of male alcoholics. *Quarterly Journal of Studies on Alcohol,* **19,** 269–302.

James, W. (1978). *Varieties of religious experience.* New York: Doubleday and Co.

Jindra, N. J., & Forslund, M. A. (1978). Alcoholics Anonymous in a western U.S. city. *Journal of Studies on Alcohol,* **39,** 110–120.

Johnson, V. (1973). *I'll quit tomorrow.* New York: Harper & Row.

Jones, R. K. (1970). Sectarian characteristics of Alcoholics Anonymous. *Sociology,* **4,** 181–195.

Jourard, S. (1964). *The transparent self.* New York: Harcourt-Brace and Co.

Jung, C. G. (1936). *Modern man in search of a soul.* New York: Harcourt-Brace and Co.

Killilea, M. (1976). Mutual help organizations: Interpretations in the literature. In G. Caplan & M. Killilea (Eds.), *Support systems and mutual help: Multidisciplinary explorations.* New York: Grune & Stratton.

Kirkpatrick, J. (1982). Self-help programs for women alcoholics. *Alcoholic Health and Research World,* **6,** 10–12.

Kurtz, E. (1980). *Not-god: A history of Alcoholics Anonymous* (2nd ed.), Center City, MN: Hazelden Educational Services.

Kurtz, E. (1981). Why A.A. works: The intellectual significance of Alcoholics Anonymous. *Journal of Studies on Alcohol,* **43,** 38–80.

Leach, B., & Norris, J. L. (1977). Factors in the development of Alcoholics Anonymous (A.A.). In B. Kissin & H. Begleter (Eds.), *Treatment and rehabilitation of the chronic alcoholic.* New York: Plenum Press.

Lieberman, M. A. (1980). Group methods. In F. Kanfer & A. Goldstein (Eds.), *Helping people change: A textbook of methods.* (pp. 470–536). New York: Pergamon Press.

Lieberman, M. A., Yalom, I., & Miles, M. (1973). *Encounter groups: First facts.* New York: Basic Books.

Lindbeck, V. (1975). *The woman alcoholic.* (Public Affairs Pamphlet No. 529), New York: Public Affairs Committee.

MacLennan, B., Beryce, W., & Levy, N. (1970). The group psychotherapy literature. *International Journal of Group Psychotherapy, 21,* 345–380.

Madsen, W. (1979). Alcoholics Anonymous as treatment and as ideology: Comments on the article by R. E. Tournier. *Journal of Studies on Alcohol, 40,* 323–327.

Mullan, H., & Sanguiliano, I. (1966). *Alcoholism: Group Psychotherapy and rehabilitation.* Springfield, IL: Charles C. Thomas.

Narcotics Anonymous. (1982) Van Nuys, CA: C.A.R.E.N.A. Publishing Company.

Norris, A. J. (1976). Alcoholics Anonymous and other self-help groups. In R. E. Tarter & A. A. Sugarman (Eds.), *Alcoholism: Interdisciplinary approaches to an enduring problem.* Reading, MA: Addison-Wesley.

Norris, A. J. (1982). The gap between active treatment and normal living—AA involvement. *Alcohol Health and Research World, 6,* 6–9.

Oden, T. C. (1972). *The intensive group experience: The new pietism.* Philadelphia: Westminster Press.

Pattison, M. (1979). The selection of treatment modalities for the alcoholic patient. In J. Mendelson & N. Mello (Eds.), *The diagnosis and treatment of alcoholism.* New York: McGraw-Hill Book Co.

Robinson, D. (1979). *Talking out alcoholism: The self-help process of Alcoholics Anonymous.* Baltimore, MD: University Park Press.

Rogers, C. (1957). The necessary and sufficient conditions of therapeutic personality change. *Journal of Consulting Psychology, 21,* 95–103.

Rosenberg, C. M. (1979). Alcoholics Anonymous as treatment and as ideology: Comments on the article by R. E. Tournier. *Journal of Studies on Alcohol, 40,* 330–333.

Sands, P., & Hanson, P. (1971). Psychotherapeutic groups for alcoholics and relatives in an outpatient setting. *International Journal of Group Psychotherapy, 21,* 23–33.

Sanguiliano, I. (1966). Quasi-group cohesion: Early anti-therapeutic trends. In H. Mullan and I. Sanguiliano (Eds.), *Alcoholism: Group Psychotherapy and Rehabilitation.* Springfield, IL: Charles C. Thomas.

Schulman, G. D. (1979). Alcoholics Anonymous as treatment and as ideology: Comments on the article by R. E. Tournier. *Journal of Studies on Alcohol, 40,* 335–338.

Siegler, M., & Osmond, H. (1974). *Models of madness, models of medicine.* New York: MacMillan.

Snyder, S. H. (1980). *Biological aspects of mental disorders.* New York: Oxford University Press.

Sobell, M. B., & Sobell, L. C. (1979). Alcoholics Anonymous as treatment and as ideology: Comments on the article by R. E. Tournier. *Journal of Studies on Alcohol, 40,* 321–323.

Soloman, S. (1981). *Tailoring alcoholism therapy to client needs.* (Publication No. ADM 81–1129). U.S. Department of Health and Human Services.

Stein, A., & Friedman, E. (1971). Group therapy with alcoholics. In H. Kaplan and B. Sadock (Eds.), *Comprehensive group psychotherapy* (pp. 652–690). Baltimore, MD: Williams and Wilkins Co.

Stierlin, H. (1973). Group fantasies and family myths: Some theoretical and practical aspects. *Family Process, 12,* 111–125.

Tamerin, J. S., Tolor, A., Holson, P., & Newmann, C. P. (1974). The alcoholic perception of self: A retrospective comparison of mood and behavior during states of sobriety and intoxication. *Annals of the New York Academy of Sciences, 233,* 48–60.

Thoreson, R. W. (1978, October). *Alcoholics Anonymous: A paradoxical blend of the behavioral and mystical.* Paper delivered at the Illinois State Conference on Alcoholism Treatment, Springfield, IL.

Thoreson, R. W. (1984). The professor at risk: Alcohol abuse in academe. *The Journal of Higher Education,* **55,** 56–72.

Thune, C. E. (1977). Alcoholism and the archetypal past: A phenomenological perspective on Alcoholics Anonymous. *Journal of Studies on Alcohol,* **38,** 75–88.

Tibout, H. M. (1949). The act of surrender in the therapeutic process with special reference to alcoholism. *Quarterly Journal of Studies on Alcohol,* **10,** 48–58.

Tournier, R. E. (1979). Alcoholics Anonymous as treatment and as ideology. *Journal of Studies on Alcohol,* **40,** 230–239.

Trice, H. M. (1959). The affiliation motive and readiness to join Alcoholics Anonymous. *Quarterly Journal of Studies on Alcohol,* **20,** 313–320.

Trice, H. M., & Roman, P. M. (1972). *Spirits and demons at work: Alcohol and other drugs on the job.* (ILR paperback, No. 11). New York State School of Industrial and Labor Relations, Cornell University.

Truax, C. B., & Carkhuff, R. R. (1967). *Toward effective counseling and psychotherapy: Training and practice.* Chicago: Aldine.

Ulrich, J. (1982). Socially supportive persons in the rehabilitation of alcoholics. *Zeitschrift für Klinische Psychologie und Psychotherapie,* **30,** 40–51.

Vaillant, G. (1983). *The natural history of alcoholism: Causes patterns and paths to recovery.* Cambridge, MA: Harvard University Press.

Vannicelli, M. (1982). Group psychotherapy with alcoholics: Special techniques. *Journal of Studies on Alcohol,* **43,** 17–37.

Vogel, S. (1957). Some aspects of group psychotherapy with alcoholics. *International Journal of Group Psychotherapy,* **7,** 302–309.

Wallace, J. (1977). Alcoholism from the inside out: A phenomenological analysis. In N. Estes & N. Heinemann (Eds.), *Alcoholism: Development, consequences and intervention* (pp. 3–14). St. Louis: C. V. Mosby Co.

Wallace, J. (1978a). Working with the preferred defense structure of the recovering alcoholic. In S. Zimberg, J. Wallace, & S. Blume (Eds.), *Practical approaches to alcoholism psychotherapy* (pp. 19–29). New York: Plenum Press.

Wallace, J. (1978b). Critical issues in alcoholism therapy. In S. Zimberg, J. Wallace, & S. Blume (Eds.), *Practical approaches to alcoholism psychotherapy,* (pp. 31–43). New York: Plenum Press.

Wegscheider, S. (1981). *Another chance: Hope and health for the alcoholic family.* Palo Alto, CA: Science & Behavior Books, Inc.

Whitley, O. R. (1977). Life with Alcoholics Anonymous: The Methodist class meeting as a paradigm. *Journal of Studies on Alcohol,* **38,** 831–848.

Yalom, I. (1974). Group psychotherapy and alcoholism. *Annals of the New York Academy of Sciences,* **233,** 85–103.

Yalom, I. (1975). *The theory and practice of group psychotherapy.* New York: Basic Books.

Zimberg, S. T., Wallace, J., & Blume, S. (Eds.), *Practical approaches to alcoholism psychotherapy,* New York: Plenum Press.

Zinberg, N. E. (1977). Alcoholics Anonymous and the treatment and prevention of alcoholism. *Alcoholism,* **1,** 91–102.

9

Craving for Alcohol: Theoretical Processes and Treatment Procedures

LAURENCE H. BAKER,* NED L. COONEY,†
AND OVIDE F. POMERLEAU‡

*Psychology Service
Veterans Administration Medical Center
Portland, Oregon 97207
and
†Department of Psychiatry
University of Connecticut School of Medicine
Farmington, Connecticut 06032
and
‡Behavioral Medicine Program
Department of Psychiatry
University of Michigan School of Medicine
Ann Arbor, Michigan 48105

Clinicians and researchers working with alcoholics are devoting increased attention to the problem of relapse after treatment (Marlatt & Gordon, 1985). Because only 26% of alcohol-dependent individuals remain improved 1 year after treatment (Miller & Hester, 1980), clinicians continue to search for treatment approaches that will not be followed by relapse.

The concept of craving has often been used in constructing models of relapse. In this chapter, we discuss craving and its implications for preventing relapse, focusing on the evolution of the concept and relevant empirical studies. Using a case example, we describe treatment procedures that are designed to modify craving and prevent relapse. Finally, we discuss future directions for research on craving.

TREATMENT AND PREVENTION
OF ALCOHOL PROBLEMS: A RESOURCE MANUAL

I. THE CONCEPT OF CRAVING

The term *craving* and its synonyms (temptation, desire-to-drink, urge, need) are often used in descriptions of alcoholic drinking. *Craving* has been used to describe an emotional state experienced by alcoholics and to explain the resumption of problem drinking following abstinence. In our treatment program, patients have often expressed concerns about resuming drinking — concerns that they refer to as *craving*. These concerns may include persistent thoughts about drinking and its pleasant effects, pleasant and unpleasant affective reactions, physical responses such as tremor, headache, and gastrointestinal upset, and, sometimes, increases in drink-seeking behavior.

Several surveys have examined alcoholics' experiences of craving, and have found that craving is a common experience. Flaherty, McGuire, and Gatski (1955), in a retrospective survey of sober alcoholics, found that most respondents described the experience as an obsessive desire for alcohol. Descriptions of craving episodes included feelings of nervousness, fatigue, and depression. In another survey, Hore (1974) found that 33% of 349 alcoholic respondents said they had experienced craving during the past week. Sixty-nine percent of the respondents reported physical symptoms and 41% described psychological symptoms. Craving was significantly more frequent among respondents with more symptoms of alcohol dependence during the previous year and among respondents who drank during the preceding month. However, generalization of the findings of both these studies is limited by the fact that a significant proportion of the alcoholics who were contacted did not respond to the questionnaires.

A phenomenological description of *craving* is provided by a 40-year-old man with a 15-year history of alcohol dependence. During treatment with one of the authors (L.H.B.), this patient related a particularly poignant episode that occurred after a year of abstinence. He was house-sitting for friends in a town where he had lived (and drunk) prior to treatment. After spending a day alone in the house and going for a walk on the beach, he reported that he began having repeated thoughts about the pleasant taste of beer and the relaxed feeling he expected from drinking it. He also felt restless and had an unsettled feeling in his stomach and a mild tremor in his hands. At times, these feelings were very intense and unpleasant and reminded him of feelings he had prior to previous drinking episodes. In planning his evening, he found himself looking through the local paper at listings for music playing at bars in the area. He fully anticipated that drinking would relieve these unpleasant feelings and struggled with the conflict between desiring to remain sober and wanting to relieve his craving. This patient's description of his experience illustrates cognitive, physiological, and behavioral aspects of craving. We return to this patient in the section on treatment in order to illustrate procedures to cope with craving.

II. THEORIES OF CRAVING

The concept of craving has a role in various theories that account for relapses following abstinence from alcohol. One theory that utilizes the concept of craving is a disease model espoused by Alcoholics Anonymous and is widely followed by professionals and lay persons. This model is attributed to William Silkworth, a physician who was influential in the founding of Alcoholics Anonymous (Alcoholics Anonymous, 1976). According to this model, alcoholism is a biological illness. The action of alcohol on the vulnerable individual is described as an allergy that elicits craving. Only alcohol can set off craving and only in those who are biologically vulnerable. Furthermore, alcoholics will inevitably experience craving whenever they consume alcohol. The problem drinking itself is taken as evidence that craving occurs. It follows from this model that the treatment for the "disease" of alcoholism is abstinence from alcohol.

In his pioneering work, Jellinek (1960) formally presented the disease model as a "working hypothesis" to the scientific community. Despite Jellinek's suggestion that his formulations need to be tested experimentally, they have often been treated by both lay persons and professionals as if they were established facts.

Various biological mechanisms have been suggested to explain craving. For example, Williams (1948) proposed that an inherited pattern of abnormal metabolism causes alcoholics to seek the vitamins in alcohol. Another view is that as a result of their heavy drinking, alcoholics develop a biological "cell hunger" for alcohol. Neither of these views has been supported empirically.

Mello (1975) and Marlatt (1978) have criticized the concept of craving derived from the disease model of alcoholism. They argued that it is tautological to infer that craving is the cause of alcoholism merely by observing abnormal drinking. Moreover, it has been demonstrated empirically that consumption of alcohol by alcoholics does not always lead to craving (Mello & Mendelson, 1972) or loss of control (Marlatt, Demming, & Reid, 1973).

In 1954, the psychological dimension of craving was acknowledged when the World Health Organization (Isbell, 1955) proposed a distinction between craving associated with physical withdrawal from alcohol and that which occurs after withdrawal is completed. The former was said to have both a physiological and psychological basis, while the latter was said to have only a psychological basis. This distinction is important because the alcoholic's continued obsession with alcohol and drinking has important implications for the management and prevention of relapse.

Craving has been defined by behavioral psychologists as a multidimensional response consisting of subjective, behavioral, physiological, and biochemical components (Rankin, Hodgson, & Stockwell, 1979). Several behavioral theorists have advanced models to explain the origins of psychological craving and its role in relapse. These theorists see either (1) respondent conditioning or (2) cognitive mediational processes as the mechanism underlying craving.

Ludwig and Wikler (1974) proposed a respondent conditioning model to explain craving for alcohol that was based on Wikler's (1965) model of opiate relapse. They proposed that when certain environmental stimuli are repeatedly paired with physical withdrawal symptoms, these previously neutral stimuli become capable of producing conditioned withdrawal reactions, even long after physical dependence has been eliminated. In this model, craving represents the cognitive component of this conditioned withdrawal syndrome. Ludwig and Wikler speculated about the range of stimuli that might evoke conditioned withdrawal; they include stimuli arising from the ingestion of alcohol, physiological arousal cues resembling the alcohol withdrawal syndrome, and a variety of situations associated with prior heavy drinking. This model has been criticized by other behavioral theorists (Heather & Robertson, 1981; Marlatt, 1978) for being so imprecise in defining conditioned stimuli that it is untestable. By invoking broad conditioned stimuli such as arousal, almost any event that precedes relapse can be seen as fitting the model.

Poulos, Hinson, and Siegel (1981) have proposed a different respondent conditioning model of alcohol craving and relapse that extends Siegel's (1979) model of opiate tolerance and withdrawal. They suggested that the consumption of an alcoholic beverage constitutes a conditioning trial. The conditioned stimuli include the sight and smell of a drink, while the unconditioned stimuli include the physiological effects of alcohol such as hypothermia. However, the conditioned responses are opposite the unconditioned responses. These compensatory conditioned responses help the organism to maintain homeostatic balance. When the conditioned stimuli are not followed by ingestion of alcohol, the conditioned responses may be experienced as craving or withdrawal symptoms. Animal studies have supported this model of conditioned withdrawal. Newlin (1984) has demonstrated what appear to be conditioned physiological responses to alcohol cues in humans—responses which seem to be opposite from acute alcohol effects. Six male nonproblem drinkers drank 0.5 g/kg ethanol in a distinctive laboratory environment on 4 days and a placebo on the fifth day. Although alcohol increased finger-pulse transit time and temperature, the placebo lead to decreased finger-pulse transit time and temperature. This was interpreted as a conditioned compensatory response to alcohol administration cues.

A two-factor model has been proposed by Pomerleau (1981). In this model, craving is not restricted to situations which elicit withdrawal-like responses. Instead, conditioned stimuli (cues associated with alcohol consumption or withdrawal) elicit various classically conditioned responses which can serve as discriminative stimuli for alcohol self-administration (operant responses). *Craving* is defined as the cognitive component of the classically conditioned responses.

Marlatt and Gordon (1980) and Wilson (1978) have argued for the importance of cognitive variables, such as expectations, in understanding craving and relapse. The expectation of favorable (or unfavorable) effects may be a more powerful determinant of behavior than actual consequences (Bandura, 1977). Positive outcome expectancies have been found to be important determinants of alcohol use (Marlatt & Rohsenow, 1980). In the context of social learning theory, *craving* is defined as the anticipation of the reinforcing effects of alcohol (Marlatt, 1978).

While there has been theoretical interest in the concept of craving, two caveats are in order: First, craving is a *construct* that can be used by clinicians and researchers to help them understand and treat alcoholism, but, like all constructs, it is only as valid as its empirical base. Craving itself is not the *cause* of relapse. Second, by helping patients to cope with or avoid craving responses one does not "cure" alcoholism. Craving accounts for some, but certainly not all, determinants of relapse. Treatments should be directed at all determinants of problem drinking.

III. BASIC RESEARCH RELEVANT TO CRAVING

Recent research on craving has used diverse measures and methodologies. Investigators have operationalized craving and have regarded it as a dependent variable, an independent variable, or a correlate of other patient characteristics. The subjective indices of craving have included self-reported desire to drink and expectations about the consequences of drinking (Cooney, Baker, Pomerleau, & Josephy, 1984). Behavioral measures of craving have included speed of drinking (Rankin et al., 1979), amount of beverage consumed during a taste-rating task (Miller, Hersen, Eisler, Elkin, 1974), and number of operant responses made in order to acquire a drink (Funderbunk & Allen, 1977). Physiological indices of craving have included hand tremor (Rankin et al., 1979), skin conductance level (Kaplan et al., 1985), swallowing rate (Pomerleau, Fertig, Baker, & Cooney, 1983), and heart rate (Kaplan, Meyer, & Stroebel, 1983). Biochemical indices such as plasma insulin levels (Dolinsky et al., 1986) may provide additional measures of craving.

A. Cognitions and Craving

Research investigating cognitive determinants of alcoholics' drinking may shed light on craving. Using a balanced placebo design, Marlatt et al. (1973) separated the pharmacological effects of drinking from the expectation of effects. Alcoholics were placed in one of four conditions: They were (1) told they were drinking alcohol and were actually given alcohol, (2) told they were drinking alcohol but in fact were given a nonalcoholic drink, (3) told they were given a nonalcoholic drink but actually were given an alcoholic one, or (4) told they were given a nonalcoholic drink and actually were given one. This was followed by a "taste-test" of an alcoholic beverage in which the amount consumed was surreptitiously recorded. Alcoholics who *believed* that they had just consumed an alcoholic beverage, regardless of the actual alcohol content of the beverage, drank more in the taste test than those who believed that they had consumed a nonalcoholic drink.

Stockwell, Hodgson, Rankin, and Taylor (1982) used a balanced placebo design to study patients who varied in their degree of alcohol dependence. Moderately dependent alcoholics who believed they were consuming alcohol drank significantly faster than those who believed they were drinking a nonalcoholic beverage, regardless of the actual alcoholic content of the drink. Severely dependent subjects, on the other hand, drank faster when the drink contained alcohol, no matter what they were told about the contents of the drink. Both moderately and severely dependent subjects showed an elevated heart rate after consuming the first alcoholic drink. However, Laberg (1984) reported a different pattern of results for moderate and severely dependent alcoholics. Using a balanced placebo design, Laberg found that a severely dependent group was clearly influenced by instructions that they had been given an alcoholic drink. The moderately dependent group was influenced by both instructions and alcohol content, and nondependent group was influenced only by the actual presence of alcohol in the priming dose. The reason for these inconsistent results is unknown, but it is clear that future research should take severity of dependence of alcoholic subjects into account when studying expectancies.

In the three preceding studies, the amount drunk or speed of drinking provided a behavioral measure of motivation to drink. These studies demonstrated that this aspect of craving can be manipulated by beliefs about whether one has consumed alcohol, though a history of alcohol dependence may mediate this effect.

B. Physiological Aspects of Craving

Other studies have employed physiological measures of craving. Pomerleau et al. (1983) compared the responses of alcoholics in treatment and nonalcoholic controls to the sight and smell of their favorite alcoholic beverage. Swallowing rate (indicated by electromyographic activity of the digastricus muscles) and self-report ratings of desire to drink were significantly greater in alcoholics than in nonalcoholics. The authors also found that salivation (as measured with dental rolls) increased when alcoholics were exposed to alcohol. In an extension of this research, Kaplan et al. (1985)

demonstrated that skin conductance level was higher in alcoholics than nonalcoholics during exposure to the sight and smell of beverage alcohol. Among alcoholics, those who reported more pretreatment withdrawal symptoms had a higher skin conductance level to alcohol cues. These two studies demonstrate how physiological assessment of craving can discriminate alcoholics from nonalcoholics.

Physiological responses to drinking cues have also been used to predict treatment outcome. In an unpublished doctoral dissertation, Kennedy (1971) measured the change in pupil diameter of alcoholics in treatment while they were exposed to the smell of alcohol. He found that a decrease in pupillary reactivity over the course of treatment discriminated those patients who remained abstinent for 3 months from those who relapsed.

Physiological measures have also been used to predict behavior in the laboratory. Kaplan et al. (1983) required alcoholics in treatment to drink a glass of malt beverage that they were told was either beer or a nonalcoholic drink. Later, subjects could choose either another beer or a lottery ticket as a reward for an operant task. Those subjects with greater cardiac rate change during the initial beverage presentations were more likely to choose the beer. These studies suggest that physiological reactivity to drinking cues can be used to discriminate between alcoholics and nonalcoholics, and to predict alcoholics' drinking behavior and treatment outcome.

C. Concordance and Craving

Studies investigating the relationships between subjective and behavioral responses are important in research and treatment of craving. Rachman and Hodgson (1974) used the term *concordance* to describe an emotional reaction in which response systems are strongly correlated. They argued that high concordance occurs during strong emotional arousal, while discordance occurs during mild arousal. It follows from their theory that in situations in which both self-reported craving and physiological measures of craving are high, subjects are experiencing a strong emotional response. By measuring cognitive, physiological, and behavioral responses, researchers can use measures of concordance to validate craving experiences in alcoholics. This is especially important as researchers are just beginning to explore the role of craving in both analogue and clinical studies of relapse. Kaplan et al. (1985) found significant concordance between self-reported craving and skin conductance levels among alcoholics presented with the sight and smell of their preferred alcoholic beverage but not among nonalcoholic controls. Concordance was especially strong for those alcoholics who reported more severe withdrawal symptoms during their last month of drinking.

Cognitions relevant to craving have been found to be correlated with measures of salivary responding during exposure to the sight and smell of alcohol. Cooney et al. (1984) observed that amount of salivation in the presence of alcohol was significantly correlated with alcoholics' expectations of positive outcome of drinking (Southwick, Steele, Marlatt, & Lindell, 1981).

Synchrony, the degree to which response systems change at the same rate during and after treatment, may be important to assess in the treatment of craving. Borkovec (1982) reported that synchronous change across response systems is associated with greater treatment effects among phobic patients treated with in vivo exposure procedures. The effects of treatments designed to change craving may be better understood by looking at the synchrony among several measures of craving.

The preceding review of basic research on craving suggests that there is growing scientific study of this frequently observed clinical phenomenon. There is evidence that different aspects of craving can be assessed using behavioral, cognitive–attitudinal, and psychophysiological measures. Craving can be manipulated by environmental factors, is predictive of subsequent behavior, and is correlated with relevant patient characteristics. Considerably more research will need to be conducted, however, before an unambiguous description of methods for the assessment of craving can be translated into accurate predictors of problem drinking and relapse.

IV. TREATMENT PROCEDURES

In this section, we reveiw treatment procedures that make use of the concept of craving. In order to do so, we return to the clinical case example that we introduced earlier. This individual had participated in a skill-training group during his inpatient treatment, which was designed to prepare him to cope with craving. In this treatment group, the patient was presented with a model of relapse adapted from Marlatt and Gordon (1978, 1985). He identified situations in which he would be likely to experience craving, and he practiced skills for avoiding or coping with these situations without drinking. These skills included refusing real drinks offered to him in role-playing situations. He also learned to identify the physiological, cognitive, and behavioral components of his craving through structured therapeutic exposure to an open bottle of cold beer. While on passes away from the hospital, he practiced monitoring his craving and visualizing scenes of the aversive consequences of drinking. Finally, he identified and used several behavioral alternatives (e.g., exercise) for coping with craving.

The patient reported that he used several behavioral and cognitive techniques to diminish craving while he was alone at the beach. First, he accurately labelled the subjective experience as *craving* rather than vaguely attribute it to boredom or anxiety. This labelling made possible a detached and more objective evaluation of the situation and helped him to marshal resources to deal with the feelings. Marlatt and Gordon (1985) suggested that increasing detachment from the feeling of craving may help patients successfully cope with craving.

Our patient recognized that by sitting alone at home and looking at tavern notices in the paper, he was increasing his risk of relapse. He decided that an alternative activity would help decrease his craving, so he began some yard work. While working in the yard, he continued to have obsessive, though less intense, thoughts about drinking a beer. At this juncture, he made himself recall the negative consequences of his past drinking, invoking vivid images of going through withdrawal in his old apartment. He focused on memories of his disheveled appearance, vomiting, and having seizures. After a few minutes of this imagery, positive thoughts about drinking began to wane. He eventually took a break from work and made a large pitcher of iced-tea which he drank until he was no longer thirsty. Within a few hours, most of his craving had subsided. This case illustrates how an alcoholic can apply specific procedures for coping with craving.

Treatment procedures for reducing craving can be placed within two broad categories. First, there are procedures that are designed to decrease the likelihood of the onset of craving. These procedures include passive cue exposure, covert sensitization, aversion therapy, skill training for avoiding situations in which craving is likely to occur, and drug therapies. A second group of procedures consists of training in behavioral and cognitive skills that can be applied to decrease the intensity and duration of craving when it occurs. However, all of these procedures are of most help to patients when put to use in the context of an overall treatment program. For example, if patients report that they often experience the desire to go to the bar to drink with friends when they are bored and lonely, then teaching them how to cope with this craving by thinking about the negative consequences of drinking deals with only one aspect of their problem. Treatment should also help them examine how they can alter their way of life and/or social skills so that they have sources of companionship available other than bar friends.

A. Cue-Exposure Treatment

Previous work with phobic avoidance (Marks, 1978), as well as with obsessions and compulsions (Rachman & Hodgson, 1980), has shown that exposure to relevant cues can be effective in reducing affective reactions. There are several theoretical rationales for alcohol cue-exposure procedures. Extinction of conditioned craving responses may occur if the unconditioned stimulus (pharmacologic effect of alcohol) is not obtained. In this manner, repeated presentations of the sight and smell of an alcoholic beverage without its pharmacologic effects should eventually result in a diminution of conditioned craving. The two-factor model of craving (Pomerleau, 1981) would also predict that operant extinction procedures may also be involved. Conditioned physical reactions which previously had signaled the availability of the reinforcing effects of drinking may lose their value as discriminative stimuli through the blocking of consumatory responses. Thus, the sight and smell of an alcoholic beverage would no longer signal the availability of reinforcement.

Cue-exposure treatments are new in the treatment of alcoholism, and patients may be unclear about the purpose of exposure to something they believe they should avoid. As with all treatment, both clinician and patient should have explicit and mutually agreed-upon goals. Specifically, the patient is told that cue exposure is designed to help the patient to avoid problem drinking, rather than learning to become comfortable with the presence of alcohol. The rationale for the treatment is clearly explained to help the patient make maximum use of the training. A well-informed patient can often make contributions that help us understand and treat his or her idiosyncratic pattern of craving.

Initial applications of cue-exposure treatments for reducing craving for alcohol have appeared in the literature as case studies. Hodgson and Rankin (1983) described the treatment of a 43-year-old man with a 20-year history of problem drinking. The patient reported that one of the strongest cues for craving was having a single alcoholic drink. Over repeated sessions, the patient was given one drink and then encouraged to resist the urge to drink further. While more alcohol was available during the session, the authors reported that the presence of a therapist provided implicit response suppression. After six sessions, the patient reported his desire to drink quickly dissipated a few hours after taking a single drink. During 6 months of follow-up, six brief lapses from abstinence were reported. This was a dramatic improvement over his drinking before treatment. After 18 months, the patient was readmitted for further cue-exposure sessions, after which he reported that craving was no longer elicited by a single drink. Though the patient showed vast improvement during the 5 years since treatment, reducing heavy drinking days from 200 to 30 per year, he was not completely free of problem drinking.

Blakey and Baker (1980) have reported six cases in which patients were gradually exposed to individualized cues, including watching other patrons drink at their favorite pubs. Most patients reported a decrease in craving over repeated exposure sessions, and five of the six patients reported abstinence in follow-up periods ranging from 2 to 9 months. An important feature of this work was the individualized tailoring of cue-exposure situations. This was necessitated by the authors' finding that some patients expressed no desire to drink in the presence of alcohol in the hospital, but experienced intense craving in other situations, such as in a pub.

To our knowledge, the only controlled evaluation of cue-exposure methods for alcoholics is one conducted by Rankin, Hodgson, and Stockwell (1983). Five severely dependent alcoholics received six sessions of alcohol cue exposure in an experimental chamber. At the beginning of each session, subjects consumed 1.2 g/kg body weight of absolute ethanol of their desired alcoholic beverage. They were then asked to hold, sniff, and try to resist drinking a third drink for 45 minutes. Five other alcoholics received six sessions of what the authors called "imaginal cue exposure," which actually was a form of covert rehearsal. These subjects were asked to imagine resisting temptations to drink. The authors reported a significant increase in the amount of time taken to consume a drink from pre- to posttreatment among the alcohol cue-exposure group, but not among the imaginal treatment group. However, after their six imagery sessions, control subjects received six sessions of alcohol cue-exposure and showed significant decreases in speed of drinking. No treatment follow-up data were reported. The cue-exposure procedures applied in this study appear to have had a positive effect on a behavioral measure of craving. However, any conclusions based on this study should be tentative, given the small sample size.

These three studies of exposure procedures illustrate several different approaches to alcohol cue exposure. All three used actual alcoholic beverages. Blakey and Baker (1980) used a repeated series of in vivo exposure trials, taking patients through individually tailored hierarchies. Hodgson and Rankin (1983) and Rankin et al. (1983) used a priming dose of alcohol, and alcohol was available for further consumption. The common theme among these approaches is an attempt to present the stimuli in a manner which encourages the patient to attend to and to cognitively process the emotional and behavioral memories associated with alcohol. Borkovec and Grayson (1980) have argued that such "functional exposure" is critical to effective treatment of emotional responses.

Relaxation, verbal prompts to focus attention to the relevant stimuli, prolonged exposure trials, and imagery may also enhance functional exposure to alcohol cues. Relaxation may help patients to visualize scenes or attend to stimuli that they might otherwise avoid because of the negative feelings elicited by the sight and smell of alcohol in a treatment setting. Instructions and prompts that encourage patients to focus their attention on alcoholic stimuli may also enhance exposure, as has been shown in the treatment of obsessions and compulsions (Grayson, Foa, & Steketee, 1982). Prolonged exposure trials may prove effective in alcohol cue exposure, as they have in exposure treatment of phobias.

An evaluation of procedures to enhance cue-exposure treatment with alcoholics has been described by Baker, Cooney, and Vinnick (1984). They compared the effects of interrupted versus prolonged trials and distraction versus attention-focusing manipulations on 1 hour of alcohol cue exposure.

These authors found the lowest posttreatment skin conductance level and heart-rate response to alcohol cues after patients received prolonged exposure, in the context of verbal instructions that focused the patient's attention on the taste, smell, and expected positive effects of drinking. This finding supports the efficacy of procedures which enhance functional exposure in reducing craving.

As noted by Blakey and Baker (1980), the sight and smell of a drink in the hospital is by no means a universal cue for craving. Some cues may be difficult to present in vivo, and the clinician may need to consider supplanting laboratory cue exposure with imaginal cue exposure. Cues such as interpersonal conflict (e.g., an argument with a supervisor) may not lend themselves to in vivo exposure. It is important that the imagined stimulus arouse a sufficient emotional response to ensure functional exposure. Functional exposure is more likely, and treatment will be most beneficial, when patients experience strong craving over a prolonged trial that uses imagery.

In our clinical work, we always begin cue exposure by giving a clear rationale to the patient. We caution the patient that, although the purpose of treatment is to reduce craving, we are not trying to make them comfortable around alcohol, and we suggest that they *not* practice cue exposure in an unsupervised fashion in real-life situations by, for example, frequenting bars. However, it is inevitable that patients will eventually come into contact with some drinking cues. After successful guided exposure, it is useful with some patients to encourage homework exercises which involve graded, self-directed exposure to cues. For example, a patient reported that while working on his car, a situation previously associated with drinking, he experienced a very strong craving for a beer. He stopped working on his car and visited a friend who was a nondrinker. Recognizing that the patient would need to maintain his car in order to keep his job, the therapist encouraged the patient to return to the situation and to remain in it without drinking, until the craving subsided. After doing this several times, the patient reported that working on the car no longer elicited craving.

B. Aversion Therapy

Another method for decreasing craving is *aversive conditioning,* in which alcohol cues are paired with aversive stimuli. Although aversion therapies are discussed in Klinger's and Riley et al.'s chapters in this volume, some discussion of the relationship between aversive conditioning and craving is relevant here.

It is worthwhile to compare and contrast cue exposure therapy with aversion therapy. *Cue exposure* involves repeated exposure to alcohol cues, a procedure that is assumed to produce extinction of craving responses. *Aversion therapy,* on the other hand, involves pairing alcohol cues with an aversive stimulus, a procedure by which alcohol cues come to elicit an aversive reaction rather than craving. The goal of cue-exposure treatment is to decrease bodily reactions to alcohol cues such as salivation and skin conductance, which are presumed to underlie desire to drink or craving. A reduction in these bodily responses to alcohol cues should, therefore, accompany successful outcome with cue-exposure treatment. To our knowledge, the relationship between physiological reactions and subsequent drinking after cue-exposure treatment has yet to be studied. The goal of aversion therapy, in contrast, is to increase reactivity to alcohol cues because such reactivity is assumed to reflect conditioned nausea. Increased bodily reactions following aversion therapy should be associated with successful outcome.

These predictions have been supported in several aversion therapy studies. In his work on covert sensitization, Elkins (1980) used measured galvanic skin response, heart rate, and respiration, to document the occurrence of conditioned aversion in patients undergoing treatment. Among patients who showed conditioned nausea, 31% abstained from 5 to 62 months; patients who did not show conditioning exhibited no sustained period of abstinence. In a study of several different covert aversive stimuli, Miller and Dougher (1984) also found that conditioned aversion (documented psychophysiologically) was associated with a more favorable outcome at an 18-month follow-up. Similarly, Cannon, Baker, and Wehl (1981) found that, in chemical aversion treatments, posttreatment heart-rate acceleration to the taste and smell of an alcoholic beverage predicted abstinence at 1-year follow-up.

Global measures of "psychophysiological reactivity" are probably too coarse to distinguish between aversion-elicited and craving-elicited responses. A definitive understanding of the psychophysiological mechanisms involved in these two treatment approaches awaits more fine-gained analyses of the different patterns of responses under these different stimulus conditions. The patient's subjective responses associated with physiological reactions elicited by alcohol should be assessed in any aversion therapy or cue-exposure research to ensure a correct interpretation of physiological responses.

C. Pharmacological Approaches to Treating Craving

Several drugs have been used in treatment of alcohol problems, some of which have been thought to decrease problem drinking by modifying the intensity and frequency of craving. Disulfiram (Antabuse®) is probably the most frequently used drug in the treatment of alcoholism. A violently unpleasant physical reaction is produced when a person taking disulfiram consumes alcohol. Patients are warned to these effects when given the drug and, presumably, alter their beliefs about the consequences of drinking. It has been proposed that disulfiram reduces craving by acting on neurotransmitters in the brain (Naranjo, Cappell, & Sellers, 1981; Silver, Ewing, Rouse, & Mueller, 1979; Wilson, Davidson, & Blanchard, 1980), but there currently is no evidence to support this point of view. In contrast, one study found that disulfiram *increases* craving. Nirenberg, Sobell, Ersner-Hershfield, and Cellucci (1983) found that orally administered disulfiram resulted in a greater number of thoughts about drinking alcohol. Fifteen outpatients on disulfiram and 10 outpatients who elected not to take disulfiram recorded their thoughts about drinking on self-monitoring cards each day for 14 consecutive days. They found that on days 7–14, patients taking disulfiram had more than twice as many daily thoughts about alcohol than patients not taking disulfiram. The authors suggested that the daily pill-taking routine may serve as a cognitive stimulus prompting thoughts about alcohol. Alternatively, they speculated that the use of disulfiram allows patients to feel safe to expose themselves to environmental cues associated with drinking. These environmental cues then elicit thoughts about drinking. In either case, controlled research with random assignment is needed to confirm this interesting finding.

Lithium carbonate, a drug used to treat bipolar affective disorders, has been found to diminish the intensity of craving elicited by a priming dose of alcohol. Judd and Huey (1984) studied the responses of 35 detoxified, male, alcoholic inpatients who received lithium or placebo. In a crossover design, subjects served as their own controls. After 14 days of lithium or placebo administration, subjects participated in an experimental session in which they drank alcohol during 60 minutes, achieving a mean blood alcohol level (BAL) of 104 mg/100 ml. Prior to, and 10 minutes after the alcohol consumption period, subjects completed a series of tests which included self-reported "desire to continue drinking." Change scores indicated that subjects showed less of a pre–post increase in craving with lithium than with placebo. Because subjects also reported significantly less of an increase in feelings of intoxication during the lithium session, Judd and Huey speculated that lithium may mitigate alcohol's effect on subjective states. Alternatively, they suggested that alcoholics' craving may be a state-dependent response which is not strongly elicited in the novel state produced by lithium. The authors cautioned against prematurely translating these findings into clinical procedures.

Borg (1983), comparing a placebo with bromocriptine, a dopamine agonist used to treat movement disorders, found that chronic alcoholics maintained on bromocriptine reported significantly less craving for alcohol as well as less drinking at 3- and 6-month follow-ups. No mechanism of action is offered to explain the effects.

D. Treatments for Coping with Craving

Cognitive – behavioral therapists hold that deficits in coping skills contribute to relapse among alcoholics (Litman, Eiser, Rawson, & Oppenheim, 1977; Curry and Marlatt's chapter in this volume). Supporting evidence comes from three retrospective studies (Jones & Lanyon, 1981; Litman et al., 1977; Rosenberg, 1983), and one prospective study (Cronkite & Moos, 1980) in which a relationship between coping and relapse after alcoholism treatment was found.

The procedures discussed previously in this chapter are designed to decrease the frequency of craving. However, because it is not realistic to expect the total elimination of craving responses in persons with a history of alcoholism, alcoholic patients may benefit from treatments which help them to cope with craving. Sanchez-Craig, Wilkinson, and Walker's chapter in this volume relates how problem drinkers were asked, prior to specific training, to describe incidents in which they had successfully coped with strong urges to drink. They found that cognitive and behavioral coping techniques were used with equal frequency. Cognitive coping included remembering the consequences of drinking or not drinking, reappraisal of the situation, and remembering one's commitment to abstinence or reduced drinking. Behavioral coping included consumption of nonalcoholic drinks, food, or cigarettes, as well as recreational or distracting activities and self-assertion. These simple client-generated coping skills may provide useful guidelines for skills-training procedures. In a study of former cigarette smokers, Shiffman (1984) found both cognitive and behavioral coping strategies to be equally superior to doing nothing in response to an urge for a cigarette.

One cognitive coping skill that may be useful to alcoholics is altering their attributions about the experience of craving. A study by Cooney, Gillespie, Baker, and Kaplan (1986) measured cognitive changes associated with cue-elicited craving for alcohol. Abstinent alcoholic inpatients and social drinkers were exposed to the sight and smell of their favorite alcoholic beverage but were not permitted to consume it. Both groups showed significant increases in craving, but the alcoholics reported significantly greater guilt associated with their craving than the social drinkers. The alcoholics also reported a significant decrease in confidence about coping with future temptations to drink. These results suggest that craving for alcohol is followed by guilt, and loss of confidence — emotions which usually result from unsuccessful coping and relapse (Marlatt, 1978). It is as if craving itself represented a failure. These findings imply that one goal of treatment should be to help patients see temptation as normal and view resisting temptation as an example of successful coping.

Relaxation training procedures may give alcoholics skills to behaviorally cope with craving. Strickler, Bigelow, and Wells (1976) taught seven abstinent alcoholics to use relaxation procedures while exposing them to drinking cues (an audiotape of heavy drinking in a bar). Compared to seven abstinent alcoholics who did not receive this training, the relaxation group showed greater reduction of muscle tension in response to the alcohol-related cues. This study is noteworthy because it did not simply teach relaxation, but taught it as a coping response to craving.

A great deal of skill training in alcoholism treatment is conducted in the absence of strong craving. Yet, alcoholics will often need to perform the skills in the presence of strong feelings of craving. Social-skills training is a case in point. While social-skills training has been shown to improve treatment outcome (Watson & Maisto, 1982), we combine cue-exposure treatments with social-skills training (Cooney, Baker, & Pomerleau, 1983). For example, when learning to refuse drinks, patients refuse a real glass of beer, thereby learning to emit an appropriate response under realistic conditions—and while experiencing physiological and psychological reactions to alcohol cue exposure. The importance of alcoholic beverage exposure during social-skills training is illustrated by the work of Binkoff et al. (1984), who found that problem drinkers with strong craving (as measured by salivation to the sight and smell of an alcoholic beverage) showed significantly less skill in refusing drinks when an actual alcoholic beverage rather than an imaginary drink was used in the role-play. A significant negative correlation was also found between craving and judges' ratings of effectiveness of subjects' ability to resist drinking.

In our treatment program, we provide a clear rationale for using real alcoholic beverages with social-skills training. Patients are reminded that prohibitions against drinking apply to these sessions and that the goal is to learn how to avoid problem drinking. We have not yet formally evaluated our procedures, but patients report that role playing in the presence of alcohol is initially quite difficult. With practice, however, they report feeling more confident about their ability to use coping responses while being tempted to drink.

Finally, one skill not to be overlooked is changing the environment to reduce or eliminate cues that trigger craving. This technique is the mainstay of stimulus-control approaches (Miller & Muñoz, 1982) which teach, for example, social skills such as asking friends to forego drinking in one's presence and leaving situations known to trigger craving.

V. DIRECTIONS FOR TREATMENT RESEARCH

Research on craving in the treatment of alcoholism is still in its beginnings. As clinical researchers begin to use the concept of craving to integrate data on the physiological, biochemical, and psychological states associated with drinking behavior in alcoholics and conduct research to examine various interrelationships among these measures, increasingly effective procedures to decrease the frequency of craving responses and to provide skills for coping with craving should emerge. A good starting point for future treatment research on managing craving is to evaluate treatment techniques that have been used successfully with other disorders. An example of this approach is Baker et al.'s (1984) parametric study of attention and duration of alcohol cue exposure, which examined treatment variables associated with positive outcomes in the treatment of phobias. Another topic for future research is the experimental investigation of in vivo procedures for cue exposure (Blakey & Baker, 1980). Still a third area for study is procedures that attempt to modify cognitions about craving responses, similar to Meichenbaum's (1977) stress inoculation for fear. Finally, as more becomes known about the neuroregulatory basis of craving, pharmacological approaches to its treatment may prove to be important.

The multimodal conceptualization of craving that we have presented in this chapter suggests that research on treating craving should ideally include physiological, cognitive, behavioral, and biochemical assessments. Investigations are needed to better understand the relationships among these measures of craving. For example, does an alcohol cue that elevates heart rate signify craving (Kaplan et al., 1983) or aversion to alcohol (Cannon & Baker, 1981)? Studies that pursue these issues should generate much useful information for understanding and managing drinking behavior and reducing the odds of relapse.

ACKNOWLEDGMENT

Partial support for the preparation of this manuscript was provided by a grant from the National Institute on Alcohol Abuse and Alcoholism (#5 P50 AA03510-08).

REFERENCES

Alcoholics Anonymous World Services, Inc. (1976). *Alcoholics Anonymous.* (3rd ed.) New York.
Baker, L. H., Cooney, N. L., & Vinnick, D. M. (1984, August). *Cue exposure in alcoholism treatment.* Paper presented at the Third International Conference on Treatment of Addictive Behaviors, North Berwick, Scotland.
Bandura, A. (1977). *Social learning theory.* Englewood Cliffs, NJ: Prentice-Hall.
Binkoff, J., Abrams, D., Collins, L., Liepman, M., Monti, P., Nirenberg, T., & Zwick, W. (1984, November). Exposure to alcohol cues: Impact on reactivity and drink refusal skills in problem and non-problem drinkers. In P. Monti (Chair), *Cue exposure and self control: Implications for drinking, smoking and eating behaviors.* Symposium conducted at the

meeting of the Association for Advancement of Behavior Therapy, Philadelphia, PA.

Blakey, R., & Baker, R. (1980). An exposure approach to alcohol abuse. *Behaviour Research and Therapy*, **84**, 319–325.

Borg, V. (1983) Bromocriptine in the prevention of alcohol abuse. *Acta Psychiatrica Scandinavica*, **68**, 100–110.

Borkovec, T. (1982). Facilitation and inhibition of functional CS exposure in the treatment of phobias. In J. Boulougouris (Ed.), *Learning theory approaches to psychiatry* (pp. 95–102). New York: Wiley.

Borkovec, T. D., & Grayson, J. B. (1980). Consequences of increasing the functional impact of internal emotional stimuli. In K. R. Blankstein, P. Pliner, & J. Polivy (Eds.) *Advances in the study of communication and affect* (Vol. 6) (pp. 117–137). New York: Plenum.

Cannon, D. S., & Baker, T. B. (1981). Emetic and electric shock aversion therapy: Assessment of conditioning. *Journal of Consulting and Clinical Psychology*, **49**, 20–33.

Cannon, D. S., Baker, T. B., & Wehl, C. K. (1981). Emetic and electric shock alcohol aversion therapy: Six- and twelve-month follow-up. *Journal of Consulting and Clinical Psychology*, **49**, 360–368.

Cooney, N. L., Baker, L. H., & Pomerleau, O. F (1983). Cue exposure for relapse prevention in alcohol treatment. In K. D. Craig & R. J. McMahon (Eds.), *Advances in clinical behavior therapy* (pp. 194–210). New York: Brunner/Mazel.

Cooney, N. L., Baker, L. H., Pomerleau, O. F., & Josephy, B. (1984). Salivation to drinking cues in alcohol abusers: Toward the validation of a physiological measure of craving. *Addictive Behaviors*, **9**, 91–94.

Cooney, N. L., Gillespie, R. A., Baker, L. H., & Kaplan, R. F. (1986). Cognitive changes after alcohol cue exposure. *Journal of Consulting and Clinical Psychology*.

Cronkite, R. C., & Moos, R. H. (1980). Determinants of the posttreatment functioning of alcoholic patients: A conceptual framework. *Journal of Consulting and Clinical Psychology*, **48**, 305–316.

Dolinsky, Z. S., Morse, D. E., Kaplan, R. S., Meyer, R. E., Corry, D., & Pomerleau, O. F. (1986). Neuroendocrine and subjective reactivity to alcohol cues and consumption of a placebo beverage in alcoholic patients. (Under editorial review.)

Elkins, R. L. (1980). Covert sensitization treatment of alcoholism: Contributions of successful conditioning to subsequent abstinence maintenance. *Addictive Behaviors*, **5**, 67–89.

Flaherty, J. A., McGuire, H. T., & Gatski, R. L. (1955). The psychodynamics of the "dry drunk." *American Journal of Psychiatry*, **112**, 460–464.

Funderbunk, F. R., & Allen, R. P. (1977). Alcoholics' disposition to drink: Effects of abstinence and heavy drinking. *Journal of Studies on Alcohol*, **38**, 410–425.

Grayson, J. G., Foa, E. B., & Steketee, G. (1982). Habituation during exposure treatment: Distraction vs. attention-focusing. *Behaviour Research and Therapy*, **20**, 323–328.

Heather, N., & Robertson, I. (1981). *Controlled drinking*. London: Methuen.

Hodgson, R. J., & Rankin, H. J. (1983). Cue exposure and relapse prevention. In W. M. Hay & P. E. Nathan (Eds.), *Clinical case studies in the behavioral treatment of alcoholism* (pp. 207–226). New York: Plenum.

Hore, B. D. (1974). Craving for alcohol. *British Journal of Addiction*, **69**, 137–140.

Isbell, H. (1955). Craving for alcohol, in WHO report. *Quarterly Journal of Studies of Alcohol*, **16**, 38–42.

Jellinek, E. M. (1960). *The disease concept of alcoholism*. Highland Park, NJ; Hillhouse Press.

Jones, S. L., & Lanyon, R. I. (1981). Relationship between adaptive skills and outcome of alcoholism treatment. *Journal of Studies on alcohol*, **42**, 521–525.

Judd, L. L., & Huey, L. Y. (1984) Lithium antagonizes ethanol intoxication in alcoholics. *American Journal of Psychiatry*, **141**, 1517–1521.

Kaplan, R. F., Cooney, N. L., Baker, L. H., Gillespie, R. A., Meyer, R. E., & Pomerleau, O. F. (1985). Reactivity to alcohol-related cues: Physiological and subjective responses in alcoholics and non-problem drinkers. *Journal of Studies on Alcohol*, **46**, 267–272.

Kaplan, R. F., Meyer, R. E., & Stroebel, C. F. (1983). Alcohol dependence and responsivity to an ethanol stimulus as predictors of alcohol consumption. *British Journal of Addiction,* **78,** 259–267.

Kennedy, D. A. (1971). *Pupilometrics as an aid in the assessment of motivation, impact of treatment, and prognosis of chronic alcoholics.* Unpublished doctoral dissertation. University of Utah, Salt Lake City.

Laberg, J. C. (1984, August) *Alcohol and expectancies: Somatic and subjective responses to expectancies and intake of alcohol in severely, moderately, and nondependent drinkers.* Paper presented at the Third International Conference on Treatment of Addictive Behaviors, North Berwick, Scotland.

Litman, G. K., Eiser, J. R., Rawson, N. S. B., & Oppenheim, A. N. (1977). Towards a typology of relapse: A preliminary report. *Drug and Alcohol Dependence,* **2,** 157–162.

Ludwig, A. M., & Wikler, A. (1974) "Craving" and relapse to drink. *Quarterly Journal of Studies on Alcohol,* **35,** 108–130.

Marks, I. M. (1978). Exposure treatments: Clinical application. In W. S. Agras (Ed.), *Behavior modification: Principles and clinical applications* (2nd ed.) (pp. 204–242). Boston: Little Brown.

Marlatt, G. A. (1978). Craving for alcohol, loss control, and relapse: A cognitive–behavioral analysis. In P. E. Nathan, G. A. Marlatt, & T. Løberg (Eds.), *Alcoholism: New directions in behavioral research and treatment* (pp. 271–314). New York: Plenum.

Marlatt, G. A., Demming, B., & Reid, J. B. (1973). Loss of control drinking in alcoholics: An experimental analogue. *Journal of Abnormal Psychology,* **81,** 233–241.

Marlatt, G. A., & Gordon, J. R. (1980). Determinants of relapse: Implications for maintenance of behavior change. In P. Davidson & S. Davidson (Eds.), *Behavioral medicine: Changing health lifestyles* (pp. 410–452). New York: Brunner/Mazel.

Marlatt, G. A., & Gordon, J. R. (1985). *Relapse prevention: Maintenance strategies in the treatment of addictive behaviors.* New York: Guilford.

Marlatt, G. A., & Rohesnow, D. J. (1980). Cognitive processes in alcohol use: Expectancy and the balanced placebo design. In N. K. Mello (Ed.), *Advances in substance abuse: Behavioral and biological research* (pp. 159–199). Greenwich, CT: JAI Press.

Meichenbaum, D. (1977). *Cognitive behavior modification.* New York: Plenum.

Mello, N. K. (1975) A semantic aspect of alcoholism. In H. Capell & A. E. LeBlanc (Eds.), *Biological and behavioral approaches to drug dependence* (pp. 73–87). Toronto: Addiction Research Foundation.

Mello, N. K., & Mendelson, J. H. (1972). Drinking patterns during work-contingent and noncontingent alcohol acquisition. *Psychosomatic Medicine,* **34,** 139–164.

Miller, P. M., Hersen, M., Eisler, R. M., & Elkin, T. E. (1974). A retrospective analysis of alcohol consumption on laboratory tasks related to therapeutic outcome. *Behaviour Research and Therapy,* **12,** 73–76.

Miller, W. R., & Dougher, M. J. (1984, June). *Covert sensitization: Alternative treatment approaches for alcoholics.* Paper presented at the Second Congress of the International Society for Biomedical Research Alcoholism, Santa Fe, NM.

Miller, W. R., & Hester, R. K. (1980). Treating the problem drinker: Modern approaches. In W. R. Miller (Ed.), *The Addictive Behaviors* (pp. 11–141). New York: Pergamon Press.

Miller, W. R., & Muñoz, R. F. (1982) *How to control your drinking* (2nd ed.). Albuquerque, NM: University New Mexico Press.

Naranjo, C. A., Cappell, H., & Sellers, E. M. (1981) Pharmacological control of alcohol consumption: Tactics for the identification and testing of new drugs. *Addictive Behaviors* **6,** 261–269.

Newlin, D. B. (1984) Human conditioned response to alcohol cues. *Alcoholism: Clinical and Experimental Research,* **8,** 110.

Nirenberg, T. D., Sobell, L. C., Ersner-Hershfield, S., & Cellucci, A. J. (1983). Can disulfiram use precipitate urges to drink alcohol? *Addictive Behaviors,* **8,** 311–313.

Pomerleau, O. F. (1981). Underlying mechanisms in substance abuse: Examples from research on smoking. *Addictive Behaviors, 6,* 187–196.

Pomerleau, O. F., Fertig, J., Baker, L., & Cooney, N. (1983). Reactivity to alcohol cues in alcoholics and nonalcoholics: Implications for a stimulus control analysis of drinking. *Addictive Behaviors, 8,* 1–10.

Poulos, C. X., Hinson, R. E., & Siegel, S. (1981). The role of Pavlovian processes in drug tolerance and dependence: Implications for treatment. *Addictive Behaviors, 6,* 205–212.

Rachman, S., & Hodgson, R. I. (1974) Synchrony and desynchrony in fear and avoidance. *Behaviour Research and Therapy, 12,* 311–318.

Rachman, S., & Hodgson, R. (1980). *Obsessions and compulsions.* Englewood Cliffs, NJ; Prentice-Hall.

Rankin, H., Hodgson, R., & Stockwell, T. (1979). The concept craving and its measurement. *Behaviour Research and Therapy, 17,* 389–396.

Rankin, H., Hodgson, R., & Stockwell, T. (1983). Cue exposure and response prevention with alcoholics: A controlled trial. *Behaviour Research and Therapy, 21,* 435–446.

Rosenberg, H. (1983). Relapsed versus non-relapsed alcohol abusers: Coping skills, life events, and social support. *Addictive Behaviors, 8,* 183–186.

Shiffman, S. (1984). Coping with temptations to smoke. *Journal of Consulting and Clinical Psychology, 52,* 261–267.

Siegel, S. (1979). The role of conditioning in drug tolerance and addiction. In J. D. Keehn (Ed.), *Psychopathology in animals: Research and clinical applications.* New York: Academic Press.

Silver, D. F., Ewing, J. A., Rouse, B. A., & Mueller, R. A. (1979). Responses to disulfiram in healthy young men: A double-blind study. *Journal of Studies on Alcohol, 40,* 1003–1013.

Southwick, L., Steele, C., Marlatt, A., & Lindell, M. (1981). Alcohol-related expectancies: Defined by phase of intoxication and drinking experience. *Journal of Consulting and Clinical Psychology, 49,* 713–721.

Stockwell, T. R., Hodgson, R. J., Rankin, H. J., & Taylor, C. (1982). Alcohol dependence, beliefs and the priming effect. *Behaviour Research and Therapy, 20,* 513–522.

Strickler, D., Bigelow, G., & Wells, D. (1976). *Electromyograph responses of abstinent alcoholics to drinking related stimuli: Effects of relaxation instructions.* Paper presented at the meeting of the Association for Advancement of Behavior Therapy. New York.

Watson, D. W., & Maisto, S. A. (1982). A review of the effectiveness of assertiveness training in the treatment of alcohol abusers. *Behavioural Psychotherapy, 10,* 1–14.

Wikler, A. (1965). Conditioning factors in opiate addiction and relapse. In D. Wilner & G. Kassenbaum (Eds.), *Narcotics.* New York: McGraw-Hill.

Williams, R. J. (1948). Alcoholics and metabolism. *Scientific American, 179,* 50–53.

Wilson, A., Davidson, W. J., & Blanchard, R. (1980). Disulfiram implantation: A trial using placebo implants and two types of controls. *Journal of Studies on Alcohol, 41,* 429–436.

Wilson, G. T. (1978). Booze, beliefs, and behavior: Cognitive processes in alcohol use and abuse. In P. E. Nathan, G. A. Marlatt, & T. Løberg, (Eds.), *Alcoholism: New directions in behavioral research and treatment* (pp. 315–339). New York: Plenum.

III

Associated Problems and Special Populations

10

Marital and Family Therapy for Alcohol Problems

TIMOTHY J. O'FARRELL

Department of Psychiatry
Harvard Medical School
Boston, Massachusetts 02138
and
Alcohol and Family Studies Laboratory
Veterans Administration Medical Center
Brockton, Massachusetts 02401

I. INTRODUCTION

Marital and family treatment approaches have been called "the most notable current advance in the area of psychotherapy of alcoholism" (Keller, 1974), and enthusiasm derives from several sources. Many alcoholics have extensive marital and family problems (Billings, Kessler, Gomberg, & Weiner, 1979; Paolino & McCrady, 1977), and positive marital and family adjustment is associated with better alcoholism treatment outcomes at follow-up (e.g., Finney, Moos, & Mewborn, 1980). In addition, reviews conclude that marital and family therapy have improved the results of alcoholism treatment (e.g., Janzen, 1977).

Further, there exists growing clinical and research evidence of reciprocal relationships between marital–family interactions and abusive drinking. It is widely known that abusive drinking leads to marital and family discord, among the more serious of which are separation–divorce (O'Farrell, Harrison, & Cutter, 1981) and child and spouse abuse (Black & Mayer, 1980; Hanks & Rosenbaum, 1977). At the same time, the role played by marital and family factors in the development and maintenance of alcohol problems is considerable. Individuals reared with an alcoholic parent are at risk for

205

developing alcohol problems due to both genetic factors and to faulty role modeling. Marital and family problems may stimulate excessive drinking, and family interactions often help to maintain alcohol problems once they have developed. Excessive drinking may provide more subtle adaptive consequences for the couple or family, such as facilitating the expression of emotion and affection or regulating the amount of distance and closeness between family members (Davis, Berenson, Steinglass, & Davis, 1974). Finally, even when recovery from the alcohol problem has begun, marital and family conflicts may often precipitate renewed drinking by abstinent alcoholics (Hore, 1971; Maisto, O'Farrell, Connors, McKay, & Pelcovitz, in press; Marlatt & Gordon, 1978).

Since 1976, the present author has conducted research on marriages and families of alcoholics, and clinical experience with alcohol problems has been gained in a Veterans Administration inpatient and outpatient alcoholism treatment program and in private practice in a coastal town halfway between Boston and Cape Cod. The work on behavioral marital therapy for alcoholics (O'Farrell & Cutter, 1979, 1984a, 1984b; O'Farrell, Cutter, & Floyd, 1985) has been guided primarily by social learning theory by which much of the material in this chapter is inspired. Recent thinking about stages in the process of change for a person with a drinking problem (Curry & Marlatt's chapter in this volume; Prochaska & DiClemente, 1983) is useful for organizing the different types of marital and family therapy interventions required to meet the varied needs of alcohol-troubled couples and families. Briefly stated, the process of change for someone with a drinking (or other addictive behavior) problem has three stages: (1) initial commitment to change — recognizing that a problem exists and deciding to do something about it, (2) the change itself — stopping abusive drinking and stabilizing this change for at least a few months, and (3) the long-term maintenance of change.

This chapter discusses marital and family interventions drawn both from clinical experience and from the published literature. For the second and third stages, techniques are grouped according to primary focus, either on the drinking problem itself or on marital and family relationship issues other than drinking.

II. MOTIVATING AN INITIAL COMMITMENT TO CHANGE IN THE ALCOHOL ABUSER

A. The Johnson Institute Intervention

Vernon Johnson of the Johnson Institute in Minneapolis has developed an intervention procedure to assist family members of alcoholics who deny their alcohol problem (Johnson, 1973). The goal is to educate the family about alcoholism and to get the alcoholic and family actively involved in treatment. The present description of the Johnson Institute Intervention procedure draws heavily on material by Thorne (1983).

The intervention process consists of two to five sessions with the family members during which the alcoholic is told that the family is attending either education sessions about problem drinking or family counseling, depending on the family situation. The usual first session, attended by several families, is an educational meeting about alcohol's effects on the drinker and the family. The second session is held with the individual family to gather further information about alcohol-related problems in the family. At the third session, each family member is asked to list positive data about the alcoholic's behavior when sober and negative data about the alcoholic's drinking behavior. The negative data explain when the member observed the alcoholic's drinking behavior, what the member did or said, and how he/she felt about it.

The fourth session is the rehearsal for the confrontation session with the alcoholic during which family members rehearse as if the alcoholic were present and discuss strategies to counteract the drinker's excuses and alibis. A frequent fear of family members is that the alcoholic will cite their own faults in order to change the topic. During the rehearsal, the family member is encouraged to bring up the feared issue first in order to defuse the efforts of the alcoholic to direct the intervention away from his or her drinking. Thorne (1983) presented an example in which a son wanted to confront his mother about her alcoholism. The son had used marijuana and felt his mother would argue that he could not criticize her since he had abused drugs himself. His opening statement during the intervention was: "Mom, I'm here today because I love you and care about you. I know that I, myself, have abused drugs and caused problems in the family in the past. I am sorry for the trouble it caused. Right now, I want to discuss your drinking, because it really concerns me now."

Other techniques are planned to reduce the alcoholic's defensiveness. Family members are encouraged to present positive data before the data on drinking-related behavior are presented. In another example from Thorne (1983), a wife told her husband, "I remember when we were first married and you were in the service. You used to come home and the baby and I would be patiently waiting for you. On your days off, we'd take trips to Connecticut and play in the snow. I remember those being good times and was very happy that we were close." The alcoholic, upon hearing such messages, tends to get less angry and resentful during the intervention. Positive closing statements that conclude with the family member saying he or she wants the alcoholic to get help and expects a positive outcome are also used. Thorne described a wife who wanted to say, as part of her closing statement, "I want you to get help so that you don't end up a Skid Row bum." The sentence was changed to, "I want you to get help so we can become closer and live many happy years together." In the intervention, the revised wording received a favorable (rather than a hostile) response.

Session five, the intervention itself, is held with the alcoholic. He or she is confronted with the data about drinking and sobriety. This is done (1) in an atmosphere of care and concern ("We're here today, John, because we love and care about you"); (2) with factual information about the alcoholic's drinking pattern ("John, you came home last week and you were so drunk you fell down"); and (3) in a nonjudgmental manner (no arguing or lecturing is permitted). The therapist's role in the intervention is to be a benevolent referee who can structure the session, guide each family member, including the alcoholic, on the proper time to respond, clarify points, and encourage the flow of communication. The family often expects the therapist to confront the alcoholic, but this rarely works because unlike the family members the therapist does not have an emotional bond with the alcoholic. When the therapist remains neutral and encourages the family members to speak to each other, they are more likely to express the intense emotions that have been suppressed and the alcoholic is more likely to accept treatment. The alcoholic is also asked to seek professional help. If refused, other efforts are made and undesirable alternative consequences are presented (e.g., "If you don't get help, John, I can't go on living with you anymore").

The intervention session ends with the alcoholic's accepting of the first treatment plan (usually hospitalization), agreeing with an alternative plan (outpatient counseling or attending Alcoholics Anonymous meetings), or rejecting all treatment. The therapist meets with the family after the session to discuss future means of family involvement, or, when the alcoholic rejects help, to consider alternatives and to provide support.

B. Unilateral Family Therapy for Alcohol Abuse

Edwin Thomas and colleagues at the University of Michigan (Thomas & Santa, 1982; Thomas, Santa, & Bronson, 1984) have been developing a unilateral family therapy approach to reach and to change the uncooperative alcohol abuser by working exclusively with a cooperative family member, usually the spouse. This approach emphasizes helping the nonabusing spouse to strengthen his or her coping capabilities, to enhance family functioning, and to facilitate greater sobriety on the part of the alcohol abuser. The unilateral approach is not limited to motivating an initial commitment to change in the drinking of the uncooperative alcohol abuser because this approach also is concerned with improving spouse and family functioning and maintaining gains in drinking behavior once achieved. However, the present discussion of the unilateral approach emphasizes the initial facilitation of sobriety, and the reader is referred elsewhere for information on other aspects of this treatment method (Thomas et al., 1982, 1984).

Thomas et al. (1984) have described the criteria for applying this unilateral approach. The partner must both have a drinking problem and express an unwillingness to receive treatment and to stop drinking. The spouse must recognize that the partner has a drinking problem, be willing to help with the partner's problem, and not have a drinking problem him/herself. The approach is not recommended for couples for whom there is evidence of domestic violence, drug abuse, history of severe emotional disturbance, or immediate plans for marital dissolution.

After dealing with such difficulties as anxiety, lack of assertiveness, depression, anger, and emotional overinvolvement, the therapist works to enhance marital and family functioning. The relationship enhancement component of the unilateral approach is designed to improve the working relationship between the marital partners and to increase the capability of the spouse to influence the alcohol abuser. The therapist and spouse choose a series of particular behaviors that are designed to improve the attractiveness of the marital relationship. Such efforts have produced more pleasant and harmonious interactions and have facilitated the spouse's later efforts to influence the abuser to change his or her drinking (Thomas et al., 1982).

Facilitating sobriety, the most important part of the unilateral approach for the present discussion, involves educating the spouse about alcohol abuse, removing spouse or family conditions that promote the drinking, and inducing the abuser to change the drinking. Thomas et al. (1984) find most spouses to be poorly informed, and they often underestimate the seriousness of the drinking problem. Some persons recoil at thinking their spouses are alcoholics. Rather than to abstain, many spouses would rather have the abuser reduce his or her drinking and become a social drinker. To overcome misinformation such as that shown by these examples, education about alcohol abuse is provided. Thomas et al. (1984) report that spouse behavior that promotes or enables abusive drinking (e.g., drinking with the abuser, making excuses for the abuser's drinking-related failings) is only one, and not a major contributing, factor. Nonetheless, the unilateral approach seeks to eliminate such behavior.

The final part of the unilateral family therapy approach is to get the abuser to change his or her drinking behavior. Previously unsuccessful methods are reviewed, and the spouse is told to discontinue these. Specific advice is given on influencing the drinker to change. Available information (Thomas et al., 1984) indicates that some alcohol abusers will initiate efforts to change their drinking in response to the spouse's changed behavior by seeking treatment, joining AA, starting a formal self-control program using a self-help manual (e.g., Miller & Muñoz, 1982), or devising their own idiosyncratic method. For cases in which previous steps have not produced a change in the drinking, the final step in the unilateral approach is a programmed confrontation patterned after the Johnson approach, and adapted for use with an individual spouse. Thomas et al. (1984) indicate that programmed confrontation requires careful assessment, intervention planning, implementation, and follow-up to avoid failure or such adverse effects as domestic violence. It is a powerful and extreme procedure that should be used with great care and only when other alternatives are inappropriate. The unilateral family therapy approach provides a series of graded steps to use prior to confrontation that may be successful in their own right or which at least pave the way for a positive outcome to the programmed confrontation experience. Thomas et al. (1984) provide a more detailed account of each step of this innovative unilateral family treatment method and the specific criteria that need to be met for its successful use.[1]

III. PRODUCING SHORT-TERM CHANGES IN THE DRINKING AND IN MARITAL–FAMILY RELATIONSHIPS

A. Alcohol-Focused Interventions

After the alcohol abuser has decided to change his or her drinking, the spouse and other family members can be included in treatment designed to support the alcohol abuser in adhering to this difficult and stressful decision. The first purpose of such treatment is to establish a clear and specific agreement between the alcohol abuser and family member(s) about the goal for the alcoholic's drinking and the role of each family member in achieving that goal. If abstinence is the goal, the minimum desired length of time during which the alcoholic plans to abstain should be specified. If reduced drinking is the goal, the acceptable quantities and conditions for consumption (e.g., where, when, with whom), along with the consequences of excessive drinking, must be established, preferably in writing. Of course, treatment for the drinking, including possible attendance at AA and Al-Anon meetings when applicable, also must be agreed upon.

Specifying other behavioral changes needed in the alcohol abuser or the family requires a careful review of individual situations and conditions. Certain issues should be addressed. For instance, possible exposure to alcoholic beverages and alcohol-related situations should be discussed. The spouse and family should decide if they will drink alcoholic beverages in the alcoholic's presence, whether alcoholic beverages will be kept and served at home, if the couple will attend social gatherings involving alcohol, and how to deal with these situations. Particular persons, gatherings, or circumstances that are likely to be stressful should be identified. Couple and family interactions related to alcohol also need to be addressed, because arguments, ten-

---

[1] See Note Added in Proof on page 231 for additional information.

sions, and negative feelings can precipitate more abusive drinking. Therapists need to discuss these patterns with the family and suggest specific procedures to be used in difficult situations. For example, Lazarus (1968) and others (e.g., Cheek, Franks, Laucius, & Burtle, 1971) have used relaxation training and systematic desensitization to help spouses control their fear and anger about the alcoholic's drinking. Similarly, Eisler (e.g., Eisler, Miller, Hersen, & Alford, 1974) taught the alcoholic to request assertively that the spouse refrain from comments about drinking. The therapist frequently will need to deal with other situations identified by the couple or family as likely to cause difficulty. Finally, if the therapist identifies positive consequences of the drinking (e.g., facilitation of sexual interaction, helping family members to relax together), then specific strategies for obtaining these satisfactions without drinking will need to be planned. The remainder of this section describes specific methods and examples of how to achieve the general goals just described.

1. Behavioral Contracting to Reduce Abusive Drinking

Peter Miller (1972) used contingency contracting with an excessive drinker and his wife to shape controlled drinking and to reduce arguments about drinking. The 44-year-old husband had been consuming four to six pints of bourbon per week for 2 years prior to treatment and could not specify any anxiety-producing situations preceding his drinking episodes. He did, however, report that his wife's frequent critical comments and disapproving glances about his drinking increased his consumption. The couple signed a contract that required the husband to limit his drinking to between one and three drinks a day (in the presence of his wife before the evening meal) and the wife to refrain from negative verbal or nonverbal responses to her husband's drinking. Each partner agreed to pay the other $20.00 if he or she broke his or her part of the agreement. Each spouse received a few fines during the first few weeks of the contract, but the infractions rapidly diminished when each partner learned that the contract would, in fact, be enforced.

The present author has also used contingency contracting with alcohol-abusing adolescents and their parents. A 16½-year-old male frequently returned home intoxicated after curfew on Friday and Saturday evenings, a situation that led to heated arguments between the adolescent and his parents, especially the father, both at the time of the incident and during the next few days. The parents also reacted by grounding the teenager for the next 4–6 weeks so he could not go out on weekends. A behavioral contract was negotiated that required the teenager (1) to be at home by the agreed on curfew or within 1 hour of the curfew if he called to explain the delay and (2) to take a breath test using the MOBAT (Sobell & Sobell, 1975) on his return home. If the breath test showed a breath alcohol content (BAC) less than .10, the parents agreed he earned the right to go out the following weekend. At least three consecutive weekends returning home not intoxicated were required to earn attendance at a special event such as a concert by a big-name rock group held a considerable distance from home. The parents agreed to provide an extra week's allowance if they yelled or threatened when the teenager returned home intoxicated either at the time of or in the days following the infraction. Treatment in this case also involved alcohol education for the teenager on the relationship between BAC and the amount and spacing of drinks, drink refusal training, and rehearsal of social skills for party situations. The interested reader may wish to consult other sources (e.g., Cassady, 1975; Teicher, Sinay, & Stumphauzer, 1976) for further information on behavioral contracting with adolescent alcohol abusers.

A related recent development is the "Contract for Life" developed and promoted by Students Against Drunk Driving (1982). Teenagers and their parents sign a contract in which the teenager agrees to call home to arrange for a safe ride if he/she or the driver with whom the teenager had planned to ride has been drinking. Parents agree to provide transportation without any questions, lectures, or recriminations. This contract does not provide for positive or negative contingencies, but it does effectively specify an exchange of behaviors between parents and teenagers designed to prevent tragic accidents and loss of life due to teenage drunk driving.

The preceding examples of behavioral contracts to reduce or control drinking raise two important issues. The first concerns the ethical dilemma of condoning illegal drinking by adolescents. Most therapists who use such contracts argue that the adolescents involved are already drinking and the procedures are designed to minimize the negative effects of this drinking. Such arguments are persuasive, but, nonetheless, therapists may wish to confer with their local police and school officials to determine local practices and opinions. The second issue concerns the need to choose carefully in each individual case whether the goal of treatment should be controlled drinking or total abstinence. Although empirical data on which to base this decision are still being gathered, rational guidelines are available (Heather & Robertson, 1981, pp. 215–240; Miller & Caddy, 1977) and should be used prior to implementing the preceding behavioral contracting procedures.

2. Antabuse Contracts to Promote Abstinence

Antabuse (disulfiram), a drug that produces extreme nausea and sickness when the person taking the drug ingests alcohol, is widely used in treating alcoholics with a goal of abstinence. Antabuse therapy often is not always effective because the alcoholic discontinues taking the drug prematurely. The Antabuse Contract (O'Farrell & Bayog, in press), a procedure adapted from the work of Peter Miller (Miller & Hersen, 1975) and Nathan Azrin (Azrin, Sisson, Meyers, & Godley, 1982), is designed to maintain Antabuse ingestion and abstinence from alcohol and to decrease alcohol-related arguments and interactions between the alcoholic and his/her spouse. Before negotiating such a contract, the therapist should be sure that the alcoholic is willing and medically cleared to take Antabuse and that both the alcoholic and his/her spouse have been fully informed and educated about the effects of the drug.

In the Antabuse Contract, the alcoholic agrees to take Antabuse each day while the spouse observes. The spouse, in turn, agrees to record the observation on a calendar provided by the therapist and not to mention past drinking or any concerns about future drinking. The contract is presented to the couple as a way they can help each other. In the Antabuse Contract, the alcoholic helps reassure the spouse by letting the spouse see him/her take the Antabuse each day. The spouse helps the alcoholic establish the Antabuse habit to replace the drinking habit and refrains from nagging about drinking in order to avoid drinking-related arguments that may precipitate a relapse. After the rationale for the contract has been explained, the couple is asked during the coming week to try out the behaviors specified in the contract and to consider signing the contract during the next session. Each spouse also completes at home a worksheet in which he or she describes potential benefits and desired duration of the contract (3–12 months are recommended), the best time of the day for ingestion of the Antabuse, and any questions or reservations that he or she may have.

In the following session when discussing the worksheets and any difficulties foreseen in complying with the daily procedure, the therapist should discuss both how to *view* the contract and how to *do* the contract. *Viewing* the contract constructively includes focusing on its benefits to the individual and to the marital relationship and being very clear about areas of responsibility. The spouse is not responsible for giving the Antabuse; instead, the alcoholic freely takes the Antabuse in the spouse's presence. The spouse observes the Antabuse ingestion and freely foregoes talk about drinking. It is extremely important that both partners view the agreement as a cooperative method for rebuilding trust and not as a coercive surveillance operation. *Doing* the contract refers to linking the Antabuse observation to a well-established habit such as mealtime or brushing teeth, keeping all the materials (calendar, contract, Antabuse tablets) near where the Antabuse is taken, and planning ahead for times when the routine might be broken such as during weekends, vacations, and marital crises. After the couple and therapist discuss the contract, they usually sign an Antabuse contract that is valid for at least the time that regular therapy sessions are expected to last (see Figure 1).

Maintaining the Antabuse agreement is facilitated by monitoring compliance with the procedure at the beginning of each subsequent session. The couple brings the calendar on which the observations are recorded to each session, and the therapist probes for and discusses any lapses in compliance. The couple can be asked to role play any situations that caused difficulty and

In order to help ___John Doe___ with his own

self-control and to bring peace of mind to ___Mary___,

his wife, ___John + Mary Doe___ agree to the following

arrangement:

John's Responsibilities	Mary's Responsibilities
1. Takes Antabuse each day _at night before bed_.	1. Observes the Antabuse being taken and records that she observed it on the calendar provided.
2. Thanks wife for observing the Antabuse.	2. Thanks husband for taking the Antabuse and shows her appreciation when he takes it.
3. If necessary, request that wife not mention past drinking or any fears about future drinking.	3. Does not mention past drinking or any fears about future drinking.
4. Refills Antabuse prescription **before** it runs out.	4. Reminds when prescription needs refilling.

EARLY WARNING SYSTEM: If at any time, Antabuse is not taken for

2 days in a row, ___John or Mary___ should contact

Dr. O'Farrell (583-4500, ext. 481 or 493) immediately.

LENGTH OF CONTRACT: This agreement covers the time from today

until ___October 9, 1983___. It cannot be changed unless

all three parties discuss the changes in a face-to-face meeting

of at least 30 minutes.

Date ___10/9/82___   _John Doe_   _Mary Doe_

Timothy O'Farrell (Ph.D.)

Figure 1. Sample Antabuse contract.

provide alternative strategies for dealing with such situations in the future. Phone calls from the therapist to monitor the agreement between sessions also can be very useful in getting the procedure firmly established. Monitoring is especially important during the first month of the agreement, when couples seem to have the most difficulty with the procedure. During later therapy sessions, it is usually sufficient to review the calendar briefly and to remind the couple to refill the prescription when needed and to contact the therapist if the Antabuse ingestion is not observed for 2 consecutive days. Finally, the therapist should contact the couple a few weeks prior to the expiration of the agreement to set an appointment to discuss whether or not the couple wants to renew the contract.

3. Decreasing Spouse Behaviors that Cue or Reinforce Abusive Drinking

McCrady and colleagues (e.g., McCrady & Noel, 1982) cite procedures to decrease spouse behaviors that cue or reinforce abusive drinking. McCrady (1982) described how these procedures where implemented with a male alcoholic and his wife, who were seeking abstinence. The couple identified many of the wife's behaviors that cued drinking by the husband, including her threatening to leave her husband because of his drinking, saying the children would lose respect for him, pouring alcohol down the sink or getting rid of it in other ways, hiding alcohol and questioning her husband about where he had been. The husband reacted by becoming angry or depressed and drinking still more. Moreover, the wife unwittingly reinforced her husband's drinking by protecting him from the consequences of his drinking (e.g., by attempting to make him comfortable when drunk, cleaning up after him when he drank, getting him to bed, bringing him in from the car if he had become unconscious).

As part of a multifaceted, behavioral treatment program, McCrady worked with the husband and the wife to find mutually comfortable and agreeable methods to reverse the wife's behavior that inadvertently promoted drinking. First, the couple discussed and role-played ways in which the wife could express her negative feelings about the husband's drinking in an assertive and constructive manner that would not make him feel more like drinking. The wife also rehearsed alternative behaviors to counter her tendency to protect the husband when he was drinking. Finally, the wife was taught to provide positive reinforcers (such as verbal acknowledgement, going to movies and flea markets together, making special dinners and snacks) contingent on the husband not drinking rather than in her previous noncontingent manner.

4. Methods to Assist the Family with More than One Alcohol-Abusing Member

The situation in which more than one member in a family residing together has an alcohol problem (e.g., parent and adolescent, both spouses) presents a difficult clinical challenge because rarely are all alcohol-abusing members in a family interested in changing their drinking at the same time. Clinicians often develop an individual treatment program for the family member who is willing to change. The program may involve at least a temporary removal (through hospitalization or a stay in a halfway house or residential treatment center) of the recovering alcoholic from the family environment. Marital and family interventions need to be developed for such a situation. These situations are not uncommon, but treatment solutions are rare in the published literature. Nevertheless, two interesting examples where both spouses have had an alcohol problem and seek treatment together have appeared and are presented here briefly.

Murray and Hobbs (1977) used a self-imposed, time-out procedure to help a married couple reduce their excessive drinking. The couple especially enjoyed drinking together each night at their home, and on such occasions jointly consumed $\frac{2}{3}$ quart of vodka. After a week of self-monitoring of their drinking, the couple established three goals: (1) mixing of drinks with less than 1 ounce of alcohol per drink, (2) consuming less than four drinks per day, and (3) consuming drinks at intervals greater than 30 minutes. In the first phase of treatment, each spouse was to administer a self-imposed time-out procedure contingent upon mixing of any drink containing more than 1 ounce of alcohol. Time-out consisted of a 15-minute period in which social reinforcement associated with drinking was withdrawn. Because the clients reported that they enjoyed drinking *only* while in each other's presence, they were instructed to consume their drinks in relative isolation (e.g., in the bathroom or in a corner of the bedroom) during the time-out period. In subsequent phases of the treatment, the time-out procedure was made contingent on exceeding each of the two remaining drinking reduction goals. The Murray and Hobbs procedure may be useful for couples who drink excessively together and for whom the social reinforcement from each other's company is a primary factor in drinking.

Hay (1982) described a case in which both husband and wife wanted to decrease their excessive alcohol consumption to nonproblem levels. Their treatment program contained four major components: (1) analyzing their drinking habits; (2) goal-setting and progressive decreases in consumption to target levels by use of blood alcohol level (BAL) discrimination training (with both external and internal stimulus cues) and instruction in control procedures (e.g., counting drinks, slowing rate of drinking, decreasing volume of sips); (3) rearranging and modifying conditions that cued or maintained problem drinking; and (4) learning positive alternatives to alcohol (e.g., deep muscular relaxation, direct expression of anger) to deal with problematic situations. This four-step, behavior-change strategy was conducted in conjoint sessions with both spouses who did the same homework each week and progressed through the four components at the same rate.

B. Interventions to Improve the Marital and Family Relationship

Once the alcohol abuser has decided to change his or her drinking and has begun successfully to control or abstain from drinking, the therapist is frequently told for the first time about serious marital and family problems.

Family members' resentment about past abusive drinking and fear and distrust about the possible return of abusive drinking in the future, coupled with the alcoholic's guilt and desire for recognition of improved drinking behavior, lead to an atmosphere of tension and unhappiness in marital and family relationships. There are problems caused by drinking (e.g. bills, legal charges, embarrassing incidents) that still need to be resolved. There is often a backlog of other unresolved marital and family problems that the drinking obscured. These longstanding problems may be perceived as increasing as drinking declines, when actually the problems are being recognized for the first time and alcohol cannot be used to excuse them. The family frequently lacks the communication skills and mutual positive feelings needed to resolve these problems. As a result, many marriages and families are dissolved during the first 1 or 2 years of the alcoholic's recovery. In other cases, marital and family conflicts trigger relapse and a return to abusive drinking by the alcoholic (Hore, 1971; Marlatt & Gordon, 1978, 1985). For these reasons, many alcoholics need assistance to improve their marital and family relationships once changes in drinking have begun.

1. Procedures to Increase Positive Feelings, Good Will, and Commitment to the Relationship

a. **Increasing Pleasing Behaviors.** A series of procedures can be used to increase a couple's awareness of benefits from the relationship and the frequency with which spouses notice, acknowledge, and initiate pleasing or caring behaviors on a daily basis. *Caring behaviors* are defined to couples as "behaviors showing that you care for the other person," and a long list of pleasing behaviors taken from the Spouse Observation Checklist (Weiss, 1975) provides examples. To make the notion of pleasing behaviors more relevant to a particular couple's relationship, each spouse is asked to complete and read aloud a list of 10 pleasing things that the partner does in the relationship (e.g., Stuart & Stuart, 1973, p. 3). Then homework called "Catch Your Spouse Doing Something Nice" is assigned to assist couples in *noticing* the daily caring behaviors in the marriage. This technique, developed by Turner (1972), requires each spouse to write down one caring behavior performed by the partner each day on sheets provided by the therapist (see Figure 2). To avoid arguments about accuracy of recordings, couples are instructed not to show each other their recording sheet at home during the first week of the exercise.

The couple brings their completed lists to the subsequent session and reads the caring behaviors recorded during the previous week. Then the therapist introduces *acknowledging* caring behaviors, a procedure which requires spouses to reinforce the behaviors they prefer. The therapist models acknowledging pleasing behaviors ("I liked it when you _____. It

NAME: *Mary*   NAME OF SPOUSE: *John*

DAY	DATE	PLEASING BEHAVIOR
MON.	10/8	He emptied dishwasher and folded clothes after I went to bed early because I didn't feel good.
TUES.	10/9	Brought home a rose for me.
WED.	10/10	John cleaned up after supper so I could get an early start on food shopping.
THURS.	10/11	Gave me extra money for myself.
FRI.	10/12	Called me during the day and told me how much he loved me.
SAT.	10/13	He watched the kids in the morning so I could get my hair done.
SUN.	10/14	John told me I looked nice when I got dressed to go to church.

NAME: *John*   NAME OF SPOUSE: *Mary*

DAY	DATE	PLEASING BEHAVIOR
MON.	10/8	Mary made my favorite supper.
TUES.	10/9	She put the storm windows on the windows and doors so I would have more time on Sat.
WED.	10/10	Told me she loved me.
THURS.	10/11	Got up and fixed breakfast for me even though she was up late the night before.
FRI.	10/12	After I came home from work she filled the tub and we jumped in together, etc! (The kids were at her mother's.)
SAT.	10/13	Mary came out and looked at the work I had done in the yard and told me how nice it looked.
SUN.	10/14	Made coffee and talked with me for an hour.

Figure 2. Sample record sheets of daily caring behaviors.

made me feel _____.''), noting the importance of eye contact; a smile; a sincere, pleasant tone of voice; and only positive feelings. The last point is stressed because many couples initially compare current positive behaviors with the past or express doubt that the new behaviors will continue. Each spouse then practices acknowledging the two best caring behaviors from his or her daily list for the previous week. Although this positive acknowledging is often very difficult for many couples, repeated role-playing with extensive prompting, coaching, and modeling by the therapist is most often successful in instigating the desired behavior. After the couple practices the new behavior in the therapy session, the therapist assigns for homework a 2–5 minute daily communication session in which each partner acknowledges one pleasing behavior noticed that day. In the next session, spouses first describe how they felt at home when giving and receiving significant caring behaviors, and then repeat the role-playing practice of acknowledging the two most appreciated caring behaviors noticed during the previous week.

As couples begin to notice and acknowledge daily caring behaviors, each partner begins *initiating* more caring behaviors. It is particularly encouraging when the weekly reports of daily caring behaviors show that one or both spouses are fulfilling requests for desired change voiced before the therapy. In addition, many couples report that the 2–5 minute communication sessions serve to initiate conversation about everyday events. A final technique is the assignment that each partner give the other a caring day during the coming week by performing special acts to show caring for the spouse. The therapist should encourage each partner to take risks and to act lovingly toward the spouse rather than wait for the other to initiate a move. Finally, spouses are reminded that at the start of therapy they agreed to try to act differently (e.g., more lovingly) and then assess changes in feelings, rather than wait to feel more positively toward their partner before instituting changes in their own behavior.

b. Planning Shared Recreational and Leisure Activities. Many alcoholic couples have discontinued shared leisure activities because in the past the alcoholic has frequently sought enjoyment only in situations involving alcohol and embarrassed the spouse by drinking too much. The importance of shared leisure activities is illustrated by a recent study which found that participation by the couple and family in social and recreational activities was one of the few family characteristics associated with positive alcoholism treatment outcome (Moos, Bromet, Tsu, & Moos, 1979).

Planning and engaging in Shared Recreational Activities (SRAs) might be initiated by simply having each spouse make a separate list of possible activities. Each activity must involve both spouses, either by themselves or with their children or other adults. Couples are told to include in their lists activities they used to do and enjoyed but have stopped as well as things they have wanted to do but have not. In addition, spouses are asked to list both activities that are possible in the next few weeks and those that require much planning or expense and for which only approximations may be feasible. The therapist often finds that many activities appear on both partners' lists even when a couple has serious conflicts about recreation. Before giving the couple a homework assignment of planning an SRA, the therapist should model an SRA planning session illustrating solutions to common pitfalls (e.g., waiting until the last minute so that necessary preparations cannot be made, getting sidetracked on trivial practical arrangements). Finally, the therapist should instruct the couple to refrain from discussing problems or conflicts during their planned SRAs.

c. Core Symbols. Core symbols, or symbols of special meaning, offer another means to develop positive feelings and interactions in a relationship. A core symbol is any event, place, or object that carries special meaning for the relationship to both marital partners (Liberman, Wheeler, deVisser, Kuehnel, & Kuehnel, 1980). Core symbols can be experienced regularly — every anniversary, New Year's Eve, monthly, or annually — and bring back warm, positive memories of mutual love, romance, shared joy, and affection. A special song, the honeymoon, the place where the couple met, pictures, eating by candlelight, and wedding rings are examples of core symbols of a marriage. In addition to objects, places, and times, rituals and activities are examples of core symbols. A weekly ritual of going out for breakfast on Sunday morning, for example, can become a core symbol and represent an intimate shared time set aside for closeness. Such rituals and activities go beyond the mere recreational activities described earlier because of their special meaning to the couple.

Core symbols have the best effect with alcoholic couples if the symbols are introduced after some of the initial tension over drinking has decreased and the partners are beginning to experience some good will and positive feeling for each other. After the therapist introduces the concept of core symbols and tries to get each partner to give one example of such a symbol from their own relationship, a homework assignment is given for each spouse to list as many core symbols as possible. Subsequent sessions involve discussions of the core symbols and attempts to get the couple to choose one or more core symbols to reexperience or reestablish in their day-to-day lives together. Some relationships have been so badly damaged by alcohol that the search for core symbols that have not been poisoned by alcohol proves fruitless. In such cases, the goal is to help the couple develop and enact new core symbols in their relationship. Identifying and participating in such core symbols can help couples foster positive feelings that have been buried for years under many layers of hostility and disappointment.

d. Applications to Family Therapy. Core symbols, planning recreational and leisure activities, and increasing positive behaviors can be applied to family therapy in which one or more children are included with their parents. Family therapy sessions are particularly useful and indicated when an adolescent has an alcohol problem or when the alcoholic parent and his/her spouse have made some progress and the therapist wishes then to include the children in the therapy. Using core symbols in family therapy sessions can be very powerful because special activities and rituals forge strong family ties and traditions. Similarly, planning recreational and leisure activities for the whole family or selected members (e.g., father and son) can be quite rewarding, and the preceding procedures for couples are directly applicable. The procedures directed to increasing pleasing behavior often can lead to pronounced changes in the emotional tone of the family, especially when the therapist can get the entire family to participate.

2. Procedures to Resolve Conflicts and Problems and Negotiate Desired Changes

a. Communication Skills Training. Inadequate communication is a major problem for alcoholic couples, and the inability to resolve conflicts and problems can cause abusive drinking and severe marital and family tension to recur. Therapists can use instructions, modeling, prompting, behavioral rehearsal, and feedback to teach couples and families how to communicate more effectively. Learning communication skills of listening and expressing feelings directly, and how to use planned communication sessions are essential prerequisites for problem solving and negotiating desired behavior changes. The training starts with nonproblem areas that are positive or neutral and moves to problem areas and charged issues only after each skill has been practiced on less problematic topics.

i. Communication Sessions. A communication session is a planned, structured discussion in which spouses talk privately, face-to-face, without distractions, and with each spouse taking turns expressing his or her point of view without interruptions. Communication sessions can be introduced for 2–5 minutes daily when couples first practice acknowledging caring behaviors and in 10- to 15-minute sessions three to four times a week in later sessions when the concern is to practice a particular skill. The therapist discusses with the couple the time and place that they plan to have their assigned communication practice sessions. The success of this plan is assessed at the next session, and any needed changes are suggested. In addition to being a vehicle to cue communication practice, a communication session is a method that couples can use to exercise stimulus control over their problem-solving discussions during and after therapy. Therapists can give examples of communication that are faulty mainly because of the setting in which they occur (e.g., raising an issue of family finances in the car with the kids on the freeway when everyone is tired and hungry). Just establishing a communication session as a method for discussing feelings, events, and problems can be very helpful for many couples. Couples are encouraged to ask each other for a communication session when they want to discuss an issue or problem and to keep in mind the ground rules of behavior that characterize such a session.

ii. Listening. Adequate listening helps each spouse to feel understood and supported and slows down couple interactions to prevent quick escalation of aversive exchanges. The therapist begins by defining effective communication as "message intended (by speaker) equals message received (by listener)" (Gottman, Notarius, Gonso, & Markman, 1976). Spouses are instructed to use the listening response ("What I heard you say was . . . . Is that right?") to repeat both the words and the feelings of the speaker's message and to check to see if the message they received was the message intended by their partner. When the listener has understood the speaker's message, roles change and the first listener then speaks. Teaching a partner in an alcoholic marriage to communicate support and understanding by summarizing the spouse's message and checking the accuracy of the received message before stating his or her own position is often a major accomplishment that has to be achieved gradually. A partner's failure to separate understanding the spouse's position from agreement with it often is an obstacle that must be overcome.

As with the Antabuse contract, both how the couples *practice* listening skills and how they *view* them are important. In terms of practicing the skill, couples are instructed to keep each message to a reasonable length and to use the exact words of the listening response until they have mastered the skill. Most couples need repeated practice with feedback, stressing both the verbal and the nonverbal (eye contact, voice, tone, facial expression, posture) components of the behavior. Spouses need to be taught specifically how to respond when the listener did not receive the message intended by the speaker. The speaker first must indicate what part of the message was correctly repeated by the listener, and then state what additional information he/she was trying to convey. The interchange is complete when the speaker's intended message has been understood by the listener. The speaker may have to repeat the paraphrasing a number of times before the intended message is received accurately. Some couples view this exercise in terms of credit and blame, so when a message sent is not received accurately, one partner must be to blame — either one spouse is a bad listener or the other is an inadequate speaker who did not make his/her message clear. Therapists need to teach couples that the exercise is a cooperative task-oriented effort, that it is equally likely over the long run that unclear reception of messages will arise from unclear sending as from inaccurate hearing, and that the technique is most useful when initial communication is somewhat unclear.

iii. Expressing Feelings Directly. Therapists can teach the skill of expressing feelings directly as an alternative to the blaming, hostile, and indirect responsibility-avoiding communication behaviors that characterize many alcoholic marriages (Becker & Miller, 1976; O'Farrell & Birchler, 1985; Gorad, 1971). The therapist instructs that when the speaker expresses feelings directly, there is a greater chance that he or she will be heard because the speaker says these are his or her feelings, his or her point of view, and not some objective fact about the other person. The speaker takes responsibility for his or her own feelings and does not blame the other person for how he or she feels, thus reducing listener defensiveness and making it easier for the listener to receive the intended message. Differences between direct expressions of feelings and indirect and ineffective or hurtful expressions are presented along with examples such as the following:

Indirect	Direct
1. You're a very likeable person.	1. I like you.
2. This is the kind of situation that makes a person uneasy.	2. I feel uneasy in this situation.
3. Why can't you be on time?	3. I'm mad at you for being late.
4. Beating around the bush and hinting indirectly that feelings are hurt.	4. Owning up to feeling hurt by partner's forgetting anniversary.

The use of statements beginning with "I" rather than "you" is emphasized. After rationale and instructions have been presented, the therapist models correct and incorrect ways of expressing positive and negative feelings and elicits the couple's reactions to these modeled scenes. Then the couple role-plays a communication session in which spouses take turns being speaker and listener, with the speaker expressing feelings directly and the listener using the listening response. During this role-playing, the therapist is poised to prompt, model, stop action, and give feedback to the couple as they practice reflecting the direct expressions of feelings. Similar communication sessions, 10 to 15 minutes each three to four times weekly, are assigned for homework. Subsequent therapy sessions involve more practice with role-playing during the sessions and for homework, and the topics on which the couple practices increase in difficulty each week.

b. Problem-Solving Skills Training. After the couple has first learned basic communication skills, they should next learn problem-solving skills to solve problems stemming from both external stressors (e.g., job, extended family) and relationship conflicts. In solving a problem, the couple should first list a number of possible solutions. Then, while withholding judgment regarding the preferred solution, the couple considers both positive and negative, and short-term and long-term consequences of each solution. Finally, the spouses rank the solutions from most to least preferred and agree to implement one or more of the solutions. As with other behavioral skills, the sequence in learning problem-solving skills is as follows: (1) therapist instructions and modeling, (2) the couple practicing under therapist supervision, (3) assignment for homework, and (4) review of homework with further practice. Use of problem-solving procedures can help spouses avoid polarizing on one solution or another or the "yes, but . . ." trap of one partner pointing out the negative consequences to the other partner's solution.

 c. Behavior Change Agreements. Many alcoholics and their spouses need to learn positive methods to change their partner's behavior to replace the coercive strategies used previously. Many changes that spouses desire from their partners can be achieved through the aforementioned caring behaviors, rewarding activities, and communication and problem-solving skills. However, the deeper, emotion-laden conflicts that have caused considerable hostility and coercive interaction for years are more resistant to change. Nevertheless, changes often can be achieved through specific behavior change agreements. In addition to general communication skills and a spirit of good will, learning to make positive specific requests (PSR) and to negotiate and compromise are prerequisites for making sound behavior-change agreements to resolve such issues.

 i. Positive Specific Requests. To introduce PSR, the therapist explains that couples often complain in vague and unclear terms and they try to coerce, browbeat, and force the other partner to change. The couple is told that in order to negotiate desired changes in the relationship "each partner has to learn to state his/her desires in the form of: *positive*—what you want, not what you don't want; *specific*—what, where, and when; *requests*—not demands that use force and threats but rather requests that show possibility for negotiation and compromise." To illustrate PSR, the following sample requests (adapted from Weiss & Ford, 1975) are valuable:

I'd like my partner to:
1. Kiss me when I come home from work
2. Help out more around the house
3. Tell me about his or her work day at dinnertime
4. Stop bugging me so much
5. Do the dishes on nights that I go to class
6. Appreciate me more
7. Have sex with me more often
8. Hold my hand while we watch TV
9. Put his or her dirty clothes in the hamper
10. Spend more time with our kids
11. Stop acting like a prude when I want sex.

The couple is asked to indicate which of these requests meets the PSR criteria and, after feedback from the therapist, rewrites the incorrect requests (nos. 2, 6, 7, 10—not specific; Nos. 4 and 11— neither positive nor specific), making each into a PSR. For homework, each partner is asked to list at least five PSRs for use in future therapy sessions.

 ii. Negotiation and compromise. Spouses share their lists of requests, starting with the most specific and positive items, and the therapist gives feedback on the requests presented and helps rewrite items as needed. Then the therapist explains that negotiating and compromising can help couples reach an agreement in which each partner will do one thing requested by the other. To help couples compromise and agree to granting a stated request, they must be instructed to translate each request onto a continuum of possible activities in terms of frequency, duration, intensity, or situation rather than present the request in all-or-none terms. For example, if a husband stated his desire for more independence and time to work on his hobbies, this general, vague goal might be translated into explicit dimensions of activity such as when, how often, how long, and where. The couple can negotiate these dimensions. Perhaps the husband and his wife would agree to his spending an hour three times weekly after supper in the basement or garage. After giving instructions and examples, the therapist coaches a couple while they have a communication session in which requests are made in a positive specific form, heard by each partner, and translated into a mutually satisfactory, realistic agreement for the upcoming week. The therapist must be sure that the couple uses all the communication skills taught previously to help them reach a reasonable compromise. Agreed-to requests must be realistic, reasonable, and commensurate with previously demonstrated skills of the spouses because fanciful and optimistic promises lead to weak agreements with little chance of success. Finally, the agreement is recorded on a homework sheet that the couple knows will be reviewed during the next session.

iii. Agreements. A major portion of the therapy sessions can be devoted to negotiating written behavior-change agreements for the forthcoming week, often with very good effects on the couple's relationship. Figure 3 shows a typical example of a couple agreement. During the sessions, unkept agreements are reviewed briefly, and the therapist provides feedback as to what went wrong and suggests changes needed in the coming week. After completing agreements under therapist supervision, the couple is asked to have a communication session at home to negotiate an agreement on their own and to bring it to the following session for review. A series of such assignments can provide a couple with the opportunity to develop skills in behavior change that they can use after the therapy ends. The present author usually encourages good-faith agreements (Weiss, Birchler, & Vincent, 1974) in which each partner agrees to make his/her change independent of whether or not the spouse keeps the agreement and without monetary or other reward of punishment contingencies. This approach, which has been used by others (Turkewitz & O'Leary, 1981), is simpler than other approaches to couple agreements and stresses the need for each spouse freely and unilaterally to make the changes needed to improve the marital relationship.

d. Applications to Family Therapy. The preceding methods for training communication, problem-solving, and behavior change skills are directly applicable to family therapy sessions involving an alcoholic and his/her

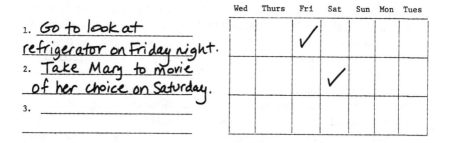

Name: __John + Mary Doe__ Week Beginning: __10/12/83 (Wed.)__

__John's__
RESPONSIBILITIES (__Mary__ checks when performed)

	Wed	Thurs	Fri	Sat	Sun	Mon	Tues
1. Go to look at refrigerator on Friday night.			✓				
2. Take Mary to movie of her choice on Saturday.				✓			
3.							

__Mary's__
RESPONSIBILITIES (__John__ checks when performed)

	Wed	Thurs	Fri	Sat	Sun	Mon	Tues
1. Serve dinner in kitchen three nights this week.	✓	✓				✓	
2. Sit down for 15-minute communication session after	✓	✓	✓			✓	
3. supper each night.							

SIGNED: __John Doe__ and __Mary Doe__

DATE: __10/11/83__

Figure 3. Sample couple agreement.

children and spouse, or an adolescent alcohol abuser and his/her parents. The present author's practice is to relabel the communication sessions as family council meetings or family meetings and to emphasize very strongly some additional ground rules that characterize such a meeting: one person speaks at a time, no interrupting is permitted, and a consensus must be reached to enact a decision. The latter is to guard against parents (or other subgroups) forcing their will on weaker family members. For more details on the use of behavioral family therapy with adolescents and parents, the reader is referred to work by Robin and colleagues on family sessions to improve the communication between adolescents and their parents (e.g., Robin, 1981). These techniques, which are similar to the ones just described for couples, can be extremely useful for families with alcohol problems because many adult alcoholics have severe problems with their adolescent offspring; and the growing number of adolescent alcohol abusers frequently have quite troubled relationships with their parents. Behavior-change agreements are also quite useful with children and their parents, but the behavior changes of the children may be more numerous than those of the parents and generally reward/punishment contingencies are useful because (unlike the marital relationship) the parent–child relationship is not one of equal partners.

IV. MAINTAINING CHANGES IN THE DRINKING AND IN MARITAL–FAMILY RELATIONSHIPS

A. Relapse Prevention

Methods to ensure long-term maintenance of the changes in alcohol problems made through marital and family therapy have received very little attention and need considerable development. The present author has a few general methods that he uses during the maintenance phase of treatment. This phase is defined somewhat arbitrarily as the phase that begins after at least 6 consecutive months of abstinence or consistent nonproblem drinking have been achieved. Maintenance must be planned prior to the termination of the active treatment phase. As a first step, a therapist can review the previous marital–family therapy sessions with the clients to determine which therapeutic interventions or behavior changes (e.g., Antabuse contract, communication sessions) have been most helpful. Once these have been identified, the therapist and couple/family can plan how long the family wants to continue the new behavior and how to ensure that they will be likely to engage in the desired behavior when needed (e.g., rehearsing how to cope with situations likely to interfere with the new behavior, rereading handouts from the therapy periodically, agreeing to periodic monitoring by the therapist).

A second method is to anticipate what high-risk situations for relapse to abusive drinking may be likely to occur after treatment and to discuss and rehearse possible coping strategies that the alcoholic and other family members can use to prevent relapse when confronted with such situations. To achieve these goals, the therapist can have the alcoholic and other family members complete a worksheet, adapted from a section of the Drinking Profile (Marlatt & Miller, 1984), for homework to help specify high-risk situations and to prepare for discussions about how to prevent relapse.

A third method is to discuss and rehearse how to cope with a relapse when it occurs. Here, the techniques suggested by Marlatt (e.g., Curry & Marlatt's chapter in this volume) can be useful: allowing a delay after the first drink, calling the therapist, and engaging in realistic and rational thinking about the slip. A specific couple–family relapse-episode plan, written and rehearsed prior to ending active treatment, can be particularly useful. Early intervention at the beginning of a relapse episode is essential and must be stressed with the couple–family. Often, spouses and family members wait until the drinking has reached dangerous levels again before acting. By then, much additional damage has been done to the marital and family relationship and to other aspects of the drinker's life. To prevent this eventuality, it can be helpful to have the alcoholic and family members identify danger signs that they consider likely precursors of a drinking episode and determine their course of action if such signs do occur. However, care must be taken to ensure that actions taken to deal with family members' perceived danger signs and fears do not produce couple–family interactions that unwittingly lead to relapse.

Given the lack of data available about how best to promote long-term maintenance, the present author continues contact with the couple/family via planned follow-up sessions at regular and then gradually increasing intervals for 3 to 5 years after a stable pattern of recovery (e.g., 6-month's abstinence) has been achieved. One schedule of follow-up contacts is office visits at 2, 6, and 12 months follow-up for the first year, and twice yearly thereafter, coupled with monthly phone calls between office visits during the first year, bimonthly calls during the second year, and quarterly phone calls thereafter. This frequent and ongoing contact with· the couple–family is a very useful method to monitor progress, to assess compliance with planned maintenance procedures, and to evaluate the need for additional preventive sessions. If continued contact is to be maintained successfully, the therapist must take responsibility for scheduling and reminding the family of follow-up sessions and for placing agreed-upon phone calls. The rationale given to couples and families for the continued contact is that alcohol abuse is a chronic health problem that requires active, aggressive, ongoing monitoring by the therapist and family members to prevent or to quickly treat relapses for 5 years after an initial stable pattern of recovery has been established. The follow-up contact also provides the opportunity to deal with marital and family issues that appear after a period of recovery.

B. Marital and Family Issues in Long-Term Recovery

Many alcohol abusers continue to experience significant marital and family difficulties after a period of stable recovery has been established. Although a wide variety of issues can present difficulties during long-term recovery, a number of concerns and life patterns predominate. Difficulties in role readjustment occur when the family members resist the alcohol abuser's efforts to regain important roles in the family (e.g., disciplinarian, equal partner and parent) that were lost through drinking. Nearly all families with a seriously alcoholic member face this problem early in the recovery process and, although many resolve it on their own, some will need help. Couples often cite problems of sex and intimacy (O'Farrell, Weyand, & Logan, 1983) somewhat later in recovery, when many of the most severe hardships due to alcohol abuse have been repaired and family roles have started to restabilize. These problems do not usually develop later in recovery, but rather the couple is willing and able to consider confronting such issues only after more pressing problems have been resolved. Problems with children, especially communication and behavior management with adolescents, frequently become a focus for intervention during long-term recovery. Finally, families during the recovery process seem particularly vulnerable to stresses created by critical transitions in the family life cycle (e.g., children leaving home), external life change events (e.g., job loss), and/or developmental changes in any of the family members (e.g., mid-life crisis). A few case examples from the author's experience illustrate these points.

A male alcoholic with 5 years' sobriety, who had seen the author in marital therapy early in the recovery process, now had yearly couple sessions to review current status and to renegotiate a yearly Antabuse contract. The client's wife called for help when the husband refused to participate in the Antbuse observation, despite their agreement, and threatened to drink and to end the marriage. Contact with the husband revealed that he was still taking Antabuse although he would not give his wife the satisfaction of knowing this. A few crisis-intervention sessions revealed the factors that had precipitated the marital crisis. Serious sexual problems, consisting of few displays of affection, infrequent attempts to have sexual contact, and the husband's difficultly in maintaining an erection, had concerned the couple for a few years. The husband's 50th birthday was approaching, and he wanted to have more sexual fulfillment and closeness in the marriage or the freedom to seek it in a new relationship "before it is too late." In addition, the couple had a mentally ill son in the early 20s who had shown in the previous year that he was not going to be able to support himself or to live outside a sheltered setting.

In another case, a male alcoholic with 12 years' sobriety, achieved through AA for himself and Al-Anon for his wife, sought help after becoming involved in an extramarital affair with a co-worker. The husband had discontinued his participation in AA a number of years previously and currently did not have any inclination to drink although his wife remained a regular Al-Anon participant. The wife attributed her husband's affair to his alcoholic personality, meaning that although he was not drinking, he was still lying and sneaking around and that the affair was a substitute for the drinking. Further assessment indicated that in the previous year the wife had started to work outside the home. In addition, the husband's job had become much more stressful, requiring him to work during evenings and on Saturdays, and the long hours made him quite irritable. These changes disrupted evening and weekend activities previously enjoyed by the couple, and the wife withdrew affection and communication in response to the husband's irritability, choosing to use her Al-Anon friends for support instead. When the husband turned to the woman at work, the couple's problems escalated.

In both examples, marital therapy was successful in resolving the marital crises. The issues in these cases are not unique to alcoholic families, and, in fact, such issues are very commonly presented for therapy by couples and families where alcohol is not a problem. Nonetheless, the therapist has two additional responsibilities when such issues are presented by alcoholic families during recovery. First, the therapist must carefully assess the current status of the drinking to determine if a relapse is imminent so that necessary preventive interventions can be instituted immediately. Second, the therapist must (1) determine each family member's view of the relationship between the former alcohol problem and the current marital/family difficulties and (2) carefully assess whether or not he/she shares the family member's view. The latter is important because family members often continue to attribute difficulties in their relationships to the previous alcohol problem rather than to their current life situation. For example, in the second case just presented, the wife incorrectly attributed her husband's extramarital affair to his alcoholic personality despite his 12 years of sobriety.

V. CONCLUDING COMMENTS

This chapter has presented a variety of techniques for marital and family therapy for alcohol problems that can be used at the various stages of the change process. Nevertheless, the paucity of available material on some important topics suggests a number of future needs in the area of marital and family therapy for alcohol problems. For example, there is clearly a need to develop and scientifically evaluate marital and family interventions specifically for adult female alcoholics, adolescent alcohol abusers, the couple–family with more than one actively alcoholic member, and homosexual couples with alcohol problems. Similarly, methods for use with alcohol problems that may not warrant a diagnosis of alcoholism or that may be presented in settings other than ones specifically for alcoholism treatment (e.g., practices of primary care physicians or marriage counselors) also need to be developed and rigorously evaluated (see Sanchez-Craig, Wilkinson, & Walker's chapter in this volume). Finally, the role of marital/family interventions for the prevention of alcohol problems should be carefully explored. For example, specific consideration should be given to family education to prevent the fetal alcohol syndrome, the role of the family in educating children in responsible drinking practices, and marital/family education of high-risk groups (e.g., children of alcoholics) prior to or early in marriage.

Note Added in Proof

When this chapter was in the final proofs, the first study to report outcome data on family-member involvement to motivate the alcoholic to stop drinking was published. Sisson and Azrin (1986) developed and evaluated a behavior therapy program for teaching the nonalcoholic family member (usually the wife of a male alcoholic) (1) how to reduce physical abuse to herself, (2) how to encourage sobriety, (3) how to encourage seeking professional treatment, and (4) how to assist in that treatment. To reduce physical abuse, she was taught how to react at the earliest sign of impending violence as well as to the violence itself. To encourage sobriety, she learned how to reinforce the alcoholic for periods of sobriety and how to arrange negative consequences of drinking through requiring the drinker to take responsibility for correcting or overcorrecting the disruption caused by his drinking. To encourage him to seek treatment, the family member learned to identify moments when the drinker was most motivated to stop drinking, generally after specific occasions when the alcohol problem had become especially severe. Examples of such occasions are after a physically debilitating drinking episode, after spending much money unwisely, after a car accident or having some contact with the law, or after the drinker did something while intoxicated which he would not do otherwise and for which he felt embarrassed or ashamed. The family member was taught to recognize such moments of high motivation and to suggest counseling. If the drinker agreed, the family members attended the professional sessions and helped the alcoholic to engage in the prescribed activities thereafter. See Azrin et al. (1982) for details of the family-involved treatment sessions.

This behavior therapy program was compared with a traditional type of counseling for the family member, which included education about the disease concept of alcoholism, supportive individual sessions, and a firm referral to Al-Anon in which the family member was accompanied by a current member. Outcome data showed that the behavior therapy program resulted in more alcoholics obtaining treatment than did the traditional type and a greater reduction in drinking before the formal treatment was obtained; drinking was reduced further during the joint treatment of the family members and problem drinkers. Sisson and Azrin (1986) concluded that the counseling of concerned family members in the use of appropriate reinforcement procedures can reduce the drinking of unmotivated alcoholics and lead to the initiation of treatment.

ACKNOWLEDGMENTS

A number of the interventions described in Section IIIB were first used by the author in a research project conducted in collaboration with Henry S. G. Cutter and Frank J. Floyd. This research project was conducted in the Alcoholism Treatment Unit (ATU) at the Brockton, Massachusetts, Veterans Administration Medical Center with the generous cooperation of the ATU's staff and director, Rogelio Bayog. Grants from the Veterans Administration and Ayerst Laboratories supported the research project.

REFERENCES

Azrin, N. H., Sisson, R. W., Meyers, R., & Godley, M. (1982). Alcoholism treatment by Disulfiram and community reinforcement therapy. *Journal of Behavior Therapy and Experimental Psychiatry,* **13,** 105–112.

Becker, J. V., & Miller, P. M. (1976). Verbal and nonverbal marital interaction patterns of alcoholics and nonalcoholics. *Journal of Studies on Alcohol,* **37,** 1616–1624.

Billings, A. C., Kessler, M., Gomberg, C. A., & Weiner, S. (1979). Marital conflict resolution of alcoholic and nonalcoholic couples during drinking and nondrinking sessions. *Journal of Studies on Alcohol,* **40,** 183–195.

Black, R., & Mayer, J. (1980). Parents with special problems: Alcoholism and opiate addiction. *Child Abuse and Neglect,* **4,** 45–54.

Cassady, J. L. (1975, September). *The use of parents and contract therapy in rehabilitating delinquent adolescents involved in drug and alcohol abuse.* Paper presented at the 26th annual meeting of the Alcohol and Drug Problems Association of North America.

Cheek, F. E., Franks, C. M., Laucius J., & Burtle, V., (1971). Behavioral modification training for wives of alcoholics. *Quarterly Journal of Studies on Alcohol,* **32,** 456–461.

Davis, D. I., Berenson, D., Steinglass, P., & Davis, S. (1974). The adaptive consequences of drinking. *Psychiatry,* **37,** 209–215.

Eisler, R. M., Miller, P. M., Hersen, M., & Alford H. (1974). Effects of assertiveness training on marital interaction. *Archives of General Psychiatry,* **30,** 643–649.

Finney, J. W., Moos, R. H., & Mewborn, C. R. (1980). Posttreatment experiences and treatment outcome of alcoholic patients six months and two years after hospitalization. *Journal of Consulting and Clinical Psychology,* **48,** 17–29.

Gorad, S. L. (1971). Communication styles and interaction of alcoholics and their wives. *Family Process,* **10,** 475–489.

Gottman, J., Notarius, C., Gonso, J., & Markman, H. (1976). *A couples guide to communication.* Champaign, IL: Research Press.

Hanks, S. E., & Rosenbaum, P. C. (1977). Battered women: A study of women who live with violent alcohol-abusing men. *American Journal of Orthopsychiatry,* **47,** 291–306.

Hay, W. M. (1982). The behavioral assessment and treatment of an alcoholic marriage. In W. M. Hay, & P. E. Nathan (Eds.), *Clinical case studies in the behavioral treatment of alcoholism* (pp. 157–182). New York: Plenum Press.

Heather, N., & Robertson, I. (1981). *Controlled drinking.* London: Methuen.

Hore, B. D. (1971). Life events and alcoholic relapse. *British Journal of Addiction,* **66,** 83–88.

Janzen, C. (1977). Families in the treatment of alcoholism. *Journal of Studies on Alcohol,* **38,** 114–130.

Johnson, V. A. (1973). *I'll quit tomorrow.* New York: Harper & Row.

Keller, M. (Ed.). (1974). Trends in treatment of alcoholism. In *Second special report to the U.S. Congress on alcohol and health.* (pp. 145–167). Washington, DC: Department of Health, Education, and Welfare.

Lazarus, A. A. (1968). Behavior therapy and marriage counseling. *Journal of the American Society of Psychosomatic Dentistry and Medicine,* **15,** 49–56.

Liberman, R. P., Wheeler, E. G., de Visser, L. A., Kuehnel, J., & Kuehnel, T. (1980). *Handbook of marital therapy.* New York: Plenum.

Maisto, S. A., O'Farrell, T. J., Connors, G. J., McKay, J., & Pelcovits, M. A. (in press). Alcoholics' attributions of factors affecting their relapse to drinking and reasons for terminating relapse events. *Addictive Behaviors.*

Marlatt, G. A., & Gordon, J. (1978). *Determinants of relapse: Implications for the maintenance of behavior change.* Alcoholism and Drug Institute: Technical Report No. 78–07, University of Washington.

Marlatt, G. A., & Gordon, J. (1985). *Relapse prevention: Maintenance strategies in the treatment of addictive behaviors.* New York: Guilford.

Marlatt, G. A., & Miller, W. R. (1984). *Comprehensive Drinker Profile.* Odessa, FL: Psychological Assessment Resources, Inc.

McCrady, B. S. (1982). Conjoint behavioral treatment of an alcoholic and his spouse. In W. M. Hay & P. E. Nathan (Eds.), *Clinical case studies in the behavioral treatment of alcoholism* (pp. 127–156). New York: Plenum.

McCrady, B. S., & Noel, N. E. (1982, November). Assessing the optimal mode of spouse involvement in outpatient behavioral treatment of alcoholism. In T. J. O'Farrell (Chair), *Spouse-involved treatment for alcohol abuse.* Symposium conducted at the annual meeting of the Association for the Advancement of Behavior Therapy, San Francisco, CA.

Miller, P. M. (1972). The use of behavioral contracting in the treatment of alcoholism: A case report. *Behavioral Therapy,* **3,** 593–596.

Miller, P. M., & Hersen, M. (1975). *Modification of marital interaction patterns between an alcoholic and his wife.* Unpublished manuscript (Available from Peter Miller, Hilton Head Hospital, Hilton Head Island, SC.)

Miller, W. R., & Caddy, G. R. (1977). Abstinence and controlled drinking in the treatment of problem drinkers. *Journal of Studies on Alcohol,* **38,** 986–1003.

Miller, W. R., & Muñoz, R. F. (1982). *How to control your drinking.* Albuquerque, NM: University of New Mexico Press.

Moos, R. H., Bromet, E., Tsu, V., & Moos, B. (1979). Family characteristics and the outcome of treatment for alcoholism. *Journal of Studies on Alcohol,* **40,** 78–88.

Murray, R. G., & Hobbs, S. A. (1977). The use of a self-imposed timeout procedure in the modification of excessive alcohol consumption. *Journal of Behavior Therapy and Experimental Psychiatry,* **8,** 377–380.

O'Farrell, T. J., & Bayog, R. D. (in press). Antabuse contracts for married alcoholics and their spouses: A method to insure Antabuse taking and decrease conflict about alcohol. *Journal of Substance Abuse Treatment.*

O'Farrell, T. J., & Birchler, G. (1985, September). *Marital Relationships of alcoholic, conflicted, and nonconflicted couples.* Paper presented at the Annual Meeting of the American Psychological Association, Los Angeles, CA.

O'Farrell, T. J., & Cutter, H. S. G. (1979). A proposed behavioral couples group for male alcoholics and their wives. In D. Upper & S. M. Ross (Eds.), *Behavioral group therapy: An annual review.* (pp. 277–298). Champaign, IL: Research Press.

O'Farrell, T. J., & Cutter, H. S. G. (1984a). Behavioral marital therapy couples groups for male alcoholics and their wives. *Journal of Substance Abuse Treatment,* **1,** 191–204.

O'Farrell, T. J., & Cutter, H. S. G. (1984b). Behavioral marital therapy for alcoholics: Clinical procedures from a treatment outcome study in progress. *American Journal of Family Therapy,* **12,** 33–46.

O'Farrell, T. J., Cutter, H. S. G., & Floyd, F. J. (1985). Evaluating behavioral marital therapy for male alcoholics: Effects on marital adjustment and communication from before to after therapy. *Behavior Therapy,* **16,** 147–167.

O'Farrell, T. J., Harrison, R. H., & Cutter, H. S. G. (1981). Marital stability among wives of alcoholics: An evaluation of three explanations. *British Journal of Addiction,* **76,** 175 – 189.

O'Farrell, T. J., Weyand, C. A., & Logan, D. (1983). *Alcohol and sexuality: An annotated bibliography on alcohol use, alcoholism and human sexual behavior.* Phoenix, AZ: The Oryx Press.

Paolino, T. J., & McCrady, B. S. (1977). *The alcoholic marriage: Alternative perspectives.* New York: Grune and Stratton.

Prochaska, J. O., & DiClemente, C. C. (1983). Stages and processes of self-change of smoking: Toward an integrative model of change. *Journal of Consulting and Clinical Psychology,* **51,** 390 – 395.

Robin, A. (1981). A controlled evaluation of problem-solving communication training with parent – adolescent conflict. *Behavior Therapy,* **12,** 593 – 609.

Sisson, R. W., & Azrin, N. H. (1986). Family-member involvement, to initiate and promote treatment of problem drinkers. *Journal of Behavior Therapy and Experimental Psychiatry,* **17,** 15 – 21.

Sobell, M. B., & Sobell, L. C. (1975). A brief technical report on the MOBAT: An inexpensive portable test for determining blood alcohol concentration. *Journal of Applied Behavioral Analysis,* **8,** 117 – 120.

Stuart, R. B., & Stuart, F. (1973). *Marital pre-counseling inventory.* Champaign, IL: Research Press.

Students Against Drunk Driving (SADD). (1982). *If we dream it, it can be done.* (Available from SADD, 110 Pleasant St., Marlboro, MA 01752.)

Teicher, J. D., Sinay, R. D., & Stumphauzer, J. S. (1976). Training community-based professionals as behavior therapists with families of alcohol-abusing adolescents. *American Journal of Psychiatry,* **133,** 847 – 850.

Thomas, E. J., & Santa, C. A. (1982). Unilateral family therapy for alcohol abuse: A working conception. *The American Journal of Family Therapy,* **10,** 49 – 60.

Thomas, E. J., Santa, C. A., & Bronson, D. (1984, March). *A treatment program of unilateral family therapy for alcohol abuse.* Paper presented at The Annual Meeting of the Council on Social Work Education, Detroit, MI.

Thorne, D. R. (1983). Techniques for use in intervention. *Journal of Alcohol and Drug Education,* **28,** 46 – 50.

Turner, J. (1972, October). *Couple and group treatment of marital discord.* Paper presented at the Sixth Annual Meeting of the Association for the Advancement of Behavior Therapy, New York.

Turkewitz, H., & O'Leary, K. D. (1981). A comparative outcome study of behavioral marital therapy and communication therapy. *Journal of Marital and Family Therapy,* **7,** 159 – 169.

Weiss, R. L. (1975) *Spouse Observation Checklist.* Unpublished questionnaire, University of Oregon, Eugene.

Weiss, R. L., Birchler, G. R., & Vincent, J. P. (1974). Contractual models for negotiation training in marital dyads. *Journal of Marriage and the Family,* **36,** 321 – 331.

Weiss, R. L., & Ford, L. (1975). *A social learning view of marriage.* Unpublished manuscript, University of Oregon, Eugene.

11

Alcohol, Gender, and Sexual Problems: An Interface

EDITH S. LISANSKY GOMBERG

*School of Social Work
and
Institute for Social Research
University of Michigan
Ann Arbor, Michigan 48109*

I. INTRODUCTION

A. The Study of Alcohol

Human beings differ in their responses to alcohol. There are not only individual differences but intra-individual differences as well. The effects of alcohol vary with the *amount* that is consumed, a small amount often improving performance while moderate and large amounts produce deterioration in performance (Carpenter, Moore, Snyder, & Lisansky, 1961). The effects of alcohol also vary with the *behavior* studied, complicated by overlearning, experience, and familiarity. In terms of norms and social acceptability, the consumption of alcohol also encompasses a wide range of drinking behaviors: Intoxication acceptable in one group is not acceptable in another. And habitual patterns must be distinguished from single incidents of drinking. On the whole, moderate, social use of alcoholic beverages is accepted by most Western countries, whereas particular societies and subcultures may not accept intoxication. In particular, patterns of drinking which are not acceptable are those labelled deviant, problematic, or alcoholic.

235

TREATMENT AND PREVENTION
OF ALCOHOL PROBLEMS: A RESOURCE MANUAL

B. The Study of Sexual Behavior

Until recently, major works on human sexual behavior dealt with medical problems like venereal disease or with aberrant sexuality, e.g., "Psychopathia Sexualis" (1866). The study of human sexual behavior as a topic of scientific interest is relatively new. In the mid-1940s, Kinsey, a zoologist who had become interested in human sexual behavior, set out to collect new information. The results of extensive interviewing were summarized in two landmark books on the sexual behavior of men and women (Kinsey, Pomeroy, & Martin, 1948; Kinsey, Pomeroy, Martin, & Gebhard, 1953). The work was criticized on the grounds that information came from volunteers who might not be representative of the population. The same objection has been raised about the more recent studies of Masters and Johnson (1966). The samples in both investigations are unquestionably selective, but it is impossible to interview those who do not volunteer.

The study of the sexual behavior of human beings has been fraught with problems. Human sexual behavior is regulated by biochemistry as well as learning, socialization, and social norms. Sexual behavior involves a wide range of activities from mating dances, flirtation, and invitational cues[1] to sexual arousal, coitus, and orgasm. Although instrumentation for study of sexual responses has become more sophisticated, many questions remain unanswered (Semmlow & Lubowsky, 1983).

II. EFFECTS OF ALCOHOL ON SEXUAL BEHAVIOR

Gantt (1952) reported that the depressant effect of alcohol on sexual response of laboratory dogs occurred in proportion to the dosage but added, "the constitution and past experience of the animal are most important factors in determining the effect on alcohol" (p. 180). The most marked effect in shortening the duration of erection occurred in an animal that had ingested large daily doses of alcohol. Of clinical relevance was Gantt's observation of two "neurotic" animals on which alcohol had a facilitating effect on sexual activity.

Almost everyone who writes about alcohol and sex quotes Shakespeare's immortal (and apparently valid) lines. MacDuff asks what three things drink provokes and the porter answers, "Marry, sir, nose-painting, sleep, and urine. Lechery, sir, it provokes, and unprovokes: it provokes the desire, but it takes away the performance" (Shakespeare, W. *Macbeth,* Act II, Scene iii). When Masters was asked by Harper's magazine (May, 1968) to comment on the effects of alcohol and other drugs on sexual behavior, he said, "Shakespeare did it years ago much better than I can. He said that a little stimulates and a lot depresses and he's right" (p. 53). Although this comment on the

---

[1]When the male octopus is sexually active, he courts the female by developing color stripes. As mating begins, the courtship colors fade (Stocker, 1978).

dose–response relationship actually is a misquote of Shakespeare, the two quotations aptly summarize the knowledge about the effects of alcohol on sexual behavior and are supported by the experimental literature. For example, Hart (1968) studying the effects of alcohol on sexual reflexes of laboratory dogs, found that large amounts of alcohol did not abolish "sexual motivation" (e.g., mounting), but that sexual potency was markedly diminished.

A. Studies of Human Males

The effects of alcohol on sexual fantasy has been studied among college males, the general conclusion being that the effect was to increase sexual thoughts (McClelland, Davis, Kalin, & Wanner, 1972). In the other direction: when college males view erotic and other slides, alcohol intake increases significantly after the erotic slides are shown (Gabel et al., 1980). The first study to use penile tumescence as the measure of sexual arousal was Farkas and Rosen (1976) who demonstrated dose-related effects: the smallest amount of alcohol was associated with maximum increase in penile diameter but larger amounts produced marked suppression of response. A series of experiments (Briddell & Wilson, 1976; Lansky & Wilson, 1981; Wilson & Lawson, 1976b) demonstrated significant inverse linear relationships between alcohol and sexual responsiveness—that is, the more alcohol ingested, the less the penile tumescence. However, subjects who *believed* they had consumed alcohol, regardless of whether they had or not, showed significantly greater levels of penile tumescence than those who did not hold this expectancy (Wilson & Lawson, 1976b). Finally, we should note that among the male subjects in Wilson's studies there was a significant positive correlation between self-reported sexual arousal and laboratory measures of penile tumescence.

There are complex interactions among pharmacological effects and beliefs about alcohol and social rules about permissible rule-breaking while under the influence. Carpenter and Armenti (1972), in a review of the effects of alcohol on sexual behavior, comment that the pharmacological effects of alcohol are confounded with "sexual opportunity and provocation." MacAndrew and Edgerton (1969) have argued that what is seen as uncontrollable alcohol-induced behavior in different societies remains within "certain culturally sanctioned albeit interculturally variable limits."

Of particular interest are those studies which report that sexual arousal in men who believe they have had alcohol is more marked when they are exposed to deviant sexual stimuli, and more marked among men with a high level of sexual guilt (Briddell et al., 1978; Lansky & Wilson, 1981; McCarty et al., 1982). Wilson (1981), in a review of the literature on alcohol and sex, discusses disavowal of deviance, a mechanism by which attribution of person-responsibility is shifted to alcohol-responsibility, particularly when deviant sexual behaviors are involved (McCaghy, 1968). The behavior is recognized as inappropriate but alcohol excuses it. Wilson also raises the question of whether alcohol enhances attention to erotic stimuli or whether it alters the manner in which the stimuli are perceived and processed.

In the laboratory, alcohol reduces penile tumescence; although artificial, this situation presumably mirrors that of the male who experiences impotence after drinking. Masters and Johnson (1966) describe men in their late 40s and early 50s who drink heavily and become impotent; it is not only the alcohol-induced loss of potency which is of clinical interest but the anxiety produced and the "concern for performance." Creative writers have provided some of the best description of alcohol-induced impotence. In Edward Albee's play, "Who's Afraid of Virginia Woolf?" (1973) the central female character and a young male character unsuccessfully attempt sexual intercourse after a night of drinking. The young man responds defensively and suggests they try again when they, "haven't been drinking for ten hours." Martha responds with contempt: "I wasn't talking about your potential; I was talking about your goddam performance."

B. Studies of Human Females

1. Sexual Arousal

As with men, a negative linear relationship between amount of alcohol and physiological indicators of sexual arousal is found among college women (Wilson & Lawson, 1978). However, women's self-reported sexual arousal was "diametrically opposed to what the vaginal pressure-pulse recordings showed" (Wilson, 1981). With increasing levels of intoxication, and in the presence of erotic stimuli, the proportion of female subjects who report enhanced sexual arousal goes up. The difference between men and women in the effect of alcohol on self-reported sexual arousal may be due to the fact that women are less accurate than men in monitoring physical sexual arousal.

The layman's view that alcohol enhances sexuality among women is contained in Ogden Nash's lines that, "candy is dandy but liquor is quicker," which fits a simplified disinhibition interpretation. While there are sound reasons for rejecting such a view (Wilson, 1981), the fact remains that both men and women do view alcohol as an aphrodisiac.[2]

2. Menstrual Cycle

Jones and Jones (1976) reported different blood alcohol level peaks for different phases of the menstrual cycle. However, in another study of menstrual phase, alcohol, and mood states, no significant relationship was found

---

[2]The drug culture is an exception: "Alcohol makes for sloppy sex " (Gay, Newmeyer, Elion, & Wieder, 1975).

among phase, alcohol, and mood (Sutker, Libet, Allain, & Randall, 1983). Nevertheless, normal menstruating women in the latter study did report drinking more frequently to relieve tensions, and they reported solitary drinking more frequently during menstrual flow. Some women do use alcoholic beverages medicinally during menstrual periods but whether tension reduction is a pharmacological or an expectancy effect has not been investigated. Heavier drinking has been linked with increased rates of menstrual problems (Russell, 1982), a finding supported by national survey data in which heavier drinkers report more heavy flow, more pain, and more premenstrual discomfort (Wilsnack, Klassen, & Wilsnack, 1984).

The problem is, of course, which comes first: the heavy drinking or the menstrual discomfort? Premenstrual difficulties have been hypothesized as *leading to* alcoholic drinking (Belfer & Shader, 1976; Lolli, 1953; Podolsky, 1963). The hypothesis has resurfaced recently with some attention to the "premenstrual syndrome" (PMS) (Hopson & Rosenfeld, 1984; Hazelden, 1983). The fact is that many women experience heightened tension and negative feelings during the menstrual cycle and that some may drink to reduce the discomfort. Considering the societal permissiveness toward women's taking medication for illness or pain, and considering the alcoholic woman's defensiveness about her drinking bouts, it is hardly surprising that some alcoholic women report PMS as a critical antecedent of their drinking bouts.

3. Pregnancy

As reported by Wilsnack et al. (1984), known complications of pregnancy do vary with drinking levels but *only* at the highest consumption level. Infertility, miscarriage, premature births, and birth defects are linked to heavy drinking. At this time, it is not clearly known what effects light or moderate drinking might have on pregnancy. However, one subgroup of women described as "temporary abstainers who had never drunk more than infrequently" were unusually high in menstrual complaints, premature births, miscarriages, and hysterectomies. Women who are presently abstainers but who used to drink moderately, were unusually likely to report sexual dysfunctions. The authors hypothesize that these abstaining groups have sexual or reproductive problems which the women see as either caused or worsened by alcohol. Temporary abstention might also be based on low estrogen levels and heightened intoxicating effects of alcohol.

Little, Schultz, and Mandell (1976) interviewed 183 women, average age 26.5, in the 4th and 8th months of pregnancy. The authors reported alcohol consumption cut to less than half its former level. Interestingly, the magnitude of decrease in alcohol use after conception was directly proportional to consumption level before pregnancy. Asked why they drank less, over half the women said that drinking had adverse physiological effects. The women who drank more heavily before becoming pregnant more frequently reported changed physiological reactions to alcohol than did the lighter drinkers.

4. Menopause

The menopause is a life transition, the biological features of which are apparently better understood than the psychosocial. Recent national survey data reported by Clark and Midanik (1982) showed that the percentage of heavy women drinkers drops precipitously after age 50, the median age for menopause. In their 40s, 18% of the women reported heavy drinking and in the 50s, this drops to 8%. The same phenomenon occurs with men a decade later. The drop in drinking and heavy drinking and the rise in abstinence may be related to changes in tolerance to alcohol (Ritzmann & Melchior, 1984) and/or to age changes in work role, social patterns, and leisure activities (Gomberg, 1981).

C. Alcohol, Sexual Activity, and Pleasure

Is sexual activity related to alcohol consumption? Two reports (Arafat & Yorburg, 1973; Curran, Neff, & Lippold, 1973) found alcohol use to be positively correlated with reported levels of past and present sexual activity for both male and female college students. Zucker, Battistich, and Langer (1981) noted that heavy-drinking college women reported the earliest and most frequent sexual activity. One reasonable explanation of these findings is that risk-taking or a generalized trend toward early acting-out underlies both drinking and sexual behaviors.

Does alcohol affect sexual pleasure? Among respondents to a questionnaire in *Psychology Today,* 68% of the men and 45% of the women reported an increase in sexual pleasure with alcohol; twice as many men (42%) as women (21%) reported a decrease in sexual pleasure with alcohol (Athanasiou, Shaver, & Tavris, 1970). One study compared the reported effects of alcohol on sexual feelings and behaviors among several different groups: alcoholic women, alcoholic men, female psychiatric patients, and normal women (Beckman, 1979). When asked whether they experienced less inhibition when drinking, there were no significant differences among the groups with a high proportion of each reporting less inhibition after drinking. Among the normal women, 31% reported that they enjoyed sexual relations most when drinking a little. Malatesta, Pollack, and Crotty (1979) reported the effects of different blood alcohol levels (BAL) on orgasmic response of 24 women volunteers: with increasing intoxication, orgasms were slower and less intense. Nonetheless, the women reported *more* sexual arousal and *more* pleasurable orgasms. A parallel study of men (Malatesta, Pollack, Wilbanks, & Adams, 1979) found the same impairment of orgasm among men, but the men showed *decreases* in self-report measures of sexual arousal and pleasure.

Like the survey and self-report data, striking differences between men and women have been found in experimental studies. Although men who believe they are drinking alcoholic beverages show increased sexual arousal, women, under the same conditions, generally do not show expectancy effects. As described, among men, significant positive correlations have been found between self-report measures of sexual arousal and measures of penile tumescence (Wilson & Lawson, 1976b). On the other hand, whereas women report increased sexual arousal as BAL rises, physiological measures suggest that alcohol impairs sexual arousal (Wilson & Lawson, 1976a; Wilson & Lawson, 1978). A sex difference also appears in the effects of alcohol on orgasm: both sexes show reduced intensity of orgasm with increasing amounts of alcohol by objective measures, but women *report* increases (Malatesta, Pollack, Crotty, & Peacock, 1982) and men *report* decreases in pleasure (Malatesta, Pollack, Wilbanks, & Adams, 1979). The gender differences described here might be explained by anatomical and/or socialization sex differences. Some authors conclude that sex differences are minimal in "expectations and subjective impressions" of alcohol as an agent of sexual arousal (Moore, 1985/1986). However, the data suggest that there are strong differences between the sexes in sexual response under alcohol conditions.

Finally, it should be noted that societal attitudes are more negative toward female intoxication than male intoxication (Lawrence & Maxwell, 1962; Stafford & Petway, 1977). Greater disapproval of female drunkenness seems linked to the view that alcohol releases women's sexual inhibitions (Knupfer, 1964). Societal attitudes link more interest in sex with women's drinking, and women apparently share those attitudes. Perhaps that is one explanation of why women report more sexual arousal and more sexual pleasure in orgasm despite the fact that objective physiological measures show the opposite (Malatesta, Pollack, & Crotty, 1979; Wilson & Lawson, 1978).

III. SEXUAL PROBLEMS THAT ANTECEDE ALCOHOL PROBLEMS

Most recent research attention has focused on sexual disorders *associated with* heavy drinking and alcoholism. However, it is also important to consider whether there are sexual behaviors, experiences, or preferences that are antecendent to alcohol problems and contribute to their development. Freudian theory hypothesized that aberrations in psychosexual development were central to the etiology of alcoholism among males. The "specific oral frustrations" of childhood produced "strong homosexual tendencies and oral cravings" (Fenichel, 1945; Lorand, 1945) which were linked to male alcoholism.

More recently, drinking and alcoholism among men have been linked to the need for power (McClelland et al., 1972):

> the central concern for the pre-alcoholic boy lies in the area of male self-esteem, in the desire to demonstrate male strength — personalized power . . . one of the chief causes of alcoholism is a concern about male superiority and power (pp. 288, 300–301).

A major area for the expression of male self-esteem and power is in sexual behavior; conflict over "male assertiveness" leads to problematic drinking because of the individual's need to feel "strong" and overcome his feelings of weakness.

Difficulties surrounding sexual preference may also be an antecedent of drinking problems. For example, conflict over repressed or denied homosexual preference may create discomforts that are alleviated by alcohol. Or choosing homosexual orientation might lead to stress which might be dealt with by drinking. Although it is true that alcohol problems appear more frequently among homosexual groups than in the population at large (Riess & Safer, 1979), it is not clear why this is so.

Sexual behavior and experience have more frequently been used to account for the development of alcoholism among women than among men. For instance, alcoholic women have been described as either promiscuous (Karpman, 1948) or frigid (Levine, 1955) before the onset of alcoholism. More recent work has suggested that early sexual experience, early life sexual trauma, or gynecological problems may give rise to alcohol problems among women (Benson & Wilsnack, 1983).

A. Women's Early Sexual Experience

A few surveys have examined the relationship between alcohol use and sexual activity, mostly among college populations. Zucker, Battistich, and Langer (1981) found, among a sample of 370 unmarried women students (mean age 18 years), that those women who engaged in heavy-escape drinking reported earlier and more frequent sexual relations, past and current. There are many ways to interpret this relationship: characterological consistency in impulsive behavior, unconventional attitudes toward societal norms, or expressions of unhappy emotional relationships.

In a sample of 301 alcoholic women (Gomberg, 1984), 5.3% reported dropping out of high school because of pregnancy; in a matched nonalcoholic group of women, 0.7% dropped out of high school because of pregnancy. In the same study, the average age at first marriage for the alcoholic women was 19.4 years; for the matched control group, it was 20.7.

B. Women's Early Life Sexual Trauma

As Wilsnack (1984) pointed out in her review on the sexuality of female alcoholics, early sexual abuse — including incest and rape — appear to predispose women to both alcoholism and to sexual dysfunction. Once the cycle has begun, alcohol-related problems and sexual problems seem to contribute to each other.

When asked about experiences with incest or rape, from 12% to over 50% of alcoholic women have reported having experienced incest and other childhood sexual abuse, and up to 74% of alcoholic women have reported all types of sexual abuse combined (Covington, 1982; Evans & Schaefer, 1980; Hammond, Jorgensen, & Ridgeway, 1979; Murphy, Coleman, Hoon, & Scott, 1980; Roth, Acker, Petersen, Perry, Shannon, & Anderson, 1981). While Kinsey et al. (1953) found only 5.5% of women respondents reporting sexual contact with a male relative during childhood, his percentages were obtained 30 years ago. More recent work (Russell, 1983) presents quite higher percentages: 38% of a sample of 930 adult women reported having been sexually abused before the age of 18, sometimes intrafamilially, sometimes extrafamilially. (While Russell reports a 50% refusal rate in her San Francisco random household sample, it is one of the first attempts to base a study of sexual behavior on respondents other than volunteers.)

During the last several decades, there have been increasing reports of sexual abuse, particularly of female children, but there are unanswered questions: Is there, indeed, a large increase in the sexual acting out of adults with children, or is there more openness in reporting behavior which was denied before now? Does sexual abuse occur more frequently in the early lives of women who later become alcoholic than it does in the general population? Is it reported more frequently by those alcoholic women who go into treatment than it would be by alcoholic women not in treatment?

Sexual dysfunction has been reported more frequently by alcoholic women with earlier histories of incest than those without such histories (Hammond et al., 1979; Hayek, 1981). The research suggests that women who are victims of incest respond to sexual relationships with discomfort and guilt and that some women use alcohol to help minimize these feelings. Childhood sexual abuse often does leave the child with feelings of guilt, shame, and anger, and while many people with such an early history make adequate adult adjustments, some may turn to alcohol and other drugs to assuage the negative feelings. It appears that childhood sexual abuse occurs more frequently among female children, but sexual abuse of boys may be a significant factor in later alcoholism. Little has been done to study the relationship of these early experiences of men to their later drinking behaviors.

The drinking status of the adult who commits incest also needs to be studied. Forrest (1982), reviewing available information about alcoholism and incest, reports rates of alcohol problems among incestuous fathers as ranging from 20% to 70% in different studies. It appears, too, that alcoholic fathers frequently report that they were intoxicated when the incest occurred. However, we refer the reader again to our discussion of the disavowal of deviance, the attribution of responsibility to alcohol and drunkenness to excuse deviant acts (MacAndrew & Edgerton, 1969; Wilson, 1981).

C. Gynecological Antecedents

In addition to anecdotal evidence, there are two scientific reports that link alcohol problems to premenstrual tension. Belfer and Shader (1976) reported that 20 of the 34 alcoholic women they studied linked their drinking to "the stress of the menstrual cycle;" the control group consisted of 10 nonalcoholic wives of alcoholic men, differing significantly from the alcoholic women in marital status and in depression. Podolsky (1963) clinically observed seven alcoholic women and reported that their alcohol problems were linked to premenstrual tension and problems accepting their femininity. These women appeared to be depressed, tense, passive–dependent, and lonely.

Animal studies of the effects of alcohol on female sex hormones bears on the gynecological antecedents of alcohol problems. In female rats (Eskay, Ryback, Goldman, & Majchrowicz, 1981) and in female monkeys (Mello, Bree, Mendelson, Ellingboe, King, & Sehgal, 1983), large amounts of alcohol disrupt the normal estrous cycle. Large amounts of alcohol also produce ovarian failure in rats (Van Thiel, Gaveler, Lester, & Sherins, 1978). Although heavy alcohol consumption has been found to affect male sex hormones, moderate amounts of alcohol have not been found to affect the follicular and midluteal phases of the menstrual cycle (Mendelson, Mello, & Ellingboe, 1981; Valimaki, Harkonen, & Ylikahri, 1983).

Jones and Jones (1976) have proposed that low estrogen level, resulting from menopause or hysterectomy, is related to high monamine oxidase levels, depression, and alcoholism in women. The hypothesis is based on the observation of relatively high BAL during premenstruum, a period during which declining levels of estrogen and progesterone are also observed. Clinically, Curlee (1969) has associated a history of menopause with the onset of alcoholism. Finally, a report of the menopausal alcoholism of 14 women suggests that the prognosis for alcoholism "that marked depressive decompensation during menopause" is good (Midenet, Midenet, & Desbois, 1974).

IV. SEXUAL PROBLEMS THAT FOLLOW THE ONSET OF ALCOHOL PROBLEMS

A. Males: Sexuality and Biology

Clinical observation of alcoholics' sexual dysfunction has been made frequently (Akhtar, 1977; Deniker et al., 1964; DeVito, R. A. & Marozas, 1981; Lemere & Smith, 1973; Levine, 1955; Mandell & Miller, 1983; Masters & Johnson, 1966; Rubin & Henson, 1976). Sexual dysfunction includes a variety of different problems: diminished interest and lowered sex drive, difficulty in erection, premature ejaculation, and impotence. Estimated incidence of impotence has varied widely from study to study: 3% by Levine (1955), 4.5% by Mandell and Miller (1983), 8% by Smith, Lemere, and Dunn (1972), 31% by Akhtar (1977). Most of these estimates were derived from self-reports. There have been differences from study to study in the definition of impotence and in the ages of the male subjects and their concomitant illnesses. Some studies report impotence under drinking conditions (Mandell & Miller, 1983), and others report impotence after detoxification (Smith, Lemere, & Dunn, 1972) and after years of sobriety (Gad-Luther, 1980). A question which needs clarification is the relative extent of sexual dysfunction before onset, during heavy drinking bouts, after detoxification and sobriety. Using the Kinsey report as baseline, Mandell and Miller (1983) reported a much higher *preonset* rate of sexual dysfunction than would appear in a general population sample.

Does treatment for alcoholism modify sexual dysfunction? Smith et al. (1972) commented that half the men who reported impotence do *not* return to their previous level of sexual competence after sobriety. In a Danish study, Jensen (1984) found a very high incidence of sexual dysfunction (63% of the alcoholic men compared with 10% of the controls), and also reported that the male alcoholics claimed that sexual dysfunction began when they started Antabuse treatment.

Does sexual interest diminish while the person is actively alcoholic, between drinking bouts, or after sobriety? The usual procedure has been to ask alcoholic men, in treatment, about their sexual drive while drinking. Levine (1955) found 70% reporting lowered interest, and Akhtar (1977) found 53% reporting "diminished sexual desire." Masters and Johnson (1966) say, of "the true alcoholic" that "his sexual tensions simply disappear." A major question is the extent to which men with drinking problems differ in lowered sex drive and impotence from other males (e.g., men in the same age group, heavy drinking nonalcoholic men, abstainers, depressed men). One investigator (Jensen, 1981) evaluated sexual dysfunction in diabetic and alcoholic men and a control group, all 30 to 45 years of age. Alcoholics and diabetics showed the same incidence and symptom pattern of sexual dysfunction, significantly higher rates of erectile dysfunction than the controls, and reduced libido.

Although few people question the generalization that "alcoholics are known to be poor sex performers" (Royce, 1981) or that "sexual activities within the alcoholic marriage are often unrewarding" (Parades, 1973), there is one report that raises a question. Burton and Kaplan (1968) studied the sexual behavior and adjustment of 16 couples (husband alcoholic) and a nonalcoholic sample of 16 couples, all in marital counseling groups. There was little difference in sexual adjustment of the two groups, and while these are small and selected samples, the number and groups involved in reports of sexual dysfunction are not much larger or better selected.

A series of papers by Van Thiel and his associates (1974, 1975, 1980, 1982) is directed toward a physiological–biochemical explanation of impaired male sexual behavior which often accompanies heavy drinking and alcoholism. These investigators report hypogonadism and feminization among male alcoholic patients; they term alcohol, "a primary testicular toxin." The men studied were hospitalized with alcohol-related liver disease. The question is how far one may generalize: the alcohol-related physical problems of the inpatient subjects were more severe than those of the typical outpatient male alcoholic.

That impotence and diminished sexual interest are significant problems for the male alcoholic is clear. Further, therapy directed toward control of the drinking may or may not be effective in restoring sexual function. It is important that the therapist help sort out those sexual problems which are directly linked to the effects of alcohol and those which are part and parcel of psychosexual problems of closeness and intimacy in relationships. Therapists should be sensitive to these issues and might refer for adjunctive treatment for alcoholics' sexual problems.

B. Females: Sexuality

In a summary of the literature on female alcoholics, Boothroyd (1980) wrote,

A number of clinical accounts report a high incidence of heterosexual inadequacy, homosexuality and frigidity . . . the erstwhile notion that sexual promiscuity is characteristic of alcoholic women has been proved false by a number of studies (page 310).

The erstwhile studies include Wall's (1937) who described 60% of his middle-class patients to be engaged in "loose heterosexual activity." Karpman (1948) presented several case histories with sexual promiscuity as a major theme. That theme continued to surface for a while, although the data consistently suggested that frigidity and lack of sexual interest characterized many of the women seen in treatment facilities (Curran, 1937; Levine, 1955). Lisansky (1957) reported that half of her sample of prison women perceived that their prostitution was related to their drinking and that 11% of her sample of women in an outpatient clinic reported that they were promiscuous. Promiscuity, however, has not been defined consistently; the variations are illustrated by Johnson's (1965, p. 380) interviews with 100 physicians.

More recent work presents various pictures of the female alcoholic's sexuality. Many describe large proportions of the women as *frigid and poorly adjusted sexually* (Kinsey, 1966; Wood & Duffy, 1966). Murphy et al. (1980) reported half the women studied as showing little interest in sex and minimal orgasmic response. Browne-Mayers and her colleagues (1976) found 5% reporting promiscuity, but 45% reported inadequate sexual response. One study reported a frequency of sexual dysfunction among women alcoholics which *does not differ* from matched nonalcoholic women, but it should be noted that these are "younger married alcoholics" (Jensen, 1984). One study shows age difference among alcoholic women with younger women reporting less sexual dissatisfaction than older ones (Gomberg, 1984). And there are recent studies which report *promiscuity:* One-third of Spalt's (1975) female alcoholics with affective disorder reported sexual relations with many sexual partners, and Hammond et al. (1979) reported half the women studied to be promiscuous.

Again the question of antecedent or consequence must be raised. Rathod and Thomson (1971) reported that a third of women alcoholics interviewed said they had engaged in repeated infidelity *before* they became alcoholic. Covington (1983) reported that 79% of alcoholic women studied said that their sexual dysfunction was *antecedent* to their alcoholism. Because clinicians have not often inquired about the client's sexual activities before and after the onset of alcoholism, the question remains open.

These studies involve small groups of women and, often, no control groups for comparison. An exception is Beckman's study (1979), in which 120 alcoholic women rated themselves significantly less sexually satisfied than did comparison groups of psychiatric female patients and normal controls. In this study, alcoholic women were more likely than the others to report wanting, participating in, and enjoying sexual relations more when drinking. In a more recent study (Gomberg, 1984), 301 alcoholic women reported willingness to have sexual relations more often and greater enjoyment of the act when drinking than did the 137 women in the control group. When alcoholic and control women were compared by age group, it was the youngest women (those in their 20s) for whom differences between alcoholics and controls were greatest.

In Beckman's (1979) study, when the 120 alcoholic women were compared with alcoholic men, few differences in sexual responsiveness emerged:

Both sexes reported desire for and enjoyment of sex while drinking. There were, however, two notable differences: Female alcoholics reported more frequent intercourse while drinking heavily than did alcoholic men, and alcoholic men reported significantly more likelihood of sexual relations "with persons with whom they would not (have sex) if not drinking." The irony of the latter finding is, of course, that male alcoholics report more promiscuity than female alcoholics!

Norms for sexual behavior have changed. For example, sexual virtue and virginity are less valued today than they were a half century ago. While some alcoholic women report sexual relations with a number of different partners, we have no idea whether that behavior is particularly deviant in their social groups. Although the question of sexual promiscuity remains moot, the evidence suggests that alcohol makes women feel freer to participate in sexual activity, and this effect may be greater for the alcoholic woman than for the nonalcoholic. Another difference involves sexual guilt; Pinhas (1980) compared alcoholic and control women on a test of sexual guilt and found alcoholics scoring higher.

In summary, alcoholic women (like alcoholic men) appear to have less interest in sexual relations than nonalcoholics. Often, alcoholic women report frigidity and impaired orgasmic response. Sexual dysfunction may be both antecedent to and a consequence of alcohol problems. It was Kinsey's viewpoint that sexual dysfunction frequently *resulted* from an unhappy marriage, and it is difficult to see how a marriage characterized by heavy drinking by one or both partners could fail to be unhappy. Drinking probably occurs, at times, to facilitate sexual relations, but the drinking compounds the sexual and marital problems (Ewing et al., 1970).

Although clinicians report sexual dysfunction to be common among female alcoholics, several clinical and research reports (e.g., Jensen, 1984) have shown that sexual dysfunction does not occur among alcoholic women to an extent greater than among women in general. Murphy et al. (1980), for example, collected self-assessments from 74 alcoholic women and 100 nonalcoholic women, and reported no greater frequency of sexual problems among the alcoholics. Potter (1979), discussing women, sex, and alcoholism, says:

> I have found nothing in the literature that noted anything different about the sexuality of the woman alcoholic than I know is true for the thousands of women of all ages who have shared information with me (Potter, 1979, p. 76).

C. Females: Gynecological Function

Besides endocrinological studies, there is little evidence on the effects of heavy drinking on the menstrual cycle. A recent report (Lumley & Wood,

1979) noted that heavy drinkers appeared to have fewer days of menstrual bleeding, but the authors noted that there was a very small number of heavy drinkers among the 1100 women studied. Women who drink (in any amount) reported significantly more dysmenorrhea than abstainers, but stillbirth rates were higher among abstainers than among drinking women, and no relationship at all appeared between drinking and menopausal symptoms.

Beginning with the reports of Jones et al. (1973, 1974), the effect of alcohol on the unborn fetus has generated more literature and more popular reports than any other issue relating to women and alcohol. Excessive maternal consumption of alcohol, particularly during early stages of a pregnancy is harmful to the fetus and is likely to produce the fetal alcohol syndrome (FAS) or fetal alcohol effects (FAE). FAS, in its severe form, includes craniofacial malformations and mental retardation. Although they do not occur frequently, these phenomena generate rather extreme responses. One physician at Baltimore City Hospital went so far as to recommend that alcoholic women have abortions during the first 12 weeks of pregnancy (Colen, 1975).

Although extensive bibliographies on the FAS have been compiled, several questions remain unanswered. How many alcoholic women have borne FAS children? How does drinking during pregnancy relate to use of nicotine, marijuana, prescribed medication, diet, and life style in general? How does the mother's age and the child's birth rank relate to FAS? Despite the incomplete evidence, the National Institute on Alcohol Abuse and Alcoholism (NIAAA) began in 1981 to issue official government warnings that "even moderate alcohol consumption during pregnancy" endangers the health of the unborn child. A controversy among physicians and researchers developed (Fetal alcohol advisory debated, Science 1981) with some challenge to the advice that *any* amount of alcoholic beverage was damaging to the fetus. According to the counterargument, there should be a sizable number of FAS cases if FAS is to be linked to moderate drinking, because pregnant women have been drinking alcoholic beverages for centuries. One may wonder whether the passions generated by the FAS controversy are not linked to attitudes about women's sexuality and roles. Intoxication among women is disapproved, and there is a good deal of hidden anger in descriptions of the sexual promiscuity of women with alcohol problems. They are described as loose women, immoral, failures in their assigned role as caretaker, nurturer, wife, and mother.

Medical effects of midlife alcoholism seem linked to the menopause (Rankin, Schmidt, Popham, & DeLint, 1975; Wilkinson, Santamaria, & Rankin, 1969). Relatively high rates of liver disease occur among midlife women who manifest alcoholic behavior. It has been hypothesized that the greater susceptibility of middle-aged women to alcoholic liver disease is linked to menopausal hormonal changes.

V. ALCOHOL AND HOMOSEXUALITY

Twenty to 30% of the homosexual population is estimated to be alcoholic (Ziebold & Mongeon, 1984). Because controversy over the origins of both homosexuality and alcoholism are rife, one would hardly expect consensus on the coexistence of the two. Bell, Weinberg, and Hammersmith (1981), after a fairly extensive interview study of men and women homosexuals and heterosexuals, concluded that their findings are "not inconsistent" with a biological explanation of sexual preference. Freudian theory has used the same explanation, oral fixation, for both alcoholism and homosexuality. Masters and Johnson (1966) viewed homosexuality as a learned phenomenon. Behavioristic models explain the homosexuality–alcoholism link as related to the life style which revolves around gay bars. These bars are often described as, "the major social institution in the gay community" (Moses & Hawkins, 1982), although the same authors point out that it is the *visibility* of the gay bars that focuses attention on them. Finally, sociocultural explanations for the homosexuality–alcoholism link focus on "how those in power structure the role of gay people and alcoholics" (Nardi, 1982) and emphasize the stigma in contemporary society attached to the labels "alcoholic" and "homosexual."

One study attributes the greater frequency of psychiatric disorders noted among lesbian than heterosexual women to alcoholism and attempted suicide (Saghir, Robins, Walberg, & Gentry, 1970). Martin, Cloninger, and Guze (1982) reported that half of a sample of 66 female felons were alcoholic, and noted that the alcoholism frequently coexisted with antisocial personality or homosexuality. Lewis, Saghir, and Robins (1982) reported a significantly higher percentage of problem drinkers among 57 lesbian women than 43 matched heterosexual women. Recent work suggests that low self-esteem and depression, prevalent among female alcoholics in general, are also common among lesbian alcoholics (Diamond & Wilsnack, 1978; Haven, 1981).

Several explanations have been offered for the strong association between alcoholism and homosexuality. A popular explanation points to the focus of gay social life in gay bars (Fifield, 1975; Hawkins, 1976). Another view hypothesizes that homosexuals' alienation resulting from their societal rejection is a major contributor to their alcohol problems (Hawkins, 1976). Whatever the view, depression, the experience of loss, and suicide attempts occur frequently among lesbian alcoholics (Saghir & Robins, 1973).

Alcohol problems have been largely ignored by many counselors working with gays. Fifield (1975) studied the personnel in 46 nongay agencies providing alcoholism treatment; three quarters of the agencies responded that "gay people have unique service needs," but few translated the sentiment into outreach, referral, or treatment groups for gay alcoholics. The staff at these agencies estimated that 1% of their clientele was homosexual; one must conclude that there are communication problems.

Treatment issues need to be candidly considered. Intervention will not be effective unless communication problems between a straight therapist and a homosexual client are efffectively resolved and counselors address *both* alcohol and sexual orientation problems. How effective will the counselor be if the goal is arresting the alcoholism while ignoring the sexual orientation of the client?

In an eclectic approach, Smith (1982) emphasizes a *combination* of treatment approaches: "responsibility building therapy, awareness therapy, medical and neurophysiological approaches, strategic therapy, utilization of altered states of consciousness, and attitudinal change therapy." Smith believes that gay alcoholics often require specialized treatment techniques, at the very least a counselor's comprehension of gay experience in childhood, adolescence, adulthood, and aging. Whitney (1982) raises an interesting question about family treatment for the homosexual alcoholic and emphasizes the importance of participation of significant others in couples and in family therapy. Treatment issues are, perhaps, best summarized by Beaton and Guild (1976): "If trust can be established between straight therapists and gay clients, group counseling can offer effective help as with heterosexual individuals" (Beaton & Guild, 1976, p. 302). A sad postscript: There is little published literature about gay male alcoholics (e.g., Ziebold & Mongeon, 1982), but there is far less written about the treatment needs of the lesbian alcoholic.

VI. SEX, ALCOHOL, AND VIOLENCE

Although people have wondered about the relationship between alcohol and violence since time immemorial, the relationship is still unclear (Løberg, 1983). A simple theory of disinhibition would posit that alcohol "dissolves the superego," thereby rendering the acting-out of unacceptable impulses more likely. A disavowal-of-deviance viewpoint posits that social norms render unacceptable acts more excusable when they are performed under the influence of alcohol. It is not uncommon for someone to drink to acquire the courage to perform some violent act (e.g., suicide).

The extent to which alcohol is involved in deviant, sexual acting-out behaviors is not at all clear. There are two different questions that need to be answered: Was the person performing the deviant act *drinking at the time* the act was performed? Was the person performing the deviant act *an alcoholic* who may or may not have been drinking at the time the act was performed?

A. Rape

Estimates that the rapist was drinking at the time of the rape range from 0 to 50% (Barbaree et al., 1983; Rada, 1975). Estimates of alcoholism rates among rapists range as high as 35%. These estimates would appear to contradict the reports that alcoholic men are low in sexual drive, uninterested in sexual activity, and often impotent. It is important to emphasize, however, that the act of rape is less an expression of sexual interest in many cases than of control, aggression, and power. As stated by Rada (1975), "Subjects (rapists) rarely seem to focus on the sexual aspects and are much more concerned with the aggressive, assertive, and controlling aspects" (Rada, 1975, p. 59). Rada sees rapists' use of alcohol as related to the need for a stimulus to increase the man's sense of power and mastery and to overcome his fears.

It has already been noted that the act of rape is judged differently when the woman raped has been drinking. Where drinking is perceived as making the man less responsible for his act, the woman who has been drinking or appears in a bar is often perceived as "asking for it."

B. Incest

Virkkunen (1974) studied 45 instances of incest; in half the cases, the men were diagnosed as alcoholic and had histories of violent behavior within and outside the family. Virkkunen cites previous studies in which estimates of alcoholism among persons involved in incestuous acts go as high as 80%; there are few reports on intervention in incest-and-alcoholism (Gunderson, 1980).

C. Child Molestation

Of 203 pedophilic sex offenders studied by Rada (1976), 49% reported drinking at the time of the offense, and one-third to one-half were estimated to be alcoholic. Alcohol was significantly more often associated with molesting a female child than a male child.

Rape, incest, and child molestation are sexual abuses in which drinking and alcoholism apparently play a significant role. These are sexual behaviors and, clearly, aggressive behaviors as well. The rising incidence of these sexual abuses and their link to drinking raises questions for therapists who will have to deal with both victims and perpetrators. It is essential that the effects of sexual abuse on the victim be assessed and treated. As for sexual offenders with alcohol problems, therapy directed toward problems both with alcohol and with impulse control is essential.

VII. IMPLICATIONS FOR TREATMENT

A number of recommendations can be made for dealing clinically with persons who have both alcohol and sexual problems (Mandell & North, 1982; Nurse, 1982; Powell, 1984; Renshaw, 1975; Schulman, 1983; Turner, 1982; Viamontes, 1974).

1. Clinicians might start by examining their own attitudes about sexuality. It would be a good idea to review the research on human sexuality in order to appreciate the wide range of human sexual behaviors. The clinician's response to such emotion-laden topics as incest, rape, and homosexual orientation would be critical in working with alcoholics with sexual problems.

2. A next step might be to gather information about sex therapy resources within the community and their willingness to work with therapists who deal with alcohol problems.

3. A clinician should be aware of the major sources of concern relating to sexuality and reproduction among men and women with alcoholic problems. Guilts and anxieties are likely to be expressed around issues such as potency, sexual adequacy, and good parenting.

4. Assessment of the client's sexual problems is a good place to begin. Questions about both sexual history and current sexual adjustment should be raised. The therapist should be prepared to deal tactfully with sexual issues that are likely to make the client feel uncomfortable. Denial of sexual problems may be anticipated because denial is a major mechanism of alcoholic clients.

5. Should the alcohol problem or the sexual problem be the initial focus of treatment? It is probably reasonable to start with an early focus on the drinking problem, but the clinician must gauge the degree of anxiety and the pressures felt by the client. Some clients will have sexual problems that preceded heavy drinking, and their sexual problems will probably need to be addressed first. For other clients who have used alcohol as a sexual facilitator, alcohol and sexual problems might best be dealt with concurrently.

6. The relationship between drinking and sexual dysfunction needs to be discussed frankly, and clients should be given information about the effects of alcohol on sexual performance. It is useful to discuss these questions: How has the drinking been related to sexual interest and pleasure? Have the sexual problems occurred during drinking episodes? Have they occurred in the absence of alcohol? How soon after resolving the alcohol problem might a client expect the sexual problems to dissipate?

7. Reassurance can be extremely valuable in treating alcohol and sexual problems. As the alcohol problem subsides, many clients will feel reassured that their sexual problems will improve as well.

8. The client's spouse or other sexual partner should be involved in treatment, whether the client's sexual orientation is heterosexual or homosexual.

REFERENCES

Akhtar, M. J. (1977). Sexual disorders in male alcoholics. In J. S. Madden, R. Walker, & W. H. Kenyon (Eds.) *Alcoholism and drug dependence: A multidisciplinary approach* (pp. 3–13). New York: Plenum.

Albee, E. (1973). *Who's afraid of Virginia Woolf?* New York: Atheneum.

Arafat, I., & Yorburg, B. (1973). Drug use and the sexual behavior of college women. *Journal of Sex Research,* **9,** 21–29.

Athanasiou, R., Shaver, P., & Tavris, C. (1970). Sex: A Psychology Today report. *Psychology Today,* **4,** 39–52.

Barbaree, H. E., Marshall, W. L., Yates, E., & Lightfoot, L. O. (1983). Alcohol intoxication and deviant sexual arousal in male social drinkers. *Behavioral Research and Therapy,* **21,** 365–373.

Beaton, S., & Guild, N. (1976). Treatment for gay problem drinkers. *Social Casework,* **57,** 302–308.

Beckman, L. J. (1979). Reported effects of alcohol on the sexual feelings and behavior of women alcoholics and nonalcoholics. *Journal of Studies on Alcohol,* **40,** 272–282.

Belfer, M. L., & Shader, R. I. (1976). Premenstrual factors as determinants of alcoholism in women. In M. Greenblatt & M. A. Schuckit (Eds.), *Alcoholism Problems in Women and Children* (pp. 97–102). New York: Grune & Stratton.

Bell, A. P., Weinberg, M. S., & Hammersmith, S. K. (1981). *Sexual preference: Its development in men and women.* Bloomington, IN: Indiana University Press.

Benson, C. S., & Wilsnack, S. C. (1983). Gender differences in alcoholic personality characteristics and life experience. In Cox, W. M. (Ed.) *Identifying and measuring alcoholic personality characteristics* (pp. 53–71). San Francisco: Jossey-Bass.

Boothroyd, W. E. (1980). Nature and development of alcoholism in women. In O. Kalant (Ed.). *Alcohol and drug problems in women: Vol. 1. Research advances in alcohol and drug problems* (pp. 299–330). New York: Plenum.

Briddel, D. W., Rimm, D. C., Caddy, G. R., Krawitz, G., Sholis, D., & Wonderlin R. J. (1978). Effects of alcohol and cognitive set on sexual arousal to deviant stimuli. *Journal of Abnormal Psychology,* **87,** 418–430.

Briddel, D. W., & Wilson, G. T. (1976). Effects of alcohol and expectancy set on male sexual arousal. *Journal of Abnormal Psychology,* **85,** 225–234.

Browne-Mayers, A. N., Seelye, E. E., & Sillman, L. (1976). Psychosocial study of hospitalized middle-class alcoholic women. *Annals of the New York Academy of Sciences,* **273,** 593–604.

Burton, G., & Kaplan, H. M. (1968). Sexual behavior and adjustment of married alcoholics. *Quarterly Journal of Studies on Alcohol,* **29,** 603–609.

Carpenter, J. A., & Armenti, N. P. (1972). Some effects of ethanol on human sexual and aggressive behavior. In B. Kissin & H. Begleiter (Eds.). *The biology of alcoholism: Vol. 2. Physiology and behavior.* New York: Plenum Press.

Carpenter, J. A., Moore, O. K., Snyder, C. R., & Lisansky, E. S. (1961). Alcohol and higher-order problem solving. *Quarterly Journal of Studies on Alcohol,* **22,** 183–222.

Clark, W. B., & Midanik, L. (1982). Alcohol use and alcohol problems among U.S. adults: Results of the 1979 national Survey. *Alcohol and health monograph No. 1, Alcohol consumption and related problems.* National Institute on Alcohol Abuse and Alcoholism. DHHS Publication No. (ADM). 82-1190, 3–52.

Colen, B. D. (1975, February 2). The infant alcoholics. *The Washington Post.*

Covington, S. S. (1982, April). *Sex and violence—the unmentionables in alcoholism treatment.* Paper presented at the National Alcoholism Forum of the National Council on Alcoholism, Washington, D.C.

Covington, S. S. (1983). Sexual experience, dysfunction, and abuse: A descriptive study of alcoholic and nonalcoholic women. *Dissertation Abstracts International,* **44** (1B), 287.

Curlee, J. (1969). Alcoholism and the 'empty nest.' *Bulletin of the Menninger Clinic,* **33,** 165–171.

Curran, F. J. (1937). Personality studies in alcoholic women. *Journal of Nervous and Mental Disease,* **86,** 645–667.

Curran, J. P., Neff, S., & Lippold, S. (1973). Correlates of sexual experience among university students. *Journal of Sex Research,* **9,** 124–131.

Deniker, P., DeSaughy, D., & Ropert, M. (1964). The alcoholic and his wife. *Comprehensive Psychiatry,* **5,** 374–383.

DeVito, R. A., & Marozas, R. J. (1981). The alcoholic satyr. *Sexuality and Disability,* **4,** 234–245.

Diamond, D. L., & Wilsnack, S. C. (1978). Alcohol abuse among lesbians: A descriptive study. *Journal of Homosexuality,* **4,** 123–142.

Eskay, R. L., Ryback, R. S., Goldman, M., & Majchrowicz, E. (1981). Effect of chronic ethanol administration on plasma levels of LH and the estrous cycle in the female rat. *Alcoholism: Clinical and Experimental Research,* **5,** 204–206.

Evans, S., & Schaefer, S. (1980). Why women's sexuality is important to address in chemical dependency treatment programs. *Grassroots,* **37,** 37–40.

Ewing, J. A., Fox, R., Carstairs, G. M., & Beaubrun, M. H. (1970). Alcohol, drugs and sex. *Medical Aspects of Human Sexuality,* **4,** 18–34.

Farkas, G. M., & Rosen, R. C. (1976). Effect of alcohol on elicited male sexual response. *Journal of Studies on Alcohol,* **37,** 265–272.

Fenichel, O. (1945). *The psychoanalytic theory of neurosis.* New York: W. W. Norton.

Fetal alcohol advisory debated. (1981). *Science,* **214,** 642–644.

Fifield, L. (1975). *On my way to nowhere: Alienated, isolated, drunk.* Los Angeles: Gay Community Services Center.

Forrest, G. G. (1982). *Alcoholism and human sexuality.* Springfield, IL: Charles C. Thomas.

Gabel, P. C., Noel, N. E., Keane, T. M., & Lisman, S. A. (1980). Effects of sexual versus fear arousal on alcohol consumption in college males. *Behavior Research and Therapy,* **18,** 519–526.

Gad-Luther, I. (1980). Sexual dysfunctions of the alcoholic. *Sexuality & Disability,* **3,** 273–290.

Gantt, W. H. (1952). Effect of alcohol on the sexual reflexes of normal and neurotic dogs. *Psychosomatic Medicine,* **14,** 174–181.

Gay, G. R., Newmeyer, J. A., Elion, R. A., & Wieder, S. (1975). Drug–sex practice in the Haight-Ashbury or 'The sensuous hippie.' In M. Sandler & G. L. Gessa (Eds.), *Sexual behavior: Pharmacology and biochemistry* (pp. 63–79). New York: Raven Press.

Gomberg, E. S. L. (1981). Women, sex roles, and alcohol problems. *Professional Psychology,* **12,** 146–155.

Gomberg, E. S. L. (1982). Alcohol use and alcohol problems among the elderly. *Alcohol and health monograph No. 4: Special population issues.* National Institute on Alcohol Abuse and Alcoholism. DHHS Publication No. (ADM) 82-1193. pp. 263–290.

Gomberg, E. S. L. (1984, May). *Women and alcoholism: Psychosocial issues.* Paper presented at the National Research Conference on Women and Alcohol, Seattle, WA.

Gunderson, I. (1980). Incest and alcoholism. *Catalyst,* **1**(3), 22–25.

Hammond, D. C., Jorgensen, G. Q., & Ridgeway, D. M. (1979). *Sexual adjustment of female alcoholics.* Manuscript submitted for publication.

Hart, B. L. (1968). Effects of alcohol on sexual reflexes and mating behavior in the male dog. *Quarterly Journal of Studies on Alcohol,* **29,** 839–844.

Haven, M. J. (1981). Alcoholism and self-esteem among women with a male sex object preference. Dissertation. California School of Professional Psychology. *Dissertation Abstracts International,* 1981, **42,** 2058-B.

Hawkins, J. L. (1976). Lesbianism and alcoholism. In M. Greenblatt & M. A. Schuckit (Eds.), *Alcoholism problems in women and children* (pp. 137–153). New York: Grune & Stratton.

Hayek, M. A. (1981). Recovered alcoholic women with and without incest experience: A comparative study. Dissertation. Reed University. *Journal of Studies on Alcohol, 42,* Abstract 146.

Hopson, J., & Rosenfeld, A. (1984, August). PMS: Puzzling monthly symptoms. *Psychology Today, 30*-38.

Jensen, S. B. (1981). Sexual dysfunction in male diabetics and alcoholics: A comparative study. *Sexuality & Disability, 4,* 215-219.

Jensen, S. B. (1984). Sexual function and dysfunction in younger married alcoholics: A comparative study. *Acta Psychiatrica Scandinavica, 69,* 543-549.

Johnson, M. W. (1965). Physicians views on alcoholism with special reference to alcoholism in women. *The Nebraska State Medical Journal, 50,* 378-384.

Jones, B. M., & Jones, M. K. (1976). Alcohol effects on women during the menstrual cycle. *Annals of the New York Academy of Sciences, 36,* 61-69.

Jones, K. L., Smith, D. W., Streissguth, A. P., & Myrianthopoulos, N. C. (1974, June). Outcome in offspring of chronic alcoholic women. *Lancet, 3,* 1076-1078.

Jones, K. L., Smith, D. W., Ulleland, C. N., & Streissguth, A. P. (1973, June). Pattern of malformation in offspring of chronic alcoholic moths. *Lancet, 1,* 1267-1271.

Karpman, B. (1948). *Alcoholic woman.* Washington, DC: The Linacre Press.

Kinsey, A. C., Pomeroy, W. B., & Martin, C. E. (1948). *Sexual behavior in the human male.* Philadelphia: W. B. Saunders.

Kinsey, A. C., Pomeroy, W. B., Martin, C. E., & Gebhard, P. H. (1953). *Sexual behavior in the human female.* Philadelphia: W. B. Saunders.

Kinsey, B. A. (1966). *The female alcoholic: A social psychological study.* Springfield, IL: Charles C. Thomas.

Knupfer, G. (1964; September) *Female drinking patterns.* Paper presented at the Annual Meeting of the North American Association of Alcoholism Programs, Portland, OR.

Lansky, D., & Wilson, G. T. (1981). Alcohol, expectations, and sexual arousal in males: An information processing analysis. *Journal of Abnormal Psychology, 90,* 35-45.

Lawrence, J. J., & Maxwell, M. A. (1962). Drinking and socioeconomic status. In D. J. Pittman & C. R. Snyder (Eds.), *Society, culture and drinking patterns* (pp. 141-145). New York: Wiley.

Lemere, F., & Smith, J. W. (1973). Alcohol-induced sexual impotence. *American Journal of Psychiatry, 130,* 212-213.

Levine, J. (1955). The sexual adjustment of alcoholics: A clinical study of a selected sample. *Quarterly Journal of Studies on Alcohol, 16,* 675-680.

Lewis, C. E., Saghir, M. T., & Robins, E. (1982). Drinking patterns in homosexual and heterosexual women. *Journal of Clinical Psychiatry, 43,* 277-279.

Lisansky, E. S. (1957). Alcoholism in women: Social and psychological concomitants. I. Social history data. *Quarterly Journal of Studies on Alcohol, 18,* 588-623.

Little, R. E., Schultz, F. A., & Mandell, W. (1976). Drinking during pregnancy. *Journal of Studies on Alcohol, 37,* 375-379.

Løberg, T. (1983). Belligerence in alcohol dependence. *Scandinavian Journal of Psychology, 24,* 285-292.

Lolli, G. (1953). Alcoholism in women. *Connecticut Review on Alcoholism, 5,* 9-11.

Lorand, S. (1945). A survey of psychoanalytical literature on problems of alcohol: Bibliography. *Yearbook of Psychoanalysis, 1,* 359-370.

Lumley, J., & Wood, C. (1979). The female reproductive system. In J. Krupinski & A. Mackenzie (Eds.). *The health and social survey of the north west region of Melbourne.* Melbourne, Australia: Health Commission of Victoria. Mental Health Division.

MacAndrew, C., & Edgerton, R. B. (1969). *Drunken comportment: A social explanation.* Chicago: Aldine.

Malatesta, V. J., Pollack, R. H., & Crotty, T. D. (1979). Alcohol effects on the orgasmic response in human females. *Annual Meeting of the Psychonomic Society,* Phoenix, Arizona, November, 1979.

Malatesta, V. J., Pollack, R. H., Crotty, T. D., & Peacock, L. J. (1982). Acute alcohol intoxication and female orgasmic response. *Journal of Sex Research,* **18,** 1–16.

Malatesta, V. J., Pollack, R. H., Wilbanks, W. A., & Adams, H. E. (1979). Alcohol effects on the orgasmic-ejaculatory response in human males. *Journal of Sex Research,* **15,** 101–107.

Mandell, L. L., & North, S. (1982). Sex roles, sexuality and the recovering woman alcoholic: Program issues. *Journal of Psychoactive Drugs,* **14,** 163–166.

Mandell, W., & Miller, C. M. (1983). Male sexual dysfunction as related to alcohol consumption: A pilot study. *Alcoholism: Clinical and Experimental Research,* **7,** 65–69.

Martin, R. L., Cloninger, C. R., & Guze, S. B. (1982). Alcoholism and female criminality. *Journal of Clinical Psychiatry,* **43.**

Masters, W. H., & Johnson, V. E. (1966). *Human sexual response.* Boston: Little, Brown and Co.

McCaghy, C. H. (1968). Drinking and deviance disavowal: The case of child molesters. *Social Problems,* **16,** 43–49.

McCarty, D., Diamond, W., & Kaye, M. (1982). Alcohol, sexual arousal, and the transfer of excitation. *Journal of Personality and Social Psychology,* **42,** 977–988.

McClelland, D. C., Davis, W. N., Kalin, R., & Wanner, E. (1972). The drinking man: Alcohol and human motivation. New York: Free Press.

Mello, N. K., Bree, M. P., Mendelson, J. H., Ellingboe, J., King, N. W., & Sehgal, P. (1983). Alcohol self-administration disrupts reproductive function in female macaque monkeys. *Science,* **221,** 677–679.

Mendelson, J. H., Mello, N. K., & Ellingboe, J. (1981). Acute alcohol intake and pituitary gonadal hormones in normal human females. *Journal of Pharmacology & Experimental Therapy,* **218,** 23–26.

Midenet, M., Midenet, J., & Desbois G. (1973). L'alcoolisme de la femme de 50 ans. *Lyon Medicin,* **229,** 479–483. (Abstract 881, *Quarterly Journal of Studies on Alcohol,* **35,** 1974. 14–52).

Moore, D. T. (1985/1986). Alcohol and sexual dysfunction. *Alcohol Health and Research World,* **10**(2), 10–13 and 51.

Moses, A. E., & Hawkins, R. O. (1982). *Counseling lesbian women and gay men: A life-issues approach.* St. Louis: Mosby.

Murphy, W. D., Coleman, E., Hoon, E., & Scott, C. (1980). Sexual dysfunction and treatment in alcoholic women. *Sexuality and Disability,* **3,** 240–251.

Nardi, P. M. (1982). Alcoholism and homosexuality: A theoretical perspective. In T. O. Ziebold & J. E. Mongeon (Eds.), *Alcoholism and homosexuality* (pp. 9–26). New York: The Haworth Press.

Paredes, A. (1973, April). Marital–sexual factors in alcoholism. *Medical Aspects of Human Sexuality,* **7,** 98–115.

Pinhas, V. (1980). Sex guilt and sexual control in women alcoholics in early sobriety. *Sexuality and Disability,* **3,** 256–272.

PMS (1983). The disease of the '80s. *Hazelden Professional Update,* **2,** 1–4.

Podolsky, E. (1963). The woman alcoholic and premenstrual tension. *Journal of the American Medical Women's Association,* **18,** 816.

Potter, J. (1979). Women and sex—it's enough to drive them to drink! In V. Burtle (Ed.), *Women who drink: Alcoholic experience and psychotherapy* (pp. 49–80). Springfield, IL: Charles C. Thomas.

Powell, D. J. (Ed.). (1984). *Alcoholism and sexual dysfunction: Issues in clinical management.*

New York: Haworth Press. Also published as *Alcoholism Treatment Quarterly*, 1(3), 1984.

Rada, R. T. (1975). Alcohol and rape. *Medical Aspects of Human Sexuality*, 9, 48–65.

Rada, R. T. (1976). Alcoholism and the child molester. *Annals of the New York Academy of Sciences*, 273, 492–496.

Rankin, J. G., Schmidt, W., Popham, R. E., & deLint, J. (1975). Epidemiology of alcoholic liver disease—insight and problems. In J. M. Khanna, Y. Israel, & H. Kalant (Eds.), *Alcoholic liver pathology* (pp. 31–41). Toronto: Addiction Research Foundation.

Rathod, N. H., & Thomson, I. G. (1971). Women alcoholics: A clinical study. *Quarterly Journal of Studies on Alcohol*, 32, 45–52.

Renshaw, D. C. (1975). Sexual problems of alcoholics. *Chicago Medicine*, 78, 433–436.

Riess, B. F., & Safer, J. M. (1979). Homosexuality in females and males. In E. S. Gomberg & V. Franks (Eds.), *Gender and disordered behavior: Sex differences in psychotherapy* (pp. 257–286). (1979). New York: Brunner/Mazel.

Ritzmann, R. F., & Melchior, C. L. (1984). Age and development of tolerance to and physical dependence on alcohol. In J. T. Hartford & T. Samorajski (Eds.). *Alcoholism in the elderly: Social and biomedical issues* (pp. 117–138). New York: Raven Press.

Roth, P., Acker, C. W., Petersen, R., Perry, W., Shannon, L., & Anderson, J. (1981, September). Skyward: A rural women's alcoholism project. Final report to the National Institute on Alcohol Abuse and Alcoholism.

Royce, J. E. (1981). *Alcohol problems and alcoholism: A comprehensive survey*. New York: Free Press.

Rubin, H. B., & Henson, D. E. (1976). Effects of alcohol on male sexual responding. *Psychopharmacology*, 47, 123–234.

Russell, D. E. H. (1983). The incidence and prevalence of intrafamilial and extrafamilial sexual abuse of female children. *Child Abuse and Neglect*, 7, 133–146.

Russell, M. (1982). Screening for alcoholic-related problems in obstetric and gynecologic patients. In E. L. Abel (Ed.), *Fetal alcohol syndrome: Volume II. human studies* (pp. 1–19). Boca Raton, FL: CRC Press.

Saghir, M., & Robins, E. (1973). *Male and female homosexuality*. Baltimore: Williams and Wilkins.

Saghir, M. T., Robins, E., Walbran, B., & Gentry, K. A. (1970). Homosexuality: IV. Psychiatric disorders and disability in the female homosexual. *American Journal of Psychiatry*, 127, 147–154.

Sanders, M. K. (1968, May). Interview with Dr. Masters and Mrs. Johnson. *Harper's*. 53–55.

Shulman, G. (1983). Sexuality and chemical dependence recovery. *Focus on Alcohol and Drug Issues*, 6, 19–25.

Semmlow, J. L., & Lubowsky, J. (1983). Sexual instrumentation. *IEEE Transactions on Biomedical Engineering*, BME-30(6), 309–319.

Smith, J. W., Lemere, F., & Dunn, R. B. (1972). Impotence in alcoholism. *Northwest Medicine*, 71, 523–524.

Smith, T. M. (1982). Specific approaches and techniques in the treatment of gay male alcohol abusers. In T. O. Ziebold & J. E. Mongeon (Eds.). *Alcoholism and homosexuality* (pp. 53–70). New York: The Haworth Press.

Spalt, L. (1975). Sexual behavior and the affective disorders. *Disease of the Nervous System*, 36, 644–647.

Stafford, R. A., & Petway, J. M. (1977). Stigmatization of men and women problem drinkers and their spouses: Differential perception and leveling of sex differences. *Journal of Studies on Alcohol*, 38, 2109–2121.

Stocker, J. (1978). Pity the poor devilfish. *International Wildlife*, 8, 28–31.

Sutker, P. B., Libet, J. M., Allain, A. N., & Randall, C. L. (1983). Alcohol use, negative mood states and menstrual cycle phases. *Alcoholism: Clinical and Experimental Research*, 7, 327–331.

Turner, D. S. (1982). An analysis of alcoholism and its effects on sexual functioning. *Sexuality and Disability*, 5, 143–157.

Valimaki, M., Harkonen, M., & Ylikahri, R. (1983). Acute effects of alcohol on female sex hormones. *Alcoholism: Clinical and Experimental Research*, 7, 289–293.

Van Thiel, D. H., Gavaler, J. S., Eagon, P. K., Chiao, Y-B., Cobb, C. F., & Lester, R. (1980). Alcohol and sexual function. *Pharmacology Biochemistry and Behavior*, 13, 125–129. Supplemental 1.

Van Thiel, D. H., Gavaler, J. S., Lester, R., & Goodman, M. D. (1975). Alcohol-induced testicular atrophy: An experimental model for hypogonadism occurring in chronic alcoholic men. *Gastroenterology*, 69, 326–332.

Van Thiel, D. H., Gavaler, J. S., Lester, R., & Sherins, R. J. (1978). Alcohol-induced ovarian failure in the rat. *Journal of Clinical Investigation*, 61, 624–632.

Van Thiel, D. H., Gavaler, J. S., & Sanghvi, A. (1982). Recovery of sexual function in abstinent alcoholic men. *Gastroenterology*, 84, 677–682.

Van Thiel, D. H., Lester, R., & Sherins, R. J. (1974). Hypogonadism in alcoholic liver disease: Evidence for a double defect. *Gastroenterology*, 67, 1188–1199.

Viamontes, J. A. (1974). Alcohol abuse and sexual dysfunction. *Medical Aspects of Human Sexuality*, 8, 185–186.

Virkkunen, M. (1974). Incest offenses and alcoholism. *Medicine, Science and The Law*, 14, 124–128.

von Kraft-Ebbing, R. (1944). *Psychopathia sexualis: A medico-forensic study*. Stuttgart, 1886. (Reprinted. New York: Pioneer Publications.)

Wall, J. H. (1937). A study of alcoholism in women. *American Journal of Psychiatry*, 93, 943–952.

Whitney, S. (1982). The ties that bind: Strategies for counseling the gay male co-alcoholic. In T. O. Ziebold & J. E. Mongeon (Eds.). *Alcoholism and Homosexuality* (pp. 37–42). New York: The Haworth Press.

Wilkinson, P., Santamaria, J. N., & Rankin, J. G. (1969). Epidemiology of alcoholic cirrhosis. *Australasian Annals of Medicine*, 18, 222–226.

Wilsnack, S. C. (1984). Drinking, sexuality, and sexual dysfunction in women. In S. C. Wilsnack & L. J. Beckman (Eds.) *Alcohol problems in women: Antecedents, consequences, and intervention* (pp. 189–227). New York: Guilford Press.

Wilsnack, S. C., Klassen, A. D., & Wilsnack, R. W. (1984). Drinking and reproductive dysfunction among women in a 1981 national survey. *Alcoholism: Clinical and Experimental Research*, 8, 451–458.

Wilson, G. T. (1981). The effects of alcohol on human sexual behavior. In N. Mello (Ed.). *Advances in substance abuse: Volume 2* (pp. 1–40). Greenwich, CT: JAI Press.

Wilson, G. T., & Lawson, D. (1976a). Effects of alcohol on sexual arousal in women. *Journal of Abnormal Psychology*, 85, 489–497.

Wilson, G. T., & Lawson, D. (1976b). Expectancies, alcohol, and sexual arousal in male social drinkers. *Journal of Abnormal Psychology*, 85, 587–594.

Wilson, G. T., & Lawson, D. M. (1978). Expectancies, alcohol, and sexual arousal in women. *Journal of Abnormal Psychology*, 87, 358–367.

Wood, H. P., & Duffy, E. L. (1966). Psychosocial factors in alcoholic women. *American Journal of Psychiatry*, 123, 341–345.

Ziebold, T. O., & Mongeon, J. E. (Eds.). (1982). Alcoholism and homosexuality. No. 5 of the Book Series. *Research on homosexuality*. New York: Haworth Press. Also published as *Journal of Homosexuality*, 7(4).

Zucker, R. A., Battistich, V. A., & Langer, G. C. (1981). Sexual behavior, sex-role adaptation and drinking in young women. *Journal of Studies on Alcohol*, 42, 457–465.

12

Culture-Specific Treatment Modalities: Assessing Client-to-Treatment Fit in Indian Alcoholism Programs

JOAN WEIBEL-ORLANDO[1]

Alcohol Research Center
Neuropsychiatric Institute
University of California at Los Angeles
Los Angeles, California 90024

I. INTRODUCTION

Americans take pride in being a nation of, or descendants of, immigrants. We, at certain prescribed times of the year, dust off our folk symbols and indulge in time-limited, but orgiastic displays of ethnic pride. In addition to obvious markers such as food, folk costumes, music, dance, language, and sports activities, the use and significance of alcoholic beverages in ritual celebrations of ethnic pride vary across groups. Ouzo, chianti, sake, Bordeaux, Dos Equis, stout, and vodka are all immediately identified with their respective national origins and for their symbolic potency. Indeed, in public ethnic displays you, metabolically, are not only "what you eat" but also "what you drink."

Certain ethnic drinking patterns persist. For instance, the Irish-American male pub culture has been well described in both academic and popular literature (Ablon, 1980; Bales, 1962; Glad, 1947; Stivers, 1971). Southern Mediterraneans are said to use alcoholic beverages (usually wines) like food,

[1]Present address: Department of Anthropology, University of Southern California, Los Angeles, California 90089-0661.

while northern Europeans are "hard drinking" consumers of grain liquors (Knupfer & Room, 1967; Lolli, Serriani, Golder, & Luzzato-Fegiz, 1958; Opler & Singer, 1956; Room, 1968; Sadoun, Lolli, & Silverman, 1965).

Ethnic differences in rates of alcohol-related problems are well documented, while the etiologies of these differences are still highly speculative. Jews are thought to have low rates of alcoholism because they incorporate alcoholic beverages into sacred ritual (Glad, 1947; Snyder, 1962). Orientals are assumed to have low rates of alcoholism because of their hypersensitivity to alcohol as evidenced by an intense vasomotor reaction upon ingestion (Reed, Kalant, Gibbons, Kapur, & Rankin, 1976; Schwitters, Johnson, McClearn, & Wilson, 1981; Wolff, 1973). And alcoholism is considered a major health problem of Native Americans because, it has been said, they simply cannot or do not know how to "hold their liquor" (Leland, 1976; MacAndrew & Edgerton, 1969).

A major problem facing the treatment field is the massive gap between our folk understandings of and research consensus about the use of alcohol and its meaning across American subcultures and the lack of culture-specific alcoholism intervention programs. Given wide-ranging and persistent segmentation of our ethnic populations, systematic appraisal of the effectiveness of alcoholism interventions (developed for Anglo populations, but directed to non-Anglos) is mandated.

In the present chapter, we outline the major problems in providing alcoholism intervention to ethnic clients described in the literature. Then we focus specifically on alcoholism interventions for Native Americans. The typological treatment model presented in this chapter is based on work during the last 6 years with urban and rural Indian alcoholism programs in California, South Dakota, Eastern Oklahoma, New Mexico, and Arizona. However, the service delivery system that developed from an analysis of these data may have broader application. Indeed, a similar typological alcoholism treatment mode may also apply to the heterogeneous Hispanic-American population, the economically and regionally segmented Black American communities, as well as to other ethnic-American subgroups now plagued by high rates of alcoholism and a lack of culture-sensitive alcoholism treatment intervention strategies.

II. ETHNICITY AND ALCOHOL

Although ethnic groups in the United States can be roughly placed into five major categories (Anglo, Hispanic, Black, Asian, and Native American), these categories are too generalized. The current literature is replete with critical reviews of studies of ethnic minorities which fail to take into consideration regional, tribal, class, and sex differences in drinking attitudes and behaviors and treatment response.

A. Hispanic Americans

Alcocer (1981) decries the use of the term, Hispanic, to describe a global drinking ethos. The range of cultural attitudes about drinking among Cubans, Mexicans, and Puerto Ricans are further crosscut by class and ethnic differences. Alcocer considers the rubric, Hispanic, practically useless as a descriptor of an ethnic category.

Much has been written about the emphasis on sex role differentiation in Hispanic cultures and its effect on drinking behavior (Alcocer, 1977; Gilbert, 1977, 1985; Guinn, 1978; Maril & Zavaleta, 1979; Paine, 1977; Trevino, 1975). Gilbert (1977), found that while bouts of public drinking serve as same-sex bonding mechanisms for the men, Mexican women usually drink in the privacy of their homes and in the company of family and family friends. The alleged double standard among Hispanics has prompted the concepts of *marianismo* and *machismo* to describe sex-associated public presentations of self (Obeso & Bordatto, 1979). As Alcocer (1981) points out, the relationship between *machismo* and *marianismo* stances and alcohol abuse is purely speculative so far. In fact, while Hispanic male drinking patterns tend to coincide with these cultural models, the Hispanic female drinking patterns do not (Alcocer, 1981).

B. Asian Americans

The need to establish criteria for determining appropriate ethnic subcategories is as apparent in studies of Asian Americans as in the Hispanics and alcohol literature. Schwitters et al. 1981, for instance, demonstrate the wide range of flushing responses across Japanese, Chinese, Filipino, and Hawaiians. Sue, Zaine, and Ito (1979) and Kitano (1981), in their studies of Asian-American drinking patterns, also warn us that differentiating between genetic and cultural models is extremely difficult. Findings suggest that alcohol consumption (and perhaps alcoholism) may be lower among Asian Americans than among the Americans in general and that Asian-American participation in alcoholism treatment is almost nonexistent. However, Kitano et al. (1985) suggest that alcohol abuse among Asian Americans may increase as a function of socialization and acculturation processes.

C. Black Americans

Similar issues can be raised about Black Americans. King (1981) and Bourne (1973) point out that most studies of Black American drinking habits concentrated on low-income, urban populations. What we think we know about drinking patterns and response to treatment among poor, urban Black communities tells us little about the rural or upwardly mobile and well-established, middle-class Black American drinking experience.

Studies have modified the early stereotypic view of the Black family (King, 1981). Since the mid-1960s, Anglos have had to accommodate the knowledge and experience of a well-established and growing Black middle class. What had been discretely ghettoed from casual view prior to the Civil Rights Movement, is now making its existence known in "front stage" activities. The significance of alcohol use in this population of Black Americans and the prognosis for treatment is yet to be depicted in any depth.

Before ethnically specific treatment modalities can be prescribed, we need studies to assess the cultural significance of drinking in the Black community across socioeconomic, age, and drinking style. We also need to know more about the cultural significance of drinking in the Black community in relationship to the larger society. Is Black drinking (as Lurie, 1971, described among the Native Americans) a thumbing of the nose at the oppressive white society, or does it constitute a viable social institution among Blacks themselves? Finally, we need to know the effect of these sociocultural and socioeconomic differences on treatment response.

D. Native Americans

Alcohol abuse has been described as the foremost medical and social problem among contemporary Native American populations (Price, 1975; Snake, Hawkins, & LaBoueff, 1977). The years since the mid-1960s have been characterized by a surge of interest in federal agencies "doing something about" this social and medical problem. At this time, the Office of Equal Opportunity, the National Institute of Mental Health and the National Institute on Alcohol Abuse and Alcoholism (NIAAA) have funded scores of Indian alcoholism intervention projects. Designed, for the most part, on alcoholism intervention strategies developed among non-Native alcoholic populations, these demonstration projects have been the foci of much experimentation and third party research and evaluation (Mail & MacDonald, 1980).

The substantial literature on alcohol use among Native Americans is also rife with warnings about facile generalizations about Native Americans drinking patterns and treatment response (Leland, 1976; Stratton, 1981; Weibel-Orlando, 1985; Weisner, Weibel-Orlando, & Long, 1984). Evaluation studies point to the disappointingly low rates of success of existing alcohol rehabilitation programs in Native American communities (Kline & Roberts, 1973; Lang, 1974; Snake et al., 1977; Towle 1975; Weibel-Orlando, 1984). Increasingly, evaluators, treatment personnel, and potential clients deplore the Anglo cultural bias of existing alcoholism intervention programs and call for integration of more traditional forms of healing practices into programs with large numbers of Native American clients (Albaugh, 1973; Bergman, 1971; Kahn, Williams, Galvez, Lejero, Conrad, & Goldstein,

1975; Shore, 1972; Stone, 1982; Weibel-Orlando, 1984). Unfortunately, however, little has been documented about the response of traditional Native American healers to the medical and social issues of alcohol abuse in their communities or the success of traditional practices in mitigating alcohol use (Mail & MacDonald, 1980). This informational void exists even though historical documents, from as early as the seventeenth century, provide graphic accounts of the social devastation wreaked by alcohol abuse among Native Americans (Dailey, 1968; Dozier, 1966).

Use of the rubrics Black, Asian, Hispanic, or Native American to identify target populations may be dysfunctional. To avoid alienating target ethnic populations through stereotyping, clear understandings of what tribal group, socioeconomic strata, age level, residential environment, and sex research findings represent and to whom treatment is being prescribed, are required.

III. THE NATIVE HEALERS IN ALCOHOLISM REHABILITATION PROJECT: DEALING WITH ETHNIC DIVERSITY IN THE TREATMENT SETTING

In 1981, as a response to the dearth of information about indigenous responses to alcohol abuse among Native American populations, the Native Healers in Alcohol Rehabilitation Project was launched by Kenneth Lincoln, A. Logan Slagle, and Joan Weibel-Orlando, University of California colleagues who shared an interest in doing something about the problem of alcohol abuse among Native Americans.[2] Kenneth Lincoln, a UCLA English professor, had grown up in a town bordering the Pine Ridge Reservation in South Dakota and is well acquainted with the problem of alcohol abuse among his Siouan-speaking contemporaries. A. Logan Slagle, a Professor of Law and Native American Studies at UC Berkeley, is part-Cherokee and a practitioner of Native American healing traditions. Weibel-Orlando, an anthropologist at UCLA, had worked with Native Americans for several years and, since 1978, has headed an Indian drinking practices study for the Neuropsychiatric Institute at UCLA. These investigators had three aims. First, they pooled collective research skills and life experiences in an attempt to identify and synthesize both primary and secondary information regarding the use of indigenous Native American healing practices in the treatment of alcoholism or problem drinking in Native American populations. Their second goal was to evaluate the potential benefits and liabilities of combining tribal medicine and Western technology in Native American alcoholism

[2]The research described in this chapter was funded by USPHS Grant AA0481701-04 from the National Institute on Alcohol Abuse and Alcoholism and was administered by the Neuropsychiatric Institute at the University of California at Los Angeles.

treatment programs. Third, they attempted to identify ways to maximize treatment effectiveness within a highly heterogeneous focal population.

IV. METHOD

A. The Survey Sample

Since July, 1981, Lincoln, Slagle, and Weibel-Orlando have interviewed traditional tribal healers, counselors, and directors of alcoholism intervention programs among the Sioux in South Dakota, the Navajo and Pueblo groups in New Mexico and Arizona, the Cherokee in eastern Oklahoma, and diverse tribal groups in both urban and rural California. Most of the alcoholism intervention programs that were surveyed were designed specifically to address the problem of alcohol abuse among Native American populations. Pan-Indian programs tended to be urban. However, many programs were more narrowly focused, dealing specifically with tribal or regional clients. These programs tended to be rural and often were located on reservations. A few experimental programs are administered by tribal governments.

Overwhelmingly, the Indian alcoholism intervention programs were initiated by grants from NIAAA. In fact, the majority of the programs had received the maximum years of funding allowable from NIAAA. Although a few had become self-sufficient, the majority of the mature treatment programs had been incorporated into the Indian Health Service Division of the U. S. Public Health Service.

To identify the full range of alcoholism treatment modalities available to Native Americans, we also interviewed alcoholism treatment personnel in off-reservation programs. Included here were alcoholism treatment units in Veteran Administrations Medical Centers, privately operated programs in urban centers close to areas of Native American concentration, and state- and county-funded alcoholism intervention programs in centers with large concentrations of Native Americans.

Personnel from all alcoholism rehabilitation programs in the selected research sites that were listed in the 1980 National Directory of Drug Abuse and Alcohol Treatment and Prevention Programs were contacted. Personnel from programs that treated Native Americans were interviewed. In turn, these persons referred us to other alcoholism programs or traditional healers, not listed in the NIAAA directory, who worked with Native American clients.

Traditional medicine people were located through personal contacts in indigenous social networks. Local people at each research site served as consultants.[3] Their knowledge of the communities and the healing personnel in them was invaluable to us, allowing us almost immediate access to the traditional healers. Working without local assistance would have taken months, or even years, of rapport-building before the traditionalists would have shared their healing knowledge with us.

The local consultants not only identified the spiritual leaders and healers, but also provided parameters by which "good" and "bad" medicine could be recognized, as well as the range of traditional healing techniques currently employed. In the course of our interviews, we asked medicine people to provide names of colleagues who may have worked with alcoholics. In this way, a roster of known healers in each region was assembled in a relatively short period of time.

Because traditional Native American healing practices are intrinsically associated with spiritual life and religious ceremony, we interviewed not only herbalists and tribal members who were primarily curers, but also religious–spiritual leaders in the Native communities we visited. Because of the impact of Roman Catholic and Protestant missionaries on Native American religious practice over the last 300 years, Christianity had to be considered one more aspect in the mosaic of contemporary Native American spiritual life. Therefore, we included both Roman Catholic and Protestant ordained and lay clergy in the survey of spiritual leaders in the selected Native American communities if they had attempted alcohol-abuse intervention among their parishioners.

B. Analytical Framework

In order to have an analytical framework to assess the effectiveness of treatment, our first step was to discover the underlying relationships among the diverse treatment approaches and philosophies we encountered. Once the analytical structure had been determined, it was necessary to decide how our large data base could be presented in a manner that could be comprehended and used by treatment personnel, funding agencies, and policy developers.

Our first solution was to develop a continuum of treatment typologies from the range of observed treatment approaches. Recognizing that typologies are, at best, approximations of reality, we used the six dimensions

[3]We are highly indebted to Mack Bettis (Cherokee), Joyce Johnson (Cherokee), John Eagleshield (Sioux), Eva Northrup (Hopi-Cherokee), Bonnie Northrup (Navajo), Glenn Allison (Navajo), Charlotte Standing Buffalo Ortiz (Sioux), and Janie Jones (Cherokee), for their assistance in the field; John Long and Marsha Gauntt, for their assistance in the data analysis; and Christopher Doyle, for typing the manuscript.

illustrated in Table 1 to establish our paradigm. We quantified the six program dimensions in the following manner:

1. Ethnicity of Personnel — The ethnicity of each staff member and client was documented and three ethnicity ratios were calculated:
   a. The proportion of Native American to non-Native clients;
   b. The proportion of Native American to non-Native staff;
   c. The proportion of Native American staff members to Native American clients.
2. Level of Involvement in Alcoholics Anonymous — The attitudinal range included program directors who strongly enforced regular attendance at AA meetings, to program directors who described AA as "unIndian" and a "cultural anathema."
3. Type of Counselor Training — Data were collected on the length, quality, and type of training counselors had received to work with alcoholic clients. Training ranged from associate and bacculaurate degrees in the social sciences, attending accredited training programs. (e.g., those administered by the University of Utah and University of South Dakota) to on-the-job training. Personnel without formal training include those with personal alcohol problems who were in remission, staff persons who had come up through the ranks in their treatment programs, and those with apprenticeships to medicine people recognized by their communities as healers or spiritual leaders.
4. Intervention Techniques — Staff members were asked to describe their intake assessment and counseling techniques and follow-up procedures.
   a. Typical programs following the medical model dealt with the physiological effects of alcohol abuse, concentrated on the restoration of the client's good health, and advocated total lifetime abstinence from alcohol.
   b. Psychosocially oriented programs used interpersonal and intrapsychic counseling approaches. Variously, staff members talked about rational–emotive, confrontation, and reality therapy. Freudian constructs, biofeedback exercises, group therapy, transactional analysis, meditation, and game playing were also used. Emphasis was placed on the development of coping strategies and marketable employment skills.
   c. Culture-sensitive counseling techniques reflected counselor's knowledge of, and sympathy with, cultural and historical influences on contemporary Native American life. Staff members usually received some training in appropriate interactional style when working with Native American clients and were encouraged to develop an understanding of and empathy with the Native American world view.

TABLE 1

Alcoholism Treatment Modality Assessment Paradigm

Ethnicity of staff and personnel	Strength of AA affiliation	Counseling training	Treatment–counseling techniques	Cultural accommodations	Traditional and nontraditional cooperation
1. All Anglo	1. Very strong	1. University degree, systematic, medical	1. Alcoholism as disease, medical, non-Indian	1. None	1. None
2. Mostly	2. Strong	2. Seminars on-the-job	2. Medical–psychosocial	2. Some	2. Some
3. Mixed	3. Mixed	3. Mixed	3. Eclectic, some Indian	3. Mixed	3. Mixed
4. Mostly Indian	4. Weak	4. Mostly on-the-job, self-experienced, some Indian	4. Major Indian influence	4. Major accommodations	4. Considerable
5. All Indian	5. None/Anti	5. Mostly life experience	5. Mostly Indian traditional healing systems	5. Mostly traditional	5. Total involvement

d. *Syncretic approaches,* that is, those that integrated two or more culturally diverse treatment modalities, tended to experiment with novel or traditional forms of healing practices. Involvement in community activities, explorations of cultural skills (e.g., bead work, silversmithing, clothes designing), sports, sweat-bath participation, and rediscovery of one's own cultural heritage are all strategies by which the Native American deviant drinker is brought back into a productive and acceptable community lifestyle.

e. At the most traditional level of counseling, entire families may be asked to participate in treatment. Some traditional curing ceremonies demand the financial, emotional, and physical participation of the primary members of the afflicted person's social network. Other traditional curing rituals demand a certain level of self-denial as well as psychic and physical trials on the part of the afflicted patient (e.g., fasting, isolation, purging through emetics, and self-mutilation as in the Sun Dance). Still others cure through the use of prayers, herbal teas, and various other forms of entreaties to the afflicting spirits.

5. Accommodation to Patient Acculturation Level — Accommodation ranged from no apparent concern with client ethnic identity to encouragement to "find one's Indian self" as the antedote to alcoholism. If Native American posters, artifacts, newspapers, or bulletins were visible, the program was judged as displaying at least a modest level of accommodation. If group sessions were spent discussing the special social conditions that might promote abusive drinking among Native Americans or the difficulties facing Native Americans in contemporary society, the program was judged as a major accommodation. If tribal languages were used in therapy, medicine men were known to treatment staff and occasionally contacted for a client, and the novel use of traditional Native American curing or health practices (e.g., sweats, teas) had been incorporated into the treatment schedule, the program was judged to be strongly accommodating.

6. Level of Cooperation between Anglo-Oriented and Tribal Treatment Modalities — At one extreme of this continuum, no cooperation was attempted or perceived useful by either modality. If some acceptance of the other system's approach to treatment (but little inclination to engage the services of the other) was voiced, we ranked the programs as somewhat cooperative. If some cooperative effort (referral of patients who request the services of the other treatment system) was demonstrated, we judged the program cooperative. Active use of both treatment systems as a syncretic approach to alcoholism recovery was judged very cooperative.

To arrive at a typological judgment, each program was rated on a five-point scale for each of the six dimensions. In this way, the range of approaches and attitudes both across and within each of the programs could be determined. Obviously, not all programs fit neatly into only one category. It is clear that, aside from certain program guidelines set by the NIAAA, Indian Health Service, Public Health Service, or tribal governments, program modalities reflect the attitudes of their personnel. Alcohol recovery program directors tend to be pragmatic in their treatment delivery, employing those counseling techniques they perceive as working and ignoring those which they do not.

V. TYPES OF TREATMENT MODALITIES

The alcoholism treatment programs were categorized into six basic types, based on the descriptive dimensions. The programs range from those that advocate the medical model with no accommodation of cultural differences among their clients, to a traditional approach that includes herbal medicine and curing rituals administered by indigenous Native American healers without host society medical interventions.

A. The Medical Model

Program administrators who advocate the disease concept of alcoholism emphasize that treatment should address the symptoms of the disease, per se. The social and psychological malaise of the client is dealt with secondarily, if at all. Further, because alcoholism is viewed as a disease, it requires specific interventions that do not take into account client age, sex, socioeconomic level, or cultural experiences. These programs tend to be strongly influenced by Alcoholics Anonymous. In fact, medical model programs are characterized by scores of 1 or 2 on all of the six program measures in Table 1.

B. The Psychosocial Model

A second approach to alcoholism treatment has a sociopsychological orientation. Although maintaining sobriety and returning to physical health are primary concerns, emphasis is also placed on identifying and resolving psychosocial problems of which abusive drinking is seen as a symptom. The goal of this approach is to develop more positive coping strategies. Program personnel in this category tend to believe that interpersonal and intrapsychic disturbances, the antecedents of abusive drinking, are pan-cultural phenomena to which certain psychotherapeutic techniques can be applied successfully, regardless of cultural experience. A mixture of Western psychotherapeutic treatment models is employed. These programs tend to have more Anglo than Native American counselors, strong AA affiliations, and scores of 2 or 3 for type of training, treatment techniques, level of cultural accommodation, and cooperation with traditional healers.

C. The Assimilative Model

A third type of alcoholism intervention program has both Native American clients and Native American personnel. These programs use the techniques of both AA and traditional psychotherapy. There is general consensus among staff members of this type of program that Native Americans treating other Native Americans makes for optimal client–counselor rapport. And if the Native American counselor is also a recovering problem drinker, he or she is viewed as a positive role model and an asset to the program. Although these programs are run by and for Native Americans, their treatment approaches are distinctively Anglo. These programs tend to have all-Native staffs, strong AA affiliations, and, as with psychosocial model programs, scores of 2 or 3 for the last four program measures shown in Table 1.

D. The Culture-Sensitive Model

A fourth type of program, which we have labeled the culture-sensitive model, modifies its treatment strategies and setting in order to make them more acceptable to patients from diverse cultural orientations. This type of program typically has one or more Native American counselors, and posters with Indian themes are hung in the living and meeting rooms. Group therapy sessions include discussion of Native American historical and cultural influences that pertain to the use of alcoholic beverages. Non-Native counselors are sensitized to the basic elements of Native American life and interactional style.

These programs are almost exclusively staffed by Native Americans. Scores on AA affiliation vary more widely in this cluster of programs than in all others. Level of training also varies but tends to be more formal than in the syncretic programs. Treatment technique scores cluster around 2 or 3 while, as might be expected, cultural accommodation scores range from 2 to 4. Cooperation with traditional healers scores, however, are similar to those of programs labeled assimilative.

E. The Syncretic Model

A fifth type of treatment program incorporates Native American values and ceremonial curing practices with standard alcoholism intervention strategies. Attempts are made to express basic tenets of alcoholism intervention in terms compatible with Native American thought and cultural experience. Consistent with the spiritual emphasis of AA, clients are encouraged to make spiritual quests based on tribal lore. A return to or intensification of the practice of traditional Native American skills (e.g., beadwork, pottery making) and social activities (e.g., pow wows, sweat baths, pipe ceremonies) is also encouraged. Membership in AA, church groups, therapy groups, and other types of social systems supportive of sobriety are also advocated.

As with assimilative and culture-sensitive programs, syncretic programs are almost totally staffed by Native Americans. They tend to have higher scores for AA affiliation (less affiliation), range widely on level of training scores, and have scores of 3 and 4 on treatment techniques and cultural accommodations. The most apparent difference between syncretic and other program types are their high scores on cooperation with traditional healers. No program labeled syncretic scores lower than 3 on this last dimension.

F. The Traditional Model

In every rural research site we visited, there were at least a dozen men and women versed in the traditional curing practices of their tribal group. Several of these traditional practitioners had developed chants, ceremonies, or herbal teas expressly for use in treating alcoholism or the medical, economic, and psychosocial consequences of alcohol abuse. Two types of clients would most often avail themselves of the traditional healers' services. The first type of client was often older, extremely isolated, and a relatively unacculturated person who had, all his/her life, believed in and employed the traditional healer in times of illness. The other type of client of the traditional healer was usually younger, better educated, and more acculturated. This client had tried repeatedly and unsuccessfully to obtain sobriety through conventional alcoholism treatment modalities. His/her reliance on a traditional healer often had the quality of a "last resort" effort. When all else had failed, the desperate Native American alcohol abuser sometimes turns to the traditional healer for help to the exclusion of other, more conventional forms of alcoholism treatment. These healers score 5 on all of the program dimensions except one: strength of AA affiliation is weak to nonexistent.

In summary, it appears that the six dimensions illustrated in Table 1 and which evolved from our ethnographic observations of Indian alcoholism intervention programs and staff interviews accurately depict differences among the treatment modalities for alcoholism that are available to Native Americans.

VI. DISCUSSION OF CLIENT-TO-PROGRAM GOODNESS
OF FIT: THE PROBLEM OF RECIDIVISM

Each of the six types of alcoholism intervention we identified was exemplified by at least one treatment program we observed. However, the majority of the programs are best described as culture-sensitive or assimilative. While most treatment program personnel voice a certain empathy for traditional forms of curing, few attempt to cooperate with tribal healers. The practicalities of administering publically funded alcoholism intervention programs that are subject to federal regulation restrict attempts at syncretism to not much more than arm's length acknowledgment of traditional healers and the efficacy of their curing powers. Experimentation is usually initiated only at the insistence of a client.

To date, there is general reluctance on the part of most Indian alcoholism recovery programs to syncretize conventional and tribal alcoholism treatment modalities. This attitude holds even though substantial numbers of Native Americans still adhere to many traditional forms of behavior and belief. Moreover, there is evidence to suggest that, under certain circumstances, indigenous treatment modalities do promote sobriety (Albaugh, 1973; Bergman, 1971; Stratton, 1981).

Programmatic rigidity is particularly disappointing considering the early recidivism that occurs after Native American involvment in conventional alcoholism treatment programs (Weibel-Orlando, 1984). Of course, high recidivism rates are not peculiar to Native American alcoholism treatment programs. Lack of follow-up, aftercare, and social supports for sobriety in the "real world" plague all alcoholism interventionists (Ablon, 1980; Alcocer, 1981; Bourne, 1973; King, 1981; Towle, 1975). However, recidivism among Native American alcoholism treatment clients is thought to be exacerbated by lack of fit between client's world view and life experience and treatment modalities into which alcoholic Native Americans are placed (Albaugh, 1973; Shore, 1972; Snake et al., 1977; Stone, 1981; Topper, 1985; Weibel-Orlando, 1984).

There is substantial documentation in the Native American and alcohol literature of those factors that shape drinking practices in the heterogeneous contemporary Native American population (Levy & Kunitz, 1974; MacAndrew & Edgerton, 1969; Price, 1975; Stratton, Zeiner, & Paredes, 1978; Topper, 1974, 1985). These factors include the time and conditions under which a tribal group first came into contact with western European settlers, the type and level of social organization and subsistance technology at the time of European incursions, family drinking patterns, educational opportunities (or lack of them), acculturation level, age, and sex.

The issue that bedevils most Indian alcoholism intervention programs is how to design a treatment program that can deal effectively with cultural heterogeneity. For instance, the middle-aged, full-blood, Navajo-speaking man who had lived (and drunk) most of his life on the reservation or in one of the border towns that cater to Native Americans may not understand or respond to conventional alcoholism treatment modalities. He may truly believe his cirrhosis of the liver is due to witchcraft practiced on the behalf of a vengeful enemy. Any alcoholism intervention with such a person would have to address his world view. Conversely, the urban-born, "street-hip," half-Navajo college student who indulges in a semester-long bout of "partying" may respond to more conventional alcoholism counseling, whereas traditional healing approaches may have no cultural validity for him.

There have been some creative attempts to come to grips with intraethnic heterogeneity in alcoholism treatment. For example, Sidney Stone-Brown (Piegan/Blood) and her associate, Rufus Charger (Lakota), during their administration of the Native American Rehabilitation Association (NARA) of Portland, Oregon, developed a seminal model for the identification of client types. They formulated a culture-specific treatment modality that seeks first to define and then to respond to world-view differences among their alcohol-abusing clients (Stone, 1981, 1982). In their intake interviews, NARA counselors placed clients along a continuum that ranges from highly traditional to highly contemporary world views.

As shown in Table 2, four main elements of world view are assessed in Stone-Brown's model: spiritual/religious, social/recreation, training/educational, familial/self.[4] Each of these elements is rated along four levels or generations that range from highly traditional to highly contemporary. Discrepancies in generational levels across the four world-view elements are considered noteworthy. The treatment paradigm is based on the assumption that self-actualization is maximized by attaining equilibrium of the four world view elements. That is to say, self-actualized individuals tend to fall in the same generational level on all four world view elements. Disequilibrium of any of the four elements produces preactualization conflicts that need to be resolved through therapy. Through the use of the world view assessment protocol, apparent preactualization conflicts are identified and treatment is individualized to address the individual's particular conflicts (Stone, 1981, 1982).

The preceding summary oversimplifies Stone-Brown's creative and ingenious attempt to assess both a client's level of acculturation and areas of world view conflict that may precede his or her alcohol abuse. Identification of an alcoholic patient's world view may have wider application. Using an amended version of the Native Self-Actualization protocol, it may be possi-

---

[4]We are highly indebted to Sidney Stone-Brown for her permission to use the generations paradigm she and Rufus Charger developed during their administration of the NARA program in Portland, Oregon as an illustration of an indigenous attempt to deal with cultural heterogeneity among Native American client populations.

TABLE 2

World View—Pre-Self Actualization Conflicts

		TRADITIONAL		
Generations	Spiritual	Social	Training	Family
1st	Attends ceremonies, sweats, or other outward signs of tribal belief system.	Spends leisure time with Native people; prefers activities centered around Indian community.	Prefers to learn in an unstructured setting; uses extended periods of listening and observation. Places greater emphasis on learning from elders.	Preceived relationships as extended family, encompassing all relations. Maintains continual contact with all family members. Ultimately includes individual's tribe.
2nd	Has knowledge of the ceremonies, sweats, or other outward signs of tribal belief system, but does not actively participate on a regular basis.	Spends leisure time with Native people; prefers activities centered around Indian community. Enjoys contemporary activities within the context of the "all-Indian" teams, rodeos or tournaments.	Prefers to learn in an unstructured setting. Uses extended listening and observation. Places greater emphasis on learning from grandparents; has received some formal education.	Perceives relationships as extended family. Maintains continual contact with all family members. Strong identification with tribal background.

	Religion	Recreation	Education	Self
3rd	Believes in a church doctrine or has participated in an organized religion; does not actively attend on a regular basis.	Spends most of their leisure time outside Indian community. Prefers activities experienced in general community. Occasionally attends Pow-Wows or other Indian community activities.	Prefers to learn in a structured classroom setting; is assisted by movies and speakers. Has had minor exposure to grandparent's and elder's teachings. Somewhat uncomfortable with assessment of skills and knowledge through written evaluation.	Perceives family relationships as restricted to parents, brothers, sisters, spouse, and children. Maintains occasional contact with grandparents and other relatives. Identifies with tribe; has had minimal contact with ancestral people or land use.
4th	Attends church or organized religious activities such as bible study.	Spends leisure time outside Indian community; prefers activities centered around general community events and social gatherings.	Prefers to learn in a structured classroom setting; is assisted by process through formal lectures, didactics and assessment of skill, and knowledge through written evaluation.	Perceives relationships as primary family; focus on relationship to spouse and children, occasionally encompassing brothers, sisters, and grandparents.

CONTEMPORARY

Note. From Stone (1982).

ble to match clients according to their life experiences, attitudes, and world views with the most appropriate alcoholism intervention strategy.

The concurrent use of a program assessment paradigm such as the typological model which our research team developed and the individual assessment paradigm developed by Stone-Brown and Charger may facilitate the administration of regional alcoholism intervention programs with diverse treatment modalities and heterogeneous clienteles. Once a client's world view has been established, the next logical step would be to determine which treatment modality, in an array of available ones, best fits that particular client's needs and world view.

Traditional tribal healing practices such as involvement in a vision quest, sweat lodge ceremony, Blessing Way cycle, or Native American Church peyote service and the belief systems which support these rites of sacred separation, purification, and renewal would not be meaningful for all Native American clients with alcohol problems. Earlier investigations have shown that the degree of the individual's ethnic group involvement, adherence to traditional belief systems, familiarity with and acceptance of indigenous healing practices, and susceptibility to the conversion experience are associated with successful traditional interventions (Stratton, 1981; Topper, 1974; Weibel-Orlando, 1984).

Conversely, conventional psychotherapeutic modalities (e.g., rational–emotive, confrontational, Gestalt) as well as AA are not inherently useless, ethnocentric superimpositions in the treatment of Native American alcoholics. Our investigations have shown that some acculturated Native Americans do respond positively to psychosocial alcoholism treatment modalities (Weibel-Orlando, 1984). Factors positively associated with success in conventional alcohol intervention are age, level of education, and relative lack of intensive involvement in Native American folkways.

VII. CONCLUSIONS

According to Gilbert and Sullivan, the Mikado's solution to outbreaks of antisocial behavior in nineteenth century Japan was to "make the punishment fit the crime." There may be a mythic message in this light-hearted lyric. A first step toward reduction of high rates of recidivism among users of Indian alcoholism treatment programs may be to match treatment modality with client profile. Some version of the treatment modality paradigm (Table 1) and a variant of the Native American Self Actualization protocol (Table 2) could be employed by a central coordinating alcoholism treatment agency (e.g., Indian Health Service or State Offices of Alcoholism and Drug Treatment Programs), to determine the optimum fit of individual clients to treatment programs. Client placement decisions would be based on the fit of client personality, sociocultural experience, spiritual beliefs, socioeconomic status, and level of acculturation to a program's modal treatment approach. In order for client-to-treatment fit to occur, lines of communication and transportation would have to be established and maintained between regional health services, mental health clinics, detoxification centers, Indian Health Service facilities, and all available alcohol treatment programs within a catchment region.

The technique for categorizing alcoholism treatment modalities, coupled with assessments of clients' world views, has broad application in a treatment field which currently lacks coordinated effort and success in promoting and sustaining lifestyles free of alcohol related problems. The notion that alcoholism treatment modalities can be typologized and utilized selectively across client types does not apply to Native Americans alone, but to other ethnic groups as well. As pointed out earlier, Hispanic, Asian, and Black Americans also are not monolithic ethnic groups. Rather, they schism along sociocultural and socioeconomic fault lines that impede and sometimes prevent intraethnic group communication.

Those criteria developed to categorize treatment programs and to assess clients' world views for Native Americans do not necessarily apply to other ethnic-American groups. For example, tribal curing ceremonies are minimally used in most Black American communities. Therefore, it seems reasonable to expect that, among Black Americans, ethnicity of treatment staff members and intensity of cooperation with Black community support systems (e.g., the churches and schools) would be more salient programmatic factors than syncretism of culture-specific treatment modalities. Location (e.g., southern/rural versus northern/urban), level of education, socioeconomic background, and level and type of personal involvement in a socioreligious community (e.g., evangelical, charismatic, conservative, Muslim) are some of the more salient sociocultural features of Black American life. These factors might influence client receptivity to various treatment approaches. Therefore, any alcoholism intake schedule designed specifically to document Black alcoholism intervention clients' preactualization conflicts should include measures of the aforementioned salient sociocultural and socioeconomic factors.

Among Hispanic Americans, the newly arrived, undocumented, and marginally employed campesino, or peasant, for instance, necessarily has a different cultural experience than the third generation, upwardly mobile, Mexican-American graduate student. Treatment personnel necessarily will have to take into account such factors as culture of origin, generational depth in the U.S., and language facility in fashioning appropriate treatment strategies for the heterogeneous Hispanic-American population. In addition, the sociopolitical status of hundreds of thousands of economically desperate illegal Hispanic aliens in the U.S. is such that their need for anonymity, fear of authority figures, and a multitude of other sociocultural factors create formidable treatment barriers for those at risk for becoming alcohol abusers. Asian Americans originate from a wide array of countries and exhibit wide cultural differences in explaining and treating illness. Because there is almost no existing research, the field of inquiry is virgin territory for those interested in developing culture-specific approaches to an apparent rise in alcohol abuse among Asian Americans.

In general, alcoholism treatment and research personnel are only beginning to understand and manipulate factors that facilitate or inhibit effective alcoholism interventions among ethnic minority populations. We had originally hoped to assess the relative effectiveness of the various program modalities once the categorization process had been completed. However, follow-up procedures of the observed programs were either totally lacking or so minimal or anecdotal in nature that no empirically based determination of relative effectiveness of treatment type could be ascertained. Systematic treatment follow-up protocols and studies that document the relative success of both conventional and nonconventional alcohol abuse treatment in maintaining sobriety in ethnic-American subpopulations are sorely needed. Additionally, studies to identify client types that either transcend ethnic boundaries or are unique to specific ethnic groups, are in order. The prototypical model for assessing client-to-treatment fit presented in this chapter could serve as a catalyst for further systematic work in this area.

REFERENCES

Ablon, J. (1980). The significance of cultural patterning for the "alcoholic family." *Family Process,* **19,** 127–144.

Albaugh, B. J. (1973). *Ethnic therapy with American Indian alcoholics as an antidote to anomie.* Paper presented at the 8th Joint Meeting of the Professional Association of the U. S. Public Health Service.

Alcocer, A. M. (1977). Alcoholism among Chicanos. In A. M. Padilla & E. F. Padilla (Eds.), *Improving mental health and human services for hispanic communities: Selected presentations from regional conferences* (pp. 35–42), Washington, DC: National Coalition of Hispanic Mental Health and Human Service Organizations.

Alcocer, A. M. (1981). Alcohol use and abuse among the Hispanic American population. In *U. S. Dept. of Health and Human Services. Fourth Special Report to the U. S. Congress on Alcohol and Health.* Washington, DC: U. S. Government Printing Office.

Bales, R. L. (1962). Attitudes toward drinking in the Irish culture. In D. J. Pittman & C. R. Snyder (Eds.), *Society, culture and drinking patterns* (pp. 157–187). New York: Wiley.

Bergman, R. L. (1971). Navajo peyote use: Its apparent safety. *American Journal of Psychiatry* **128,** 695–699.

Bourne, P. G. (1973). Alcoholism in the urban Negro population. In P. G. Bourne & R. Fox (Eds.), *Alcoholism: Progress in research and treatment.* New York: Academic Press.

Dailey, R. C. (1968). The role of alcohol among North American tribes as reported in the Jesuit relations. *Anthropologica,* **10,** 45–57.

Dozier, E. P. (1966). Problem drinking among American Indians: The role of sociocultural deprivation. *Quarterly Journal of Studies on Alcohol*, 27, 72–87.

Gilbert, M. J. (1985). Intracultural variation in attitudes and behavior related to alcohol: Mexican Americans in California. In G. Ames & L. Bennett (Eds.), *The American experience with alcohol* (pp. 225–278). New York: Plenum.

Gilbert, M. M. (1977). *Qualitative analysis of the drinking practices and alcohol-related problems of the Spanish speaking in three California locales.* (Available from Technical Systems Institute, Alhambra, CA.)

Glad, D. D. (1947). Attitudes and experiences of American Jewish and American Irish male youth as related to differences in adult rates of inebrity. *Quarterly Journal of Studies on Alcohol*, 8, 406–472.

Guinn, R. (1978). Alcohol use among Mexican American youth. *Journal of School Health*, 48(2), 90–91.

Kahn, M. W., Williams, C., Galvez, E., Lejero, L., Conrad, R. D., & Goldstein, G. (1975). The Papago Psychology Service: A community mental health program on an American Indian reservation. *American Journal of Community Psychology*, 3(2), 81–97.

King, L. M. (1981). Alcoholism: Studies regarding Black Americans, 1979–1980. In *U.S. Department of Health and Human Services*. In *U.S. Department of Health and Human Services. Fourth Special Report to the U.S. Congress on Alcohol and Health.* Washington, DC: U.S. Government Printing Office.

Kitano, H. L. (1981). Asian American drinking patterns. *Fourth Special Report to the Congress on Alcohol and Health.* Washington, DC: U.S. Government Printing Office.

Kitano, H. L., Hatanka, H., Yeung, W., & Sue, S. (1985). Japanese American drinking patterns. In G. Ames & Bennett (Eds.), *The American experience with alcohol: Contrasting cultural perspectives* (pp. 335–358). New York: Plenum Press.

Kline, J. A., & Roberts, A. C. (1973). A residential alcoholism treatment program for American Indians. *Quarterly Journal of Studies on Alcohol* 34, 860–868.

Knupfer, G., & Room, R. (1967). Drinking patterns and attitudes of Irish, Jewish and White Protestant American men. *Quarterly Journal of Studies on Alcohol* 28, 676–699.

Lang, G. M. C. (1974). Adaptive strategies of urban Indian drinkers. Unpublished doctoral dissertation, University of Missouri, Columbia, MO.

Leland, J. (1976). *Firewater myths: North American drinking and alcohol addiction.* (Monograph No. 11, available from Rutgers Center for Alcohol Studies, New Brunswick, NJ.)

Levy, J. E., & Kunitz, S. J. (1974). *Indian drinking: Navajo practices and Anglo American theories.* Wiley-Interscience, New York, NY.

Lolli, G., Serianni, E., Golder, G. M., & Luzzato-Fegiz, P. (1958). *Alcohol in Italian culture: Food and wine in relation to sobriety among Italians and Italian Americans.* (Monograph No. 3, available from Rutgers Center of Alcohol Studies, New Brunswick, NJ.)

Lurie, N. O. (1971). The world's oldest ongoing protest demonstration: North American Indian drinking patterns. *Pacific Historical Review*, 40(3), 311–332.

MacAndrew, C., & Edgerton, R. (1969). *Drunken comportment: A social explanation.* Chicago: Aldine.

Mail, P. D., & McDonald, D. R. (1980). *Tulapai to tokay: A bibliography of alcohol use and abuse among Native Americans of North America.* New Haven, CT: HRAF Press.

Maril, R. L., & Zavaleta, A. N. (1979). Drinking patterns of low-income Mexican American women. *Journal of Studies on Alcohol*, 40(5), 480–484.

Obeso, P., & Bordatto, O. (1979). Cultural implications in treating the Puerto Rican female. *American Journal of Drug and Alcohol Abuse*, 6(3), 337–344.

Opler, M. K., & Singer, J. L. (1956). Ethnic differences in behavior and psychopathology: Italian and Irish. *International Journal of Social Psychiatry*, 2, 11–23.

Paine, H. J. (1977). Attitudes and patterns of alcohol use among Mexican Americans: Implications for service delivery. *Journal of Studies on Alcohol*, 38, 544–553.

Price, J. A. (1975). Applied analysis of North American Indian drinking patterns. *Human Organization* **34**, 17–26.

Reed, T. E., Kalant, H., Gibbons, R., Kapur, B., & Rankin, J. (1976). Alcohol and acetaldehyde metabolism in Caucasians, Chinese and Amerinds. *Canadian Medical Association Journal*, **115**, 851–855.

Room, R. (1968). Cultural contingencies of alcoholism: Variations between and within nineteenth-century urban ethnic groups in alcohol-related death rates. *Journal of Health and Social Behavior*, **9**(20), 99–113.

Sadoun, R., Lolli, G., & Silverman, M. (1965). *Drinking in French culture* (Monograph No. 5, available from Rutgers Center of Alcohol Studies, New Brunswick, NJ.)

Schwitters, S. Y., Johnson, R. C., McClearn, G. E., & Wilson, J. R. (1981). Alcohol use and the flushing response in different racial-ethnic groups. *Journal of Studies on Alcohol*, **43** (11), 1259–1262.

Shore, J. (1972). Three alcohol programs for American Indians. *American Journal of Psychiatry*, **128**, 1450–1454.

Snake, R., Hawkins, G., & LaBoueff, S. (1977). *Report on alcohol and drug abuse Task Force Eleven: Alcohol and drug abuse.* (Final report to the American Indian Policy Review Commission.) Washington, DC: Author.

Snyder, C. R. (1962). Culture and Jewish sobriety: The ingroup–outgroup factor. In D. J. Pittman & C. R. Snyder (Eds.), *Society, culture and drinking patterns* (pp. 188–225). NY: Wiley.

Stivers, R. A. (1971). *The bachelor group ethic and Irish drinking.* Unpublished doctoral dissertation, Department of Sociology, University of Illinois.

Stone, S. A. (1981, April). *Cross-cultural alcoholism treatment: A model for conflicts diagnosis and treatment planning through the Native Self-actualization Chart.* Paper presented at the Annual Conference of the National Council on Alcoholism Conference, New Orleans, LA.

Stone, S. A. (1982, May). Native generations: Diagnosis and placement on the conflicts/resolution chart. Paper presented at the Annual School on Addiction Studies. University of Alaska, Anchorage, AK.

Stratton, R. (1981). Indian alcoholism problems and Native American culture. *New Directions for Mental Health Services*, **10**, 45–60.

Stratton, R., Zeiner, A., & Paredes, A. (1978). Tribal affiliation and prevalence of alcohol problems. *Quarterly Journal of Studies on Alcohol*, **39**(7), 1166–1177.

Sue, S., Zaine, N., & Ito, J. (1979). Alcohol drinking patterns among Asian and Caucasian Americans. *Journal of Cross-Cultural Psychology*, **10**, 41–56.

Topper, M. C. (1974). Drinking patterns, culture change, sociability and Navajo adolescents. *Addictive Diseases*, **1**(1), 97–116.

Topper, M. C. (1985). Navajo "alcoholism": Drinking, alcohol abuse and treatment in a changing cultural environment. In L. Bennett & G. Ames (Eds.), *The American experience with alcohol: Contrasting cultural perspectives* (pp. 227–251). New York: Plenum.

Towle, L. H. (1975). Alcoholism treatment outcomes in different populations. In M. E. Chafetz (Ed.), *Research treatment and prevention: Proceedings of the Fourth Annual Alcoholism Conference of the National Institute on Alcohol Abuse and Alcoholism.* Washington, DC: NIAAA (SUDOCS No. HE 20.8314.974).

Trevino, M. (1975). Machismo alcoholism: Mexican American machismo drinking. In M. E. Chafetz (Ed.), *Research, treatment and prevention. Proceedings of the Fourth Annual Alcohol Conference of the National Institute on Alcohol Abuse and Alcoholism.* Washington, DC: NIAAA (SUDOCS No. HE 20.8314.974).

Weibel-Orlando, J. (1984). Indian alcoholism treatment programs as flawed rites of passage. *Medical Anthropology Quarterly*, **15**(3), 62–67.

Weibel-Orlando, J. (1985). Indians, ethnicity and alcohol: Contrasting perceptions of the ethnic self and alcohol use or non-use. In L. Bennett, G. Ames (Eds.), *The American experience with alcohol: Contrasting explanatory models* (pp. 201–226). New York: Plenum.

Weisner, T., Weibel-Orlando, J., & Long J. (1984). Serious drinking, white man's drinking and teetotaling: Predictors of drinking level differences in an urban Indian population. *Journal of Studies on Alcohol, 45*(3), 237–250.

Wolff, P. H. (1973). Vasomotor sensitivity to alcohol in diverse Mongoloid populations. *American Journal of Human Genetics, 25*(2), 193–199.

IV
Early
Intervention
and Prevention

13

Theory and Methods for Secondary Prevention of Alcohol Problems: A Cognitively Based Approach

MARTHA SANCHEZ-CRAIG[*,†]
AND D. ADRIAN WILKINSON[*]

*Department of Sociobehavioral Research
Clinical Institute
Addiction Research Foundation
Toronto, Ontario, Canada M5S 2S1
and
†Division of Community Health
Faculty of Medicine
University of Toronto
Toronto, Ontario, Canada M5S 2S1

KEITH WALKER

Private Practice
Toronto, Ontario, Canada M4C 1Z1

I. RATIONALE FOR SECONDARY PREVENTION

Although alcohol problems typically emerge when people are in their 20s (Cahalan & Room, 1974; Room, 1977), alcoholism treatment programs typically have been successful in attracting only the most chronic segment of the problem-drinking population. The clients of these programs tend to be over 40 years of age, to have a history of drinking of approximately 15 years,

TREATMENT AND PREVENTION
OF ALCOHOL PROBLEMS: A RESOURCE MANUAL

and to suffer some alcohol-related medical problems (e.g., Ashley, Olin, le Rich, Kornackzewski, Schmidt, Corey, & Rankin, 1981; Lelbach, 1974). Most health professionals would suggest that a 15-year interval between the onset of any health problem and the beginning of treatment is too long, yet few concerted efforts have been made to reach problem drinkers earlier. The desirability of early intervention is indicated by results of many treatment studies which revealed that the earlier the problem is treated, the greater the chances of successful outcome (e.g., Armor, Polich, & Stambul, 1976; Orford & Edwards, 1977). Moreover, there is evidence to suggest that early-stage problem drinkers can be treated using relatively brief and inexpensive interventions (e.g., Miller & Taylor, 1980; Miller, Taylor, & West, 1980).

Recently, the concept of secondary prevention of alcohol problems has aroused the interest of many alcoholism researchers and clinicans, including the present authors. The main objectives in this area have been to develop procedures for identifying early-stage problem-drinkers, attracting them into treatment, and treating them effectively at acceptable cost. In this chapter, we describe the development of a secondary prevention program, based on a program of research conducted over the past 12 years. In the first section of the chapter, we briefly review factors which appear to have delayed the deployment of secondary prevention programs for problem drinkers. In addition, we discuss developments that have given impetus to secondary prevention and the characteristics that such programs should probably have if they are to be successful. In the second section, we outline the theoretical bases of our approach and the manner in which the procedures were developed. The third section is devoted to a description of procedures. Techniques that can be useful in recruiting and screening clients and in retaining them in treatment are discussed. Guidelines for helping clients to set appropriate drinking goals are presented, and procedures for the development of adaptive coping with tendencies to drink excessively are described. The chapter concludes with some consideration of what seem to be priorities for research in this area. It should be noted that we do not attempt to provide a review of the literature, although at various points we refer the reader to sources that may be helpful in elaborating the issues.

A. Impediments to Secondary Prevention

A major impediment to the provision of services to the early-stage problem drinker is the widespread set of beliefs about alcoholism. Though alcoholism programs vary considerably in format, length, and content, they are generally based on the following beliefs: (1) alcoholism is a disease, or the symptom of some psychopathology; (2) lifelong abstinence is essential to arrest the disease; (3) for treatment to be effective, the alcoholic must first acknowledge both having the disease and an inability to adopt control over his or her drinking; (4) such acknowledgment tends to occur only under excruciating circumstances — that is, when the alcoholic "hits bottom."

Current advocates of the disease concept usually cite Jellinek (1960) as scientific support for their views, but actually Jellinek cautiously presented this concept as a working hypothesis in need of evaluation. Some of Jellinek's ideas were compatible with the ideology of Alcoholics Anonymous, a self-help organization that has been the predominant treatment force for alcoholics in North America over the past 50 years (see Thoreson and Budd's chapter in this volume). Popularized versions of these ideas are now accepted as factual by the majority of people involved in counseling alcoholics. Expressions that exemplify the prevailing system of beliefs are, "Once an alcoholic, always an alcoholic"; "One-drink, one-drunk"; "An alcoholic needs to hit bottom before he or she is ready for sobriety"; "For an alcoholic, one drink is too many and one hundred are not enough." In short, advocates of the disease concept tend to view alcoholism as part of an all-or-none dichotomy. One can argue that this tendency to see alcoholism as an all-or-none state has been a principal deterrent to the development of secondary prevention programs. Edwards and Gross (1976) and Edwards (1977) have attempted to undermine this type of dichotomous thinking of alcoholism. They propose the existence of an "alcohol dependence syndrome," consisting of a group of symptoms typical of alcohol dependence, each of which can vary in severity within an individual. Furthermore, they suggest that for persons low in dependence, but encountering problems related to drinking, moderation may be an appropriate goal; for persons in the middle range, abstinence is recommended, but negotiable; and for severely dependent alcoholics, abstinence should be the only acceptable goal.

Many problem drinkers are extremely reluctant to entertain the notions that they are the victims of an irreversible disease and that the only appropriate goal for them is lifelong abstention. This unwillingness to admit to having the disease — namely, *denial* — has been interpreted by advocates of the disease concept as a symptom of the disease itself. Denial is the mechanism that is presumed to operate against the effectiveness of treatment. For example, Moore and Murphy (1961) stated; "Since denial is often an essential component of the syndrome of alcoholism and an opposing force to treatment, few patients are being successfully treated for alcoholism by any technique." Earlier, Tiedbout (1953) had emphasized that the surrender of the alcoholic's denial of his or her illness is absolutely necessary for treatment success. (For a critical review of issues related to denial and motivation for treatment see Miller, 1985).

Because of the central role granted to denial in the alcoholism syndrome, problem drinkers who are unwilling to admit to alcoholism, or to consider lifelong abstinence, are likely to be viewed by treatment workers as insufficiently motivated to benefit from treatment. Hence, the concept of denial and the notion of the importance of hitting bottom imply that efforts at secondary prevention are likely to be futile.

B. Empirical and Conceptual Influences on Secondary Prevention

The interest in secondary prevention has been instigated both by an array of empirical findings which directly challenge the validity of central tenets of the disease concept and by an alternative conceptualization of excessive drinking based on principles of learning.

At the empirical level, there have been many reports since the mid-1960s of persons diagnosed as alcoholic who successfully developed patterns of moderate drinking after treatment in abstinence-oriented programs. (For reviews of this literature, see Heather and Robertson, 1981, pp. 28–48; Miller & Hester, 1980, pp. 63–65.) In the most comprehensive of these studies (Polich, Armor, & Braiker, 1981), 548 patients were followed for a period of 4 years after discharge from treatment. Of this number, 13% reported that they had maintained moderate drinking without apparent problems for the entire 4 years, whereas 5% reported they had maintained abstinence during the 4 years without problems. The persistent finding that some alcoholics have successfully resumed moderate drinking on their own is at odds with two central aspects of the disease concept, namely loss of control and irreversibility. Furthermore, the consistent finding that successful outcome tends to be associated with a less chronic problem is discrepant with the notion that significant deterioration (i.e., "hitting bottom") is a prerequisite of treatment success.

The preceding observations led us and others to conclude that secondary prevention may be both feasible and desirable. Evidence to support this conclusion has emerged in recent years from a number of treatment studies with early-stage problem drinkers who were trained in techniques for achieving moderation. The rates of success reported ranged from about 60% to 80% over follow-up periods of 3 months to 2 years (see Miller & Hester, 1980, pp. 82–83).

At the theoretical level, it has been proposed that excessive drinking is to a large extent a *learned behavior* rather than a manifestation of an intrinsic abnormality (P. M. Miller, 1976). According to this view, excessive drinking (like other high-frequency behaviors) can be modified, so as to become a low-frequency behavior, by the application of methods based on principles of learning. Hence, in theory, abstinence is a possible but not a necessary objective of treatment. Furthermore, an accepted general principle of learning is that weakening of learned behaviors is more readily accomplished when the level of learning is at an early stage (Hilgard & Bower, 1975). The notion that alcoholism is principally a learned behavior is congenial both with the finding that some alcoholics have successfully resumed moderation of alcohol use and with the finding that alcoholics treated at an early stage of dependence have better prognosis than those treated later on. Moreover, this conception of alcoholism clearly suggests the desirability of intervention in drinking problems at an earlier stage than heretofore has been the case.

The view that excessive drinking is largely something that the person learns to do, and hence that the person can change (also by learning), is less deterministic and stigmatic than the view that it is the result of an incurable disease. Nevertheless, it is important to keep in mind that the learning model of alcoholism is, like the disease model, a working hypothesis. It is not incompatible with the idea that biological differences are important determinants of risk of excessive alcohol consumption[1]; however, excessive drinking may only be revealed under conditions in which the behavior can be acquired and environmentally sustained.

C. Desirable Features of Secondary-Prevention Programs

If programs of secondary prevention are to be successfully implemented, it is important to keep in mind the following considerations in their development: (1) What are the needs of the clients they are meant to serve? (2) What types of programs might best be suited to meet these needs? (3) How can these programs best be integrated with existing community resources?

1. Client Needs

In a program of secondary prevention (Sanchez-Craig, Annis, Bornet, & MacDonald, 1984), information was obtained about some of the clients' perceived needs and hopes regarding treatment. The research objective in this program was to assess the relative appropriateness of abstinence and moderation as treatment goals for early-stage problem drinkers. Hence, the 70 clients were randomly assigned to one or the other of these drinking goals. A set of screening criteria was used to ensure that the alcohol problem of the participants was, in fact, at an early stage of development. Later in the chapter, we describe the characteristics of these clients. For now, it suffices to say that their history of problem drinking was 5 years on average, and that all of them were receiving treatment for their alcohol problem for the first time.

In the first treatment session, the 70 clients were asked to rate the acceptability of the assigned drinking goal (i.e., accepts, rejects, accepts only temporarily). Also, they were asked if they had considered treatment before and, if

[1]There is a growing scientific literature on genetic contributions to risk of alcoholism (Goldstein, 1983, 124–140). This literature indicates that intrinsic individual differences determine levels of risk of alcoholism. The demonstration of genetically determined risk of alcoholism is not inconsistent with the hypothesis that the development of the condition among persons at risk, and others, is governed by principles of learning.

so, what were their reasons for postponing it. The ratings of the assigned drinking goal indicated that most of the clients (86%) who were assigned to moderation reacted favorably to this goal, whereas only a minority (34%) of those who were assigned to abstinence accepted it as a lifelong objective (Sanchez-Craig, 1980a; Sanchez-Craig et al., 1984). With regard to their needs for treatment, most clients reported that they had considered treatment before. Predominant among reasons for postponing it were concerns that the time commitments required by available programs would interfere with their jobs and family responsibilities; rejection of the notion that they were alcoholic; fear that they would be stigmatized by attending an alcoholism treatment program; and unwillingness to consider the goal of total abstinence, which they believed would be imposed on them. The belief that their drinking represented a serious threat to their jobs or to their relationships with members of their family or friends finally motivated them to seek help. A priority for these clients was to do something about their drinking as soon as possible. These expressed needs suggest characteristics that would be desirable in secondary-prevention programs.

2. Program Characteristics

The information obtained during the initial therapy session indicated that the clients entertained clear notions about the nature of programs that would be appropriate for them. *We propose that programs of secondary prevention must accommodate the clients' perceived needs if they are to have the face validity to attract the target population.* Specifically, we suggest that programs be flexible in terms of goals — that clients be given the choice of either abstinence or moderation of alcohol consumption. Programs should avoid the premature labelling of the client as alcoholic and (where possible) should not be directly associated with existing alcoholism or drug addiction services. Programs should be minimally intrusive to the clients' vocational and social life, and their emphasis should be on the modification of harmful drinking practices.

An important additional consideration in the development of programs with face validity for clients is the program content itself. The theoretical rationale and procedures derived therefrom should make sense to the person in treatment. Of course, face validity per se is an insufficient criterion for the adoption of particular programs. They should also be effective.

3. Integration with Existing Community Resources

Workers in all helping professions typically encounter problem drinkers in the course of their practice. Many of these persons are likely to be early-stage problem drinkers, who outnumber severe alcoholics (Room, 1977). As indicated, traditional alcoholism treatment programs are likely to be unsuitable or unacceptable to early-stage problem drinkers, for whom specialized services are rare. Thus, at present, the responsibility for assisting such clients falls mainly on professionals in a primary-care or general-practice role, such as physicians in general practice, public health nurses, clinical psychologists, social workers, pastoral counselors, probation officers, and school guidance counselors. Most of these professionals are unlikely to have received specific training in secondary prevention of alcohol problems.

Given the differing orientations of professionals who encounter persons with alcohol problems, it is necessary to develop procedures that are readily understandable and acceptable to a multidisciplinary audience. An elaborate account of the etiology of drinking problems may not be essential, but the basic theoretical principles and the assumptions from which the procedures are derived should be clear. For psychological procedures, the description should make theoretical sense to professionals without formal training in psychology. However, in making the description, the theoretical and empirical underpinnings of the procedures should not be compromised by reducing the psychological literature to a series of clichés or commonsensical notions.

If professionals in primary-care or general-practice roles are to work with persons who are experiencing problems due to excessive alcohol use, it is clear that the amount of time available for each case will be limited. Hence, the recommended intervention should be brief. Moreover, because funds for health-care services are limited, and problems of substance abuse tend to receive few of these funds, in communities intent upon sponsoring preventive programs for alcohol abuse, cost-effectiveness should be a consideration of paramount importance. The emphasis must be on the development of low-cost procedures of demonstrated effectiveness.

A prominent feature of established programs for the treatment of alcohol abuse has been the segregation of the clients from other persons requiring health-care services. This is usually accomplished either by the establishment of specialized clinics or specialized units in hospitals. Such segregation increases fear in potential clients of being stigmatized. Programs of secondary prevention should have low visibility and, ideally, should be represented in facilities that offer primary-care services. In this sense, all communities potentially contain the necessary basic resources for secondary prevention of alcohol problems. What they lack is personnel specifically trained in the management of these problems.

II. CONCEPTUAL BASES AND PROGRAM DEVELOPMENT

The objectives in the present section are (1) to provide a brief description of the conceptual model that has influenced the development of our approach to problem drinking; (2) to describe how the approach has been developed through a program of research which has involved populations of nonalcoholics, chronic alcoholics, and early-stage problem drinkers; and (3) to present a cognitively oriented model of alcohol abuse that we have been gradually formulating.

A. Cognitive Model of Human Emotions and Action

The principal conceptual influence in the development of the present approach to problem drinking has been the cognitive model of emotions and action described by M. B. Arnold (1960, 1969) and, more specifically, the elaboration of this model by R. S. Lazarus and his colleagues to explain psychological stress and the coping process (Lazarus, 1966, 1968, 1980; Lazarus, Averill, & Opton, 1974). For these authors, the concepts of appraisal and coping are central to the understanding of human emotions and behavior. Their main assumptions can be summarized as follows:

1. Coping

"Coping" refers to efforts at exerting control over one's environment in circumstances in which the person's resources are taxed or exceeded. Frequently, such circumstances will be those which threaten the person's well-being, but they may also include situations that hold the promise of future gratification.

Coping can serve two main fuctions. One is that the person may *act instrumentally* so as to change a situation for the better. The person may, for example, act on the social environment to eliminate danger or to increase gratification. The second function of coping is to *regulate the distressing emotion itself* through cognitive processes (e.g., denying, accepting, detaching). In this manner, the person may attenuate the negative emotions without changing the stimulus situation.

It is important to note that coping responses can be effective or ineffective in the immediate situation. Over the long term, they can be either adaptive or maladaptive independently of their effectiveness. Over time, some forms of coping may become habitual and largely automatized — that is, little reflective thinking precedes the coping response.

2. Appraisal

The central feature of this formulation is that appraisals, rather than emotions, constitute the central mediating processes between perception and action. The term *appraisal* refers to "the evaluation of information regarding the relevance of an event to the individual's welfare" (Lazarus et al., 1974, p. 285). Two basic types of appraisal are distinguished as follows:

The *primary appraisal* involves the judgment of stimulus events as either beneficial, harmful, or irrelevant. When an event is appraised as beneficial, the appraisal is accompanied by positive emotions, and some kind of approach may follow. In contrast, when an event is appraised as potentially harmful, the emotions experienced are negative and the tendency is to react by some form of attack or avoidance (active or passive).

A *secondary appraisal* involves considering alternatives for coping. When behavioral options are not perceived to be available, coping efforts may be cognitive. If no coping response is readily available, the response tendency is expressed as emotion (e.g., as grief, anger, guilt).

Appraisals are, of course, highly subjective in nature; they are influenced by past experiences, cultural and personal values, beliefs, preferences, and coping dispositions. Also, appraisals are not always appropriate because the person may either ignore, distort, or attribute imaginary properties to stimulus events.

3. Reappraisal

As a result of repeated exposures to the same (or similar) events, or as one continues to think about them, new evidence may become available that can radically change the meaning of the events. Reappraisal of an event (from aversive towards beneficial and vice versa) may follow from the discovery of new properties in the event itself (e.g., that it is less dangerous than previously believed), or from the person's assessment of his or her coping ability. In Lazarus's view, reappraisal of an event most often results from a change in one's perceived ability to cope.

The reader may recognize that the theoretical constructs employed by Lazarus bear some resemblance to Bandura's social learning theory (1977). For Lazarus, coping and adaptation depend upon the mutual interaction of cognitions and actions. Similarly, Bandura has developed the important notion of reciprocal determinism to describe the mutual interaction of cognitions and behaviors. In addition, there is at least a superficial resemblance between the notions of secondary appraisal and reappraisal, and Bandura's concepts of self-efficacy and changes in efficacy expectations (Bandura, 1977). To our knowledge, no one has formally contrasted the logical properties of these two theoretical descriptions of human behavior.

B. Development of a Cognitive–Behavioral Treatment Program

The first application of Arnold and Lazarus's concepts to psychotherapy was carried out by the first author in a doctoral dissertation (Sanchez-Craig, 1972, 1976). The aim of this study was to assess the relative effectiveness of cognitive and behavioral coping strategies in the reappraisal of aversive interpersonal situations. The clients were children and adolescents who wished to improve their relationships with significant persons (e.g., parents, teachers, peers, siblings). The application of the cognitive and behavioral strategies to interpersonal problems served as the basis of the problem-solving strategies that were subsequently developed with populations of chronic alcoholics and early-stage problem drinkers.

1. Research with Chronic Alcoholics

The research took place in a halfway house for homeless and unemployed alcoholics. The overall objective of the research was (1) to gain a better understanding of the role that alcohol plays in the alcoholic's (often unsuccessful) attempts to cope with life problems, and (2) to teach clients coping skills that would help them in maintaining abstinence, finding gainful employment, developing recreational activities, and establishing a social network supportive of a goal of abstinence.

An important initial feature of our research with this chronic population was to inquire about their appraisals of alcohol and alcohol-related activities when drinking was associated with problems. To this end, we designed a questionnaire in which the antecedents and consequences of incidents of problem drinking were systematically recorded. Clients were asked to describe incidents which they remembered well. For each incident, they specified (1) the events preceding drinking (i.e., physical and social context, the client's feelings and thoughts); (2) whether the client made a conscious decision to drink and, if so, how he or she came to the decision; and (3) the consequences of drinking (i.e., those experienced after consuming the initial few drinks, and after the drinking episode). Such descriptions were obtained from over 160 clients involved in the evaluation of the project.

Alcohol was depicted as a means for coping with stressful situations in about 90% of the incidents described. Most of these situations were social, or related to feelings and thoughts about social situations. The *feelings* most frequently associated with these incidents were depression, anger, loneliness, boredom, fear, anxiety, and guilt. Nonsocial stressful situations were mainly related to loss of jobs, anxieties about serious illnesses, chronic pain, and consequences of previous drinking (withdrawal reactions). The *thoughts* typically associated with these events were catastrophic, self-derogatory, or self-defeating (e.g., "I feel so lonely and depressed that life is not worth living"; "I've been rejected again, so I must not be good enough"; "It is useless to try, so I might as well drink again"). *Functions* attributed to alcohol when it was used for coping were to relieve the intensity of the negative emotions and thoughts and/or to increase the clients' confidence to act in ways that would be less probable in a sober state (e.g., express anger or affection, talk to strangers, engage in sexual behavior). The relatively few incidents in which chronic alcoholics did not use alcohol for coping were related to celebrations and to the desire to have a good time with their friends. Clients often reported that they did not remember having made a conscious decision to drink. On the basis of past experience, clients knew that they seldom stopped after having a few drinks, or after 1 day of drinking. Thus, when the decision was conscious, it was often justified by faulty rationalizations such as "I'll only have one or two" or "I'll drink today and then stop." Regarding the *consequences,* clients tended to consider the immediate beneficial effects of drinking and to disregard the negative longer-term consequences.

Cognitive and behavioral strategies were used to teach clients how to deal more effectively with interpersonal conflicts and with the tendency to drink during negative emotional states. Basically, they were taught to identify problem situations, to generate alternative cognitive and behavioral responses, to select responses most likely to succeed, and to assess the effectiveness of selected responses. An innovative feature of the program was the attempt to use cognitive coping strategies to help alcoholics bring under control the immediate tendency to drink in the presence of strong eliciting cues (Sanchez-Craig, 1975; Sanchez-Craig & Walker, 1974, 1975, 1982). Cognitive coping took the form of self-statements that would serve the following purposes: inhibit the immediate tendency to drink, counteract rationalizations for drinking, reappraise the necessity of drinking in response to particular cues, consider the consequences of using alcohol for coping, and motivate oneself for actions other than drinking.

An important finding of this research was that clients tended to forget the coping strategies within a month of program completion, even though assessment conducted during programs suggested that they had mastered the strategies and considered them helpful. Also, most clients were unable to give convincing examples of applications to real-life situations. The failure to consolidate and transfer gains made during therapy may in part be attributable to the fact that about half of the clients had cognitive deficits of the sort that interfere with the learning of problem-solving skills (Sanchez-Craig, 1980b). Furthermore, as indicated, the clients reported that they seldom remembered making self-conscious decisions to drink. This lack of self-conscious control may be related to alcohol-induced cognitive deficits, and may interfere with the establishment of new coping behaviors. In short, the nature of cognitive deficits common in chronic alcoholics may mitigate against the application with them of cognitively oriented treatment strategies. We return to this issue in a later section of the chapter.

The halfway house program was assessed with a sample of 104 males and 56 females. The outcome was poor, but it was similar to outcomes usually reported with alcoholic populations (e.g., Costello, 1975). In follow-up interviews conducted at 6, 12, and 18 months after discharge from the house, about 15% of the sample reported abstinence for each of the 6-month blocks, and about 8% reported drinking small quantities of alcohol without problems. A detailed description of the halfway house program, and the results of the research can be found in Sanchez-Craig and Walker (1982) and in Walker, Sanchez-Craig, and Bornet (1982).

2. Research with Early-Stage Problem Drinkers

A further elaboration of the cognitive and behavioral coping strategies took place in an outpatient clinic, where 70 (52 males and 18 females) early-stage problem drinkers were treated on an individual basis. The discouraging results obtained with the chronic alcoholics, plus the bulk of empirical evidence indicating that problem drinkers who were more socially stable and less chronic have a better prognosis, motivated the application of the coping strategies to a population that was less debilitated and more cognitively intact. As mentioned earlier, the principal objective of this research was to assess the relative appropriateness of abstinence and moderation as treatment goals for early-stage problem drinkers. The cognitive and behavioral coping strategies were used to aid clients in the achievement of these goals (Sanchez-Craig et al., 1984).

The clients were asked to specify the antecedents and consequences of incidents of problem drinking, which they could remember well. Analyses of 297 descriptions revealed that the conditions associated with problem drinking (including the appraisals of the function of alcohol) were in some ways similar to those described by the chronic alcoholics. However, there were also salient differences. Like the chronic alcoholics, the problem drinkers drank excessively (although less frequently) in response to aversive events in which feelings of anxiety, boredom, depression, fatigue, and anger were most commonly experienced. Negative and self-defeating thoughts were frequently associated with these emotions. Many of these incidents involved interpersonal events, but stresses arising from work or home responsibilities were equally represented. In a few instances, alcohol was used as medication to aid sleep or to relieve physical pain. The functions most commonly attributed to alcohol when it was used as a coping device were to relieve the intensity of negative feelings or thoughts and/or to facilitate performance of some kind (e.g., to become more sociable, to increase one's confidence to speak up, or to disclose personal matters). A salient difference between the chronic alcoholics and the problem drinkers was the extent to which the latter group depicted heavy drinking as a source of pleasure or recreation when they were in a relaxed or pleasant mood (e.g., to have fun with friends, to enhance social situations, to enjoy the taste and the effects of alcohol). Another difference noted was the extent to which the problem drinkers reported having made a conscious decision to drink. Self-statements used to justify drinking included "I need a drink to relax and unwind," "I deserve a few drinks after having worked so hard," "Why not, there is nothing better to do," "It is a special occasion." Regarding the consequences of drinking, those associated with the first two or three drinks were largely the positive consequences that had been anticipated (e.g., increased relaxation, decreased boredom, greater sociability, increased tolerance for tedious tasks or social events). In contrast, the consequences of continued drinking tended to be negative. The most frequently reported were drunkenness, hangover, guilt, fatigue, concerns among family members or friends, absenteeism, depression, passing out, and making a fool of oneself.

With regard to drinking behavior, the main findings of the study can be summarized as follows: During treatment, clients who were assigned to a goal of moderation drank significantly less than clients who were assigned to abstinence. By the end of treatment, drinking had been reduced from an average of 51 drinks per week in both groups, to an average of 13.6 drinks in the abstinence group and 6.6 drinks in the moderate-drinking group. The significantly lower consumption observed in the moderate-drinking group may have resulted from the initial effects of random assignment to drinking goal. During the first 3 weeks of treatment, the conditions of the experiment were the same for *all* clients, except for assignment to drinking goal. Training in moderation was initated after the third week of treatment, and clients in this condition were requested to abstain until then. It is possible that the greater acceptability of the goal of moderation caused the greater reduction by clients assigned to this condition (Sanchez-Craig, 1980a).

At follow-up, no significant differences in reported alcohol consumption were found between the groups. Six months after discharge from treatment, the average weekly consumption in both groups was around 13 or 14 drinks. On drinking style, about 70% in each group were categorized as moderate drinkers (using an average of 20 drinks per week as cutoff); two clients in the abstinence group and one in the moderate group reported that they had abstained for the entire 6 months. The levels of alcohol consumption and drinking styles observed at 6 months posttreatment were maintained by the two groups throughout the 2 years of follow-up. The drinking reported by clients during treatment and at follow-up was validated with biochemical and neuropsychological measures as well as reports by collaterals (Sanchez-Craig et al., 1984).

It was concluded that for most early-stage problem drinkers, a goal of moderation may be more suitable than a goal of abstinence. First, moderation was more acceptable for the majority of the clients; second, clients in the moderate-drinking condition drank less during treatment; third, most of the clients who were assigned to abstinence developed moderate drinking on their own; and lastly, the clients in the abstinence group requested more aftercare appointments.

C. Cognitively Oriented Model of Alcohol Abuse

When we considered the notions presented by Arnold and Lazarus and the incidents of problem drinking described by the chronic alcoholics, a model of alcohol abuse was formulated in which excessive drinking was viewed primarily as a means for coping with stressful events (Sanchez-Craig, 1975; Sanchez-Craig & Walker, 1974, 1975). As descriptions by early-stage problem drinkers became available, the model was further elaborated. In its present form the assumptions of the model are as follows:

Excessive drinking frequently represents an attempt to cope with a variety of events appraised by the drinker as aversive. The functions attributed to alcohol are to reduce the aversiveness of the events themselves (whether present or anticipated) and/or to increase the person's confidence to act in ways that would be less probable in a sober state.

Some excessive drinking also occurs, not for purposes of coping, but because alcohol or alcohol-related activities are appraised as a source of pleasure or recreation while the person is relaxed or in a pleasant mood. The person may claim, for example, that he or she enjoys the taste or the effects of alcohol, or that drinking with friends is highly enjoyable.

Continued reliance on alcohol, either as a means for coping or as a recreational activity, can result in the development of a habitual and generalized way of responding that may have the following consequences: reduced awareness of the conditions leading up to drinking and of the amounts consumed; increased dependence on alcohol (evidenced by the generalization of the response), which may impede the development of more appropriate coping or recreational activities; and development of social and physical consequences which can provoke further drinking to cope.

The use of alcohol may be reappraised upon discovery of new information concerning its negative effects on the life of the person. However, because of the important functions that have been attributed to alcohol, it is unlikely to be reappraised except upon the experience of rather dramatic negative consequences (e.g., being threatened with loss of job, family, or health; causing accidents or legal charges due to impaired driving). Such discoveries tend to counteract positive appraisals of the more immediate consequences of drinking, and to motivate people to change.

After a decision to abstain or to reduce alcohol intake has been made, a desire to drink is likely to be experienced, especially in situations where alcohol was frequently used in the past. Relapse to inappropriate drinking is not unexpected at this stage. Such situations can be used to gain further understanding of the functions served by alcohol. Relapse to inappropriate drinking may be prevented by the development of cognitive and behavioral coping responses and recreational activities that can lead to reappraisal of the importance of alcohol. The risk of inappropriate drinking decreases as a function of time in drinking moderately, but nonetheless occasional relapses may occur for a protracted time after the decision to abstain or to moderate drinking.

Although the preceding model is based on hundreds of descriptions of incidents associated with problem drinking, it is limited in a number of respects. First, the chronic alcoholics and early-stage problem drinkers from whom the descriptions were obtained cannot be considered to be representative of the problem-drinking population at large. Second, some of the clients gave multiple descriptions and others gave very few. Finally, the instruction given to clients to describe only incidents that they remembered well may have produced some kind of bias (i.e., it is difficult to say whether incidents were well remembered because of their frequency or because of the seriousness of their consequences). Nonetheless, these descriptions have been extremely useful. Not only have they increased our understanding of the conditions associated with problem drinking and the functions attributed to alcohol, but also they have permitted the refinement of instruments for conducting these assessments more efficiently.

Following from this conceptualization of alcohol abuse, the treatment approach that we have developed involves procedures whereby the problem drinker can learn: (1) to recognize the situations under which excessive drinking tends to occur and the functions he or she attributes to alcohol; (2) to develop new ways of responding in those situations so that the role of alcohol may be reappraised; and (3) to develop the habit of more objectively observing the drinking behavior and associated contexts, cognitions, and consequences. This approach shares many elements of other cognitive–behavioral approaches directed toward a wide variety of maladaptive behaviors—for example, Beck's (1976) cognitive therapy, D'Zurilla and Goldfried's (1971) problem-solving skills training, Ellis' (1962) rational–emotive therapy, and Meichenbaum's (1977) self-instructional training. Common denominators of cognitive-behavioral therapies are (1) that cognitions importantly influence the way people feel and behave, (2) that identifying maladaptive thoughts and their behavioral consequences is frequently a prerequisite for behavioral change, and (3) that competent actions in the natural environment can serve to test and undermine the maladaptive thoughts.

III. TREATMENT PROGRAM FOR EARLY-STAGE PROBLEM DRINKERS

Our approach to problem drinking is similar in many respects to the multimodal behavioral therapies developed by others working with problem drinkers (e.g., Alden, 1983; Duckert, 1982; Miller & Mastria, 1977; Miller & Muñoz, 1976). As in these therapies, the principal focus of treatment is the client's drinking behavior and the problems directly associated with excessive drinking. A major difference of our approach, however, lies in the emphasis placed upon people's cognitions, not only as determinants of excessive drinking, but also as instruments of behavior change.

The specific procedures that we use in treating early-stage problem drinkers is not described in detail because such description has already been made in a manual for therapists (Sanchez-Craig, 1984). Instead, our intention in this section is to discuss procedures that we think may be useful in (1) attracting early-stage problem drinkers into treatment, (2) retaining clients in treatment, (3) helping them set appropriate drinking goals, and (4) assisting them in the development of more adaptive coping in situations where there is a risk of excessive drinking.

A. Procedures for Recruiting and Screening Suitable Clients

1. Recruiting Strategies

At present, one cannot precisely predict the type of problem drinker who will, or will not, be able to learn moderation of alcohol use. However, the bulk of empirical evidence indicates that those who succeed tend to be younger, more socially stable, and to have fewer alcohol-related symptoms (see Heather & Robertson, 1981, pp. 216–219; Miller & Hester, 1980, pp. 100–103). Because of this evidence, we have aimed our recruiting strategies at early-stage problem drinkers.

In testing the program on which the present approach is based (henceforth referred to as our program), two strategies to recruit appropriate clients were adopted. The first recruiting strategy was to provide two alcoholism clinics in our vicinity with a set of selection criteria reflecting the characteristics that are peculiar to early-stage problem drinkers. Eighteen months after the inception of our program, these clinics had referred 45 of the planned total of 70 clients.

The second recruiting strategy was adopted because the flow of clients was slow, and we were repeatedly advised by staff of the clinics that very few of those requesting treatment met the admission criteria. The following advertisement was placed in two local newspapers:

The Addiction Research Foundation is currently offering a program of early intervention for people whose consumption of alcohol has recently begun to interfere with work, school, family, and other important responsibilities. Successful applicants for the program must be regular heavy drinkers still maintaining their work (or school) and home situation, prepared to attend approximately 8 weekly, 1 1/2 hour sessions of individual counseling, and to be contacted for follow-up purposes over a 2-year period after completion of the program. Before admission to the program, candidates would undergo a comprehensive assessment.

In a single weekend, this advertisement attracted the 25 clients we needed to complete the sample. Other preventive programs in North America and Europe have relied upon advertisements and announcements in the local media for purposes of recruitment (Alden, 1978; Duckert, 1982; Miller & Taylor, 1980; Miller, Taylor, & West, 1980; Miller, Gribskov, & Mortell,

1981; Miller, Pechacek, & Hamburg, 1981; Pomerleau, Pertschuck, Adkins, & Brady, 1978; Vogler, Weissbach, & Compton, 1977). Clearly, therapists interested in employing preventive techniques would be ill-advised to rely upon local alcoholism treatment facilities for many of their referrals. Heather and Robertson (1981) examined the characteristics of clients of controlled-drinking studies according to whether the samples were recruited through alcoholism clinics or through media advertisements and the courts. They concluded that clients recruited through the media had a less severe problem and, on average, their daily consumption was lower than that documented for clinic alcoholics (pp. 168–171). In our study, some unexpected differences were observed between the group of clients referred by the clinics and the group recruited through the advertisment when the groups were compared on the intake variables included in Table 1. The advertisement group was significantly older (41.2 vs. 31.7 years) and brighter, as evidenced by higher scores in the Raven's Progressive Matrices (Raven, 1960) and the two subtests of the *Wechsler Adult Intelligence Scale* (WAIS; Wechsler, 1958). The advertisement also tended to attract more females; 50% of the females in the study were recruited through the advertisement. These findings suggest that brighter persons perhaps take longer to present to treatment, and that more females could be attracted into treatment by this procedure.

Two other case-finding techniques deserve mention. One technique involves widespread routine employment of psychosocial and biological indicators of alcohol intake (e.g., Bernadt, Mumford, Taylor, Smith, & Murray, 1982; Kristenson, Trell, Fex, & Hood, 1980). This approach, however, has problems of feasibility and specificity. The second technique involves widespread health screening. This approach is uncommon because it involves a substantial financial governmental commitment. The biological markers that have been employed are not specific to alcohol intake, and the psychosocial markers, although more specific, do not exclude the more serious cases. Another option for recruitment of clients is referral from courts and community primary-care health professionals. This option, although promising in theory, has not been evaluated. Overall, the most fruitful method currently available seems to be local advertising and media publicity.

It should be noted that the advertisement used in our program did not allude to the treatment goal because the design of the study involved random assignment to abstinence or moderation. Given the common belief that treatment of alcohol problems always involves abstinence as the goal, providing information about the moderate-drinking option might have increased the recruitment of subjects. Generally speaking, the use of public media for recruitment purposes should involve being as specific as possible about the nature of the program and the characteristics of the clients for whom it has been developed.

TABLE 1

Characteristics of the 70 Clients Who Participated in the Evaluation of the Program

SOCIAL AND DEMOGRAPHIC		COGNITIVE FUNCTIONING	
Age	$\overline{X} = 34.8$, SD $= 10.5$	Raven's Progressive Matrices	$\overline{X} = 85.2$, SD $= 18.5$
Sex		Clarke WAIS Vocabulary Test	$\overline{X} = 12.4$, SD $= 1.8$
Males	74.3%	Digit Symbol Test (WAIS)	$\overline{X} = 11.8$, SD $= 2.2$
Females	25.7%	Benton Visual Retention Test	$\overline{X} = 8.0$, SD $= 1.3$
Marital status		ALCOHOL USE	
Single	35.7%	Years of problem drinking	$\overline{X} = 5.0$, SD $= 1.3$
Divorced/separated	17.1%	Drinks per drinking day[a]	$\overline{X} = 9.5$, SD $= 4.8$
Married/common-law	47.1%	(past 3 months)	
Present accommodation		Days drinking per week	$\overline{X} = 5.5$, SD $= 2.0$
Rents house/apartment	62.8%	(past 3 months)	
Owns house	37.2%	Drinking pattern	
Occupation		Occasional	1.4%
Unemployed	1.4%	Weekend	7.1%
Blue collar	22.8%	Binge	4.3%
Sales/clerical	22.8%	Frequent	27.1%
White collar/professional	40.0%	Daily	60.0%
Student	7.2%		
Housewife	5.8%	SEVERITY OF ALCOHOL USE	
Weeks worked full-time (past 6 months)	$\overline{X} = 23.7$, SD $= 5.9$	MAST score	$\overline{X} = 18.7$, SD $= 6.5$
Present income (thousands/year)	$\overline{X} = 18.5$, SD $= 13.5$	ADS score	$\overline{X} = 14.2$, SD $= 7.1$
Years of education	$\overline{X} = 13.9$, SD $= 3.1$	USE OF OTHER DRUGS[b]	
Parental alcoholism	40.0%	Cannabis (past year)	35.7%
Source of referral		Barbiturates (past year)	4.3%
Alcoholism clinics	64.0%	Amphetamines (past year)	1.4%
Newspaper advertisements	36.0%	Tranquilizers (presently using)	14.3%

[a] For the clients one drink was defined as 1.5 oz of liquor 40%, 5 oz of wine 12%, 3 oz of fortified wine 20%, and 12 oz of beer 5%. Each one of these units contains .60 oz or 13.6 g of ethanol.

[b] Consumption of drugs other than alcohol during the year preceding treatment was rare; clients using tranquilizers (except for one of them), reported taking them as prescribed.

2. Criteria for Identification of Suitable Clients

As previously indicated, our program was designed to include subjects with the kind of characteristics that are predictive of a successful moderate-drinking outcome. The screening criteria employed yielded a group of clients with characteristics outlined in Table 1. Before admission, the 70 clients were assessed by a physician to ensure that they had no medical problems for which any drinking was contraindicated. The set of screening criteria employed served to identify clients who had relatively short histories of problem drinking, and who were socially stable, and normal in cognitive abilities. This group of clients was new to treatment of alcohol problems, nonpartici-pants in Alcoholics Anonymous, and not adherent to the disease concept of alcoholism. Cutoff scores on the Michigan Alcoholism Screening Test (MAST) (Selzer, 1971) or the Alcohol Dependence Scale (ADS) (Horn, Skinner, Wanberg, & Foster, 1984) were not used to screen clients. However, the scores that emerged are significantly lower than those obtained for two clinical populations, one receiving outpatient individual counseling and the other undergoing conventional alcoholism treatment (Skinner & Allen, 1982).

In addition to criteria of social stability, intact health and cognitive func-tioning, and relatively low chronicity and dependence on alcohol, there are other criteria that we believe should be taken into account in screening clients who opt for goals of moderation: (1) The client's family and close friends should be supportive of the goal. If, for example, the spouse believes that total abstinence is the only solution to the problem, it will be difficult for the client to achieve moderation. (2) The client should be ready both to make the achievement of the goal a first priority, and to invest the time and effort that is typically required. (3) The client's excessive drinking should be the main presenting problem. Criteria similar to the preceding have have recom-mended by other authors to screen clients for whom goals of moderation are most appropriate (see Heather & Robertston, 1981, pp. 216–24; Miller & Hester, 1980, pp. 100–103).

B. Introductory Procedures to Enhance Compliance

The first treatment session is extremely important because its content will frequently determine whether the client decides to persist with treatment or to withdraw. We believe that several components should be included in this session so as to maximize the probability of the client making an appropriate decision in this respect. We expect that if a client is to persist with treatment, he or she should, by the end of the first session, be able to answer the following questions in the affirmative: (1) Are the demands of the program compatible with my other obligations? (2) Does the structure of the program indicate that my anonymity will be protected? (3) Does the proposed treatment make sense to me as a possible solution to my problem? (4) Are the objectives of the program consistent with my own? (5) On the basis of what was done in this session, do I feel closer to the solution of my problem? (6) Do I have a clear understanding of what I can expect from my therapist and of what my therapist can expect from me?

In the program, a number of procedures were incorporated into the first treatment session, so as to permit clients to make such judgments, but the effectiveness of these procedures has not been formally tested. However, we suspect that the 96% completion rate in the evaluation of our program was influenced by the clients' impressions of the first treatment session. Zweben and Li (1981) found that two factors were associated with continuation in treatment for substance abuse: (1) Clients were more likely to persist with treatment if their expectations of the program were concordant with those of the staff. (2) Furthermore, clients with concordant expectations were more likely to remain in treatment when a pretreatment session was devoted to describing and explaining various aspects of the treatment procedures. These findings are consistent with a variety of evidence that clients receiving treatment are more likely to be successful if their expectations of the treatment process are accurate (see Miller, 1985). Hence, it is probably important that programs for treatment of substance abuse anticipate the expectations of their clientele and incorporate procedures in the initial session that will permit clients to make informed decisions about the concordance of the proposed treatment with their expectations. Next, we indicate how we have attempted to achieve this objective.

1. Offering a Flexible Treatment Schedule

Most early-stage problem drinkers have vocational and family responsibilities that they are unwilling to compromise as a consequence of committing themselves to treatment. Programs that make light demands on the clients' time and are flexible in respect to appointed sessions should be appropriate for this population. When our program was evaluated, one session of approximately 90 minutes per week was arranged at the clients' convenience. It was observed that the average number of treatment sessions was six, and that these were distributed over 7 weeks. Apparently, the clients found that the demands on their time were not exorbitant, and that the time spent in treatment was sufficient for their needs.

2. Ensuring Confidentiality

A number of the clients expressed concern about the possibility of being discovered to be receiving counseling for problem drinking. Some were resolved that no one, not even family members, should know. The clients asserted that this concern did not arise from shame about their condition, but rather from a self-protective prudence. They feared the prejudicial and stigmatizing appraisals of people who became aware of their involvement in treatment. They believed that individual counseling would reduce the risk of breach of anonymity. However, they expressed some concerns about attending sessions at an addictions treatment center. It is likely that these concerns would be allayed to some extent if programs of this nature are offered in various community health centers, rather than in clinics exclusively devoted to the treatment of problems of substance abuse.

3. Avoiding Stigmatic Explanations of Excessive Drinking

Many clients of our program said that they had postponed treatment because of two fears: (1) that they would be identified as alcoholic, and (2) that they would be obliged to admit to having the disease of alcoholism. Such clients were relieved to discover that no such demands would be placed upon them. Our practice is to inform clients that there are divergent views about the nature of alcoholism (e.g., that it is the result of a metabolic or biochemical imbalance, of faulty upbringing and bad influences, of having no meaning in one's life, of unresolved oral conflicts), but that no one knows for certain which, if any, of these views is correct. Indeed the most prevalent view in North America is that alcoholism is a disease that can be arrested only by total abstinence, and that the source of the disease is a special body chemistry that prevents the person from drinking moderately. However, there is abundant evidence to suggest that heavy drinkers can learn to control their drinking, especially when their alcohol problem is treated at an early stage.

Clients are informed that we adhere to the view that excessive drinking is to a large extent a learned behavior that can be modified by methods based on principles of learning. According to this view, high-frequency heavy drinking should be modifiable to moderate consumption or to abstinence. Hence, in theory, total abstinence is not essential to solve the problem. We recommend to our clients that they evaluate these notions in light of their own experiences, and that they decide whether the assumptions underlying our program are consistent with their beliefs, or whether they would prefer referral to an alternate treatment program.

Clients opting for goals of moderation are warned about conflicting opinions likely to be offered by persons who consider themselves knowledgeable about alcoholism. Some may assert that moderation is ill-advised or unachievable, and that those who try it will be harmed. Clients should therefore be discreet about freely discussing a chosen goal of moderate drinking.

4. Focusing Immediately on the Client's Drinking

A priority for the clients of our program was to take immediate action to produce change in the identified problem behavior of excessive drinking. Our practice is to address this need by focusing extensively on the client's drinking behavior during the initial treatment session. This involves (1) discussion of the immediate and longer-term drinking goal, (2) introducing the client to procedures for systematic self-observation of incidents of drinking and tendencies to drink, and (3) preliminary analysis of the functions that the client has attributed to alcohol. These discussions lead to the assignment of specific tasks designed to maintain the client's attention on selected goals and probable determinants of drinking until the subsequent session. The therapist emphasizes the great importance of accurate self-observation and description of drinking tendencies and events, because this information will form the basis of the strategies that are developed to bring drinking behavior under the client's deliberate control.

5. Clarifying Client–Therapist Expectations

Clients are advised of the therapist's expectations of them, and of what they can expect from the therapist. They are expected to complete homework assignments, to attend sessions regularly, and not to cancel sessions without notice. They are advised that discontinuation of further sessions will be considered if these expectations are not met.

Clients are told that the principal focus of treatment will be on the problem behavior of drinking; if additional problems are identified during treatment that are beyond the scope of the program, referral to a specialized treatment resource will be considered. In addition, if the goals of treatment are not achieved after a reasonable period of treatment (10–12 sessions), the client will be asked to consider an alternative goal (e.g., abstinence instead of moderation), or referral to a more intensive treatment will be recommended. It should be emphasized that shifting the treatment goal from moderation to abstinence does not entail lifetime commitment to the latter objective. The client and therapist may agree to work for a specified period of abstinence, at the end of which the feasibility and the attractiveness of moderation can be reassessed.

6. Offering Alternative Treatment Goals

The goals of problem drinkers presenting to treatment vary along two independent dimensions. The ultimate goal of treatment may be either abstinence or moderation of consumption. Regardless of which of these goals applies, the client can resolve to achieve the goal either by an abrupt change, or by tapering off. In our experience, any combination of these goals may be selected by a particular client. Thus, for example, a client who regularly consumes 12 drinks per day may elect to taper his or her drinking over 4 weeks, with an ultimate goal of complete abstinence. Another client may wish to shift immediately from high consumption to abstinence, with an ultimate goal of moderation. For early-stage problem drinkers, there is no evidence that a particular procedure for approaching the selected goal is superior, although the desirability of an initial period of abstinence is discussed here later. Whether early-stage problem drinkers initially aim for moderation or abstinence, in evaluating our program we found that the most probable outcome was moderation of drinking (Sanchez-Craig et al., 1984). This finding suggests that the most reasonable course in preventive programs is to be flexible about the goals of treatment and to accept the clients' judgments. Of course, this recommendation does not preclude guidance from the therapist about the nature of the goal, the level of consumption if moderation is the goal, and the most advisable route for approaching the goal. In the evaluation of our program, total flexibility about treatment goals was impossible because of constraints imposed by the experimental design. Clients were randomly assigned to the goal of either moderation or abstinence; nevertheless, assignment to goal did not determine outcome.

The ultimate importance of the client determining the goal of treatment can be illustrated by an anecdote. The client in question was assigned to abstinence. He returned to the second session with self-monitoring records showing daily drinking. The therapist proceeded in the client's presence to calculate the number of drinks he had consumed over the week, which added to 11 drinks. The client was reminded that his goal was abstinence, but he erupted with excitement and said, "Isn't that beautiful! Over the whole week I drank less than I used to drink on a single day." Later in treatment, this client mentioned that keeping records about his drinking and risk situations had given him "a much better understanding of what is behind my drinking."

It is interesting to note that of 35 clients assigned to the goal of abstinence, only two withdrew from treatment, despite the high rate of rejection of this goal. This suggests, as indicated in the preceding anecdote, that clients in the abstinence condition perceived elements in our program that seemed useful in better understanding their problem and in helping them achieve a goal that they had selected (i.e., to cut down on drinking). Apparently these clients were quite comfortable in adopting what was useful to them in our program, and in ignoring what was irrelevant. However, they drank more during treatment and required more of aftercare than clients assigned to moderation who did not have a treatment goal imposed upon them (Sanchez-Craig et al., 1984). We provisionally conclude that although clients may overcome rigidity in the treatment program, flexibility from the outset is the preferable treatment strategy. Miller (1985) reviewed evidence indicating that providing clients with choices in regard to treatment programs and treatment goals increases compliance and improves the overall effectiveness of treatment. Evidence consistent with this position has been produced recently in a Swedish study of alcoholics (Öjehagen & Berglund, 1986).

C. Guidelines for Setting Drinking Goals

We make recommendations about guidelines for moderate drinking on the basis of the levels of consumption that the most successful clients of our program reported. An alternative procedure would be to rely upon estimates of safe levels culled from epidemiological studies. However, such estimates are inconsistent and tend to be related to a particular risk (e.g., cirrhosis, hypertension). Furthermore, such guidelines are *representative* figures and take no account of *individual* variation. Similarly, the recommendations we make are no more than guidelines, and the final estimate of what constitutes an appropriate goal should derive from a frank discussion between the client and the therapist.

The guidelines that we recommend arose from analyses of the levels of consumption reported by the clients of our program before treatment (Sanchez-Craig & Israel, 1985) and after treatment (Sanchez-Craig, 1986). These guidelines are as follows: (1) We discourage clients from adopting goals where quantity exceeds 4 drinks per day (each drink is equivalent to 13.6 g of ethanol). (2) We discourage clients from drinking daily, even if they wish to restrict their consumption to one or two drinks per day. We stress the importance of maintaining abstinence at least on one day of the week; this day of planned abstinence should serve to reinforce the idea that the client can be in total control and, also, it should reduce the probability of developing a habitual pattern of drinking. (3) We recommend that consumption be limited to no more than 20 drinks per week. Note that some clients of our program reported problems associated with their drinking (e.g., intoxication, sleep disturbances, missed meals, quarrels), although their week consumption did not exceed 20 drinks. Problem-free clients drank no more than 12 drinks per week. (4) We strongly advise clients to avoid drinking before noon, to avoid drinking in situations where drinking has caused problems, and to avoid using alcohol for coping. Finding a drinking pattern that fits well with the client's lifestyle may take time; thus, as treatment progresses it may be necessary to make adjustments to the goal until a suitable pattern is established.

Therapists are alerted to the fact that some clients change their mind about drinking goals, either at the inception of treatment or later on. Some heavy drinkers (i.e., usually people who have been consuming 10 or more drinks per day) who present to treatment with a goal of moderation in mind, reappraise this goal when they are informed that it usually involves very conservative levels of drinking. They indicate that since limited amounts (such as those we recommend) do not give them enjoyment, they will try to abstain on most days and leave drinking for special social occasions (e.g., birthdays, weddings, Christmas celebrations). Other clients who come to treatment with a goal of abstinence in mind reappraise the goal as treatment progresses. Clear examples are the five clients who rejected the goal of moderation that was assigned to them at random in our program. All these clients were sensitized against drinking because in the year preceding treatment they had experienced a traumatic event in which drinking was associated with death or serious injuries (e.g., a client's mother died of an alcoholic coma; a client's brother died in a car accident under the influence of alcohol; a client injured himself while drinking). These clients were trained in procedures for abstinence; however, within the first 6 months of their discharge from treatment, four of them contacted their therapist to discuss a goal of moderation. It is interesting to note that these clients were among the youngest in the sample, with ages ranging from 18 to 27 years. Failure to maintain moderation or abstinence, either during or after treatment, also causes some clients to reappraise the feasibility of the selected goal. Such reappraisals, however, tend to occur on the instigation of the therapist, the spouse, or someone close to the client.

At this point, it is useful to review briefly how the guidelines that we are recommending were derived. When our program was evaluated, it was found that some clients, though reporting mean consumption of less than 20 drinks per week, were nonetheless reporting problems related to their drinking. This finding prompted two analyses. First, the information collected (at admission to our program) on the Lifetime Drinking History (Skinner & Sheu, 1982) was examined to find the levels of drinking reported at the inception of regular drinking (presumed to be problem-free) and the levels reported at the alleged onset of problem drinking. The level of consumption that best discriminated problem-free from problem drinking was a quantity–frequency average of 4 drinks, 3 days per week (Sanchez-Craig & Israel, 1985).

Subsequently, the levels of drinking of all clients reporting some problems at 6 months follow-up were compared with those of all clients reporting no such problems. The analyses indicated that the average consumption of those who reported problems was 5.55 ($SD = 2.14$) drinks per day, for an average of 4.21 ($SD = 1.57$) days per week. In contrast, the average consumption of problem-free clients was 2.97 ($SD = 2.28$) drinks, 2.26 ($SD = 2.02$) days per week (Sanchez-Craig, 1986). This finding is consistent with the preceding recommended guidelines.

D. Aids for Goal Achievement

Aids that we have used to facilitate the achievement of drinking goals and to ensure that drinking is under the client's deliberate control, include the following:

1. Self-Monitoring of Drinking Behavior

Asking clients to keep a daily record of their drinking behavior has important advantages, both from the clinical and research point of view. An accurate record of drinking behavior permits clients and therapists to make an objective assessment of progress from session to session, and to identify situations where clients may be at risk of drinking excessively. We have found that clients who self-monitor their drinking give more reliable reports than clients who reconstruct their consumption from memory (Sanchez-Craig & Annis, 1982). Furthermore, regular self-monitoring can focus the client's attention on deliberate control of the problem behavior. Several clients of our program spontaneously asserted that fear of "spoiling the record" helped to keep them within the preset drinking limits.

Self-monitoring forms can be designed according to the needs of particular programs. However, in order to increase the client's compliance with the procedure, it is important to keep self-monitoring forms as simple as possible. At present, we ask clients only to record for each day (1) the number of standard drinks consumed and (2) the number of these drinks that were consumed before 12 noon. We stress to clients the importance of *accurately* recording their drinking daily. We point out that self-monitoring of problem behaviors can have beneficial reactive effects in and of itself (Nelson, 1977).

2. Pacing Drinking

Because early-stage problem drinkers do not generally perceive themselves as being alcoholic, informing clients of documented differences between the drinking practices of alcoholics and social drinkers lends credence to the notion of pacing consumption. Alcoholics tend to pour straight drinks and to gulp them, but social drinkers tend to mix their drinks and to sip them (Sobell, Schaeffer, & Mills, 1972). Also, whereas social drinkers tend to measure their drinks, alcoholics do not. We propose to clients that the following measures can be helpful to slow their drinking and to avoid intoxication: (1) measuring, (2) diluting, (3) sipping, and (4) spacing drinks (e.g., by alternating alcoholic and nonalcoholic beverages, by letting at least 1 hour pass before taking the next drink), and (5) drinking along with meals.

3. Preparation for Drinking Events

Until new drinking patterns are well established, it is important to teach clients to prepare themselves in advance for situations where alcohol will be available and where pressures to drink are likely to occur. This will increase the probability of drinking in moderation. Before attending a social event, the client should have a plan about (1) the maximum number of drinks that will be taken and (2) the strategies that will be used to keep within this limit (e.g., diluting drinks, alternating alcoholic and nonalcoholic drinks, requesting help from others, using mnemonic devices to keep count of drinks consumed). The client should also prepare strategies for coping with social pressures and with his or her own temptations to go over the limit. Initially, these preparations are made in the treatment sessions.

4. Engaging in Activities Incompatible with Heavy Drinking

The clients of our program often drank excessively either for recreational purposes or to cope with boredom. Hence, a priority for many clients in similar programs would be the re-establishment or the development of social and recreational activities which do not involve heavy drinking. The large majority of the clients of our program for whom this objective was indicated proved capable of resolving the issue satisfactorily themselves. Failure to compensate for the loss of recreational activities associated with heavy drinking can prove a serious impediment to the achievement of the principal treatment goal. Thus, if clients fail to progress independently in this area, referral for leisure counseling is indicated.

E. Development of Adaptive Coping in High-Risk Situations

Our principal objective in treatment is to help clients attain the goals they have with respect to their drinking. To this end, we systematically guide them (1) to recognize the circumstances of problem drinking and (2) to develop forms of coping that are both effective and adaptive over the long-term. To facilitate these activities, we motivate clients to abstain for the first 3 weeks of treatment. Although moderation of alcohol use could be achieved by tapering down consumption, or by introducing a moderate-drinking pattern from the inception of treatment, we discuss with clients the advantages of maintaining an initial period of abstinence.

1. Potential Advantages of an Initial Period of Abstinence

When heavy drinkers abstain for a short period of time, they frequently improve in cognitive abilities that can be dulled by habitual heavy drinking (Wilkinson & Sanchez-Craig, 1981). Because the emphasis in therapy is on learning problem-solving skills, improved cognitive functioning may facilitate this process. Also, a short period of abstinence is likely to cause the client to experience urges or temptations to drink. Such experiences provide the opportunity not only to identify situations where the client is at risk of excessive drinking, but also to observe the manner in which he or she copes.

Of the 35 clients of our program who were assigned to the goal of moderation, 17 complied with an initial 3-week period of abstinence: 5 rejected the goal of moderation and elected to pursue abstinence, 9 complied with the request to abstain, and 3 contracted with the therapist for some ceremonial drinking not in excess of two drinks on a single occasion. For example, one client was getting married and resolved to have a glass of champagne. There were 11 clients who agreed to the request to abstain, but then consumed small amounts, with a daily average per client of no more than one drink, and no day with more than six drinks. The remaining 7 clients (except one) also agreed to abstain, but consumed more than one drink per day on average (range 2.0 to 5.4 drinks). Although the mean consumption of these clients was within the conventional limits of moderation (weekly average not exceeding 20 drinks), some of them had occasional days of heavy drinking (defined as 6 or more drinks per drinking day).

In summary, about 50% of the clients of our program who were assigned to the goal of moderation were successful in abstaining for the first 3 weeks of treatment; another 30% reduced their consumption to no more than one drink per day on average, and 20% consumed higher levels, although some of them were tapering their drinking down.

Examination of the performance of the preceding groups for the second phase of treatment (when controlled-drinking training was initiated) showed the following pattern: Of 28 clients who abstained or who drank very small amounts in the first 3 weeks of treatment, *all* moderated their drinking during the second phase of our program. In contrast, of the 7 clients who initially consumed higher amounts, 4 were categorized as heavy drinkers in the second phase. A subsequent analysis revealed that alcohol consumption during treatment was a significant predictor of outcome drinking for this group of clients (Sanchez-Craig & Lei, 1986). On the basis of these findings, we suggest that clients who are offered a goal of moderation and are unable to reduce their consumption drastically in the initial stages of treatment, or to stay within conventional limits of moderation during training in controlled drinking, should be referred to more intensive treatment.

At this point, one can only speculate about the meaning that a drastic reduction in drinking may have for the clients in the initial stages of treatment. Success at this time can be a strong stimulus to the reappraisal of high-risk situations and the role of alcohol. Many clients view the prospect of abstaining for the initial 3 weeks as a real challenge, but not beyond their capabilities. In terms of social-learning theory, this might be conceptualized as a procedure for enhancing self-efficacy with respect to the avoidance of drinking. Bandura and Cervone (1983) indicate that challenging but achievable goals constitute an effective component of the treatment process.

Informing clients about improvement in cognitive abilities that often occurs after 3 weeks of abstinence or very limited drinking (Wilkinson & Sanchez-Craig, 1981) seems to motivate them to abstain, or to drastically reduce their consumption. This is particularly the case when they have jobs or recreational activities that make intellectual demands. Furthermore, this initial period of abstinence provides an opportunity for physical recuperation, including significant improvements in the quality of sleep, according to some clients' self-reports. The experience of a greater sense of physical well-being and sharpened mental awareness can serve itself as a stimulus for the reappraisal of the value of drinking.

For the preceding reasons, we recommend that therapists suggest to their clients that they attempt to abstain for a period of 3 weeks at the inception of treatment. One should recognize that a significant proportion of clients will accede to this request, but yet drink small amounts on some days during this period. This pattern is usually associated with successful moderation of drinking at the end of treatment. However, clients who continue to drink larger amounts during the initial phase tend to have difficulty in moderating their drinking later on (Sanchez-Craig & Lei, 1986). As previously indicated, therapists have at their disposal the options of tapering off or aiming for immediate moderation for those clients who prefer one or the other of these routes.

2. Identification of High-Risk Situations

By *high-risk situations,* we mean those circumstances under which excessive drinking is most likely to occur. The riskiest circumstances tend to be those for which the client attributes important functions to alcohol (e.g., to palliate negative emotions), and those that tend to arise as a result of abstaining or to reducing drinking (e.g., social pressures, urges to drink). To help clients recognize high-risk situations, we assign them two tasks. One task involves specifying incidents of problem drinking in terms of their antecedents (physical and social context, the client's feelings and thoughts, including the function attributed to drinking) and their consequences (those experienced after 1 – 3 drinks were consumed and after continued drinking). The second task involves specifying incidents of successful coping with urges to drink in terms of their antecedents (physical and social context and the client's feelings) and the coping responses used (cognitive and behavioral).

From the 297 incidents of problem drinking described by the 70 clients in our program, we were able to abstract the following six classes of high-risk situations: (1) where clients experienced negative feelings or emotions (often related to social situations in which they felt powerless or incompetent to change their circumstances) and alcohol was mainly used as a palliative (42% of the descriptions); (2) where clients experienced positive feelings and believed that the situations would be enhanced by drinking (33%); (3) where clients believed that alcohol would serve to aid some kind of performance such as expressing anger, becoming more sociable, or completing unwelcome tasks (18%); (4) where drinking was habitual, for no particularly identified purpose (4%); (5) where clients experienced difficulty refusing invitations to drink or where alcohol was freely available (2%); and (6) where clients believed that alcohol would serve as a medication for pain or sleeplessness (2%). Some of the incidents described occurred while clients were in treatment, but the vast majority preceded treatment. The descriptions were sometimes ambiguous; however, two independent raters could allocate descriptions to the six classes of situations with acceptable reliability (81% concordance).

Within our program, the clients completed 180 descriptions of incidents of successful coping with urges to drink. Coping with negative emotions and interpersonal problems was the most frequent category identified (40% of the incidents described). About one-third of the incidents involved coping with the urge to drink in the presence of alcohol or social pressure. This contrasts with the relatively infrequent retrospective identification of problem drinking in such situations (34% vs. 2%). Thus, after reducing their consumption in our program, clients were more likely to experience social pressures to drink and to experience urges to drink where drinking was the norm. Coping with urges to drink for hedonic reasons was reported less frequently (13%) than incidents of such drinking were recollected (33%). In contrast, the necessity of coping with the urge to drink based on habit (13%) was more frequently reported than incidents involving such drinking were recalled (4%). In short, urges to drink for hedonic purposes were less frequently coped with than might have been expected on the basis of recalled incidents. On the other hand, as might be expected, there was an increase, during our program, in the frequency with which clients were obliged to deal with urges to drink related to alcohol cues, social pressure, and old habits. Reports of the salience of negative emotions were consistent between the two procedures for assessing high-risk situations.

As descriptions of incidents of problem drinking and successful coping accumulate, the therapist works with the client to synthesize the information and to abstract from it descriptions of areas of risk. In our experience, these are most commonly negative emotions and interpersonal conflicts. This finding is consistent with Marlatt's evaluation of risk situations for relapse (Marlatt, 1978). The functions attributed to alcohol in circumstances of problem drinking provide the fastest route to identification of areas of difficulty. For example, in the area of interpersonal problems, the client may have difficulty in expressing anger to various people. When drinking is described as habitual, and no function is attributed to it, then specification of the circumstances of drinking may give an indication of the function that alcohol serves.

3. Development of Cognitive and Behavioral Coping

In helping clients to develop alternative responses for high-risk situations, we make them aware of the distinction between cognitive and behavioral coping. Because problem drinking is most frequently associated with negative emotions, the use of cognitive coping strategies makes good sense to the clients, particularly when they feel powerless to alter the circumstances provoking the emotions. Clients of our program often reported problem drinking in response to emotions engendered by situations where there was little or nothing they could do instrumentally to produce change—for example, having been left by a spouse for another person, having a serious illness either in themselves or in a loved one, or losing a job after many years when the company went bankrupt. Under such circumstances, some kind of reappraisal (cognitive coping) is the most immediately available response to regulate the distressing emotions and to forestall drinking.

Similarly, in situations where "out of the blue" clients experience strong urges to drink, cognitive coping can immediately serve to reappraise the aversiveness of the urge, and to motivate the undertaking of actions other than drinking. Teaching clients how to cope with unexpected urges to drink should be an important aspect of therapy simply because many of the cues or conditions that have been associated with problem drinking are likely to remain unidentified during treatment. In situations of relapse, cognitive coping is also extremely useful to counteract the negative thoughts and emotions typically associated with these situations (Marlatt & Gordon, 1980) and to prevent clients from giving up on their drinking goals.

The description of incidents in which clients of our program spontaneously coped with strong urges to drink during the initial stages of treatment indicates that they readily understand the distinction between cognitive and behavioral coping and that they actually used both forms of coping. Cognitive coping was as extensively used as behavioral coping; in about 90% of the incidents described, at least one self-statement was reported. The self-statements that clients used more frequently to forestall drinking had the following functions: (1) to remind the client of the consequences of drinking or not drinking (e.g., "If I drink now, I'll be disappointed in myself tomorrow"); (2) to reappraise the situation and the role of alcohol (e.g., "There must be a better way to solving problems than having a drink"; "I don't really need it to enjoy myself or to add to the situation"); and (3) to remind oneself about the commitment to maintain abstinence (e.g., "I made a commitment to myself and I'll stick to it"). It should be noted that the most successful self-statements tended to be simple and straightforward.

Behaviors more frequently reported by clients as an alternative to drinking were (1) consummatory behaviors (i.e., consumption of nonalcoholic beverages and, to a lesser extent, eating and smoking); (2) sedentary recreation (e.g., watching television, reading, listening to music, and going to movies); (3) active recreation or distracting activities (e.g., physical exercise, working or studying, visiting friends, going shopping); and (4) asserting oneself in the presence of social pressures (e.g., "I'm not going to drink tonight"). During treatment, clients were asked to comment on the appropriateness and effectiveness of their coping behaviors. Where responses produced undesirable consequences (e.g., alienation of friends), alternative responses were considered.

We view cognitive coping not only as an alternative response in its own right, but as a means of facilitating behavioral coping. Depending on the nature of the problem situation at hand, cognitive or behavioral coping may become the initial or primary form of response. In situations where clients cannot change the circumstances producing the negative emotions, cognitive coping becomes the primary form of response. The self-statements that they are encouraged to develop are designed to palliate the negative emotions, and thus to set the emotional tone required for initiating activities that will compete with the disruptive emotions and excessive drinking. In cases where clients wish to and can do something to change the problem situation for the better, behavioral coping is emphasized. This form of coping is designed to produce immediate changes in the social environment, and to forestall the old coping responses of drinking. The development of behavioral coping is frequently instigated by teaching clients to make the connection between thinking and doing. In other words, for new appraisals or reinterpretations of stimulus events, clients are asked to specify the behaviors that would naturally follow from such interpretations. This method frequently seems to accelerate the process of identifying appropriate strategies for behavioral coping.

In summary, the principal respect in which our approach to the treatment of problem drinking differs from other behavioral approaches in the psychological literature is in the major emphasis that we place upon cognitive coping. As indicated, there are several important attributes of this coping method: It can be discretely used in any circumstance; it can be employed when behavioral options are apparently unavailable; it can serve as the initial stage in the elaboration of behavioral coping; and, lastly, it makes very good sense to clients.

IV. FUTURE CONSIDERATIONS

A. Abbreviation of the Treatment Program

Shortly after the initial evaluation of our program, accounts appeared in various newspapers around Canada. This publicity prompted inquiries from persons who believed that the program as described in the media was appropriate to their needs. Generally, such persons were not able to commit as much time to treatment as clients in our program. In response to such requests, the treatment was abbreviated to its barest essentials, which were conveyed in one or two brief counseling sessions. The elements selected for this purpose were (1) brief assessment of current drinking practices and functions attributed to alcohol, (2) goal setting and self-monitoring of drinking, (3) advice about aids for goal achievement, (4) instruction to avoid drinking for coping, and (5) recommendation that the client take steps either alone or with help to resolve problems in other life areas. This pilot work suggested that significant abbreviation of our program might be feasible without sacrificing effectiveness. This finding is consistent with Miller's findings that self-administered treatment involving similar components is as effective as more extensive programs (Miller & Taylor, 1980; Miller, Taylor, & West, 1980). Furthermore, a developing body of literature suggests that goal setting and feedback about performance are very important features of effective psychological treatments (Bandura & Cervone, 1983; Locke, Frederick, & Lee, 1984). The use of this abbreviated approach also seemed justified at the time it was attempted because data collected in our program showed that clients frequently generated effective coping techniques spontaneously.

A second consequence of the initial description of our program was the expression of interest by other professionals working with problem drinkers. These included physicians, social workers, and nurse practitioners working at the Addiction Research Foundation and other agencies. Initially, some of these professionals were trained in the procedures of our program, using a manual for therapists (Sanchez-Craig, 1984). However, the complete treatment package proved to be more extensive than many primary-care professionals could readily accommodate into their practice. In light of the apparent success of the abbreviated package, and scientific evidence of the effectiveness of brief interventions, the abbreviated treatment was formally specified. The feasibility of the abbreviated treatment for use by physicians in general practice has been evaluated (McIntosh & Sanchez-Craig, 1984). A controlled trial has been planned for implementation in the family practice unit of a large general hospital, with physicians as therapists. The abbreviated treatment will be compared to a brief session of advice comparable to the most extensive of the advice procedures employed in a preventive program for smoking (Russell, Wilson, Taylor, & Baker, 1979).

B. Generalization of Our Program to Other Client Populations

1. Long-Term Benzodiazepine Users

Except for nicotine and caffeine, the clients of our program were not simultaneously abusing alcohol and other psychoactive drugs. In theory, clients with an early-stage problem of abuse of other substances (e.g., cannabis) should respond as well as alcohol abusers to a similar treatment approach. The procedures of the program have been evaluated with clients who wished to discontinue their use of prescribed tranquillizers. These clients were selected for social stability, normal cognitive functioning, and daily consumption not exceeding 40 mg diazepam. The design of the study involved random assignment to either a drug condition or a placebo condition in a double blind trial. During treatment, clients were guided to identify risk situations and to develop cognitive and behavioral coping, to set goals of reduction, and to maintain daily records of drug use. Typically, five 60-minute sessions were required to help clients reduce their drug consumption to zero (or to occasional use of no more than 5 mg per day). Results obtained for 20 clients treated by the first author recently have been published, (Sanchez-Craig, Kay, Busto, & Cappell, 1986). The drug group (N = 11) and the placebo group (N = 9) were not found to differ significantly at any point in treatment outcome, although the placebo group reported more withdrawal symptoms. Overall, 75% of the clients were successful in discontinuing their use of tranquillizers over the two year follow-up, 15% did not change, and 10% dropped out. Self-reports of drug use at follow-up were corroborated by benzodiazepine levels in plasma. These findings suggest that the procedures of the program can be useful in the management of persons who are dependent on relatively low doses of benzodiazepines.

2. Multiple-Drug Abusers

A treatment study of 201 multiple-drug abusers was recently completed at the Addiction Research Foundation. Seventy-eight of these clients were randomly assigned to a brief outpatient program (three treatment sessions and six follow-up sessions), which incorporated a number of procedures found in the abbreviated version of our program. These included: goal setting, self-monitoring, analysis of the functions attributed to drug use, and indication of possible methods of coping in risky situations. Evaluation of the program after 1 year revealed that 64% of the clients had reduced their drug consumption by at least 50%. This brief program was as effective as a broad-spectrum residential behavioral program involving contingent reinforcement of individual therapeutic progress over a period of 4 to 6 weeks (Wilkinson & Martin, 1983). Subsequent analyses showed that the most successful clients receiving the brief treatment were heavy users of alcohol and/or cannabis, but did not use other psychoactive drugs very extensively. In addition, the more successful clients in this program perceived themselves as being relatively competent to resolve problems of their drug abuse and other life problems without much professional assistance. These data suggest that even for clients using a variety of psychoactive substances, a relatively brief treatment is effective, especially for those who do not view their problem as particularly severe (Wilkinson & LeBreton, in press).

3. Chronic Alcoholics

There is general consensus that the most appropriate candidates for a goal of moderation are early-stage problem drinkers. However, one should note that evidence reviewed by Heather and Robertson (1981) indicates that many alcoholism programs apparently contain a significant proportion of clients for whom moderation is an appropriate goal. This interpretation is supported by the rates of success achieved when selected clients of such programs are trained in moderation (pp. 196–197).

In clinical practice, there are two types of cases for whom it might be considered that objectives of moderation are contraindicated. These are the chronic alcoholic who has repeatedly failed in abstinence-oriented programs, and the heavy drinker or alcoholic with medical complications who adamantly refuses to abstain despite the risks of unaltered consumption. In such cases, the therapist has no option but to treat the client according to his or her wishes. A case example is useful in illustrating how such an eventuality can result in satisfactory outcome.

A chronic alcoholic in his mid-40s was referred to the physician for possible disulfiram treatment after 12 sessions in an alcoholism program in which he was considered unsuccessfully treated. The medical examination revealed that disulfiram should not be prescribed, mainly due to hypertension. Furthermore, the client adamantly asserted that he would not abstain. The attending physician, who had been trained in the abbreviated version of our program, observed that the client had reduced his alcohol consumption by about 50% from the time of his admission, although he was still a heavy drinker (consuming about 60 drinks per week). The physician suggested "cutting down," to which the patient agreed. Goals of reduction were set with him in sessions scheduled at steadily increasing intervals. The sessions were contingent on the client's presenting his drinking records to the physician, who gave him feedback regarding improvements in health (reductions in hypertension). After five visits (3 months later) the client had reduced his alcohol consumption to about 12 drinks per week, and his blood pressure had returned to normal levels. Six months later he returned to discuss a bout of heavy drinking. He was asked to set a goal and to resume daily self-monitoring of drinking. The client was followed-up for about 2 years, by which time he had become an extremely conservative drinker, typically restricting his consumption to two drinks once or twice per week.

4. Offspring of Alcoholics

There is some indication that a history of familial alcoholism might be a contraindication to a goal of moderation. In an analysis of data collected from several controlled-drinking studies, Miller and Joyce (1979) found that successful controlled-drinking subjects were less likely to have parental alco-holism. Among the clients of our program, 28 of the 70 reported having an alcoholic parent. These 28 clients did not differ significantly from the rest of the sample on any of the variables presented in Table 1, nor did they differ on other variables such as inception of regular drinking, onset of problem drinking, time in treatment, or drinking during treatment. There was, how-ever, a trend toward greater dependence and severity in the group with alcoholic parentage, as indicated by their higher mean scores in the ADS ($16.2\,SD = 7.0$ vs. 12.9, $SD = 7.0$, $p = .058$) and the MAST (20.4, $SD = 7.1$ vs. 17.4, $SD = 5.8$, $p = .067$). Interestingly, over the 2-year follow-up, the clients with alcoholic parentage reported drinking approximately half the amount reported by the other group. It is possible that observing the negative consequences of drinking in a parent, and experiencing themselves more of these consequences, sensitized them to the risks associated with heavy drinking and motivated them to adopt more conservative goals.

Miller and Joyce (1979) found that parental alcoholism was a predictor of either heavy drinking or abstinence, indicating the selection of more con-servative goals by some of their clients with alcoholic parents. However, in the present study, this variable was not predictive of the outcome of heavy drinking. This difference between the studies is problematic, and the issue clearly merits further investigation.

C. Cognition and Conditioning

Earlier experimental analyses of drinking behavior and alcoholism were grounded on the hypothesis that alcohol consumption is an instrumental behavior that can be analyzed within the paradigms of conditioning (Bige-low, Stitzer, Griffiths, & Liebson, 1981; Cohen, 1975; Mello, 1975; Mello & Mendelson, 1965, 1972). More recently, a variety of studies has demon-strated the importance of cognitive variables as determinants of alcohol consumption and alcohol effects (see Marlatt & Rosenhow, 1980). This reintegration of cognitions into experimental clinical psychology was not unique to alcohol studies, and was generally occurring in the treatment field under the influence of Bandura's work (1969). An important theoretical issue concerns the nature of these cognitive processes: Are they the result of the operation of the same associative principles that underly simple condi-tioning, or do they reflect the operation of some qualitatively distinct pro-cess? Clearly, this issue is of importance when a behavioral problem is being treated, and when it is clear that both simple associative processes and cognitions are important determinants of the behavior. If cognitive pro-cesses and conditioning processes are separate and distinct, then cognitive treatments might effectively alter cognitive determinants of the problem behavior, while leaving the associative determinants unaffected. This possible distinction between self-conscious, reflective cognitive evaluations, and automatized, unreflective responses to stimulation is indicated within the present formulation by the notions of primary and secondary appraisals mentioned earlier in this chapter.

Evidence for the possible qualitative distinctiveness of the aforementioned two aspects of mind has arisen out of studies of memory. In particular, studies of amnesia have revealed that the amnesic deficit in Korsakoffian alcoholics is a circumscribed deficit. It leaves a variety of skilled behaviors unaffected, while obliterating the aware remembrance of the events of skill acquisition (Moscovitch, 1982). A recent theoretical analysis has led to the proposal that the manner in which this well-established dichotomy of memory processes can be operationalized is by viewing the residual abilities of amnesics as based in associative processes (associative memory). In contrast, the memory system in which they are impaired (imaginal memory) is presumed to have nothing to do with associative processes, to operate as a perceptual system for the past, and to be largely responsible for short-term rapid adaptive changes in behavior (Poulos & Wilkinson, 1984).

This analysis has clear implications, in principle, for the treatment of behaviors that are determined by the operation of both of the two distinct systems of memory. Because it is postulated that imaginal memory and associative memory are distinct with respect to their underlying processes, it follows that a behavior principally controlled by one system could be affected by a treatment, while the same behavior under the principal control of the second system would be unaffected. As previously indicated, there is evidence that alcohol consumption is regulated both by reflective consciousness and by fairly automatized responses to alcohol cues. Hence, a cognitive treatment may provide the client with satisfactory self-control procedures with respect to drinking, while failing to extinguish some highly automatized responses to specific cues for consumption. The risk of this eventuality would depend upon the extent to which drinking behavior was automatized via associative processes. Of course, this argument is speculative and as yet untested. Nonetheless, these concepts may be useful to therapists in selecting cognitive strategies, in making recommendations to clients about how protracted the use of such strategies should be, and in cautioning clients about the possibility of the unexpected triggering of tendencies to drink. In theory, these tendencies can lie dormant for very long periods of time if the releasing stimuli happen not to be encountered. Thus, our practice is to prepare clients for such unanticipated urges to drink, even after strong cravings have not been experienced for weeks or months. We prepare them to use cognitive coping strategies as soon as the urge to drink is experienced, and not to be sanguine about such urges.

D. Relapse

The preceding considerations suggest a possible theoretical elaboration of current conceptualizations of the phenomenon of relapse. *Relapse* is a process that bedevils programs for the treatment of alcohol problems and other addictive behaviors. Marlatt (1978) focused the attention of clinical researchers on the issue of relapse prevention, and, currently, such enterprise is a central feature of much psychological treatment (Marlatt, 1985). Marlatt advanced two important theoretical notions in analyzing relapse. In essence, these can be summarized as the person's interpretation of violations of drinking goals and the adequacy of the person's resources for coping with situations of high risk.

The previous analysis of the processes underlying the control of behaviors suggests a possible additional interpretation for some situations of relapse. If clients cope successfully by cognitive or cognitive and behavioral strategies, over time they are likely to relax their preparedness to employ such strategies because of the decreased frequency with which these strategies are required. In contrast, tendencies to drink that were based on associative memory would not weaken over time, if such tendencies, though strong, were of low-frequency. For example, a client may, very predictably in the past, have engaged in heavy drinking in specific low-frequency situations such as: on holiday, when travelling by plane, at professional conferences, or in the face of strong emotional distress. Because such situations will probably not be encountered during treatment or shortly thereafter, they will not be coped with. Hence, the opportunity for weakening of any associatively based tendency to drink in these situations (via extinction by cue exposure while coping) will not occur. After a period without any drinking problems, cognitive vigilance is likely to be relaxed. When the client re-enters the low-frequency, high-risk situations, associatively-based processes may fairly automatically re-initiate drinking while the client's "cognitive guard" is down. What Marlatt terms "apparently irrelevant decisions" (AIDS, Marlatt & Gordon, 1980) may well be involved in such situations. Furthermore, the notion that reduction of cognitive vigilance may be an important determinant of relapse is suggested in recent empirical work by Litman, Eiser, Rawson, and Oppenheim (1979).

The foregoing elaboration of the concept of relapse has implications for alcoholism treatment in general, as well as programs of secondary prevention. Specifically, the greater the extent to which drinking is regulated by associative learning (as distinct from conscious reflection), the greater the risk of relapse of the kind just described. The more chronic the pattern of excessive drinking, the more probable that associatively based processes will be the major determinants of the behavior. Thus, for more chronic populations, treatment procedures based on associative learning would seem to be more suitable. Such procedures would include cue exposure, aversive conditioning, and concrete methods of skill acquisition. In contrast, for earlier-stage problem-drinkers, cognitive manipulations such as those described in this chapter may be simpler and more suitable. Data consistent with this view have been collected by Rankin (1984), who has demonstrated that cue exposure is a useful component to treatment for severely dependent alcoholics, but of much less relevance to the treatment of moderately dependent persons.

A second issue is the relevance of alcohol-related neuropsychological impairment to treatment procedures. Analyses of neurophychological deficits in alcoholics suggest that processes of abstraction and visuospatial problem-solving requiring rapid adaptive capabilities are much more affected than well-established procedural skills (Wilkinson & Carlen, 1981). Hence, treatments involving adaptive cognitive coping strategies may be especially difficult to implement with alcoholics who are impaired. On the other hand, because their associatively based capacities are likely to be relatively intact, treatments based on associative learning should remain effective. In a recent study of attrition, alcoholics deficient in visuospatial problem-solving were more likely to drop out from treatment, and tended to indicate that cognitive manipulations were not helpful to them (Erwin & Hunter, 1984).

Clients of our program differed from those described by Erwin and Hunter, in that they readily and spontaneously employed cognitive procedures for coping, and analyses of successful coping with urges to drink revealed that cognitive coping was as likely to be employed as behavioral coping. It should be noted, however, that the successful use of cognitive coping is not exclusive to early-stage problem drinkers. Litman et al. (1979) found that alcoholics treated in conventional abstinence-oriented programs also spontaneously used cognitive coping strategies, and that the use of such strategies was the best predictor of avoidance of relapse. The results from our program showed that the pattern of findings on drinking was atypical, in that within clients, the outcome was very stable from follow-up to follow-up. In short, there was little relapse to problem drinking, and the patterns of drinking established during the treatment phase were maintained. One possible reason for the stability of the outcome is that clients were deliberately prepared in a variety of ways for each of the conditions that might be associated with relapse. They were taught to use coping skills for identified high-risk situations, and a central feature of the procedures was the making of such identifications and evaluating the effectiveness of coping responses. In addition, all clients were explicitly taught to interpret slips or violation of the drinking goal as opportunities for learning how to enhance their capabilities to cope in the future. Thus, the possibility of abstinence or drinking-rule violations effects should have been minimized. Lastly, clients were prepared to expect sudden urges to drink for weeks and months after the conclusion of treatment, and they were urged to employ cognitive coping strategies on any occasion in which such urges were experienced. Clients were provided with a conceptual model of the possible mechanisms underlying such unexpected dormant tendencies to drink. In short, our program, as specified, contained components which addressed each of the three processes that we suggest may underly relapse.

V. CONCLUSIONS

Problem drinkers with the characteristics of the clients of our program are generally reluctant to attend conventional alcoholism treatment programs. They fear that participation in such programs will compromise their anonymity and that the time commitments typically required will interfere with their work or family responsibilities. Moreover, they tend to reject the notion that they are alcoholic or diseased, and they are unwilling to consider abstinence as a lifelong objective. Although there is a substantial number of persons with an alcohol problem at an early stage, programs for secondary prevention are virtually nonexistent. Interest in this area among behaviorally oriented clinicians has developed since the mid-1960s, but their research has had a negligible impact on general clinical practice (Litman & Topham, 1983). We suggest that if secondary prevention efforts are to be successful, programs should be well publicized in the community but should be implemented in facilities that offer general primary-care services, to protect the clients from stigmatization. Procedures such as those proposed in the chapter seem to constitute sufficient treatment for early-stage problem drinkers, and an initial assessment indicates that persons without formal training in psychotherapy readily assimilate these procedures. Furthermore, completed studies indicate that these procedures are appropriate for treating persons reporting problems with other substances, such as benzodiazepines, cannabis, and multiple drugs (Wilkinson & Martin, 1983).

A second general consideration relates to whether purely behavioral, rather than cognitive and behavioral, self-control procedures might be more appropriate for the client population. We have opted for the latter formulation, both because we are persuaded that a cognitive–behavioral synthesis is necessary for an adequate description of behavior and because clients of the type treated in our program spontaneously employ cognitive coping strategies to forestall heavy drinking. We suggest that procedures that do not stress the crucial role of cognitions in self-control would be considered conceptually inadequate by such clients.

REFERENCES

Alden, L. (1978). Evaluation of preventive self-management programme for problem drinkers. *Canadian Journal of Behavioural Science,* 10, 258–263.

Alden, L. (1983). *An ounce and a half of prevention.* Vancouver, B.C., Canada: Evergreen Press Limited.

Armor, D. J., Polich, M., & Stambul H. B. (1976). *Alcoholism and treatment.* Santa Monica, CA: The Rand Corporation, R-1739-NIAAA.

Arnold, M. B. (1960). *Emotions and personality* (Vols. 1 & 2). New York: Columbia University Press.

Arnold, M. B. (1969). Human emotion and action. In J. Mischel (Ed.), *Human action* (pp. 167–197). New York: Academic Press.

Ashley, M. J., Olin, J. S., le Rich, W. H., Kornaczewski, A., Schmidt, W., Corey, P. N., & Rankin, J. G. (1981). The physical disease characteristics of inpatient alcoholics. *Journal of Studies on Alcohol,* 42, 1–14.

Bandura, A. (1969). *Principles of behavior modification.* New York: Holt, Rinehart, and Winston, Inc.

Bandura, A. (1977a). Self-efficacy: Toward a unifying theory of behavioral change. *Psychological Review,* 84, 191–15.

Bandura, A. (1977b). *Social learning theory.* Englewood Cliffs, NJ: Prentice Hall.

Bandura, A., & Cervone, D. (1983). Self-evaluative and self-efficacy mechanisms governing the motivational effects of goal systems. *Journal of Personality and Social Psychology,* 45, 1017–1028.

Beck, A. (1976). *Cognitive therapy and emotional disorders.* New York: International Universities Press.

Bernadt, M. W., Mumford, J., Taylor, C., Smith, B., & Murray, R. M. (1982, February 6). Comparison of questionnaire and laboratory tests in the detection of excessive drinking and alcoholism. *The Lancet,* 325–328.

Bigelow, G. E., Stitzer, M. L., Griffiths, R. R., & Liebson, I. A. (1981). Contingency management approaches to drug self-administration and drug abuse: Efficacy and limitations. *Addictive Behaviors,* 6, 241–252.

Cahalan, D., & Room, R. (1974). *Problem drinking among American men.* New Brunswick, NJ: Rutgers Center of Alcohol Studies.

Cohen, M. (1975). Suppression of drinking and facilitation of prosocial behavior in residential treatment programs for alcoholics. In H. D. Cappell & A. E. LeBlanc (Eds.), *Biological and behavioural approaches to drug dependence* (pp. 115–132). Toronto: Addiction Research Foundation.

Costello, R. (1975). Alcoholism treatment and evaluation: In search of methods. *International Journal of Addictions,* 10, 251–275.

Duckert, F. (1982). *Control training in the treatment of alcohol abusers.* Oslo: National Institute for Alcohol Research, Mimeograph No. 62.

D'Zurilla, T. J., & Goldfried, M. R. (1971). Problem solving and behaviour modification. *Journal of Abnormal Psychology,* 78, 107–126.

Edwards, G. (1977). The alcohol dependence syndrome: Usefulness of an idea. In G. Edwards & M. Grant (Eds.). *Alcoholism: New knowledge and new responses,* London: Croom Helm.

Edwards, G., & Gross, M. M. (1976). Alcohol dependence: Provisional description of a clinical syndrome, *British Medical Journal,* 1, 1058–1061.

Ellis, A. (1962). *Reason and emotion in psychotherapy.* New York: Lyle Stuart.

Erwin, J. E., & Hunter, J. J. (1984). Prediction of attrition in alcoholic aftercare by scores on the Embedded Figures Test and two Piagetian tasks. *Journal of Consulting and Clinical Psychology*, **52**, 343–353.

Goldstein, D. B. (1983). *Pharmacology of alcohol*. New York: Oxford University Press.

Heather, N., & Robertson, I. (1981). *Controlled drinking*. London: Methuen.

Hilgard, E. R., & Bower, G. H. (1975). *Theories of learning*. Englewood Cliffs, NJ: Prentice Hall.

Horn, J. L., Skinner, H. A., Wanberg, K. W., & Foster, F. M. (1984). *Alcohol dependence scale (ADS)*. Toronto: Addiction Research Foundation.

Jellinek, E. M. (1960). *The disease concept of alcoholism*. New Haven, CT: Hillhouse Press.

Kristenson, H., Trell, E., Fex, G., & Hood, B. (1980). Serum-glutatmyltransferase: Statistical distribution in a middle-aged population and evaluation of alcohol habits in individuals with elevated levels. *Preventive Medicine*, **9**, 108–119.

Lazarus, R. S. (1966). *Psychological stress and the coping process*. New York: McGraw-Hill.

Lazarus, R. S. (1968). Emotions and adaptation: Conceptual and empirical relations. In M. Arnold (Ed.), *Nebraska symposium on motivation* (Vol. 16, pp. 175–270). Lincoln: University of Nebraska Press.

Lazarus, R. S. (1980). Cognitive behavior therapy as psychodynamics revisited. In M. J. Mahoney (Ed.), *Psychotherapy process* (pp. 121–126). New York: Plenum.

Lazarus, R. S., Averill, J. R., & Opton, E. M. (1974). The psychology of coping: Issues of research and assessment. In G. V. Colho, D. A. Hamburg, & J. A. Adams (Eds.), *Coping and adaptation* (pp. 249–315). New York: Basic Books.

Lelbach, W. K. (1974). Organic pathology related to volume and patterns of alcohol use. In R. J. Gibbins, Y. Israel, H. Kalant, R. E. Popham, W. Schmidt, & R. Smart (Eds.), *Research advances in alcohol and drug problems* (Vol. 1) (pp. 93–198). New York: Wiley.

Litman, G., Eiser, J. R., Rawson, N. S. B., & Oppenheim, A. M. (1979). Differences in relapse precipitants and coping behavior between alcohol relapsers and survivors. *Behavior Research and Therapy*, **17**, 89–94.

Litman, G. K., & Topham, A. (1983). Outcome studies on techniques in alcoholism treatment. In M. Galanter (Ed.), *Recent developments in alcoholism* (pp. 167–194). NY: Plenum.

Locke, E. A., Frederick, E., & Lee, C. (1984). Effect of self-efficacy, goals, and task strategies on task performance. *Journal of Applied Psychology*, **69**, 241–251.

Marlatt, G. A. (1978). Craving for alcohol, loss of control, and relapse: A cognitive–behavioral analysis. In P. E. Nathan, G. A. Marlatt, & T. Løberg (Eds.), *Alcoholism: New directions in behavioral research and treatment* (pp. 271–314). New York: Plenum.

Marlatt, G. A. (1985). Relapse prevention: General overview. In G. A. Marlatt & J. Gordon (Eds.), *Relapse prevention* (pp. 3–70). New York: The Guilford Press.

Marlatt, G. A., & Gordon, J. R. (1980). Determinants of relapse: Implications for the maintenance of behavior change. In P. Davidson & S. Davidson (Eds.), *Behavioral medicine: Changing health lifestyles* (pp. 410–452). New York: Brunner/Mezel, Inc.,

Marlatt, G. A., & Rosenhow, D. J. (1980). Cognitive processes in alcohol use: Expectancy and the balanced placebo design. In N. K. Mello (Ed.), *Advances in substance abuse: Behavioral and biological research* (pp. 159–199). Greenwich, CT: JAI Press.

McIntosh, M., & Sanchez-Craig, M. (1984). Moderate drinking: An alternate treatment goal for early-stage problem drinkers. *Canadian Medical Association Journal*, **131**, 873–876.

Meichenbaum, D. (1977). *Cognitive behavior modification*. New York: Plenum.

Mello, N. K. (1975). A semantic aspect of alcoholism. In H. D. Cappell & A. E. LeBlanc (Eds.), *Biological and behavioural approaches to drug dependence*. Toronto: Addiction Research Foundation.

Mello, N. K., & Mendelson, J. H. (1965). Operant analysis of drinking habits of chronic alcoholics. *Nature*, **206**, 43–46.

Mello, N. K., & Mendelson, J. H. (1972). Drinking patterns during work contingent and noncontingent alcohol acquisition. *Psychometric Medicine, 34,* 139–164.

Miller, P. M. (1976). *Behavioral treatment of alcoholism.* New York: Pergamon Press.

Miller, P. M., & Mastria, M. A. (1977). *Alternatives to alcohol abuse.* Champaign, IL: Research Press.

Miller, W. R. (1978). Behavioral treatment of problem drinkers: A comparative outcome study of three controlled drinking therapies. *Journal of Consulting and Clinical Psychology, 46,* 74–86.

Miller, W. R. (1985). *Motivation for treatment: A review. Psychological Bulletin, 98,* 84–107.

Miller, W. R., Gribskov, C. J., & Mortell, R. L. (1981). Effectiveness of a self-control manual for problem drinkers with and without therapist contact. *International Journal of Addictions, 16,* 1247–1254.

Miller, W. R., & Hester, R. (1980). Treating the problem drinker: Modern approaches. In W. R. Miller (Ed.), *The addictive behaviors: Treatment of alcoholism, drug abuse, smoking and obesity* (pp. 111–142). Oxford: Pergamon.

Miller, W. R., & Joyce, M. A. (1979). Prediction of abstinence, controlled drinking, and heavy drinking outcomes following behavioral self-control training. *Journal of Consulting and Clinical Psychology, 47,* 773–775.

Miller, W. R., & Muñoz, R. (1976). *How to control your drinking.* Englewood Cliffs, NJ: Prentice Hall.

Miller, W. R., Pechacek, T. F., & Hamburg, S. (1981). Group behavior therapy for problem drinkers. *International Journal of Addictions, 16,* 829–839.

Miller, W. R., & Taylor, C. (1980). Relative effectiveness of bibliotherapy, individual and group self-control. *Addictive Behaviors, 5,* 13–24.

Miller, W. R., Taylor, C. A., & West, J. (1980). Focused versus broad-spectrum behavior therapy for problem drinkers. *Journal of Consulting and Clinical Psychology, 48,* 590–601.

Moore, R. C., & Murphy, T. C. (1961). Denial of alcoholism as an obstacle to recovery. *Quarterly Journal of Studies on Alcohol, 22,* 597–609.

Moscovitch, M. (1982). Multiple dissociations of function in amnesia. In L. S. Cermak (Ed.), *Human memory and amnesia* (pp. 337–370). Hillsdale, NJ: Erlbaum.

Nelson, R. A. (1977). Assessment and therapeutics functions of self-monitoring. In H. Hersen, R. Eisler, & R. Miller (Eds.), *Progress in behavior modification* (Vol. 5) (pp. 264–209). New York: Academic Press.

Öjehagen, A., & Berglund, M. (1986). To keep the alcoholic in out-patient treatment: A differentiated approach through treatment contracts. *Acta Psychiatrica Scandnavica, 73,* 68–75.

Orford, J., & Edwards (1977). *Alcoholism.* Maudsley Monograph No. 26, Oxford University Press.

Polich, J. M., Armor, D. J., & Braiker, H. B. (1981). *The course of alcoholism: Four years after treatment.* New York: Wiley.

Pomerleau, O. F., Pertschuck, M., Adkins, D., & Brady, J. P. (1978). A comparison of behavioral and traditional treatment methods for middle-income problem drinkers. *Journal of Behavioral Medicine, 1,* 187–200.

Poulos, C. X., & Wilkinson, D. A. (1984). A process-theory of remembering. In L. Squire & N. Butters (Eds.), *Neuropsychology of memory* (pp. 67–82). New York: Plenum.

Rankin, H. J. (1984). Dependence and compulsion: Experimental models for change. Paper presented at the Third International Conference on Treatment of Addictive Behaviours, North Berwick, Scotland.

Raven, J. C. (1960). *Guide to the standard progressive matrices.* London: H. K. Lewis.

Room, R. (1977). Measurement and distribution of drinking patterns and problems in general populations. In G. Edwards, M. M. Gross, M. Keller, J. Moser, & R. Room, (Eds.), *Alcohol related disabilities.* Geneva: WHO Offset Publication No. 32.

Russell, M. A. H., Wilson, C., Taylor, C., & Baker, C. D. (1979). Effect of general practitioners' advice against smoking. *British Medical Journal,* **2,** 231–235.

Sanchez-Craig, M. (1972). Reappraisal procedures in the modification of unsatisfactory social interactions. Unpublished doctoral dissertation, University of Toronto.

Sanchez-Craig, M. (1975). A self-control strategy for drinking tendencies. *The Ontario Psychologist,* **7,** 25–29.

Sanchez-Craig, M. (1976). Cognitive and behavioral coping strategies in the reappraisal of stressful social situations. *Journal of Counseling Psychology,* **23,** 7–12.

Sanchez-Craig, M. (1980a). Random assignment to abstinence or controlled drinking in a cognitive-behavioral program: Short-term effects on drinking behavior. *Addictive Behaviors,* **5,** 35–39.

Sanchez-Craig, M. (1980b). Drinking pattern as a determinant of alcoholics' performance on the Trail Making test. *Journal of Studies on Alcohol,* **41,** 1082–1090.

Sanchez-Craig, M. (1984). *A therapists' manual for secondary prevention of alcohol problems: Procedures for teaching moderate drinking and abstinence.* Toronto: Addiction Research Foundation.

Sanchez-Craig, M. (1986). How much is too much? Estimates of hazardous drinking based on clients' self reports. *British Journal of Addiction,* **81,** 263–268.

Sanchez-Craig, M., & Annis, H. M. (1982). Self-monitoring and recall measures of alcohol consumption: Convergent validity with biochemical indices of liver function. *British Journal of Alcohol and Alcoholism,* **17,** 117–121.

Sanchez-Craig, M., Annis, H. M., Bornet, R., & MacDonald, K. R. (1984). Random assignment to abstinence and controlled drinking: Evaluation of a cognitive-behavioral program for problem drinkers. *Journal of Consulting and Clinical Psychology,* **52,** 390–403.

Sanchez-Craig, M., Kay, G., Busto, U., & Cappell, H. (1986, February 15). Cognitive-behavioural treatment for benzodiazepine dependence. *Lancet.* (Letter to the Editor).

Sanchez-Craig, M., & Israel, Y. (1985). Pattern of alcohol use associated with self-identified problem drinking. *The American Journal of Public Health,* **75**(2), 178–180.

Sanchez-Craig, M., & Lei, H. (1986). Disadvantages to imposing the goal of abstinence on problem drinkers: An empirical study. *British Journal of Addiction.*

Sanchez-Craig, M., & Walker, K. (1974). *Teaching alcoholics how to think defensively: A cognitive approach for the treatment of alcohol abuse.* North American Congress on Alcohol and Drug Problems, San Francisco, CA.

Sanchez-Craig, M., & Walker, K. (1975). I feel lonely but that doesn't mean I have to drink. *Addictions,* **22,** 2–17.

Sanchez-Craig, M., & Walker, K. (1982). Teaching coping skills to chronic alcoholics in a coeducational halfway house: I. Assessment of programme effects. *British Journal of Addiction,* **77,** 35–50.

Selzer, M. L. (1971). The Michigan Alcoholism Screening Test: The quest for a new diagnostic instrument. *American Journal of Psychiatry,* **127,** 1653–1658.

Skinner, H. A., & Allen, B. A. (1982). Alcohol dependence syndrome: Measurement and validation. *Journal of Abnormal Psychology,* **91,** 199–209.

Skinner, H. A., & Sheu, W. (1982). Reliability of alcohol use indices: The Lifetime Drinking History and the MAST. *Journal of Studies on Alcohol,* **43,** 1157–1170.

Sobell, M. B., Schaefer, H. H., & Mills, K. C. (1972). Differences in baseline drinking behavior between alcoholics and normal drinkers. *Behavior Research and Therapy,* **10,** 257–267.

Tiedbout, H. M. (1953). Surrender vs. compliance in therapy: With special reference to alcoholism. *Quarterly Journal of Studies on Alcohol,* **14,** 58–68.

Vogler, R. C., Weissbach, T. A., & Compton, J. V. (1977). Learning techniques for alcohol abuse. *Behavior Research and Therapy,* **15,** 31–38.

Walker, K., Sanchez-Craig, M., & Bornet, R. (1982). Teaching coping skills to chronic alcoholics in a coeducational halfway house: Assessment of outcome and identification of outcome predictors. *British Journal of Addiction,* **77,** 185–196.

Wechsler, D. (1958). *The measurement and appraisal of adult intelligence.* Baltimore: Williams and Wilkins.

Wilkinson, D. A., & Carlen, P. L. (1981). Chronic organic brain syndrome associated with alcoholism: Neuropsychological and other aspects. In Y. Israel, F. Glaser, H. Kalant, R. Popham, W. Schmidt, & R. Smart (Eds.), *Research advances on alcohol and drug problems* (Vol. 6) (pp. 108–138). New York: Plenum.

Wilkinson, D. A., & LeBreton, S. (in press). Early indications of treatment outcome in multiple drug users. In W. R. Miller & N. Heather (Eds.), *Treating addictive behaviors: Processes of change.* New York: Plenum.

Wilkinson, D. A., & Martin, G. W. (1983, December). *Experimental comparison of two behavioural treatments of multiple drug abuse.* Paper presented at Annual Conference of the Association for the Advancement of Behavior Therapy, Washington, DC.

Wilkinson, D. A., & Sanchez-Craig, M. (1981). Relevance of brain dysfunction to treatment objectives: Should alcohol-related deficits influence the way we think about treatment? *Addictive Behaviors,* **6,** 253–260.

Zweben, A., & Li, S. (1981). The efficacy of role induction in preventing early dropout from outpatient treatment of drug dependency. *American Journal of Drug and Alcohol Abuse,* **8,** 171–183.

14

Prevention of Alcohol Problems

PETER E. NATHAN* AND RAYMOND S. NIAURA†

*Center of Alcohol Studies
†Department of Clinical Psychology, Graduate School of
    Applied and Professional Psychology
Rutgers, The State University of New Jersey
Piscataway, New Jersey 08854

I. INTRODUCTION

The well-known distinction among primary, secondary, and tertiary prevention appears to be less apt for alcohol problems than for either physical or psychiatric ones. Because most people drink in our society and because the relationship between drinking pattern and risk for alcoholism is a complex one, it is impossible to identify individuals at risk for development of alcoholism simply by virtue of drinking pattern (For example, in the absence of data on how many heavy-drinking persons progress to problem drinking or alcoholism, it is even impossible to say with confidence that heavy drinking beyond a certain level places a person at risk.) While we do know that there is, likely, a genetic component to alcoholism (Goodwin, 1983) and that ethnic factors are also associated with risk (Vaillant, 1983), only a distinct minority of persons possessed of such risk factors ever actually develop clinical alcoholism. Hence, it is not possible to design prevention programs that *focus* either on all individuals at risk (primary prevention) or on those at special risk for alcoholism (secondary prevention). Moreover, as some of the material reviewed here suggest, differences between treatment and prevention are especially difficult to draw when it comes to alcoholism: Programs that are designed as treatment have important prevention consequences and vice versa. Accordingly, we suggest that distinctions among primary, secondary, and tertiary alcoholism prevention programs are probably unnecessary to make.

TREATMENT AND PREVENTION
OF ALCOHOL PROBLEMS: A RESOURCE MANUAL

Our overview of primary and secondary prevention efforts in this country includes programs with only a prevention thrust as well as those which combine prevention with either a treatment or an education focus. We review programs serving individuals as well as those which aim to prevent alcoholism by increasing the costs of consumption, by making beverage alcohol more expensive, by changing laws governing its sale and consumption, or by making drunken driving more likely to result in apprehension and punishment.

II. OVERVIEW OF PREVENTION EFFORTS: PREVENTION AS A NATIONAL PRIORITY

Of a total of 584.1 million dollars in federal funds expended on alcohol-related actions in 1980, only $24.4 million (4%) was allocated to prevention efforts. These efforts were largely restricted to the three federal agencies for whom alcoholism is a central concern—the National Institute on Alcohol Abuse and Alcoholism (NIAAA), the Department of Defense (which must provide prevention and treatment services for members of the armed forces), and the National Highway Safety Administration. The federal government's commitment of these funds meant, surprisingly, that it was responsible for 63.5% ($24.4 million of $38.4 million) of all public funds expended for the purposes of alcoholism prevention. Viewed this way, the federal involvement in prevention is both substantial and impressive. Viewed another way, the fact that only 4% ($24.4 million of $584.1 million) of all federal funds for alcohol-related activities were spent on prevention activities, the prevention fraction appears scandalously low, given primary prevention activities' potential to return their costs many times over.

Efforts to prevent alcoholism and alcohol-related problems are accorded lower priority in this country than elsewhere—notably, in the Scandinavian countries. Nowhere, though, is prevention accorded emphasis comparable to that given treatment. Primary and secondary prevention are always funded at significantly lower levels than tertiary prevention, despite the widely recognized differences in their cost–benefit ratios in favor of prevention. Why this paradox continues is unclear. Perhaps it is best explained by pointing to the absence of empirical support for the efficacy of prevention programs (a research lacuna that is revealed here subsequently), despite their theoretical advantages in costs. If prevention works only in theory and never in fact, it is little wonder that policymakers put their money—and that of their constituents—into treatment, whose efficacy, however modest, has nonetheless been documented.

III. EFFORTS THAT FOCUS ON THE INDIVIDUAL

One of the most encouraging recent developments in prevention programming is a focus on groups of persons at risk but not previously the focus of either prevention or treatment.

A. Women and Prevention

Although the data are in some question, most observers believe that rates of alcoholism among women have increased during much of the twentieth century (Shaw, 1980), although this rise has either slowed or stopped in recent years (Bower, 1980; Braiker, 1982).

Some of the most damaging behavioral and biological effects of alcohol abuse affect men and women differentially (Hill, 1982; Knupfer, 1982). To this end, successful suicide, death from accidents, and death from liver cirrhosis associated with alcoholism is significantly greater among women than men. Women also appear to develop drinking-related cancers, cardiovascular disorder, and brain damage at higher rates than men at equivalent levels of alcohol dependency. Differences in genetic predisposition to alcoholism have been offered in explanation of these differences in susceptibility to alcohol-related disease: Although both men (Goodwin, Schulsinger, Knop, Mednick, & Guze, 1977) and women (Goodwin, 1983) can be predisposed to develop alcoholism on a genetic basis, there may be some difference in heritability that favors greater morbidity from alcoholism for women. On the other hand, because women drink less than men on average, the overall severity of alcoholism among female alcoholics is less than that among men, mitigating the apparent difference in susceptibility to the behavioral and biological effects of alcoholism. Women with high rates of abusive drinking include young women with young children, women with alcoholic husbands, and employed women in stressful occupations.

Prevention workers have only recently taken into account these data on comparative prevalence and morbidity rates by developing programs designed specifically for women. Among the earliest of such efforts were behavioral programs that saw alcoholism among women as a consequence of deficits in assertiveness, self-esteem, and ability to handle stress. According to this view, alcoholism among women would diminish to the extent that women received training in these skills (Irwin, 1976; Sandmaier, 1976). Unfortunately, empirical data supporting this approach and its assumptions have not been reported: It is not certain that alcoholic women do lack assertiveness or self-esteem or that, if they do, their lack is associated with the development of alcoholism.

Alcohol education has also been targeted specifically for women. The

National Center for Alcohol Education course, "Reflections in a glass," for example, is designed to provide information to women without current alcohol problems, in order to help them make more rational decisions on the role they wish alcohol to play in their lives. While the course has been found to increase participants' knowledge of alcohol and alcoholism, its role in reducing alcoholism was not assessed and is not known.

The Los Angeles County Alcoholism Center for Women undertook identification of and delivery of prevention services for women at special risk for alcoholism following an extensive needs assessment reported in 1982. Special attention was paid to high-risk women to heighten the effectiveness of the multimedia and multimodal prevention strategy. Unfortunately, no assessment of the effectiveness of this program has been reported.

Prevention efforts among women also encompass efforts to raise the minimum drinking age, on the assumption that young women are more likely than young men to obey laws on age of consumption (Whitehead & Ferrance, 1977). In the same vein, prevention strategies designed to alter the drinking context are more likely to be effective for women than for men because women are more apt to be influenced by the environmental context of their drinking than are men (Harford, Wechsler, & Rohman, 1980; Morrissey & Schuckit, 1979; Rosenbluth, Nathan, & Lawson, 1978).

To summarize: Much more is now known about alcoholism among women than ever before. It suggests strongly that alcohol-related morbidity and mortality among women are at least as discouraging as those among men — if not somewhat more so. Despite these new findings, however, prevention efforts directed toward women, though increasing modestly, remain relatively rare. As well, few of the projects for women that have been undertaken have been evaluated and, of them, none has reported success in actually reducing drinking by women who abuse alcohol.

B. Youth and Prevention

Most prevention programs for youth have consisted largely of alcohol education; these programs have typically been offered either to unselected youth groups or to youth at high risk for alcoholism (including those from alcoholic families, disadvantaged youth, and the delinquent, the dropout, and the troubled.) For both categories of youth, programs have been designed that have little or no alcohol content (these are supposed to foster healthy emotional development in order to head off serious alcohol problems later on), though most alcohol education programs set out to inform fully on alcohol, alcohol problems, and alcoholism. Alcohol education efforts have also been provided adults who interact with youth — including parents, other family members, teachers, and other community professionals and laypeople — on the assumption that providing these key gatekeepers information on alcohol and alcoholism is a cost-effective way to convey the information to the youth with whom these individuals interact (Hewitt, 1982).

Those few alcohol education programs for youth which have been evaluated report (1) significant increases in knowledge about alcohol and its effects (Fullerton, 1979; Staulcup, Kenward, & Frigo, 1979), (2) marked changes in attitudes toward alcohol or toward self and others in relation to alcohol, especially when attitude change is an explicit goal of the program (Evans, Steer, & Fine, 1979; Weisheit, Kearney, Hopkins, & Mauss, 1979), and (3) few or no changes in actual alcohol consumption.

Elementary-age children were recently the target of two promising but unproven prevention programs. The first, a substance abuse prevention program for elementary and junior high school students in Napa (California), was also designed to investigate etiologic factors in substance abuse among these youth (NIDA, 1982). Unfortunately, the absence of a carefully conceived evaluation component prevented assessment of the program's worth. The same must be said of another program designed for elementary-age children, the Alpha Center Prevention Model, implemented in two Florida counties (Pringle, Gregory, Ginkel, & Cheek, 1981). Assuming that alcoholism, like other behavioral problems, stems from early developmental problems, the developers of the Alpha Centers established special classes for 8- to 12-year old children who had displayed maladaptive behavior at home and school. The classes were designed to improve social and academic skills. Their teachers applied classroom behavior management techniques and taught interpersonal communication skills while counselors worked with parents in the home. As before, however, a promising prevention strategy remains essentially unproven on an empirical basis because an assessment component was not a part of the program design.

Adolescents have received more attention from developers of prevention programs because most youth begin to drink during these years. Adolescence is also the time when youth are involved in the worst behavioral consequences of drinking, including drunken driving. Moreover, recent data indicate that (1) alcohol is the drug used most widely by adolescents, (2) problem drinking increases sharply with advancing age during adolescence, (3) adolescent problem drinkers use illicit drugs much more often than do nondrinkers, (4) heavy drinking during adolescence is typically accompanied by antisocial behavior, (5) both parents and peers influence problem drinking, and (6) adolescent problem drinkers are less religious, more tolerant of deviance, less successful academically, and more drawn to independence than nonproblem-drinking adolescents (Braucht, 1982). The most frequent cause of death and disability for American youth is traffic accidents, many of them alcohol-related (Douglass, 1982).

Several innovative prevention programs have focused on adolescent drinking. (1) An intensive alcohol problems training program was developed for the staff of the Partners Program, a nonprofit volunteer organization designed to provide service to youth in trouble with the law in Denver (Resource Alternatives Corporation, 1982). An evaluation of this program revealed that youths' perceptions of the negative consequences of drug and alcohol use increased after their counselors had received alcohol education, although no change in actual drug or alcohol use was observed. (2) A diverse group of state prevention programs for adolescents ranging from alcohol education alone to health promotion projects aiming to develop health-conscious lifestyles incompatible with problem drinking through legislative and other efforts to reduce adolescent accessibility to alcohol have been developed. These projects remain unexamined and, hence, unproven. (3) A drunken driving prevention program designed to identify primary alcoholics from among drunken adolescents seen on the emergency service of a general hospital in Ohio has recently been tried out. When such persons are identified, they and their parents are encouraged to participate in drinking and driving intervention programs (*Medical World News,* 1980). (4) Programs in New York, Wisconsin, and Oklahoma requiring teenagers applying for a driver's license to view an alcohol education film in high school driver education classes, on the assumption that adolescents at this stage are maximally motivated to cooperate with alcohol education programs, has been evaluated. The evaluation indicated that students retained the information acquired (although for an undetermined period of time). (5) Lectures were given to almost 1000 junior and senior high school students on the pharmacology of drugs; the physiology of drug action, including alcohol; and the legal, social, and psychological ramifications of their use (Stuart, 1980). Information levels increased—as did drug and alcohol use, suggesting that the program had produced better-informed drug and alcohol users. Whether or not these users were less likely to become abusers was not assessed. (6) Lectures were given to 7th- through 10th-grade students on myths about alcohol, reasons for drinking, and effects of alcohol on the family, driving, sports, fitness, and sexuality. The lectures increased knowledge but had mixed effects on attitudes toward alcohol. They were also associated with lower future alcohol use and decreases in current alcohol use, according to one of the few studies in this vast literature reporting such behavioral changes (Goodstadt, Sheppard, & Chan, 1982).

A particularly innovative prevention program for adolescents placed teams of 5 to 7 high school students in a California junior high school after the students had received intensive alcohol education. Another junior high school served as a control for the intervention. The teams of students in the experimental junior high school led class discussions of alcohol-related issues during 2 consecutive years (McAlister, Perry, Killen, Slinkard, Maccoby, 1980). The project was designed to increase students' commitment not to smoke or use alcohol and other drugs. A 21-month follow-up indicated that students in the experimental school were drinking and smoking at lower rates than students in the control school.

Programs for college-aged students have been slower to develop, even though college students consider alcohol and other drug problems to be the most serious of the 24 mental health problems with which they must wrestle (Henggeler, Sallis, & Cooper, 1980). As with younger individuals, alcohol education programs typically increase college students' level of information but do little or nothing to change drinking behavior (Donovan, 1980; Leavy, 1980; Portnoy, 1980).

One of the most innovative and comprehensive alcoholism prevention programs for college students was implemented at the University of Massachusetts and the University of North Carolina between 1975 and 1980. The University of Massachusetts project provided (1) mass media appeals in order to raise awareness of drinking and driving, accidental injuries, and the alcoholic content of various beverages; (2) group discussions, lectures, and special courses, to enable small groups of students to explore various alcohol-related topics more intensively; (3) community development techniques, to influence ways in which alcohol was consumed by target groups; and (4) efforts to influence institutional norms and practices involving alcohol, to modify alcohol consumption at campus parties. Well over half the students on campus recalled at least one message from this massive campaign; environmental, knowledge, and attitude changes also took place. Unhappily, however, changes in drinking behavior did not accompany changes in knowledge or attitudes (Kraft, 1982).

Similarly, despite equally innovative programming (which included a student-run tavern designed to improve student participation in the prevention program as well as a direct mail campaign), students' attitudes and information levels changed for the better — but their drinking behavior did not.

To summarize: Both the number and the sophistication of prevention activities directed at youth have increased in recent years. Unfortunately, however, while these efforts typically yield desired changes in information about alcohol and attitudes towards abusive drinking, they rarely produce measurable changes in drinking behavior.

C. Minorities and Prevention

The problem of alcoholism among Blacks in this country has been — and remains — bleak. Treatment of Black alcoholics, for example, remains clearly less adequate than that for nonminorities (King, 1982), in part because social norms in the Black community promote heavier alcohol usage than do these norms in other subcultures. The drinking behavior of youth and the elderly in the Black community remains largely undocumented, though many believe these two groups ought to be targets of prevention efforts because of especially heavy alcohol abuse potential (Payton, 1981; Scott, 1981). Black youth (Crisp, 1980; Miranda, 1981) and women (Gaines, 1976) have recently been the targets of a few prevention programs, though none of them has proven effective on an empirical basis. Overall, the situation does not encourage the view that either treatment or prevention of alcoholism among Blacks is a high priority issue either within the Black community or to the surrounding community of which it is a part.

Problems of alcoholism among Asian-Americans continue to be minimal; this is fortunate, because this minority group (actually, a very diverse one) makes little use of existing prevention and treatment resources designed for the surrounding majority community (Kitano, 1982).

The situation is very different for Hispanic-Americans, whose rates of alcoholism are higher than the national average (Garza, 1979). At the same time, Hispanic-Americans, like other minority group members, underutilize existing treatment and prevention resources and are served by few resources specifically designed for them (Alcocer, 1982). An NIAAA-funded clinical alcoholism project sponsored by the School of Social Work of the San Jose (California) State University (Arevalo & Minor, 1981) was one of the few programs designed specifically for this group. Charged with the goal of developing a Hispanic-oriented alcohol education curriculum for social workers, the project revealed the special difficulties and problems associated with the design of such a curriculum, which had to meet the needs of a very diverse group of persons ranging from Chicanos and Chicanas in the western United States to Puerto Ricans and Cubans in the east.

Alcoholism among Native Americans continues to be epidemic in its proportions (Merker, 1981). Despite this continuing fact of life for both American Indians and native Alaskans, effective treatment and prevention programs for these people have not been developed (Lewis, 1982). Interestingly, as high as rates of alcoholism among American Indians on the reservation are, they are that much worse among American Indians living in urban centers of this country (Weibel, 1982).

To summarize: Data on incidence and prevalence of alcoholism and alcohol problems among minority groups in this country reveal rates that are higher than for the nonminority population among three leading minority groups—the Blacks, Hispanic-Americans, and Native Americans. These rates are, unfortunately, accompanied by fewer and less effective treatment and prevention programs than for nonminority Americans. Increased attention to this situation has begun to attract the attention of policymakers—with no tangible results thus far.

D. The Elderly and Prevention

Although the percentages of drinkers and of heavy drinkers declines beyond the age of 50, some persons who have been lifelong abstainers or moderate social drinkers develop drinking problems as they age (Brody, 1982). Three groups of the elderly have been identified as at risk: (1) the aging, long-term alcoholic, (2) the elderly problem drinker whose problem developed recently, and (3) the elderly problem drinker with a lengthy history of intermittent alcohol abuse. Because older alcoholics are more heterogeneous than younger ones and because many professionals maintain negative attitudes towards older persons seeking help, the prevention and treatment of alcoholism among the elderly is a particularly difficult problem. One solution appears to be self-help groups among the elderly designed to permit a sharing of the financial, psychological, and physical difficulties of the aging process; another may be increased emphasis on preretirement counseling to help prepare the newly retired for the stresses as well as the pleasure of retirement (Gomberg, 1982).

IV. EFFORTS THAT FOCUS ON THE HOST

A. The Fetal Alcohol Syndrome and Prevention

The fetal alcohol syndrome (FAS) comprises an abnormal pattern of growth and development in both animals (Randall, 1982; Riley, 1982) and humans (Landesman-Dwyer, 1982) that is found more frequently in the offspring of heavy drinking mothers than in those of nondrinking or light drinking mothers. Major mental and motor retardation may accompany the developmental anomalies. While accurate incidence and prevalence figures are unavailable, best estimates are that one in every 750–1000 live births is an FAS infant.

One of the best-documented FAS prevention programs, of the many that have arisen in response to the widespread publicity the FAS has received, is the Fetal Alcohol Syndrome Demonstration Program at the University of Washington School of Medicine (Little, Streissguth, & Guzinski, 1980; McIntyre, 1980). Incorporated in the program are public and professional education on FAS, clinical services for pregnant women, and assessment of FAS children. A special strength of the program is a commitment to thorough evaluation throughout. The program is associated with a decrease in reported alcohol use among pregnant women in Seattle, suggesting (but not proving) that it has been effective.

B. Drunk Driving and Prevention

As many as 25,000 deaths and 75,000 injuries a year in the U.S. are attributed to drunk driving. Many of those injured and killed are youthful drivers, and drunk driving is a leading cause of death among the nation's young people. During 1983, in belated recognition of the immensity of the problem of drunk driving in this country, especially among youth, a Presidential Commission on Drunk Driving was appointed. The National Highway Safety Administration was challenged to develop more effective programs to control the problem, and the Health and Human Services Secretary announced an initiative to reduce teenage drinking. As well, many states have passed legislation to raise the minimum drinking age and to mandate stringent minimum penalties for drunk driving.

Borkenstein (1981) has suggested that the incidence of drunk driving might be reduced by simultaneously (1) reducing per capita alcohol consumption (by increasing price or raising drinking age), (2) increasing enforcement efforts to bring about general deterrence of drinking and driving, and (3) constructing streets and highways in such a way that they place fewer demands on drivers. While such a massive program would doubtless affect rates of drunken driving, it is not likely that legislative bodies could be mobilized anytime soon to authorize the monumental expenditure of public funds necessary to put this program into operation. Selected aspects of the program, put into place in selected regions of the country, are probably more realistic to expect in the near future.

The impact of raising or lowering the legal drinking age on drinking and driving remains uncertain despite a number of studies designed to determine this relationship. To this end, an investigation of alcohol-related motor vehicle crashes in Michigan between 1972, when the legal drinking age in Michigan was lowered from 21 to 18, and 1978, when it was again raised to 21, indicated that lowering the drinking age was associated with an increase in crashes, while raising it was associated with a decrease. Unfortunately, concurrent environmental happenings so obscured the real effects, if any, of these changes that an unequivocal judgment about the relationship between drinking age and automobile accidents was not possible (Douglass, 1980; Wagenaar, 1980, 1982b). Despite the uncertainty surrounding this relationship, many state officials (e.g., Lillis, Williams, Chupka, & Williford, 1982) recommend increasing the drinking age to control alcohol-related motor vehicle accidents. As well, the U.S. Congress is currently considering a similar piece of legislation that would extend a uniform drinking age of 21 nationally.

A survey of the international literature on "Scandinavian-type" laws (Rose, 1981), which promote prevention of drunk driving by very rigid enforcement of strict laws on drunk driving, suggests that this approach to prevention nearly always produces a decrease in drunk driving in the short-run; the long-term deterrent effects of this enforcement method, however, are diminished if drunk drivers can expect to avoid apprehension every time they drink and drive.

V. EFFORTS THAT FOCUS ON THE AGENT

A. Price and Consumption

In 1956, Ledermann proposed that the distribution of alcohol is *lognormal* in all populations — meaning that a direct and unchanging relationship between consumption and heavy drinking exists and that, accordingly, the incidence of alcohol problems can be reduced by lowering per capita consumption (for example, by limiting the availability of alcoholic beverages). Although many of the assumptions underlying Ledermann's theory have been widely questioned (e.g., Parker & Harman, 1978; Pittman,1980; Sulkunen, 1978), increasing the price of alcoholic beverages in order to reduce consumption — and the problems associated with it — is still considered a viable alcoholism control policy (Plymat, 1979; Schmidt & Popham, 1978).

While most authorities on the subject subscribe to the view that alcohol consumption is affected by price, few can point to data to support the related assumption that consumption by heavy or abusive drinkers is sufficiently sensitive to price to be amenable to change simply by price increase. The data are complex and inconsistent. Ornstein (1980), for example, found that beer sales in the United States, Canada, and several European countries were *price inelastic* (that is, an increase in price did not significantly lower demand), that distilled spirits sales were price elastic in the United States and inelastic in Europe, and that wine sales were variable in elasticity; he concluded, accordingly, that these data could not resolve the controversy between those who would and those who would not use price as a control measure. Smith (1981) reported that liquor consumption does appear to be moderately responsive to price in the United States. A slightly different view is held by the World Health Organization (1979) and by Colon (1980). Their position was that, while the consumption of alcoholic beverages is affected by price, complicated interactions between the availability of alcohol and the density of the distribution network, on the one hand, and the pricing of alcohol, on the other, prevent one from assuming that a simple linear relationship links these variables.

These data notwithstanding, the regulatory authorities of most countries have tended to adopt the view that increasing price is a viable control strategy. Accordingly, Sweden (Somervuori, 1977), Finland (Koski, 1977), Australia (Luey, 1979), Poland (Malec, 1980), and some of the countries in the European Economic Community (Sulkunen, 1978) have chosen to employ some form of price policy as a consumption control.

B. Drinking Age and Consumption

A time-series analysis of beverage alcohol distribution in Michigan from 1969 through 1980 revealed changes in alcohol consumption associated with, first, a decrease in the legal drinking age, then an increase in it, during the same time that a mandatory beverage container deposit law was enacted (Wagenaar, 1982a). This analysis provides an empirical answer to the question of whether increasing the legal drinking age leads to a decrease in drinking by youthful drinkers. Wagenaar reported that a statistically significant, but temporary, increase in aggregate draft beer sales followed the reduction in legal minimum drinking age from 21 to 18 in 1972; no such changes in total beer, package beer, or wine sales were associated with the lowered drinking age. Significant decreases in total beer and package beer distribution and large increases in draft beer distribution occurred in 1979 – 1980, after the legal drinking age was raised from 18 to 21 and the mandatory beverage container deposit law was implemented; no concomitant change in wine distribution was observed. While Wagenaar believes that these data provide modest support for the availability theory, he acknowledges that simultaneous changes in several other variables affecting availability, including the effects of a major economic recession in Michigan, make it impossible to interpret these data unequivocally. Accordingly, we conclude that firm conclusions on the relationship between price or drinking age and alcohol consumption, especially by abusive drinkers, cannot be drawn at this time.

VI. EFFORTS THAT FOCUS ON THE ENVIRONMENT

A. Alcohol Education

A variety of alcohol education programs continue to be a prime source of alcoholism prevention efforts worldwide. Despite this fact, a recent critical review of educational strategies for alcoholism prevention (Hochheimer, 1981) concludes that behavior change is induced by alcohol education methods only when they are accompanied by efforts to change the behaviors associated with consumption. In other words, the standard alcohol information program does not induce behavior change — a change in consumption levels — because it does not focus on that ultimate goal of all prevention programs.

Also helpful in development of alcohol education programs that work is Milgram's (1980) evaluation of alcohol education materials. She concludes that the strongest of these materials are those directed at professionals, educators, and counselors; weakest are those designed for the general public. Is it any wonder that most of the latter materials have little impact on behavior?

B. Mass Media

A comprehensive review of the impact on alcohol consumption of advertising and other controllable marketing factors — which also include relative price, taxation level, number of distribution outlets, legal drinking age, and introduction of breath testing capabilities by law enforcement agencies — in the 10 Canadian provinces between 1951 and 1974 was recently completed (Bourgeois & Barnes, 1979). The review indicated that, during a period when per capita consumption of alcoholic beverages almost doubled (from 1.28 to 2.30 gallons), consumption nonetheless was unaffected by total print or broadcast advertising, relative beverage price, or number of outlets. However, consumption was negatively related to taxes and positively related to the lowering of the drinking age and the introduction of breath testing. The authors of this survey conclude — somewhat surprisingly, given the level of expenditure for alcoholic beverage advertising — that advertisements and other controllable marketing factors influence alcohol consumption less than uncontrollable factors like employment status, ethnicity, and the like.

VII. PREVENTION IN THE WORKPLACE

In a recent volume on alcoholism prevention, Nathan (1984) drew the following conclusions about alcoholism prevention in the workplace:

> Alcoholism prevention efforts in the workplace are still modest, imperfect, and variable in quality. Many or most corporations have moved no farther than recognition that the alcoholism problems of their employees may be costing them money; some have progressed a bit farther, to the point where Employee Assistance Programs of one sort or another have been funded. But treatment, despite its problems, still seems far more cost-effective than prevention to most managers. In other words, to this time, industry has failed to recognize the dollars and cents value of alcoholism prevention; as a consequence, when prevention efforts are undertaken, they are usually a small, ineffective afterthought grafted onto a treatment program. It is clear that data on the cost-effectiveness of prevention *per se* are essential before hard-headed managers will heed our appeals to heighten efforts at prevention of alcoholism (Nathan, 1984, p. 404).

This chapter's first author drew these rather pessimistic conclusions following three separate experiences as a consultant to alcohol-related service programs that each had the clear potential to provide important prevention programming alongside the intervention or training services that had been contracted for. In all three instances, however, the prevention component made a much smaller impact than it might have made, because prevention was considered of lesser import than treatment. The lessons learned from these experiences illustrate well the problems those who would develop alcoholism prevention programs in the workplace will experience.

A. An EAP Consortium

The first of these experiences stemmed from the first author's involvement in the development of an Employee Assistance Program (EAP) to serve employees of 11 federal agencies in the Atlanta area. Ranging in size and diversity from the Federal Aviation Administration and the Center for Disease Control (both with over 2000 employees in the Atlanta area, many of whom were highly educated and highly paid) to the Railway Retirement Agency and the Bureau of Firearms, Tobacco, and Alcohol (each with fewer than two dozen employees, most of whom were poorly paid clerks with little formal education), the agencies presented formidable problems for the developers of the EAP consortium. Because support for the program among managers at the several agencies also varied markedly, these problems were compounded. Nonetheless, a comprehensive and effective EAP did emerge from these efforts.

The EAP initially employed three people. A full-time M.S.W. (Masters in Social Work) clinical social worker and a part-time advanced graduate student in clinical psychology provided counseling and referral resources for the clients of the EAP. A penetration rate of over 3% of the 14,000 employees of the agencies in the consortium was reached the first year of the program; this rate yielded more than 450 telephone calls and office visits from federal employees in distress. Despite the good utilization rate of 3% the first year, however, fewer alcoholics than expected either self-referred or were referred by others to the EAP. As a consequence, an experienced alcoholism counselor was added to the staff, on the assumption that he would be able to generate more referrals for alcohol problems than the other two clinicians, neither of whom was interested in alcohol and drug abuse problems, had been able to generate.

Carefully developed, separate training programs for the managers, the first-line supervisors, and the employees in utilization of the EAP described the program, stressed the confidentiality that was necessary to its successful functioning and reaffirmed the primacy of the performance criterion in deciding on a referral. That is, supervisors and employees were reminded that referrals to the EAP were to be made when or if decrements in performance on the job were observed—but only then. Supervisors were not to function as counselors. Instead, they were to observe performance and recommend referral if performance deteriorated. In turn, if a troubled employee accepted referral to the EAP, he or she would not be subject to usual disciplinary actions, including termination, so long as he or she remained involved in the program, working on the performance problem.

Because about 30% of referrals to the EAP were ultimately for alcoholism or alcohol-related problems (e.g., marital difficulties, spouse or child abuse, job performance decrement, excessive absenteeism), the EAP was investing heavily in tertiary prevention of alcohol problems. Unfortunately, resources and personnel could not be mobilized to heighten the program's primary and secondary prevention components. To this end, none of the federal agencies served by the EAP consortium were willing to pay extra for formal alcohol education programs, while the alcoholism counselor hired to heighten the appeal of the EAP to those with alcohol problems was quite unwilling to spend time in prevention activities "when so many out there need treatment." When told that prevention was part of his job, the counselor promised to do prevention when and as he could—but his heart was clearly never in prevention. The attitudes of management and supervisory personnel were similar; prevention was a luxury that had to await the time that all serious alcoholism problems had been dealt with. That that time would almost certainly never come was clearly recognized by most of those who took that position.

As a consequence, the prevention component of this EAP was much less effective than it might have been. Brown-bag lunches were held periodically for those employees who wished to learn something about alcoholism and were willing to be identified by peers and supervisors as having this interest. Occasional alcohol education programs were held; most of them were sparsely attended because management and supervisory personnel made no effort to make it easy for employees to attend. A newsletter designed to maintain employee awareness of the EAP was developed; it occasionally reprinted articles on alcoholism in the effort to heighten awareness of the problem. But, overall, it was clear that prevention was a minor and relatively unimportant part of this EAP—despite the program's enormous potential for primary prevention at very reasonable cost. Indifference toward prevention rather than active opposition to it on the part of agency personnel and EAP employees accounted for the failure of this EAP consortium to exploit its prevention opportunities.

B. A Training Program for Alcohol Servers

Several years ago, the first author of this chapter agreed to develop a training program for alcohol servers working for the casinos of Atlantic City. Sponsored by the Casino Control Commission, a New Jersey State Agency, the training program was designed in recognition of the casinos' potential liability for property damage, personal injury, and death caused by intoxicated patrons. The Casino Control Commission recognized that many or most patrons leaving the casinos after a night of gambling were drunk—after having been served virtually unlimited quantities of free beverage alcohol on the casino floor, so long as they continued to gamble. Accordingly, the commission wanted a program that would (1) sensitize alcohol servers to their own liability if they served an intoxicated patron, (2) buttress them in their resolve to refuse service to intoxicated patrons, and (3) equip them with the skills necessary to do so.

The program that was ultimately developed provided detailed information on alcohol and its psychological, behavioral, and psysiological effects and on the laws governing the sale and service of alcoholic beverages to sober and drunken patrons. The program also employed videotapes of drunken comportment, to detail the varieties of drunken behavior that might be encountered, and role-playing, designed to give alcohol servers the opportunity to try out various techniques to let a patron know he or she would no longer be served an alcoholic beverage. Role-playing also gave the alcohol servers the chance to experience the consequences, which were often quite heated, even in the role-played scene, of a drink refusal.

Alcohol servers evaluated the program very positively on forms that permitted anonymous evaluations. The training program foundered, though, and was ultimately terminated, over the refusal of casino managers and owners to recognize the dimensions of their potential legal liability for serving alcohol to intoxicated patrons. This refusal to face up to the problem of drunken patrons was best illustrated by the unwillingness of casino owners and managers to encourage their employees to limit drinks to drunken patrons who could still gamble. Owners and managers agreed that patrons who were so drunk that they could not continue to bet, patrons who were betting small amounts, or patrons who were playing slot machines were all suitable targets for drink refusal by alcohol servers. But drunken patrons who were betting heavily were not to be refused drinks because they might become angry at the casino and take their business elsewhere. As a consequence, alcohol servers were placed in a difficult conflict every time they were called upon to serve a drunken patron: Refuse him or her a drink and avoid legal liability and the wrath of the Casino Control Commission — but, in so doing, earn the wrath of the employer and, possibly, lose the job!

A similar message was conveyed by management when they were asked about the possibility of expanding the training program to convey prevention information to casino employees who might be becoming alcohol abusers. At first, refusing to acknowledge that alcoholism was a problem among employees at any level, the casino owners and managers then admitted that they probably did have a problem but added that the easiest and best solution to it was simply to discharge employees whose work had been affected by alcohol. Because the casino workforce had not yet been unionized, this plan would not meet with opposition from any organized group representing the employees. As well, casino managers added, if the casinos were to acknowledge that an alcohol problem exists among casino employees, the Casino Control Commission would respond with strong actions and great concern, a consequence that was unacceptable to the owners because it would involve undue intrusion into management prerogatives. To this time, no coherent primary, secondary, or tertiary alcoholism prevention program has been instituted in the casinos of Atlantic City, despite what is almost certainly an extraordinarily high rate of alcoholism among casino employees.

C. A Positive Lifestyle Change Program

A few years ago, the chapter's first author agreed to help Johnson & Johnson, one of the nation's leading health care products companies and central New Jersey's largest employer, develop an innovative positive lifestyle change program. The program, called Live for Life, was to make Johnson & Johnson's employees' "the healthiest in the world" according to the company's Board Chair, who was the program's prime mover from the start. Live for Life was to focus on the reduction of cardiovascular risk, since it is with cardiovascular risk factors that lifestyle intervention has the greatest chance to reduce preventable disease and death.

The program that ultimately emerged from the design efforts provided exercise, smoking cessation, weight control, stress management, and nutrition information options, in the context of a program with strong motivational and educative components. Initially offered to employees of Johnson & Johnson companies in the New Brunswick area, the program has now been extended, several years later, to all of Johnson & Johnson's 60,000 employees worldwide.

The program's key elements include an introductory Lifestyle Seminar to which all employees are invited when their unit contracts for Live for Life. The seminar informs employees on the central role lifestyle factors play in health and quality of life and the extent to which serious health problems, including cardiovascular disease, can be prevented by alterations in lifestyle. The Live for Life program is also detailed in the seminar, and opportunities to sign up for one or more of its associated programs are offered.

Seminar participants also receive feedback on a Lifestyle Screen in which they participated earlier, at which a wide range of demographic, personal, and medical history, and current biometric and behavioral information is taken in order to permit assessment of the health risks associated with their present lifestyle. The Lifestyle Profile employees receive at the Lifestyle Seminar is designed to represent an additional inducement for employee involvement in the Live for Life Action Groups on exercise, weight control, smoking cessation, nutrition, and stress management. These action groups typically meet 1 hour a week (either during lunchtime or after work) for 8 to 12 weeks.

When Live for Life was in the planning stages, serious consideration was given to an Alcohol Action Group for persons interested in learning more about alcohol and alcoholism. The Action Group would be explicitly enjoined from providing therapy for confirmed alcoholics; an Employee Assistance Program for that purpose already existed in the company. However, when the plan for the Alcohol Action Group was set forth, it was met with very strong opposition from the alcoholism counselors working in the several Johnson & Johnson Employee Assistance Programs, on the grounds that it would duplicate their efforts, lead to confusion among alcohol-abusing employees on where to go for help, and otherwise deflect the impact of the effective network of programs for alcoholism already in place in the company. From the point-of-view of those in favor of an alcoholism component of Live for Life, the Alcohol Action Group would function as a prevention rather than an intervention medium. Because virtually none of the company's EAPs invested in prevention activities, it appeared that there would, in fact, be little duplication of effort.

Unfortunately, from the perspective of those interested in prevention, the EAP coordinators at Johnson & Johnson won out. Claiming that they could do the prevention job along with their assigned triage, diagnosis, and treatment responsibilities, they were successful in preventing development of the Alcohol Action Group within Live for Life. And to this time, several years later, meaningful prevention programming has not been a part of any of Johnson & Johnson's Employee Assistance Programs!

VIII. A FINAL WORD

Not surprisingly, the very modest infusion of federal dollars into alcoholism prevention has not had an impact on alcohol abuse and alcoholism in this country. While prevention programs typically increase levels of information about alcohol and its effects, and sometimes change attitudes toward excessive drinking, they rarely change consummatory behavior among those who drink most heavily and are most responsible for drunken driving, automobile accidents, FAS children, and serious disease secondary to chronic alcoholism. As well, debilitating political struggles that obscure or prevent rational policy-formation with regard to drinking age, taxation levels, and the availability of alcoholic beverage have successfully prevented development of a comprehensive national policy toward alcohol distribution and consumption. Finally, for a variety of reasons, including a priority system that seems often to put profits before people, industry has been slow to add prevention components to existing, treatment-oriented Employee Assistance Programs.

Despite rhetoric to the contrary, this nation does not take prevention of alcoholism seriously.

REFERENCES

Alcocer, A. (1982). Alcohol use and abuse among the Hispanic American population. In *Alcohol and Health Monograph No. 4: Special Population Issues* (pp. 361–382). Rockville, MD: National Institute on Alcohol Abuse and Alcoholism.

Arevalo, R., & Minor, M. (Eds.). (1981). *Chicanas and alcoholism: A socio-cultural perspective of women*. Monograph from San Jose State University School of Social Work.

Borkenstein, R. F. (1981). Problems of enforcement. In L. Goldberg (Ed.), *Alcohol, drugs, and traffic safety* (pp. 239–252). Stockholm: Almqvist & Wiksell International.

Bourgeois, J. C., & Barnes, J. G. (1979). Does advertising increase alcohol consumption? *Journal of Advertising Research, 19,* 19–29.

Bower, S. (1980). Tools for change: Issues, strategies, and resources: Prevention of alcohol-related problems. *Journal of Addictions and Health, 1,* 242–249.

Braiker, H. (1982). The diagnosis and treatment of alcoholism in women. In *Alcohol and Health Monograph No. 4: Special Population Issues* (pp. 111–139). Rockville, MD: National Institute on Alcohol Abuse and Alcoholism.

Braucht, G. (1982). Problem drinking among adolescents: A review and analysis of psychosocial research. In *Alcohol and Health Monograph No. 4: Special Population Issues* (pp. 143–164). Rockville, MD: National Institute on Alcohol Abuse and Alcoholism.

Brody, J. A. (1982). Aging and alcohol abuse. *Journal of the American Geriatrics Society, 30,* 123–126.

Colon, I. (1980). *Alcohol control policies and their relation to alcohol consumption and alcoholism.* Unpublished doctoral dissertation, Brandeis University, Waltham, MA.

Crisp, A. D. (1980). Making substance abuse prevention relevant to low-income black neighborhoods. II. Research findings. *Journal of Psychedelic Drugs, 12,* 139–156.

Donovan, B. (1980). Collegiate group for the sons and daughters of alcoholics. Paper presented at NADC Conference, Washington, DC.

Douglass, R. L. (1980). Legal drinking age and traffic casualties: A special case of changing alcohol availability in a public health context. *Alcohol and Health Research World, 4,* 18–25.

Douglass, R. L. (1982). Youth, alcohol, and traffic accidents. In *Alcohol and Health Monograph No. 4: Special Population Issues* (pp. 197–223). Rockville, MD: National Institute on Alcohol Abuse and Alcoholism.

Evans, G. B., Steer, R. A., & Fine, E. W. (1979). Alcohol value clarification in sixth graders: A filmmaking project. *Journal of Alcohol and Drug Education, 24,* 1–10.

Fullerton, M. A. (1979). A program in alcohol education designed for rural youth. *Journal of Alcohol and Drug Education, 24,* 58–62.

Gaines, J. J. (1976). Alcohol and the black woman. In F. D. Harper (Ed.), *Alcohol abuse and black America* (pp. 153–162). Alexandria, VA: Douglass Publishers.

Garza, R. (1979). El alcoholico. *Impact, 9,* 4–5.

Gomberg, E. (1982). Alcohol use and problems among the elderly. In *Alcohol and Health Monograph No. 4: Special Population Issues* (pp. 263–290). Rockville, MD: National Institute on Alcohol Abuse and Alcoholism.

Goodstadt, M. S., Sheppard, M. A., & Chan, G. C. (1982). An evaluation of two schoolbased alcohol education programs. *Journal of Studies on Alcohol, 43,* 352–369.

Goodwin, D. W. (1983). The genetics of alcoholism. In E. Gottheil, K. A. Druley, T. E. Skoloda, & H. W. Waxman (Eds.), *Etiologic aspects of alcohol and drug abuse* (pp. 5–13). Springfield, IL: Charles C. Thomas.

Goodwin, D. W., Schulsinger, F., Knop, J., Mednick, S., & Guze, S. B. (1977). Alcoholism and depression in adopted-out daughters of alcoholics. *Archives of General Psychiatry, 34,* 751–755.

Harford, T. C., Wechsler, H., & Rohman, M. (1980, April). *Contextual drinking patterns of college students: The relationship between typical companion status and consumption level.* Paper presented at the annual meeting of the National Council on Alcoholism, Seattle.

Henggeler, S. W., Sallis, J. F., & Cooper, P. F. (1980). Comparison of university mental health needs priorities identified by professionals and students. *Journal of Counseling Psychology, 27,* 217–219.

Hewitt, L. (1982). Current status of alcohol education programs for youth. In *Alcohol and Health Monograph No. 4: Special Population Issues* (pp. 227–260). Rockville, MD: National Institute on Alcohol Abuse and Alcoholism.

Hill, S. (1982). Biological consequences of alcoholism and alcohol-related problems among women. In *Alcohol and Health Monograph No. 4: Special Population Issues* (pp. 43–73). Rockville, MD: National Institute on Alcohol Abuse and Alcoholism.

Hochheimer, J. L. (1981). Reducing alcohol abuse: A critical review of educational strategies. In M. H. Moore & D. R. Gerstein (Eds.), *Alcohol and public policy* (pp. 286–335). Washington, DC: National Academy Press.

Irwin, K. D. (1976, May). *Women, alcohol, and drugs: A feminist course focusing on causes and prevention of abuse.* Paper presented at the annual meeting of the American Public Health Association, Miami.

King, L. (1982). Alcoholism: Studies regarding black Americans. In *Alcohol and Health Monograph No. 4: Special Population Issues* (pp. 385–407). Rockville, MD: National Institute on Alcohol Abuse and Alcoholism.

Kitano, H. (1982). Alcohol drinking patterns: The Asian Americans. In *Alcohol and Health Monograph No. 4: Special Population Issues* (pp. 411–430). Rockville, MD: National Institute on Alcohol Abuse and Alcoholism.

Knupfer, G. (1982). Problems associated with drunkenness in women. In *Alcohol and Health Monograph No. 4: Special Population Issues* (pp. 3–39). Rockville, MD: National Institute on Alcohol Abuse and Alcoholism.

Koski, H. (1977). Labor market and alcohol prices. *Alkoholpolitik, Hels.,* **40**, 37–38.

Kraft, D. P. (1982, August). *A program to prevent alcohol problems among college students: Success and failures.* Paper presented at the annual meeting of the American Psychological Association, Washington, DC.

Landesman-Dwyer, S. (1982). Drinking during pregnancy: Effects on human development. In *Alcohol and Health Monograph No. 2: Biomedical Processes and Consequences of Alcohol Use* (pp.335–358). Rockville, MD: National Institute on Alcohol Abuse and Alcoholism.

Leavy, R. L. (1980 July-August). First steps in campus prevention programs. *CAFC News.*

Ledermann, S. (1956). *Alcool, alcoolisme, alcoolisation.* Donnees scientifiques de caractere physiologique, economique et social. Institut d'Etudes Demographiques, Cahier No. 29. Paris: Press Universitaire.

Lewis, R. (1982). Alcoholism and the Native Americans — A review of the literature. In *Alcohol and Health Monograph No. 4: Special Population Issues* (pp. 315–328). Rockville, MD: National Institute on Alcohol Abuse and Alcoholism.

Lillis, R. P., Williams, T. P., Chupka, J. Q., & Williford, W. R. (1982). *Highway safety considerations in raising the minimum legal age for purchase of alcoholic beverages to nineteen in New York State.* Albany, NY: New York State Division of Alcoholism and Alcohol Abuse.

Little, R. E., Streissguth, A. P., & Guzinski, G. M. (1980). Prevention of fetal alcohol syndrome: A model program. *Alcoholism: Clinical and Experimental Research,* **4**, 185–189.

Luey, P. (1979). Can alcohol taxes reduce consumption? *Australian Journal of Alcoholism and Drug Dependence,* **6**, 119–122.

Malec, J. (1980). Methods of reducing alcohol consumption. *Problemy Alkoholizmu,* 27, 3–4.

Malec, J. (1980). Methods of reducing alcohol consumption. *Problemy Alkoholizmu,* **27**, 3–4.

McAlister, A., Perry, C., Killen, J., Slinkard, L. A., & Maccoby, N. (1980). Pilot study of smoking, alcohol and drug abuse prevention. *American Journal of Public Health,* **70**, 719–721.

McIntyre, C. E. (1980, April). *Evaluating prevention and education: Fetal alcohol syndrome.* Paper presented at the annual meeting of the National Council on Alcoholism, Seattle.

Medical World News. (1980, May). Inpatient care can rescue many alcoholic teenagers. *Medical World News*, **12**, 46–47.

Merker, J. F. (1981, April). *Indians of the Great Plains: Issues in counseling and family therapy*. Paper presented at the annual meeting of the National Council on Alcoholism, New Orleans.

Milgram, G. G. (1980). Descriptive analysis of alcohol education materials, 1973–1979. *Journal of Studies on Alcohol*, **41**, 1209–1216.

Miranda, V. L. (1981, February). Paper presented at NIAAA Skills Development Workshop: Agenda for Black Alcoholism Programs, Jackson, MS.

Morrissey, E. R., & Schuckit, M. A. (1979, April). *Drinking patterns and alcohol-related problems in a population of alcoholic detoxification patients: Comparison of males and females*. Paper presented at the annual meeting of the National Council on Alcoholism, Washington, DC.

Nathan, P. E. (1984). Alcoholism prevention in the workplace: Three examples. In P. M. Miller & T. D. Nirenberg (Eds.), *Prevention of alcohol abuse*. New York: Plenum.

NIDA. (1982). Napa Project. Rockville, MD: National Institute on Alcohol Abuse and Alcoholism.

Ornstein, S. I. (1980). The control of alcohol consumption through price increases. *Journal of Studies on Alcohol*, **41**, 807–818.

Parker, D. A., & Harman, M. S. (1978). Distribution of consumption model of prevention of alcohol problems: A critical assessment. *Journal of Studies on Alcohol*, **39**, 377–399.

Payton, C. R. (1981). Substance abuse and mental health: Special prevention strategies needed for ethnics of color. *Public Health Reports*, **96**, 20–25.

Pittman, D. J. (1980). *Primary prevention of alcohol abuse and alcoholism: An evaluation of the control of consumption policy*. Unpublished manuscript, Washington University, Social Science Institute, St. Louis, MO.

Plymat, W. N. (1979, September). *Economic strategies for prevention*. Paper presented at the Third World Congress for the Prevention of Alcoholism and Drug Dependency, Acapulco.

Portnoy, B. (1980). Effects of a controlled-usage alcohol education program based on the Health Belief Model. *Journal of Drug Education*, **10**, 181–195.
Belief Model. *Journal of Drug Education*, **10**, 181–195.

Pringle, H. Gregory, J., Ginkel, K., & Cheek, C. (1981). Alpha Centers: A viable prevention model for substance abuse agencies and public schools. In A. J. Schechter (Ed.), *Drug dependence and alcoholism* (Vol. 2) (pp. 183–189). New York: Plenum.

Randall, C. (1982). Alcohol as a teratogen in animals. In *Alcohol and Health Monograph No. 2: Biomedical Processes and Consequences of Alcohol Use* (pp. 291–307). Rockville, MD: National Institute on Alcohol Abuse and Alcoholism.

Resource Alternatives Corporation (1982). *Prevention of alcohol abuse among pre-delinquent youth: An overview of the evaluation results*. Washington, DC: Resource Alternatives Corporation.

Riley, E. (1982). Ethanol as a behavioral teratogen: Animal models. In *Alcohol and Health Monograph No. 2: Biomedical Processes and Consequences of Alcohol Use* (pp. 311–332). Rockville, MD: National Institute on Alcohol Abuse and Alcoholism.

Rosenbluth, J., Nathan, P. E., & Lawson, D. M. (1978). Environmental influences on drinking by college students in a college pub: Behavioral observations in the natural environment: *Addictive Behaviors*, **3**, 117–121.

Ross, H. L. (1981). *Deterrence of the drinking driver: An international survey*. Washington, DC: National Highway Safety Administration, Department of Transportation.

Sandmaier, M. (1976, May). *Women and alcohol abuse: A strategy for prevention*. Paper presented at the annual meeting of the American Public Health Association, Miami.

Schmidt, W., & Popham, R. E. (1978). Single distribution theory of alcohol consumption: A rejoinder to the critique of Parker and Harman. *Journal of Studies on Alcohol*, **39**, 400–419.

Scott, B. M. (1981, October). *Alcohol prevention for black communities.* Paper presented at the Alcoholism in the Black Community Seminar, Newark, NJ.

Shaw, S. (1980). The causes of increasing drinking problems amongst women: A general etiological theory. In *Women and alcohol* (pp. 1–40). New York: Tavistock Publications.

Smith, R. (1981). Relation between consumption and damage. *British Medical Journal*, **283**, 895–898.

Somervuori, A. (1977). Pricing as an instrument of alcohol policy. *Alkoholpolitik, Hels.*, **40**, 85–93.

Staulcup, H., Kenward, K., & Frigo, D. (1979). A review of federal primary alcoholism prevention projects. *Journal of Studies on Alcohol*, **40**, 943–968.

Stuart, R. B. (1980). Teaching facts about drugs: Pushing or preventing? In D. A. Ward (Ed.), *Alcoholism: Introduction to theory and treatment* (pp. 211–225). Dubuque, IA: Kendall/Hunt.

Sulkunen, P. (1978). *Developments in the availability of alcoholic beverages in the EEC countries.* Helsinki: Social Research Institute of Alcohol Studies.

Vaillant, G. E. (1983). *The natural history of alcoholism.* Cambridge, MA: Harvard University Press.

Wagenaar, A. C. (1980, May). *Raised legal drinking age and motor vehicle accidents in Michigan.* Paper presented at the annual meeting of the American Public Health Association, Detroit.

Wagenaar, A. C. (1982a). Aggregate beer and wine consumption: Effects of changes in the minimum legal drinking age and a mandatory beverage container deposit law in Michigan. *Journal of Studies on Alcohol*, **43**, 469–487.

Wagenaar, A. C. (1982b). Raised legal drinking age and automobile crashes: A review of the literature. *Abstracts and Reviews in Alcohol and Driving*, **3**, 3–8.

Weibel, J. (1982). American Indians, urbanization and alcohol: A developing urban Indian drinking ethos. In *Alcohol and Health Monograph No. 4: Special Population Issues* (pp. 331–358). Rockville, MD: National Institute on Alcohol Abuse and Alcoholism.

Weisheit, R. A., Kearney, K. A., Hopkins, R. H., & Mauss, A. L. (1979). *Evaluation of a model alcohol education project for the public schools: Phase II, An overview of the first year's activities and results.* Pullman, WA: Washington State University.

Whitehead, P. C., & Ferrance, R. G. (1977). Liberated drinking: New hazard for women. *Addictions*, **24**, 36–53.

World Health Organization. (1979). Alcohol control policies. In D. Robinson (Ed.), *Alcohol problems.* New York: Holmes and Meier Publishers.

Index